AUTOCAD 2000
IN A NUTSHELL

A Command Reference Guide

AUTOCAD 2000
IN A NUTSHELL

A Command Reference Guide

Dorothy Kent

O'REILLY®

Beijing • Cambridge • Farnham • Köln • Paris • Sebastopol • Taipei • Tokyo

AutoCAD 2000 in a Nutshell
by Dorothy Kent

Published by O'Reilly & Associates, Inc., 101 Morris Street, Sebastopol, CA 95472.

Editor: Troy Mott

Production Editor: Melanie Wang

Cover Designer: Hanna Dyer

Printing History:

February 2000:   First Edition.

ISBN: 1-56592-690-0
[M]

[3/00]

Table of Contents

Part III: Appendixes

Preface

AutoCAD is the most widely used PC-based, 2D/3D design and drafting environment. And the newest version, AutoCAD 2000, contains hundreds of new commands and features, which are covered in this book. Whether you are a beginning AutoCAD user, a part-time user, or even a long-standing user, it is virtually impossible to remember every nuance and every option for every AutoCAD command, variable, and express tool. We have all had questions like "Can I do it this way with that command?" or "How do I get this sequence to work?" It is more important to know where to find information about AutoCAD commands than to remember it all. This reference guide is designed to give you fast access to AutoCAD's commands, variables, and express tools. Their complexities are explained, along with tips and warnings learned from years of experience.

Why This Book Is Different

This book pulls AutoCAD commands, express tools, and variables into one easy-to-use alphabetical reference and isn't limited to a mere listing of what these features do. It also helps you:

- Find commands, express tools, and variables quickly to get key descriptions.

- Get tips and warnings that will save you time.

- See example sequences and screenshots illustrating how to use commands, variables, and express tools.

- Identify variables for use with commands, express tools, menu macros, scripts, and AutoLISP programs.

Years ago, the variables were actually options from within a command named *setvar*. You could not type variables at the command prompt. Now all the variables (except for a couple) can be accessed at the command prompt. Although experienced users who have used older versions of AutoCAD may still think of the variables as being a subset of *setvar*, they can be typed at the command prompt like any other command, which is why they are also included in Chapter 3, *Alphabetical Reference.*

Express tools were called "bonus tools" in past releases, and most of the AutoCAD releases left them undocumented. In Release 14, the bonus tools were finally documented, and in Release 2000, they are documented and grouped in their own toolbars and pull-down menus. Although the express tools are grouped by function, you won't, for instance, find all the dimension commands located in the dimension toolbar or pull-down menu. For this reason, we've included the express tools throughout Chapter 3.

Whom This Book Benefits

This book has been crafted for AutoCAD 2000 users having basic knowledge of the program. It describes each command and the various options available for that command, along with tips and warnings that help save time and increase productivity. This book also is helpful to experienced users who need quick answers to AutoCAD questions and to those who provide AutoCAD support but don't use the product on a daily basis.

We recommend that you periodically log onto Autodesk's web site (*http://www.autodesk.com/*) for updated technical information. You may find information concerning bugs, software patches, and revised and new AutoCAD routines that are available free of charge.

How This Book Is Organized

This book is divided into three main parts.

Part I, Getting Acclimated

Chapter 1, *What's New in AutoCAD 2000*, describes AutoCAD 2000's screen display and new features.

Chapter 2, *Command Index and Global Topics*, breaks down the main commands found in Part II by function (e.g., 3D Objects, Dimensioning, etc.).

Part II, Alphabetical Reference

Chapter 3, *Alphabetical Reference*, references each AutoCAD command, express tool, and variable in alphanumeric order (A–3D). New and modified AutoCAD 2000 commands and variables are labeled with a **2000** or **2000mod** icon next to the appropriate command or variable. Each command section in the reference contains some or all of the following elements.

Command Name and Description

You will find the commands, express tools, and variables arranged alphabetically with a general description.

A transparent command or variable is one that can be started when another command is already in progress. These commands must be prefaced with an apostrophe (') in order to work transparently, and we have marked them in this same fashion throughout the book. For example, if you are using the *-insert* command, you can start the *redraw* command transparently by prefacing it with an apostrophe.

Some AutoCAD commands can be either command-line or dialog-box driven. For those users who prefer to stick with the command line, you can enter a hyphen (-) before the command. This is especially useful when taking advantage of wildcard characters and when writing scripts, macros, and lisp routines. We have indicated these commands in this book by prefacing them with a hyphen (-). *-linetype* is an example of such a command.

Commands referencing Visual Basic and Visual Lisp have been omitted since they are beyond the scope of this book.

Initiate Command By

This section lists the available methods for accessing each command, express tool, and variable. You can access them by entering the command, variable name, or alias (keyboard shortcut) on the command line, by navigating through the pull-down menu bar, or by selecting the toolbar button (listed on the same line as the command in the reference). You can't initiate all of the commands via the pull-down menu, an alias, or a toolbar button, but you can always type the command out on the command line. On the first line, which reads "Command," we list all command names and any function keys (e.g., F6) that will initiate a given command. On the line that reads "Alias," we provide all command aliases (e.g., **x** for *explode*) and any control keys (e.g., Ctrl-D) that can initiate a given command.

Options

This section demonstrates the prompting text that AutoCAD displays at the command line when input is requested. It also lists the various options, including a description, that are available for each command, express tool, and variable. We have omitted some of the more obvious options such as the length, width, and height options for creating a box. Since dialog boxes often set system and environment variables, we have included the variable names with the dialog boxes when appropriate.

Tips & Warnings

This section provides time-saving tips and helpful warnings to prevent user problems and to increase productivity.

Variable Settings

This information is provided for the different types of system and environment variables:

Initial Default
Lists the default AutoCAD setting.

Subsequent Default
Tells you whether the setting applies to the current drawing session only, whether it's saved with the drawing file, or whether it's saved to the registry

file, thereby making it the default setting no matter what drawing you are editing.

Value

Tells you whether the variable is stored as an integer, real number, 3D or 2D point, or a text string.

Related Variables

This section lists system variables found in this book that are related to the command, express tool, or variable.

Associated Commands

This section provides cross-references to other commands found in this book that interact with or are similar to the command, express tool, or variable.

Example

This section gives a command line and response and/or an illustration to demonstrate how the command is used.

Part III, Appendixes

Appendix A, *Command Shortcuts*, describes the keyboard shortcuts and aliases for AutoCAD 2000.

Appendix B, *Scale Factor Chart and Drawing Limits*, describes various scale factors and drawing limits for architectural, mechanical, and civil disciplines.

Conventions Used in This Book

This book uses the following typographic conventions:

Apostrophes (')

are used to preface transparent commands, which can be run from the command line when another command is in progress.

Hyphens (-)

are used to preface those commands that display dialog prompts on the command line (note that there are some differences between options in the dialog box and those available on the command line).

Constant width bold

is used to indicate user input from the command line.

Constant width

is used for options from the command line.

Italic

is used for commands and variables throughout the book. Italic is also used to a show a command and its options, for example, *pedit–join.*

Square brackets ([ ])

are used to indicate that one of the options separated by slashes can be typed at the command line, for example, [ON/OFF].

Angle brackets (<>)
> are used to illustrate default AutoCAD command-line options, for example, <ON>.

MiXed capitalization
> is used in the command-line prompts to indicate the shortcut alias (e.g., you only need to type x and select the Enter key to initiate eXit).

Arrows (→)
> are used between cascading menu commands (e.g., View → Zoom → Previous).

2000
> is used to indicate every command that is new to AutoCAD 2000.

2000mod
> is used to indicate every command that has been modified for AutoCAD 2000 but is not a new command.

Acronyms Found in This Book

The following acronyms are used frequently throughout this book:

ACIS	Alan Charles Ian System
ADC	AutoCAD DesignCenter
AME	Advanced Modeling Extension
ARX	AutoCAD Runtime Extension
HLS	hue, lightness, saturation
ISO	International Standards Organization
OLE	Object Linking and Embedding
UCS	User Coordinate System
URL	Uniform Resource Locator
WCS	World Coordinate System

How to Contact Us

We have tested and verified all the information in this book to the best of our ability, but you may find that features have changed (or even that we have made mistakes). Please let O'Reilly know about any errors you find, as well as your suggestions for future editions, by writing to:

> O'Reilly & Associates, Inc.
> 101 Morris Street
> Sebastopol, CA 95472
> 800-998-9938 (in the United States or Canada)
> 707-829-0515 (international/local)
> 707-829-0104 (fax)

You can also send messages electronically. To be put on our mailing list or to request a catalog, send email to:

> *info@oreilly.com*

To ask technical questions or comment on the book, send email to:

bookquestions@oreilly.com

We have a web site for the book, where we'll list errata and any plans for future editions. You can access this page at:

http://www.oreilly.com/catalog/autocadnut/

For more information about this book and others, see the O'Reilly web site:

http://www.oreilly.com

Acknowledgments

Throughout the years I have had the privilege to come into contact with many people who have shared their thoughts, ideas, and experiences. This has ultimately provided me with the knowledge to write this book. I would especially like to thank Grace Gallego, Wayne Hodgens, and Denis Kadu from Autodesk and the staff at Cadalyst Magazine. A special thanks to the technical reviewers Frank Angelini, Michael Beall, Troy Carbone, Randy Cook, Harry Hellerman, Herb Schwarz, and Lydia Stokes.

I wish to express my appreciation to the many individuals at O'Reilly who were instrumental in producing the book, and especially to Troy Mott, Bob Herbstman, and Melanie Wang.

A very personal thank you goes to my husband, Harry, who provided encouragement and support and made sure I balanced my personal and professional goals. I'd also like to thank all my family and friends, especially to my parents, Florence and Harry Kent, for their continued love and support.

PART I

Getting Acclimated

CHAPTER 1

What's New in AutoCAD 2000

In this chapter, we cover some of the basics, but we focus mainly on the new AutoCAD 2000 features and commands, such as the improved drawing tools and 3D dimensioning enhancements. We also list the new, modified, and obsolete or renamed AutoCAD 2000 commands and variables. With this preview, you can then use Chapter 3, *Alphabetical Reference*, as the place to go for all the information you'll need about these new AutoCAD 2000 commands and variables.

Using AutoCAD 2000

Because of AutoCAD's flexibility, there are many ways to create and edit drawings. You should experiment using different combinations of commands and drawing tools.

Draw full size and define the drawing scale when you are ready to plot. Drawing full size gives you the following advantages:

- Editing is accomplished using the actual dimensions.

- You can easily merge other drawing files that also have been created full size.

If your drawing contains multiple scales, use layout tabs and create viewports. Assign different scales to each viewport with the *zoom* command.

The same drawing can be plotted as often as you want on any size paper and at any scale. Of course, paper size is limited to your output device (printer or plotter). When plotting to different scales, you probably will need to modify the height of your annotation (text and dimension text). See Appendix B, *Scale Factor Chart and Drawing Limits*, for a listing of plot scale factors, text heights, and the amount of space available for the different paper sizes.

Enter the exact sizes for all the geometry or objects. When you dimension, you can set up parameters to have the dimensions automatically rounded to your specification. Since AutoCAD retains the original values, you can always revert to the original values if necessary.

Create prototype or template files. Preset information that is typical to the different types of drawings you create (i.e., titleblocks, layers, colors, line types, line weights, dimension styles, layouts, and plot styles) and save that information to one or more template files. Whether or not you use template files, you will find that almost everything you do can be changed after the fact by using the various editing commands.

Application Details

When you first start AutoCAD 2000, a Startup wizard is provided for your convenience. This Startup wizard lets you open an existing drawing or begin a new drawing. There are three different methods for starting a new drawing: from scratch, from a template, or by answering a series of questions. In addition, you can assign English or metric units to each new drawing and disable this feature the next time you activate AutoCAD. You can always turn this wizard back on through the System tab of the *preferences* command. Figure 1-1 shows how your AutoCAD drawing screen looks the first time you initiate the software.

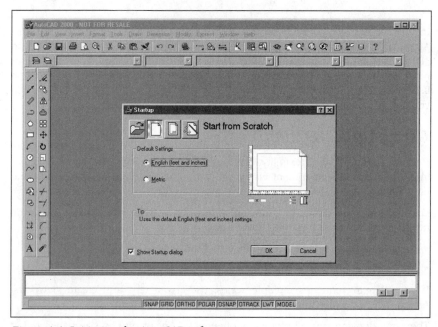

Figure 1-1: Initiating the AutoCAD software

Once you have one or more drawing files activated, your AutoCAD screen may resemble something similar to Figure 1-2.

The items in the following list correspond to the numbered callouts in Figure 1-2 and will help familiarize you with the various items displayed on the screen:

1. **Docked toolbars.** You can move docked and floating toolbars by clicking the mouse on the small gray area surrounding the toolbar icons. After you've clicked on the point, do not release the mouse button until you have dragged

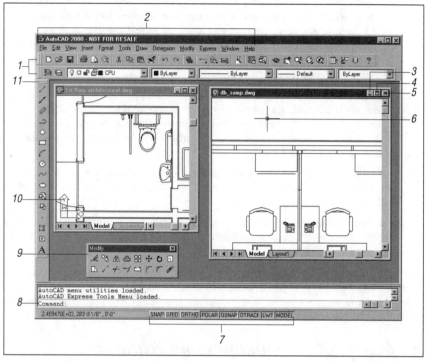

Figure 1-2: Editing existing AutoCAD drawing files

the toolbar to a new location. You can also click on the grab bar located on the toolbar's top or lefthand side.

2. **Pull-down menus.** If a command located in a pull-down menu or dialog box contains an ellipsis (...), a dialog box will appear if you choose the command. If a command located in a pull-down menu contains an arrow pointing to the right (>), the menu is cascading, or another menu will open when moving the pointing device over the command.

3. **Minimize the drawing.** You can also minimize drawing files using the standard Window icon located on the upper-right side of the drawing file.

4. **Maximize the drawing.** You can also maximize drawing files using the standard Window icon located on the upper-right side of the drawing file.

5. **Close the drawing.** You can also close drawing files using the standard Window icon located on the upper-right side of the drawing file.

6. **Crosshairs.** The crosshairs display the location of the pick and drawing points.

7. **Status bar.** The status bar on the bottom of the screen toggles the coordinates, snap, grid, ortho, polar tracking, object snap, object snap tracking, lineweight, and model space/paper space features on and off. Activating the shortcut menu (by right-clicking) on most of those buttons lets you change their values.

8. **Command line.** The command line, or prompt, located at the bottom of the screen, is where you can issue a command or respond to information necessary to complete a command. If you want to repeat the last command, you can press the spacebar or the Enter key. If you use the keyboard to enter commands, you can use the up or down arrow keys to scroll through the list of keyboard entries that have been typed.

9. **Floating toolbars.** You can move floating and docked toolbars by clicking the mouse on the small gray area surrounding the toolbar icons. After you've clicked on the point, do not release the mouse button until you have dragged the toolbar to a new location. You can also click on the top of the toolbar containing the toolbar's name.

10. **UCS icon.** The icon in the lower-lefthand corner orients you to the current coordinate system. This icon is replaced when paper space is active or when working in perspective projection.

11. **Grab bar.** Double-clicking on a toolbar's grab bar automatically makes it floating. Double-clicking on a floating toolbar's banner automatically docks the toolbar.

The express tools are loaded onto your computer only if you installed AutoCAD with the Full option or if you choose that feature with the Custom install. If you didn't load the express tools, you can rerun the AutoCAD installation program using the Add option and install the express tools.

AutoCAD 2000 Commands and Features

There have been a significant number of changes to this latest release of AutoCAD. These changes impact end users, programmers, CAD managers, and those individuals providing support. Although this release can be used in a similar fashion to previous releases, you should take the time to understand the differences and perhaps make changes to the way you currently use the software. This section describes some of the new features and concepts in AutoCAD 2000 and lists the new, modified, and obsolete commands and variables. The details of all the commands and variables can be found in Chapter 3.

Windows-like Features

You can now select more than one item in a dialog box list (when appropriate) by using the Shift and Ctrl keys. Commands such as *open, matlib, appload,* and *scene* take advantage of this Windows feature.

The right mouse button offers a shortcut menu that constantly changes based on the current command and the expected input. Right-clicking on different areas produces different shortcut menus (see the "Drawing Tools" section later in this chapter).

AutoCAD supports the multiple document interface (MDI) feature of Windows. This means you can have multiple files open during the same AutoCAD session. Use the Window pull-down menu to quickly rearrange the open files. Use Ctrl-Tab or Ctrl-F6 to switch between open drawings. The cut (*cutclip*), copy (*copyclip*, *copybase*, *copylink*), and paste (*pasteblock, pasteclip, pasteorig, pastespec*) features allow you to easily transfer objects from one drawing into another.

From Windows Explorer, you can drag and drop files into the current AutoCAD session. Using the right mouse button, you can select the properties option and read drawing information entered with the new *dwgprops* command. You can also search for that information using the Windows Explorer Find Files feature.

AutoCAD DesignCenter

The AutoCAD DesignCenter (*adcenter*) lets you drag and drop drawing files and named objects within other drawing files into any of the drawings already opened. Using the right mouse button, you can open, insert, and externally reference a drawing or image file into another drawing file. The drawing files can be local, on remote network drives, or on the Internet. You can search for files based on named objects (such as layer and block names), information inputted with the *dwgprops* command (title, subject, author, keywords, etc.), date, blocks, or attributes.

Drawing Tools

AutoSnap provides the means to create geometry from existing objects by displaying temporary markers, tooltips, construction lines, and graphical points. AutoTrack lets you draw objects at specific angles or in relationship to other objects. You access these tools using the new *dsettings* command.

The *ucsman* and *view* commands let you assign a User Coordinate System (UCS) to a viewport and to a saved view.

The right mouse button pops up the shortcut menu, providing quick access to many of the commands and their options. The shortcut menus are divided into six modes:

Edit menu
   The Edit menu appears when objects are selected without an active command.

Default menu
   The default menu is displayed when no objects are selected and no command is active.

Dialog mode
   The Dialog menu is active when a dialog box is activated.

Command menu
   The Command menu appears when a command is in progress.

Toolbar menu
   The Toolbar menu is displayed when right-clicking on any toolbar button.

Other menus
   Command-specific menus appear when you right-click on the command line.

Page Layouts

You can create multiple layouts using the new *layout* command. Each layout can contain one or more paper space viewports. You can control layer visibility (*vplayer*), assign a different plot scale factor (*psvpscale, zoom xp*) and lock that value to each viewport (*mview*), and create irregular-shaped viewports (*mview*). You also can assign different plotting parameters, including plotters, to each layout (*pagesetup*). These layouts can be imported into other drawing files (*psetupin*). You can use this feature to split drawings into different disciplines, create construction documents, and display different views of 3D drawings.

When an AutoCAD 2000 drawing containing multiple layouts is saved to a Release 14 format, only the last active layout is recognized. However, when that drawing is brought back into a Release 2000 format, all the other layouts are restored.

Plotting

Plotting probably presents the biggest impact to end users and CAD managers. Before you migrate existing drawings into this latest version, you should evaluate the new plotting options and your current standards. There are now two different ways to plot drawings (*plotstyle*): color-dependent plot styles and named plot styles. Color-dependent plot styles (the method closest to what was used prior to this release) assign lineweights, linetypes, and the color of a drawing when plotted based on an object's color. Named plot styles provide more flexibility since you can assign objects, layers, and layouts to different plot style tables, regardless of the object's color. This method does not work for pen plotters. You also can preview plots that accurately display the plotting output WYSIWYG regardless of the method chosen; each drawing retains its own plot settings.

Properties Dialog

The Properties dialog box displays most of the current settings for new objects. You can set the dialog box to be visible always, or you can turn it off. You can change most of the current settings using this feature. If you select objects, the dialog box changes to show the properties of those selected objects, or you can use the quick select feature and find all the objects based on specific properties.

In-Place Reference Editing and Block Editing

Using the *refedit* command, you can modify an external reference file without having to exit the drawing file and open the reference file. This command also lets you modify blocks without having to explode and then reblock the symbol.

Dimensioning Enhancements

Changing dimension variables through the Dimension Style dialog box (*dimstyle* or *ddim*) automatically updates the preview pane. The quick-dimensioning feature (*qdim*) lets you create multiple horizontal and vertical dimension lines by merely selecting a group of objects. The quick-leader (*qleader*) function creates more intelligent leader lines than in past releases.

3D Enhancements

The *3dorbit* command provides a new way to view 3D objects. It is interactive and more intuitive than the *ddvpoint* and *dview* commands. In addition, you can shade the object and continuously rotate it using the *3dcorbit* command.

3D solids can be modified without having to re-create the geometry. You can edit solid objects by extruding, moving, rotating, offsetting, tapering, copying, coloring, separating, shelling, cleaning, checking, and deleting faces and edges using *soledit.*

Object Display

You can assign lineweights to objects, layers, and plot styles. You can instruct visible layers not to plot. You can determine line spacing for multiline text, and you have more control over stacked fractions by defining the size and text location. Zooming and panning a shaded drawing does not cause the drawing to revert to its wireframe display.

New Commands and Variables

The following commands and variables are new to AutoCAD 2000 and are detailed in Chapter 3:

acadlspasdoc	dimldrblk	-linetype (was linetype)
adcclose	dimlunit	logfilepath
adcenter	dimlwd	lwdefault
adcnavigate	dimlwe	lwdisplay
-attdef (was attdef)	-dimstyle	-lweight
-attext (was attext)	dimtmove	lweight
bindtype	dsettings	lwunits
-block (was block)	dwgcheck	laydel
blockicon	dwgprops	-layer (was layer)
bmod (see -block)	expresstools	mbuttonpan
camera	extnames	mkltype
celweight	find	mkshape
close	fullopen	model
-color (was color)	fullscreen	-mtext
compass	hideprecision	nomutt
copybase	-hyperlink	offsetgaptype
cplotstyle	hyperlink	olequality
cprofile	hyperlinkbase	olescale
ctab	hyperlinkoptions	olestartup
dbcclose	imagehlt	options
dbconnect	-insert (was insert)	-osnap (was osnap)
deflplstyle	insunits	pagesetup
defplstyle	insunitsdefsource	paperupdate
dimaltrnd	insunitsdeftarget	partiaload
dimatfit	laymrg	-partialopen
dimazin	-layout	partialopen
dimdsep	layout	pasteblock
dimfrac	layoutwizard	pasteorig

pcinwizard	refset	ucsman
pljoin	-rename (was rename)	ucsname
-plot	rtedit	ucsortho
plotstyle	rtext	ucsview
plottermanager	savefilepath	ucsvp
plquiet	sdi	-units (was units)
polaraddang	shademode	-view (was view)
polarang	shortcutmenu	vpclip
polardist	showurls	-vports
polarmode	snaptype	-wblock (was wblock)
properties	solidedit	whiparc
propertiesclose	stylesmanager	whohas
psetupin	superhatch	wmfbkgnd
pstylemode	tducreate	writestat
pstylepolicy	tduupdate	xedit
psvpscale	textunmask	xfadectl
pucsbase	trackpath	zoomfactor
qdim	tspacefac	3dclip
qleader	tspacetype	3dcorbit
redir	tstackalign	3ddistance
refclose	tstacksize	3dorbit
-refedit	txt2mtxt	3dpan
refedit	ucsaxisang	3dswivel
refeditname	ucsbase	3dzoom

Modified Commands and Variables

The following commands and variables have been modified in AutoCAD 2000 from previous CAD versions and are detailed in Chapter 3:

acisoutver	ddim	imageattach
apbox	ddinsert	insert (was ddinsert)
appload	ddselect	layer (was ddlmodes)
attdef (was ddattdef)	dducs	limits
attdia	dducsp	linetype (was ddltypes)
attext (was ddattext)	ddunits	lman
autosnap	ddview	logfilename
bcount (was count)	delobj	maxactvp
bhatch	dimadec	mtext
blipmode	dimblk1	osmode
block	dimblk2	osnap (was ddosnap)
bmake (see block)	dimstyle	pack
boundary	dragmode	plot
bpoly (see boundary)	dragp1	preferences (see options)
change	dragp2	qselect
chprop	dwgname	rename (was ddrename)
clipit	dxfin	revcloud
color	dxfout	savefile
coords	extrim	shade
ddgrips	facetratio	snap

textmask	ucsorg	vports
tilemode	ucsxdir	wblock
ucs	ucsydir	wipeout
ucsicon	units (was ddunits)	worldview
ucsname	view (was ddview)	xplode

Obsolete Commands and Variables

The following commands and variables are obsolete or have been renamed in AutoCAD 2000 from previous CAD versions. We've provided you with the alternate command or variable, and you can find details about them in Chapter 3.

ai_propchk (see properties)
aliasedit
ascpoint
cht (see properties)
convertplines (see convert)
count (renamed to bcount)
dbtrans
ddattdef (see attdef)
ddattext (see attext)
ddchprop (see properties)
ddcolor (see color)
ddemodes (see properties)
ddlmodes (see layer)
ddltype (see linetype)
ddmodify (see properties)
ddosnap (see osnap)
ddrename (see rename)
ddrmodes (see properties)
dimfit (maintained for compatability; see dimatfit and dimtmove)
dimsho (maintained for compatability)
dimunit (maintained for compatability; see dimlunit and dimfrac)
exchprop (see properties)
end (see quit)
files
hpconfig
hpmplot
inethelp (see help)
inserturl (see hyperlink)
makepreview (see rasterpreview)
plotid
plotter (maintained for compatability; see plot)
saveasr12 (see saveas)
selecturl (see hyperlinkoptions)
tiffin (see image)

CHAPTER 2

Command Index and Global Topics

We have grouped many of the key AutoCAD commands by function in this chapter. Some of the commands are multifunctional and depending on your application can be used in many different ways. Therefore, this list is at times subjective. Once you look up a command in Chapter 3, *Alphabetical Reference*, you will find associated commands and related variables to help you understand the overall context of the command and how it functions in the program. In this chapter, we also cover the major global topics, such as selection sets and transparent commands and variables, that are crucial to using AutoCAD 2000 effectively.

Creating Accurate Drawings

There are various tools available to help create accurate drawings, and these commands are crucial in creating them. It is far easier to spend the time creating the drawing accurately than to try to fix it up later.

dsettings   ucsman

Drawing

The following commands increase productivity by letting you use existing objects to create new geometry.

array	block	copy	grips	insert
minsert	mirror	mirror3d	offset	3darray

Hatching

Cross-hatching is often used to enhance sectional views and to show the type of material the geometry represents. Architectural drawings often show glass, roofing, and brick materials; mechanical drawings may show steel, iron, and bronze; and structural detail drawings frequently show earth, concrete, and steel.

bhatch   hatch   hatchedit   superhatch

Dimensioning

Dimensioning commands automatically construct the appropriate dimension lines, arrowheads, extension (witness) lines, and dimensional text to drawings. Depending on how you set up your drawing's dimensioning features, you can automatically update the dimensions without having to re-create them.

Dimensioning commands are grouped into three major categories: construction, edit, and style. These categories are supported by more than 60 dimension variables, whose values you can set to control dimension appearance. The following is a breakdown of the three dimensioning command categories and dimension variables. Each list shows the command name when activated at the Command prompt and its counterpart when activated at the Dim prompt. When looking up individual commands, use the Command prompt name.

Creating associative dimensions is the most important feature of dimensioning. Associative dimensions can be dynamically updated individually or as part of a group. Nonassociative dimensions cannot be updated unless you edit each component of the dimension or redimension the object. It is strongly recommended that you create associative dimensions and dimension styles (*ddim*). If necessary, convert only those that you feel should be nonassociative. Use the *explode* or *xplode* command to convert associative dimensions to nonassociative. The variable to keep dimensions associative is named *dimaso*.

Construction

dimaligned	dimcenter	dimlinear	leader	qleader
dimangular	dimcontinue	dimordinate	qdim	tolerance
dimbaseline	dimdiameter	dimradius		

Edit

dimedit	dimim	dimtedit	dimtmove	qldetachset
dimex	dimstyle			

Style

dimoverride	dimstyle

Variables

dimadec	dimaso	dimclre	dimjust	dimscale
dimalt	dimasz	dimclrt	dimldrblk	dimsd1
dimaltd	dimatfit	dimdec	dimlfac	dimsd2
dimaltf	dimaunit	dimdle	dimlim	dimse1
dimaltrnd	dimazin	dimdli	dimlunit	dimse2
dimalttd	dimblk	dimdsep	dimlwd	dimsoxd
dimalttz	dimblk1	dimexe	dimlwe	dimstyle
dimaltu	dimblk2	dimexo	dimpost	dimtad
dimaltz	dimcen	dimfrac	dimrnd	dimtdec
dimapost	dimclrd	dimgap	dimsah	dimtfac

dimtih	dimtofl	dimtolj	dimtvp	dimtzin
dimtix	dimtoh	dimtp	dimtxsty	dimupt
dimtm	dimtol	dimtsz	dimtxt	dimzin

Drawing Annotation

Annotation includes the various methods of placing text and notes on a drawing. Although dimensions are also a form of annotation, I left that as a separate item due to its complexity. There are five different methods for creating annotation:

- *text* and *dtext* create lines of text where each line of text is a separate object.

- *mtext* maintains one or more lines of text as one object.

- Attributes are similar to *text* and *dtext*, but the text height, justification, and font are preset. They help maintain drafting standards and are often used in titleblocks. Attribute information can be exported from the AutoCAD drawing and imported into database and spreadsheet programs.

- *arctext* creates text about an arc.

- *rtext* references the content of ASCII text files or the value of Diesel expressions.

Displaying Annotation

attdisp	fontalt	fontmap	qtext	style

Creating Annotation

arctext	dtext	mtext	rtext	text
attdef	leader	qleader		

Editing Annotation

attedit	find	mtprop	spell	textunmask
attredef	gatte	properties	textfit	txt2mtxt
ddatte	mtexted	rtedit	textmask	txtexp
ddedit				

Drawing Information

The following commands provide specific information about objects and more general information concerning the drawing file. These commands are especially useful when working on a drawing that hasn't been worked on for a while or one that was created by someone else.

area	distance	list	status	whohas
bcount	id	stats	time	xlist
dblist				

Drawing Display

Drawing display commands control how objects appear on the screen. This includes the object's screen resolution, viewing size, and color. The commands in the "Rendering and Shading" section also control the drawing display, but they are specifically for 3D objects.

clipit	hide	redraw	viewres	3dclip
ddvpoint	layer	redrawall	vpclip	3dcorbit
draworder	lman	regen	vplayer	3ddistance
dsviewer	pan	regenall	vpoint	3dorbit
dview	plan	syswindows	wipeout	3dpan
edge	psdrag	transparency	xclip	3dswivel
fill	psfill	view	zoom	3dzoom

Rendering and Shading

Although the following commands are part of the drawing display category, we kept them separate since they specifically refer to 3D objects.

background	matlib	rpref	scene	shademode
fog	render	saveimg	shade	showmat
light	rmat			

Paper Space and Plotting

You can use paper space to prepare drawings for plotting, or you can simply plot in model space. However, the benefits of using paper space far outweigh the more traditional and less flexible model space plots.

layout	pcinwizard	plotstyle	preview	stylesmanager
pagesetup	plot	plottermanager	psetupin	

Sharing Information

You can copy geometry from one drawing into another. In addition, you can import other file types into AutoCAD and export different file types from AutoCAD to be used by other programs. Files can reference other files, and they can be linked to addresses and files on the Internet.

acisin	copyhist	imageattach	pasteblock	showurls
acisout	copylink	imageclip	pasteclip	stlout
adcenter	cutclip	import	pasteorig	wblock
ameconvert	dxbin	insertobj	pastespec	xattach
attext	export	lslib	psetupin	xbind
bmpout	hyperlink	lsnew	refclose	xref
copybase	hyperlinkoptions	olelinks	refedit	3dsin
copyclip	image	olescale	refset	3dsout

Global AutoCAD Topics

We have included the following AutoCAD topics since they are crucial to creating accurate drawings and increasing productivity. These topics contain options that are used as modifiers to the various AutoCAD commands.

Point and Coordinate Entry

Point entry is based on the Cartesian coordinate system; every point has an X, a Y, and a Z value. The X axis is the horizontal distance; the Y axis is the vertical distance; and the Z axis is at a right angle to the plane defined by the X and Y axes. If you do not specify a Z value, it defaults to the current elevation.

Nearly all AutoCAD commands require you to identify points. Most prompts typically request "Specify first point" and "Specify next point." Use the following methods to identify points:

Pointing device
> Pick a point on the screen with your pointing device. You can use any of the following to help locate specific points: grid, grips, ortho, object snap, polar tracking, point filters, and snap.

Direct distance entry
> When asked to specify a second point, move your pointing device in the intended direction and enter the distance.

Absolute coordinates
> Specify a point by entering its absolute coordinates. Absolute coordinates are based on the current UCS origin. Examples are 3,2 or 3,2,0.

Relative coordinates
> Specify a point by entering its relative coordinates. Relative coordinates are relative to the last entered point and are preceded with the @ symbol. Examples are @-5,0 or @-5,0,0.

Polar coordinates
> Specify an absolute or relative point by entering polar coordinates. Polar coordinates specify a distance and angle or direction. The format for an absolute polar coordinate is *distance<direction*; precede with an @ for a relative polar coordinate. Examples are 3<90 or @3<90.

Spherical coordinates
> Specify a spherical point. This is a 3D variation of the polar format. A point is specified by its distance from the current UCS origin, its angle in the XY plane, and its angle up from the XY plane. Use the < symbol between each value. The format for an absolute spherical point is *distance<direction in the XY plane<direction up from XY plane*; precede with an @ for a relative spherical point. Examples are 4<90<30 or @4<90<30.

Cylindrical coordinates
> Specify a cylindrical point. This is another 3D variation of the polar format. A point is specified by its distance from the current UCS origin, its angle in the XY plane, and its Z distance. Use the < symbol to separate the distance and angle; use a comma to separate the angle and Z distance. The format for an

absolute cylindrical point is *distance<direction in the XY plane,Z value*; precede with an @ for relative cylindrical points. Examples are 8<22,5 or @8<22,5.

The following tips will help you use point and coordinate entries in AutoCAD:

- The status bar displays the current coordinates if *coords* is enabled. The coordinates are displayed with the current *units* settings.

- If *limits* checking is on and you enter a point outside the limits, you will receive the message, "**Outside limits." Either re-enter a point inside the limits, turn limits checking off, or change the limits.

- Using direct distance entry and polar coordinate entry (*@distance<direction*) is easy and fast since you do not have to remember to use negative numbers.

- Points are expressed in relation to the current UCS. If you are working in an UCS and want to enter a point based on the World Coordinate System (WCS), precede the coordinates with an asterisk. This entry can be used for relative as well as polar input. If used for relative points, the format is @*X,Y or @*distance<direction.

- *lastangle* and *lastpoint* are related variables.

Point Filter

Point filter lets you use the coordinate components of existing points in your drawing to build a new point. You can use any combination of existing X, Y, and Z values and new values entered from the keyboard. Use filters to specify a Z value easily when working in 3D.

There are two different ways you can access point filter in AutoCAD. From the command line you can type the following commands: **.X**, **.Y**, **.Z**, **.XY**, **.XZ**, and **.YZ**. Using your mouse or other pointing device, you can Shift-right-click and choose Point Filters from the context menu.

The following prompts can be defined from the command line:

.X Accept the *X* value of the next point.

.Y Accept the *Y* value of the next point.

.Z Accept the *Z* value of the next point.

.XY Accept the *X,Y* value of the next point.

.XZ Accept the *X,Z* value of the next point.

.YX Accept the *Y,Z* value of the next point.

The following is an example of using point filter:

```
Command: Circle
Specify center point for circle or [3P/2P/Ttr (tan tan radius)]: .X
of Mid
of (need YZ): Mid
of
Specify radius of circle or [Diameter]: .5
```

Selection Sets

Selection sets are used to locate objects for editing and inquiry commands. You form a selection set at the "Select objects" prompt displayed by most commands. Create selection sets using one or more of the various choices listed in this section. As a selection set is formed the objects usually are highlighted on the screen.

You also can select objects with *filter*, *qselect*, and *getsel*. *filter*, and *qselect* let you select objects based on the object type, layer, color, lineweight, linetype, linetype scale, hyperlink, and plot style assignments. *qselect* is more user-friendly than *filter*, but *filter* lets you save your search criteria for future use. *getsel* lets you select objects based on their layer assignment and object type.

The following list uses uppercase and lowercase letters. The uppercase letters show what must be entered at the command line in order to be understood by AutoCAD.

Add

Allows you to add objects to the selection set. Use this option only after you have used the *remove* option and you want to include more objects in the selection set. Once you are back in the Add mode, you can include any of the other selection set options. This is the default mode for creating selection sets.

ALL

Selects all objects in the drawing except those on locked or frozen layers. Be careful when using this option since it will select objects on layers that are unlocked and turned off.

AUto

Changes the selection method to *box* if the pick fails to select an object.

BOX

Allows you to move the crosshairs to the right to define a window and to the left to define a crossing window.

Crossing

Selects objects crossing or totally enclosed within a rectangular area. The rectangular area is created by picking two diagonal points. You know you are creating a crossing when the rectangle is made up of dashed lines. This selection set method is the opposite of '*exc*.

CPolygon

Selects all objects crossing or totally enclosed within an irregular polygon boundary. The polygon cannot intersect itself. The *pickadd* setting does not affect this command. This selection set method is the opposite of '*excp*.

'EXC

Selects all the objects in a drawing except those crossing or totally enclosed within a rectangular area. The rectangular area is created by picking two diagonal points. This locates even those objects on layers turned off or frozen. Make sure that you include the apostrophe (') when using this selection set method transparently. This selection set method is the opposite of *crossing*. When *pickfirst* is set to 1, you can enter *exc* at the command line before using a command requiring you to select objects.

'EXCP

Selects all the objects in a drawing except those crossing or totally enclosed within an irregular polygon border. The polygon cannot intersect itself. This locates even those objects on layers turned off or frozen. Make sure that you include the apostrophe (') when using this selection set method transparently. This selection set method is the opposite of *cpolygon*. When *pickfirst* is set to 1, you can enter *excp* at the command line before using a command requiring you to select objects.

'EXF

Selects all the objects in a drawing except those located by drawing a line through them. This even locates those objects on layers turned off or frozen. Make sure that you include the apostrophe (') when using this selection set method transparently. This selection set method is the opposite of *fence*. When *pickfirst* is set to 1, you can enter *exf* at the command line before using a command requiring you to select objects.

'EXP

Selects all the objects in a drawing except those that were last defined in the previous selection set. This even locates those objects on layers turned off or frozen. Make sure that you include the apostrophe (') when using this selection set method transparently. This selection set method is the opposite of *previous*. When *pickfirst* is set to 1, you can enter *exp* at the command line before using a command requiring you to select objects.

'EXW

Selects all the objects in a drawing except those totally enclosed within a rectangular area. The rectangular area is created by picking two diagonal points. This even locates those objects on layers turned off or frozen. Make sure that you include the apostrophe (') when using this selection set method transparently. This selection set method is the opposite of *window*. When *pickfirst* is set to 1, you can enter *exw* at the command line before using a command requiring you to select objects.

'EXWP

Selects all the objects in a drawing except those totally enclosed within an irregular polygon border. The polygon cannot intersect itself. This locates even those objects on layers turned off or frozen. Make sure that you include the apostrophe (') when using this selection set method transparently. This selection set method is the opposite of *wpolygon*. When *pickfirst* is set to 1, you can enter *excp* at the command line before using a command requiring you to select objects.

Fence

Selects all objects located by drawing a line through them. This is similar to the *cpolygon* option except the lines do not form a closed polygon and can cross over themselves. The *pickadd* setting does not affect this command. This selection set method is the opposite of *'exf*.

Group

Selects all objects within a specified group. See *group* in Chapter 3, *Alphabetical Reference*, for more detailed information.

Last

Selects the last object drawn and displayed in the current viewport. If the last object is on a locked layer, it cannot be chosen.

Multiple

Allows you to pick multiple points before the drawing searches for objects at those points. This is used to speed up the selection set process.

pick point

Allows you to select one object at a time. The size of the target box is determined by the *pickbox* value. Use the Ctrl key to locate overlapping objects. During object selection, you can press the Ctrl key at the "Select objects" prompt to sequentially highlight each object located near the pick point. Once the intended object is highlighted, press Enter to turn cycling off.

Previous

Selects the previous selection set. Selecting *undo* and closing the drawing clears the previous selection set. This selection set method is the opposite of *'exp.*

Remove

Removes objects from the selection set. Once you are in the Remove mode, you can include any of the other selection set options. You can include more objects in your selection set by returning to the Add option. As an alternative, you can temporarily activate the Remove mode by pressing the Shift key. Releasing the key returns you to the Add mode.

pressing Enter

Completes the selection set process unless the *single* option is active.

SIngle

Ends the selection process after the object or objects are found. Once you are in the Single mode, you can include any of the other selection set options. This option is most commonly used when creating macros, scripts, or LISP routines.

Undo

Removes the last group of selected objects from the selection set.

Window

Selects objects totally enclosed within a rectangular area. The rectangular area is created by picking two diagonal points. You know you are creating a window when the rectangle is made up of continuous or solid lines. The results from this selection set method are the opposite of *'exw.*

WPolygon

Selects all objects totally enclosed within an irregular polygon boundary. The polygon cannot intersect itself. The *pickadd* setting does not affect this command. This selection set method is the opposite of *'exwp.*

The following tips will help you use selection sets:

- You cannot select objects from model space that were created in paper space, and vice versa. You cannot select objects on locked layers.

- When *pickfirst* is set to 1, you can either select objects before or after issuing commands. If you pick objects before issuing an edit or inquiry command, you can select objects individually and use the auto method. The rest of the choices are not available.

- If objects do not highlight during the select set process, check the *highlight* setting. When *highlight* is set to 1, the objects should appear with dashed lines.

Transparent Commands and Variables

Transparent commands and variables can be accessed while in the middle of other commands. An apostrophe must precede the command or variable name.

You know you are using a command transparently when two arrows (>>) are shown at the command line. Most of the transparent changes will not take effect until after you complete the original command.

The following tips will help you use the transparent commands and variables in AutoCAD:

- Filters (*.X, .Y, .Z, .XY, .XZ, .YZ*) and the individual object snap modes are always transparent.

- You cannot use transparent commands during *dtext, dview, sketch, text,* or *vpoint,* for any command that is dialog-box-driven, or while you are already working in a transparent mode.

- *setvar* is a related variable.

Wildcard Characters

Wildcard characters are available for certain commands that retain lists of information or named objects. They help you search for information by using approximate criteria instead of exact criteria and provide complete or partial lists based on those criteria. Sometimes you can include more than one wildcard parameter by placing a comma between search patterns. Do not enter any spaces.

The following commands take advantage of wildcard characters:

adcenter	-group	matlib	-style
-bhatch	hatch	menu	ucs
-block	imageattach	minsert	-view
blockicon	import	open	vplayer
compile	-insert	-plotstyle	-vports
dim: Restore	-layer	psetupin	whohas
dim: Save	layout	rename	xattach
dim: Variables	-linetype	setvar	-xbind
-dimstyle	load	shape	-xref

Typically a question mark (?) is the option that activates use of wildcards. The default, an asterisk, displays a complete list of information. There are 10 different wildcard characters that can be used to form specific search patterns:

? (question mark)
   Matches any single character.

* (asterisk)

Matches any string. It can be used anywhere in the search pattern.

~ (tilde)

When used as the first character in the pattern, matches everything but the characters in the string.

 # (number or pound sign)

Matches a single numeric character.

@ (at sign)

Matches a single alpha character.

. (period)

Matches a single nonalphanumeric character.

[..]

Matches any one of the characters enclosed in the brackets.

[~...]

Matches any of the characters not enclosed in the brackets. Characters such as # or @ are taken literally.

- (hyphen)

Specifies a range when used within brackets.

` (reverse quote)

Escapes special characters (reads next character literally).

PART II

Alphabetical Reference

CHAPTER 3

Alphabetical Reference

'ABOUT

Displays a dialog box containing the following information: AutoCAD copyright, release number, serial number, licensed to, and obtained from. This information is determined during the initial AutoCAD installation procedure and is modified when you run incremental patch updates. Once the software is installed, you cannot change the information.

Initiate Command By

Command: **about**
Help → About AutoCAD

Related Variables   acadver, loginname

'ACADLSPASDOC [2000]

Determines whether the *acad.lsp* file is activated only at the beginning of an AutoCAD drawing session or activated each time a drawing is opened. This variable is set when checking the "Load *acad.lsp* with every drawing" box in the *options* System tab. The *acad.lsp* file does not come with AutoCAD; it is a file created by programmers wanting to add more functionality to AutoCAD.

Initiate Command By

Command: **acadlspasdoc**

Options

0   The *acad.lsp* file is activated only at the beginning of an AutoCAD drawing session.

1   The *acad.lsp* file is activated each time a drawing is opened.

Variable Settings

Initial default:	0
Subsequent default:	Registry file
Value:	Integer

Tips & Warnings

Changes to this setting won't take effect until you restart AutoCAD.

Associated Commands   options, preferences

'ACADPREFIX

Displays the AutoCAD support folder path. This *acadprefix* path is set with the "Support file search path" and "Device driver file search path" options from the *options* Files tab. Setting the path enables AutoCAD to locate support files such as font definitions and AutoLISP routines. You should set the folder path to locate any customized support and font files.

Initiate Command By

Command: **acadprefix**

Variable Settings

Initial default:	System default, read-only
Subsequent default:	Last value set
Value:	String

Tips & Warnings

acadprefix truncates the path if it has more than 63 characters. Select the Files tab of the *options* command to determine the complete path setting.

Associated Commands   options, preferences

'ACADVER

Displays the AutoCAD release or version number.

Initiate Command By

Command: **acadver**

Variable Settings

Initial default:	System default, read-only
Subsequent default:	Initial default
Value:	String

ACISIN   *see IMPORT*

ACISOUT   *see EXPORT*

'ACISOUTVER 2000mod

Defines the ACIS version of *.sat* files that are created with the *acisout* command. The version's value can be set to 15–18, 20, 21, 30, or 40. ACIS files are based on 3D modeling technology developed by Spatial Technology.

Initiate Command By

Command: **acisoutver**

Variable Settings

Initial default:	System default
Subsequent default:	Initial default
Value:	Integer

Associated Commands

acisout, export

ADCCLOSE 2000

Closes the AutoCAD DesignCenter window. You can also pick the Windows close button to close the window. See the *adcenter* command for more detailed information.

Initiate Command By

Command: **adcclose**
Alias: Ctrl-2

Associated Commands

adcenter, adcnavigate

ADCENTER 2000   Standard toolbar

Starts AutoCAD DesignCenter, which is a multipurpose program that displays drawing files and raster images. The drawing files can be inserted as a block or external reference into any of the drawing files that are already open. You also can open additional drawing files for editing. Use the shortcut menu to define the method or drag the file into an empty drawing area. Named objects (blocks, dimension styles, layers, layouts, linetypes, text styles, and external references) can be inserted from one drawing into another. Dragging a raster image (*bil, bmp, cal, cg4, dib, flc, fli, gif, gp4, ig4, igs, jpg, mil, pct, pcx, png, rlc, rle, rst, tga, tif*) into an open drawing is equivalent to using the *imageattach* or *image* command.

Initiate Command By

Command: **adcenter**, **adc**
Alias: Ctrl-2
Tools → AutoCAD DesignCenter

Options

The AutoCAD DesignCenter is split vertically into two sections. The section on the left is known as the navigation pane or tree view, and the section on the right is known as the palette or content pane.

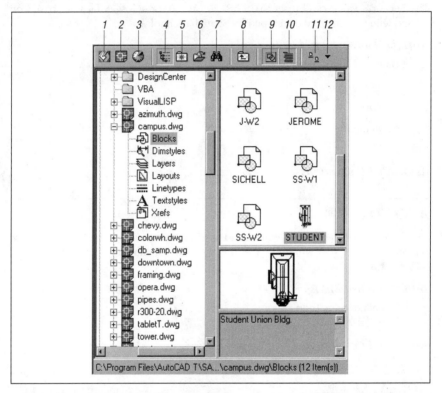

1. **Desktop.** Displays in the tree view all the files and folders you can access from your computer. Depending on your hardware and software setup, this may include network drives and access to the Internet. When you highlight a drawing file in the tree view, a listing of all the named objects for that drawing are listed in the content pane.

2. **Open Drawing.** Displays in the tree view all the files currently opened in your AutoCAD session.

3. **History.** Displays in the tree view a list of files that were selected from the content pane. The list length varies depending on your computer hardware. Selecting an item automatically sets the tree view to that file's location.

4. **Tree View.** Displays or hides the tree view.

5. **Favorites**. Displays in the tree view the contents of the Autodesk Favorites folder. This folder is located in the \ *Windows* directory.

6. **Load**. Displays the Load Design Center Palette dialog box, which lists AutoCAD drawing files and file types available for use with the AutoCAD DesignCenter program. Selecting a file automatically displays that file's location in the tree view.

7. **Find**. Displays the Windows Find dialog box with which you can search for drawing files and named items contained within drawings. These named items include layers, blocks, dimension styles, layouts, linetypes, text styles, and external references. You can use wildcard characters (see "Wildcard Characters" in Chapter 2, *Command Index and Global Topics*) to gain more control over your search efforts.

8. **Up**. Displays the contents of the tree view one level above the active tree view.

9. **Preview**. Activates the Preview box in which you can preview drawing files and blocks within drawing files. If the Preview box is empty, a preview image was never saved with the selected item. You can quickly create preview images for blocks within drawings using the *blockicon* command.

10. **Descriptions**. Activates the Description box in which you can read a description of the selected file or named object. If the box is empty, a description was never saved with the selected item. Descriptions for drawing files are created with the *dwgprops* command; descriptions for blocks are created with the *block* command. You can copy the description information into the clipboard by right-clicking in the description box and choosing copy. You can then place that information into other files using the *paste* command.

11. **Views**. Determines if the content information is displayed with large icons, small icons, a list, or details. This option is a four way toggle. Large icons display the actual drawing as it was displayed on the screen the last time it was saved. However, the drawings must have been saved with Release 13 or later.

12. **View list**. Enables you to choose one of four ways to have your content displayed. This is the same as the Views icon except that instead of toggling through each of the four choices, you can select the display view from a drop-down list.

Tips & Warnings

Whether AutoCAD DesignCenter is active when starting a new session is based on its status from the previous session.

Related Variables	adcstate, insunits, insunitsdefsource, insunitsdeftarget
Associated Commands	adcclose, adcnavigate, copy, dwgprops, imageattach, import, insert, layout, xref

ADCNAVIGATE 2000

Activates the Desktop mode for the ADC (AutoCAD DesignCenter) window and lets you preset a directory path, image filename, or a Universal Naming Convention (UNC) network path to use as your default. When referencing a drawing or image file, you must include the file extension. The first time you run *adcnavigate*, it activates only the design center. The next time you run *adcnavigate*, it lets you enter the path.

Initiate Command By
Command: **adcnavigate**

Associated Commands   adcclose, adcenter

'ADCSTATE

Maintains the on/off setting for the AutoCAD DesignCenter window. The *adcstate* value is set every time the *adcenter* and *adcclose* commands are used.

Initiate Command By
Command: **adcstate**

Options

0   AutoCAD DesignCenter is inactive.

1   AutoCAD DesignCenter is active.

Variable Settings

Initial default:	0, read-only
Subsequent default:	Registry file
Value:	Integer

Associated Commands   adcclose, adcenter

'AFLAGS

Retains the setting of invisible, constant, verify, or preset for each attribute definition. This value is set using the *attdef* command.

Initiate Command By
Command: **aflags**

Options

aflags is bit-coded, and its value is the sum of the following:

0   No attribute mode chosen.

1   Invisible.

2 Constant.

4 Verify.

8 Preset.

Variable Settings

Initial default:	0
Subsequent default:	Initial default
Value:	Integer

Related Variables   attdisp

Associated Commands   attdef

AI_BOX

Surfaces toolbar

Creates a 3D polygon mesh (surface) box.

Initiate Command By

Command: **ai_box**
Draw → Surfaces → 3D Surfaces

Options

```
Specify corner point of box:
Specify length of box:
Specify width of box or [Cube]:
Specify height of box:
Specify rotation angle of box about the Z axis or [Reference]:
```

corner
Define the center of the box.

Cube
Sets the height and width to same value given for the length.

rotation angle
Define the rotation angle of the box about the *Z* axis.

Reference
Prompts for a reference angle and a new rotation angle relative to the reference angle.

Tips & Warnings

Use the *rectang* command to create a 2D box and the *box* command to create a solid box. Extruding a polyline creates a solid box with the option to include a taper.

Associated Commands   box, rectang, 3d, 3dmesh

Example

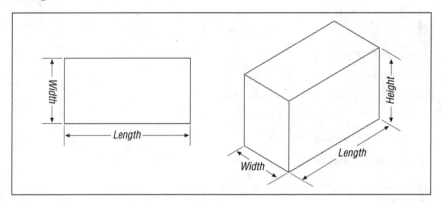

AI_CONE

Surfaces toolbar

Creates a 3D polygon mesh (surface) cone.

Initiate Command By

> Command: **ai_cone**
> Draw → Surfaces → 3D Surfaces

Options

```
Specify center point for base of cone:
Specify radius for base of cone or [Diameter]:
Specify radius for top of cone or [Diameter] <0>:
Specify height of cone:
Enter number of segments for surface of cone <16>:
```

radius for top of cone

> 0   Default radius for nontruncated cone.

> *radius*
>> A value greater than 0 defines a truncated cone.

Diameter

> A value greater than 0 defines a truncated cone.

segments for surface of cone

> Determines the number of line segments generated for each spline.

Tips & Warnings

Use the *cone* command to create a solid cone. Extruding a circle and including a taper angle creates a solid cone shape.

Associated Commands   cone, 3d, 3dmesh

Example

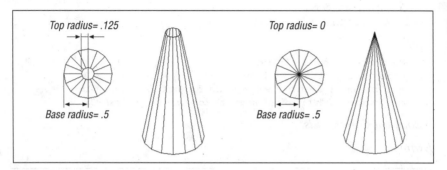

Top radius= .125

Base radius= .5

Top radius= 0

Base radius= .5

AI_DISH

Surfaces toolbar

Creates a 3D polygon mesh (surface) dish.

Initiate Command By

Command: **ai_dish**

Draw → Surfaces → 3D Surfaces

Options

```
Specify center point of dish:
Specify radius of dish or [Diameter]:
Enter number of longitudinal segments for surface of dish <16>:
Enter number of latitudinal segments for surface of dish <8>:
```

Associated Commands   3d, 3dmesh

Example

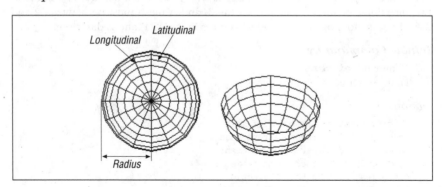

Longitudinal

Latitudinal

Radius

AI_DOME

Surfaces toolbar

Creates a 3D polygon mesh (surface) dome.

Initiate Command By

Command: **ai_dome**

Draw → Surfaces → 3D Surfaces

Options

```
Specify center point of dome:
Specify radius of dome or [Diameter]:
Enter number of longitudinal segments for surface of dome <16>:
Enter number of latitudinal segments for surface of dome <8>:
```

Associated Commands   3d, 3dmesh

Example

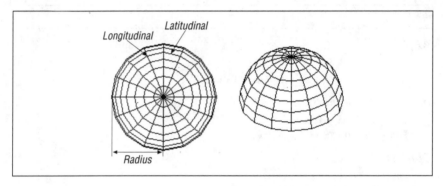

AI_MESH   Miscellaneous toolbar

Creates 3D polygon meshes. These meshes are actually 3D faces fused together to act as one object. You specify the mesh size in terms of the number of vertices in two directions, M and N. The size for the M and N mesh must be between 2 and 256. Use grips to move the individual vertices in the X, Y, and Z directions.

Initiate Command By

Command: **ai_mesh**

Draw → Surfaces → 3D Surfaces

Options

```
Specify first corner point of mesh:
Specify second corner point of mesh:
Specify third corner point of mesh:
Specify fourth corner point of mesh:
Enter mesh size in the M direction:
Enter mesh size in the N direction:
```

first, second, third, and fourth corner points

Define the mesh's boundary.

mesh size in the M direction

Specifies the number of vertices on the M direction.

---

mesh size in the N direction
Specifies the number of vertices on the *N* direction. The *N* direction is considered the direction in which you begin to define the mesh.

Associated Commands   3d, 3Dmesh

Example

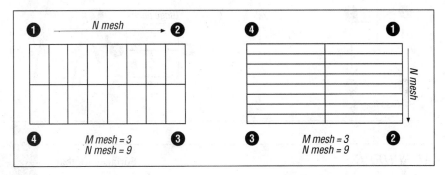

AI_PROPCHK (obsolete)   *see PROPERTIES*

AI_PYRAMID   Surfaces toolbar

Creates three- and four-sided 3D polygon mesh (surface) pyramids. All the sides can meet in a single point at the top, or you can have a three- or four-pointed top.

Initiate Command By
Command: **ai_pyramid**
Draw → Surfaces → 3D Surfaces

Options
```
Specify first corner point for base of pyramid:
Specify second corner point for base of pyramid:
Specify third corner point for base of pyramid:
Specify fourth corner point for base of pyramid or [Tetrahedron]:
Specify apex point of pyramid or [Ridge/Top]:
```

first, second, third, and fourth corner points
Define the base of the pyramid.

Tetrahedron
Creates a three-sided pyramid.

apex point
Defines the top point of the pyramid.

Ridge
Creates a ridge line at the top of a pyramid.

Top
Defines the pyramid's top.

Associated Commands   3d, 3dmesh

Example

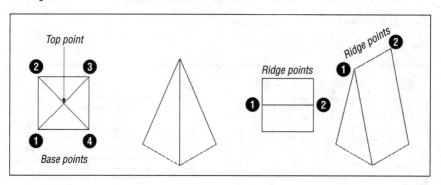

AI_SPHERE

Surfaces toolbar

Creates a 3D polygon mesh (surface) sphere.

Initiate Command By

Command: **ai_sphere**
Draw → Surfaces → 3D Surfaces

Options

```
Specify center point of sphere:
Specify radius of sphere or [Diameter]:
Enter number of longitudinal segments for surface of sphere <16>:
Enter number of latitudinal segments for surface of sphere <16>:
```

Associated Commands   3d, 3dmesh

Example

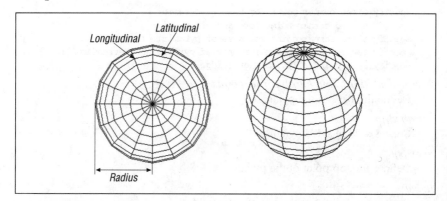

AI_TORUS

Surfaces toolbar

Creates a 3D polygon mesh (surface) torus.

Initiate Command By

Command: **ai_torus**
Draw → Surfaces → 3D Surfaces

Options

```
Specify center point of torus:
Specify radius of torus or [Diameter]:
Specify radius of tube or [Diameter]:
Enter number of segments around tube circumference <16>:
Enter number of segments around torus circumference <16>:
```

Associated Commands   3d, 3dmesh, torus

Example

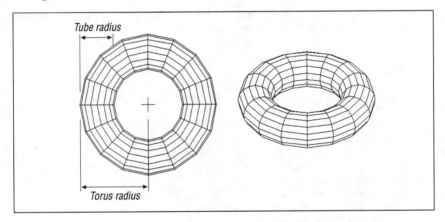

AI_WEDGE

Surfaces toolbar

Creates a 3D polygon mesh (surface) wedge.

Initiate Command By

Command: **ai_wedge**
Draw → Surfaces → 3D Surfaces

Options

```
Specify corner point of wedge:
Specify length of wedge:
Specify width of wedge:
Specify height of wedge:
Specify rotation angle of wedge about the Z axis:
```

Associated Commands   3d, 3dmesh, wedge

Example

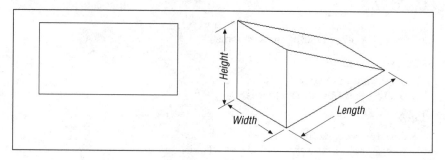

ALIASEDIT (obsolete)

ALIGN

Moves and rotates objects in 2D and 3D space. Additionally, you can scale the objects based on alignment points when using the 2D option.

Initiate Command By

Command: **align**
Alias: **al**
Modify → 3D Operation → Align

Options

```
Select objects:
Specify first source point:
Specify first destination point:
Specify second source point:
Specify second destination point:
Specify third source point or <continue>:
Specify third destination point:
```

first source and destination points
Objects move from the source point to the destination point.

second source and destination points
Once you've defined the first and second source and destination points, press Enter. The rotation angle is based on the second set of points and on the *XY* plane of the current UCS.

Scale objects based on alignment points? [Yes/No] <N>:
If the response is "yes," the source objects will automatically scale to fit the destination points. The scaling is equal in the *X* and *Y* directions.

3D
Objects are rotated in the plane defined by the two destination points and the second source point translated along the vector from the first source point to the first destination point.

Associated Commands   grips, mocoro, move, rotate, rotate3d, scale

---

Example

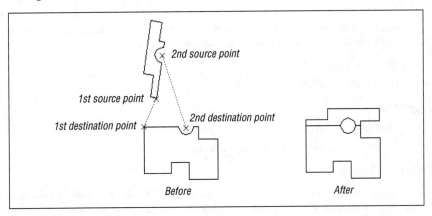

2nd source point

1st source point

1st destination point

2nd destination point

Before

After

AMECONVERT

Converts solids or regions created from AME (Advanced Modeling Extension) Release 2 or 2.1 to AutoCAD's newer version of solid objects. Since the new solids modeler is much more exact than its earlier version, you may have to modify or re-create the converted geometry.

Initiate Command By

Command: **ameconvert**

'ANGBASE

Sets the direction for angle 0. AutoCAD's default settings assume that angle 0 is at 3 o'clock and that angles are measured in a counterclockwise direction. This value is set with the *units* command.

Initiate Command By

Command: **angbase**

Variable Settings

Initial default:	0 (East, 3 o'clock)
Subsequent default:	Last value used in the drawing
Value:	Real

Tips & Warnings

You may get unexpected results if you both set the *aunits* variable (systems of angle measure) to surveyor's units and you change the *angbase* variable (direction for angle E). Try changing only one of the settings and see whether you get the desired results.

Related Variables   angdir, aunits, auprec, lunits, luprec

Associated Commands   rotate, rotate3d, units

'ANGDIR

Determines whether positive and negative angles are referenced clockwise or counterclockwise. This value is set with the *units* command.

Initiate Command By

Command: **angdir**

Options

0   Angles are positive in a counterclockwise direction.

1   Angles are positive in a clockwise direction.

Tips & Warnings

Regardless of the units settings, you can always default the angle to decimal degrees, 0 at 3 o'clock, and positive angles referenced counterclockwise by using two left angle brackets (<<) before a numeric angle. For example, inputting the length of a line at @3<<90 forces the line upward regardless of the units settings.

Variable Settings

Initial default:	0
Subsequent default:	Last value used in the drawing
Value:	Integer
Related Variables	angbase, aunits, auprec, lunits, luprec
Associated Commands	rotate, rotate3d, units

'APBOX 2000mod

Determines the visibility of the AutoSnap aperture box when using the AutoSnap feature. This value is set when selecting the "Display AutoSnap aperture box" option from the *options* Drafting tab. See *autosnap* and *osnap* for more detailed information.

Initiate Command By

Command: **apbox**

Options

0   Aperture box is invisible.

1   Aperture box is visible.

Variable Settings

Initial default:	0
Subsequent default:	Registry
Value:	Integer

Tips & Warnings

Regardless of this setting, when AutoSnap has the marker option turned off, the aperture box is invisible.

Related Variables   aperture, autosnap, osmode

Associated Commands   dsettings, options, osnap, preferences

'APERTURE

Controls the size of the aperture box located at the intersection of the crosshairs during object snap selection. The size of the aperture box may be changed by specifying its height in pixels (1–50). A pixel is the smallest dot visible on the screen. Set the default to 4 or 6 pixels for the best visibility. This value is set when selecting the Aperture Size option from the *options* Drafting tab.

Initiate Command By

Command: **aperture**

Tips & Warnings

- This box is sometimes confused with the pickbox, which is used during the selection set process. To avoid confusion, set *aperture* and *pickbox* to different sizes.

- Don't make the aperture setting so large or so small that it is difficult to pick objects.

Related Variables   aperture, osmode, pickbox

Associated Commands   dsettings, options, osnap, preferences, setvar

---

'APPLOAD 2000mod

Manages which applications are loaded at startup and automates the loading and unloading of applications. The applications can be AutoLISP, ObjectARX, VBA, ObjectDBX, Fast Load AutoLISP, and Visual LISP. These applications are often written by third-party vendors adding additional functionality to AutoCAD.

Initiate Command By

Command: **appload**
Alias: **ap**
Tools → Load Application

Options

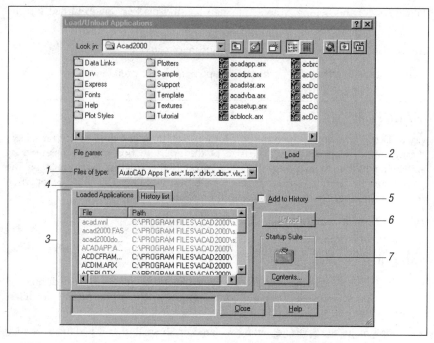

1. **Files of type**. The following files are recognized by *appload*:

.arx	ObjectARX	*.dbx*	ObjectDBX
.dvb	VBA	*.fas*	Fast Load AutoLISP
.lsp	AutoLISP	*.vlx*	VisualLISP

2. **Load**. Loads one or more files selected from the file window. Once those files are loaded, they are placed in the Loaded Applications window.

3. **Loaded Applications**. Lists the loaded application files and their locations. Applications are loaded by using the Load button or by dragging and dropping files from programs that support dragging functionality, such as Microsoft Windows Explorer.

4. **History list**. Keeps track of files that are loaded. This list is retained for future AutoCAD drawing sessions and is kept current as long as the Add to History button is checked.

5. **Add to History**. Enables the History list to track applications that are loaded with the Load button.

6. **Unload/Remove**. Lets you unload applications from the current drawing session when the Loaded Applications window is active. When the History list is active, this button permanently removes references to other applications.

7. **Startup Suite: Contents**. Lists applications that will be loaded automatically when AutoCAD starts. You can add these files by selecting the Add button or by opening Windows Explorer and dragging files into the Startup Suite

window. You also can go to the History list window and right-click on any of the files and select Add to Startup Suite. You cannot include applications loaded through AutoCAD's web browser.

Tips & Warnings

undo has no effect on this command.

ARC   Draw toolbar

Draws a segment of a circle. Arcs, like circles, may be constructed only in the counterclockwise direction (except those created by the three-point method). You can continue drawing arcs and lines from the last point of an arc or line by immediately pressing Enter at that command's first prompt. Using object snaps, you can locate the arc's center, midpoint, and endpoints.

Initiate Command By

    Command: **arc**
    Alias: **a**
    Draw → Arc

Options

    Specify start point of arc or [CEnter]:
    Specify second point of arc or [CEnter/ENd]:
    Specify end point of arc:

There are 10 options for the *arc* command. Combining these options with the ability to continue an arc tangent to the last arc or line provides 11 ways to construct an arc:

    Three-pointed arc
    Start point, center, and endpoint
    Start point, center, and length of chord
    Start point, endpoint, and starting direction
    Center, start point, and endpoint
    Start point, endpoint, and included angle
    Start point, center, and included angle
    Start point, endpoint, and radius
    Center, start point, and included angle
    Center, start point, and length of chord
    Continue, creates an arc tangent to the last line or arc drawn

Prompts display the available options based on the order of the arc's construction.

Tips & Warnings

• If arcs look like polygons, this may be because of a low *viewres* setting. You can verify that the objects are arcs by changing the *viewres* setting and regenerating the display. Regardless of their appearance on-screen, the plotted output of the arcs will be smooth.

- Arcs also are created with the *pline, ellipse,* and *fillet* commands or by editing circles with *break* or *trim.* You can convert an arc into a polyline arc with the *pedit* command.

- When grips are enabled, the arc's grip definition points are the endpoints and midpoint. You can change the size of arcs using the *grips, lengthen, properties,* or *scale* commands.

Related Variables   lastangle, lastpoint

Associated Commands   ellipse, fillet, pline, properties

ARCTEXT

Express Text toolbar

Creates and edits text about an arc.

Initiate Command By

Command: **arctext, atext**
Express → Text → Arc Aligned Text

Options

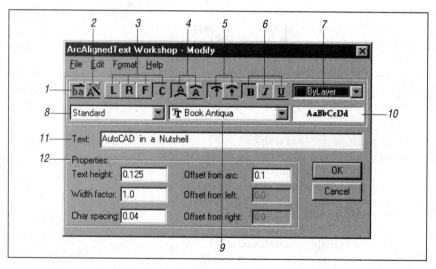

1. **Reverse Text.** Reverses the text reading order.

2. **Drag Wizard.** Determines the text location when its associated arc is modified. When the wizard is enabled, manipulating the arc with grips causes the arc text to adjust accordingly.

3. **Left, Right, Fit, Center.** Determines where the text starts in relation to the arc.

4. **Convex, Concave.** Determines if the text is placed outside or inside the arc.

5. **Inward, Outward.** Determines if the bottom of the text is pointing toward the center of the arc (inward) or away from the center of the arc (outward).

---

6. **Bold, Italic, Underline**. Applies properties to the text string only, not individual characters. Not all fonts can display these properties.

7. **Color**. Assigns one color to the text string only, not individual characters.

8. **Style**. Applies a text style. Regardless of the text style's settings, you can change the font. This option doesn't alter the original text style definition.

9. **Font**. The default font is based on the current text style. You can change the font without permanently altering the style definition.

10. **Font Preview**. Displays a sample of the selected font. If the display is empty, select a different color and then reset back to the intended color.

11. **Text**. Allows you to enter the text string.

12. **Properties**. Assigns the text height, width, and character spacing. You can also determine how far away the text is from the arc and where it starts in relation to the arc's endpoints.

Tips & Warnings

- *ddedit, spell,* and *find* do not recognize arctext. You must use *arctext* or *properties* to edit arctext.

- *arctext* converts each character to single line text when a text string is exploded. The characters take on the values of their style assignment.

Related Variables   textstyle

Associated Commands   dtext, expresstools, mtext, text

Example

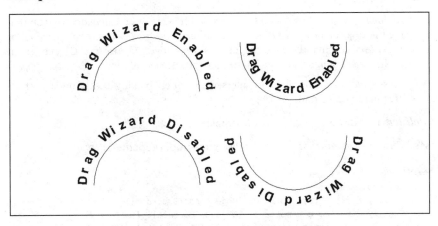

AREA   Object Properties toolbar

Calculates the area of either an object (circle, polyline, region, solid, or spline) or a series of points that define an area. In addition to the area, the perimeter of a closed object or the length of an open polyline is displayed. 3D points may be used, but points and objects must lie in a plane parallel to the *XY* plane of the current UCS. A running total may be calculated by adding and subtracting areas.

When calculating an area, enter *area* at the command line; when requesting the area's last computed value, you must first enter the command *setvar* and then ask for area. This is because *area* is both a command and a system variable.

Initiate Command By

Command: **area**
Alias: **aa**
Tools → Inquiry → Area

Options

Specify first corner point or [Object/Add/Subtract]:

corner point
Accepts points that define a closed area.

Object
Determines the area of circles, polylines, regions, solids, and splines. If this option is used on a polyline that is not closed, the area is computed as though a straight line is drawn from the starting point to the ending point.

Add
Keeps a running total of the area.

Subtract
Subtracts an area from the running total. Before an area value can be subtracted, it must be added.

Tips & Warnings

• An area composed of contiguous arcs and lines may be calculated by combining the objects into a polyline or region using the *pedit–join, pljoin, region,* or *boundary* command. Once the objects are converted, use the Object option of the *area* command to quickly retrieve the area's value.

• Preset *snap* to endpoint and intersection when picking the boundary of an area made up of multiple objects.

Related Variables
area, perimeter

Associated Commands
dblist, list, massprop, properties, setvar

Example

```
Command: area
Specify first corner point or [Object/Add/Subtract]: A
Specify first corner point or [Object/Subtract]: Pick point 1
Specify next corner point or press ENTER for total (ADD mode): Pick point 2
Specify next corner point or press ENTER for total (ADD mode): Pick point 3
Specify next corner point or press ENTER for total (ADD mode): Pick point 4
Specify next corner point or press ENTER for total (ADD mode): Press Enter
Area = 4.59 square in. (0.0319 square ft.), Perimeter = 0'-9 1/16"
Area = 4.50, Perimeter = 9.00
Total area = 4.50
```

```
Specify first corner point or [Object/Subtract]: S
Specify first corner point or [Object/Add]: O
(SUBTRACT mode) Select objects: Select the circle
Area = 0.20, Circumference = 1.57
Total area = 4.30
(SUBTRACT mode) Select objects: Select the rectangle
Area = 0.50, Perimeter = 3.00
Total area = 3.80
```

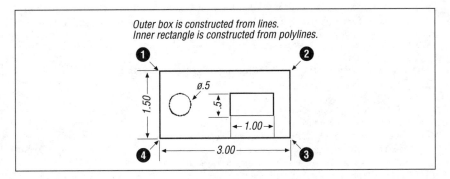
Outer box is constructed from lines.
Inner rectangle is constructed from polylines.

ARRAY

Modify toolbar

Copies objects in rectangular or polar (circular) patterns. Use this option when you need to copy a group of objects that are equidistant from one another, for example, bolt holes on flanges or columns in a building. The maximum number of rows, columns, and objects for polar arrays is 32,767.

To show the row and column spacing for a rectangular array, pick a point at the "Enter the distance between rows or specify unit cell (---):" prompt and move your crosshairs and pick another point, indicating row and column spacing as well as direction.

Initiate Command By
Command: **array**
Alias: **ar**
Modify → Array

Options
```
Enter the type of array [Rectangular/Polar] <R>:
Enter the number of rows (---) <1>:
Enter the number of columns (||||) <1>
Enter the distance between rows or specify unit cell (---):
```

Rectangular
Designates the number of rows and columns and the distance between rows and columns for a rectangular array. There must always be at least two rows or two columns. Entering a negative distance causes the array to be located in the negative direction—down and to the left.

Polar

Specifies a center point and two of the following: the number of items; the number of degrees to fill; or the angle between items. The objects in the array may optionally be rotated.

Tips & Warnings

- Create diagonal arrays by changing your UCS or snap rotation.

- A polar array rotates about a center point in a counterclockwise direction if you specify a positive angle, clockwise if your response is a negative angle.

Related Variables   snapang

Associated Commands   3darray, copy, grips, minsert

Example

```
Select objects: Select lines at 1
Select objects: Press Enter
Enter the type of array [Rectangular/Polar] <R>: P
Specify center point of array: Pick point 2
Enter the number of items in the array: 20
Specify the angle to fill (+=ccw, -=cw) <360>: Press Enter
Rotate arrayed objects? [Yes/No] <Y>: Press Enter
```

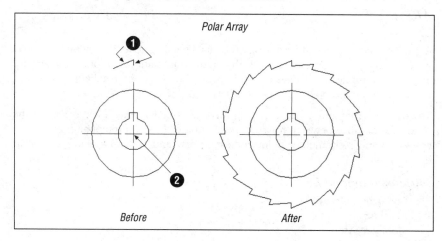

Polar Array

Before   After

ARX

Loads and unloads ObjectARX applications, which are internal applications such as the multiline text editor and render. AutoCAD Runtime Extension is a programming environment for developing AutoCAD applications. Many programs that are purchased to enhance AutoCAD software are ObjectARX applications.

ASCPOINT (obsolete)

-ATTDEF 2000

see ATTDEF

ATTDEF 2000mod

Defines how attribute text will be displayed, prompted for, and stored. Once you define one or more attributes, you save it with the *block* command. Other objects can be saved with the attribute. The attribute data is requested when the block is inserted into the drawing.

You can achieve the same results using the *-attdef* (*-att*) command so all prompts and options appear on the command line.

Initiate Command By

Command: **attdef**
Alias: **att** or **ddattdef**
Draw → Block → Define Attributes

Options

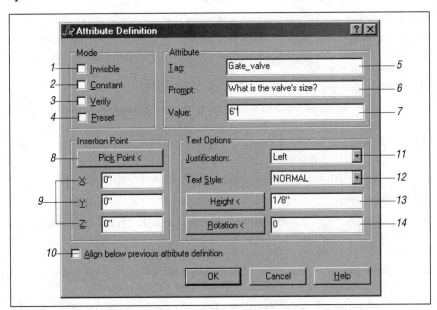

1. **Invisible.** Regardless of this setting, you can make all attributes visible or invisible or return them to their original visibility assignment with the *attdisp* (attribute display) command. This setting is maintained by the *aflags* variable.

2. **Constant.** Sets a fixed, uneditable value for the attribute. Since you cannot edit constant attributes and they do not take advantage of the *mirrtext* variable, you should use the Preset option for greater flexibility. This setting is maintained by the *aflags* variable.

3. **Verify**. Prompts you to confirm your responses when you insert a block containing attributes. Any values defined as constant are not verified. This setting is applicable only if you enter attributes on the command line. This value is maintained by the *aflags* variable.

4. **Preset**. Sets inserted attributes to take on their default settings automatically. Unlike constant values, these settings can be modified. This value is maintained by the *aflags* variable.

5. **Tag**. Assigns a name to the attribute. This tag is sometimes used as a link to an external database. There can be no spaces in a tag name. You may want to keep tag names unique for each drawing or for groups of drawings assigned to the same project.

6. **Prompt**. Becomes the text you see during attribute insertion. Typically, this is in the form of a question or statement. If no prompt is assigned, the tag becomes the prompt.

7. **Value**. Determines the default attribute value. This is optional.

8. **Pick Point <**. Temporarily hides the dialog box and lets you pick a location on your drawing for the attribute's location.

9. **X, Y, Z**. Sets the *X, Y,* and *Z* coordinates for the attribute location.

10. **Align below previous attribute definition**. This option can only be used if you have already entered at least one attribute definition during the current drawing session.

11. **Justification**. Specifies the attribute's text justification.

12. **Text Style**. Specifies the attribute's text style. See the *style* command for more detailed information.

13. **Height <**. Specifies the attribute's height. If the style is preset with a height, this option is not accessible.

14. **Rotation <**. Specifies a rotation angle for the attribute text.

Tips & Warnings

- If you want the attributes to appear in a certain order, you should select each attribute individually in the order you want them to appear; otherwise, you may get unexpected results.

- When inserting a block with attributes, attribute prompts do not appear until the normal prompts for a block insertion have been answered.

- If you want to edit the information assigned to an attribute definition, use the *change, ddedit,* or *properties* command. You can do this before you include the attribute in a block definition or *insert* and *explode* an attribute. Using *ddedit* lets you edit only the tag, prompt, and default values. *change* is similar to *ddedit* but also lets you change the information concerning text style, height, rotation, and location. Using the *properties* command lets you change all values assigned to the attribute.

Related Variables   aflags, attdia, attmode, attreq

Associated Commands   attdisp, attedit, attext, attredef, properties

'ATTDIA 2000mod

Controls whether the Attribute dialog box is activated during the insertion of blocks containing attributes. This is valid only when using the *-insert* command.

Initiate Command By

Command: **attdia**

Options

0   Prompts for attribute information on the command line.

1   Prompts for attribute information with the *attedit* dialog box.

Variable Settings

Initial default:	0
Subsequent default:	Last value used in the drawing
Value:	Integer

Tips & Warnings

- If *attreq* is set to 0, you will receive neither the Attribute dialog box nor the *attribute* command prompts. The attributes are inserted based on their default values. However, you can always edit the attributes with the *attedit* command.

- If, after inserting a block defined with attributes, the attributes do not appear, check the *attdisp* setting.

- Depending on the *extnames* setting, the tag's value can contain up to 255 characters.

Related Variables   attmode, attreq, extnames

Associated Commands   attdisp, attedit, -insert

'ATTDISP

Controls the display of all inserted attributes in the current drawing. *attdisp* overrides the visibility settings defined with *attdef* and *-attdef*. The *attmode* variable maintains the value of *attdisp*.

Initiate Command By

Command: **attdisp**
View → Display → Attribute Display

Options

Enter attribute visibility setting [Normal/ON/OFF] <Normal>:

Normal
Displays attributes the way they were originally defined.

Tips & Warnings

- You may want to create all attributes as visible and control their display by placing them on different layers. Turn the layers off or freeze them if you want to have invisible attributes.

- If you change the *attdisp* mode and *regenauto* is off, you will need to regenerate your drawing to see the result.

Related Variables	aflags, attmode
Associated Commands	attdef, layer

-ATTEDIT

Enables you to edit attributes individually, or globally if they have the same block names, tag names, or value. Executing *attedit* (without the hyphen) only lets you edit attributes individually.

Initiate Command By

Command: **-attedit**
Alias: **atte** or **-ate**
Modify → Attribute → Single or Global

Options

```
Edit attributes one at a time? [Yes/No] <Y>:
Enter block name specification <*>:
Enter attribute tag specification <*>:
Enter attribute value specification <*>:
Select Attributes:
Enter an option [Value/Position/Height/Angle/Style/Layer/Color/Next] <N>:
```

one at a time (Yes)

Specifies the attributes to edit by their block name, attribute tag, attribute value, and selection set. If you respond with an asterisk, you can edit all attributes regardless of block name, attribute tag, and attribute value. Only attributes visible on the screen may be edited. You can edit the following properties: value, position, height, angle, style, layer, and color.

one at a time (No)

Only attribute values may be edited. You may choose to edit only those attributes visible on the screen or all the attributes regardless of visibility. You are asked to enter the text string to change and the new text string. A screen regeneration is performed after the command has completed unless *regenauto* is off. If *regenauto* is off, you will need to wait until the drawing is regenerated or force a regeneration with the *regen* command.

Tips & Warnings

- Edit attribute values with a dialog box by using the *attedit* command. *gatte* edits any text string assigned to the same block and tag with a new text string.

- Wildcard characters can be used to specify the block names, tags, and values of attributes to edit. These characters are treated literally if used within a string to change or new string prompt.

- Attributes defined as constant cannot be edited. Attribute values are case sensitive.

- See "Wildcard Characters" in Chapter 2, *Command Index and Global Topics*, for more information.

References A–C

Related Variables	attmode
Associated Commands	attdef, attedit, gatte

ATTEDIT   Modify II toolbar

Edits each block definition containing attributes individually. Executing the *-attedit* command lets you edit attributes individually or globally. Attributes defined as constant cannot be edited. Enter `multiple attedit` if you wish to edit more than one block containing attribute information.

Initiate Command By

Command: **attedit** or **ddatte**
Alias: **ate**
Modify → Attribute → Single

Tips & Warnings

See "Wildcard Characters" in Chapter 2, *Command Index and Global Topics*, for more information.

Related Variables	attmode
Associated Commands	attdef, -attedit

-ATTEXT 2000   *see ATTEXT*

ATTEXT 2000mod

Provides a method for letting you extract attribute data from your drawing. This information is written to an ASCII text file in one of three possible formats: comma delimited (CDF), space delimited (SDF), or format extraction (DXX). Other programs, such as databases or spreadsheets, can usually read the extracted file in one of those formats for analysis and report generation. Either all or selected attributes can be extracted. The program you will use to manipulate the extracted data determines which format to use.

You can achieve the same results using the *-attext* command so all prompts and options appear on the command line.

Initiate Command By

Command: **attext**
Alias: **ddattext**

Options

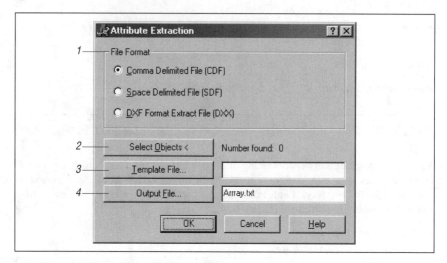

1. **File Format.** Specifies the file format: comma delimited (CDF), space delimited (SPF), or format extract (DXX).

2. **Select Objects <.** Select all or specific objects to extract.

3. **Template File.** Required for CDF and SDF files. In order to extract a CDF or SDF file, you must create an ASCII template file. The template file specifies the type and order of data to be extracted. Each data item is listed on its own line, specifying field name, character width, and precision for numeric fields.

4. **Output File.** The CDF and SDF output gets written to a file with the default extension *.txt*. The DXF option creates a file with the default extension *.dxx*. This makes it easier to distinguish the *dxfout* and *dxfin* files, which have the file extension name *.dxf*.

Associated Commands   attdef, attdisp, attedit, export

'ATTMODE

Controls the display of all inserted attributes in the current drawing, overriding the visibility settings defined with the *attdef* command. This value is set with the *attdisp* command.

Initiate Command By

Command: **attmode**

Options

0 (off)
All attributes are invisible.

1 (normal)
All attributes default to their original settings.

---

2 (on)

All attributes are visible.

Tips & Warnings

- You may want to create all attributes as visible and control their display by placing them on layers turned off or frozen.

- If you set *attmode* and *regenauto* to off, you will need to regenerate your drawing to see the result.

Variable Settings

Initial default:	1 (normal)
Subsequent default:	Last value used in the drawing
Value:	Integer
Related Variables	aflags
Associated Commands	attdef, attdisp

ATTREDEF

Modifies existing attribute definitions (*attdef*) contained in blocks and updates any existing blocks. New attributes added to existing blocks receive their default value; existing attributes maintain their values; and deleted attribute tags are removed.

Initiate Command By

Command: **attredef**

Options

```
Enter name of the block you wish to redefine:
Select objects for new Block...
Select objects:
Specify insertion base point of new Block:
```

Related Variables	aflags
Associated Commands	attdef, attedit, attdisp, block

'ATTREQ

Determines whether you are prompted for attribute values during the *insert* command or whether the attribute's default values are used.

Initiate Command By

Command: **attreq**

Options

0   Attributes are inserted with their default values. Use *attedit* to edit those values.

1   You are prompted for attribute values. The *attdia* setting determines whether the prompts are offered via a dialog box or at the command line.

Variable Settings

Initial default:	1
Subsequent default:	Last value used in the drawing
Value:	Integer
Related Variables	aflags, attdia
Associated Commands	attdef, attedit, insert

AUDIT

Examines a drawing's integrity, checking for errors. The errors can be automatically corrected or left alone. Use the *recover* command if *audit* is unable to fix any errors.

An ASCII report file describing any problems and actions taken can be generated by turning *auditctl* on. This report is created in the same folder as the current drawing. Its name is the same as the drawing file, with the extension *.adt.* You can delete an *.adt* file without doing any harm to its associated drawing file. Every time an audit report is created, it overwrites any existing audit report for that same drawing file.

Initiate Command By

Command: **audit**
File → Drawing Utilities → Audit

Options

Fix any errors detected? [Yes/No] <N>:

Related Variables	auditctl
Associated Commands	options, preferences, recover

'AUDITCTL

Determines whether an ASCII file is created when you issue the *audit* and *recover* commands. This file is a log of actions and is created in the same folder as the current drawing. Its name is the same as the drawing file, with the extension *.adt.* You can delete *.adt* files without affecting the associated drawing file. Every time an audit report is created, it overwrites any existing audit report for that same drawing file.

Initiate Command By

Command: **auditctl**

Options

0   Disables *auditctl* and doesn't create *.adt* files.

1   Enables *auditctl* and creates *.adt* files.

Variable Settings

Initial default:	0
Subsequent default:	Registry file
Value:	Integer

Associated Commands   audit, recover

'AUNITS

Sets the drawing's angle measurement format. This value can be seen on the drawing's status bar and is set with the *units* command.

Initiate Command By
Command: **aunits**

Options

0   Decimal degrees

1   Degrees, minutes, and seconds

2   Gradients

3   Radians

4   Surveyor's units

Variable Settings

Initial default:	0 (decimal degrees)
Subsequent default:	Last value used in the drawing
Value:	Integer

Related Variables   angbase, angdir, auprec, lunits, luprec

Associated Commands   dimaunit, units

'AUPREC

Determines the precision with which angles are displayed. This value can be seen on the drawing's status bar and is set with the *units* command.

Initiate Command By
Command: **auprec**

Variable Settings

Initial default:	0
Subsequent default:	Last value used in the drawing
Value:	Integer

Tips & Warnings

Don't round off numbers when inputting values. Regardless of the current setting, a number with precision greater than *auprec*'s setting is recorded in AutoCAD's database. You never know when you may need the true number for data extraction.

Related Variables angbase, angdir, aunits, lunits, luprec

Associated Commands units

'AUTOSNAP `2000mod`

Maintains the current settings for the AutoSnap marker, tooltip, and magnet features. This value is set when selecting any of the AutoSnap Settings options from the *options* Drafting tab. See the *osnap* command for more detailed information.

Initiate Command By

Command: **autosnap**, F11, F10
Status bar: OTRACK (left-clicking toggles AutoSnap on and off; right-clicking activates the *dsettings* Object Snap tab)

Options

AutoSnap is bit-coded, and its value is the sum of the following:

0 Turns off the AutoSnap marker, tooltips, magnet, polar tracking, object snap tracking, and tooltips for polar and object snap tracking

1 Activates the AutoSnap marker.

2 Activates the AutoSnap tooltips.

4 Activates the AutoSnap magnet.

8 Activates polar tracking.

16 Activates object snap tracking.

32 Activates tooltips for polar tracking and object snap tracking.

Variable Settings

Initial default: 7

Subsequent default: Registry file

Value: Integer

Related Variables apbox, aperture, osmode

Associated Commands dsettings, options, osnap, preferences

BACKGROUND Render toolbar

Determines the type of background displayed when you use the *render* command.

Initiate Command By

Command: **background**
View → Render → Background

Options

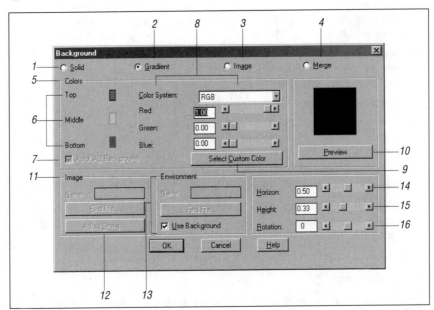

1. **Solid.** Displays a solid color as the background. The default is the color of your model space display. You can change the color by unchecking the AutoCAD Background box and setting the color with the Color System, Red, Green, Blue, or Select Custom Color option.

2. **Gradient.** Displays a two- or three-color gradient background. Use the Color System, Red, Green, Blue, and Select Custom Color options and the Horizon, Height, and Rotation controls to define the display. The default display is three colors, but you can change that to two by setting the Height button to 0.

3. **Image.** Sets a bitmap file as the background.

4. **Merge.** Uses the current AutoCAD image as the background. The viewport option must be active in the render dialog box for this to take effect.

5. **Colors.** Sets the colors when using the Solid and Gradient options.

6. **Top, Middle, Bottom.** Top sets the color when using the Solid option. Top, Middle, and Bottom set the color when using the three-color Gradient option. Top and Bottom determine the color when using the two-color Gradient option as long as the Height option is set to 0.

7. **AutoCAD Background.** This option is available when using the Solid background. It determines whether the default AutoCAD background color or the Color System, Red, Green, Blue, and Select Custom options are available.

8. **Color System**. Determines whether to use the RGB (red, green, blue) or HLS (hue, lightness, saturation) color system.

9. **Select Custom Color**. Activates the Color dialog box and is an alternative to selecting the individual RGB or HLS slider bars.

10. **Preview**. Displays the results of the background settings. Preview does not automatically update. Each time you make a change, you must reselect the Preview button.

11. **Image**. Sets an image file as the background image. This option is available only when the Image background type is active. Valid file types are *.bmp, .gif, .jpg, .pcx, .png, .tga,* and *.tif.*

12. **Adjust Bitmap**. Adjusts the bitmap offset, scale, aspect ratio, and tile setting.

13. **Environment**. Enhances photo real and photo raytraced renderings by using additional reflective and raytraced materials on objects. A mirrored effect is displayed when the rendering type is set to photo real. A raytraced environment is displayed when the rendering type is set to photo raytraced.

14. **Horizon**. Determines the center of a gradient background.

15. **Height**. Determines where the second color of a three-color gradient background begins. Its value is based on a percentage of the screen display. Setting it to 0 displays a two-color gradient.

16. **Rotation**. Determines the angle for the gradient background.

Tips & Warnings

The drawing must contain at least one object in order to display the background following the use of the *render* command.

Associated Commands   render, rmat

'BACKZ

Retains the back-clipping plane offset from the target plane when you view the objects in 3D. *viewmode* must be set to 4 for this to be displayed. *backz*'s value is set by the Clip option of *dview* or *3dclip*.

Initiate Command By
Command: **backz**

Variable Settings

Initial default:	0.0000, read-only
Subsequent default:	Last value used in the drawing
Value:	Real

Related Variables   frontz, viewmode

Associated Commands   3dorbit, dview, view

'BASE

Establishes a reference point for the current drawing. When a drawing is inserted or referenced (*xref*) into another drawing, the location of the crosshairs for the inserted drawing is determined by the base point. The default base point is 0,0,0. This base point can be changed if the drawing is *blocked* or *wblocked* or if a new base point is defined. When you merge drawing files it is much easier to use the same reference or base point for each file. This value is maintained by the *insbase* variable.

Initiate Command By

Command: **base**
Draw → Block → Base

Options

Enter base point <0.0000,0.0000,0.0000>:

Tips & Warnings

When creating write blocks, you are prompted to define an insertion base point. You can always redefine that base point by directly modifying the write block or drawing file with the *base* command.

Related Variables   insbase

Associated Commands   block, insert, wblock

BCOUNT 2000mod

Lists the names of inserted blocks and the number of times each block was inserted.

Initiate Command By

Command: **bcount**

Associated Commands   block

Example

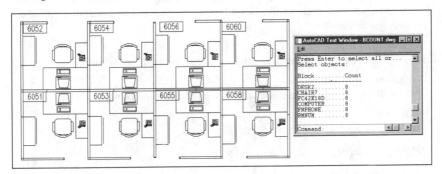

BEXTEND

Express Block toolbar

Lengthens objects to one or more boundaries. These boundaries can be individual objects or objects that are part of a block definition.

Initiate Command By

Command: **bextend**

Express → Blocks → Extend to Block Entities

Options

```
Select edges for extend:
Select objects:
Select object to extend or [Project/Edge/Undo]:
```

edges for extend

Determines the boundary location(s) for the extended object. You can pick one or more objects, including the individual objects that are part of a block definition.

objects

Selects the object(s) to lengthen. Pick closer to the endpoint being extended. You can select multiple objects by using the fence selection set method.

Project

Determines the projection mode used for finding boundary edges. This value is maintained by the *projmode* variable.

None

Specifies no projection. Only objects that intersect with the boundary edge in 3D space extend.

UCS

Specifies projection onto the *XY* plane of the current UCS.

View

Specifies the projection in the direction of the current view. All objects that intersect with the cutting edge in the current view are extended.

Edge

Determines whether the object extends to the implied intersection or whether it must actually intersect the boundary edge. This value is maintained by the *edgemode* variable.

Extend

Extends to the boundary edge or to the implied intersection.

No extend

Extends only if the object actually intersects the boundary edge.

Undo

Restores the last object extended.

Related Variables   edgemode, projmode

Associated Commands   block, expresstools, extend

-BHATCH   *see BHATCH*

BHATCH 2000mod   Draw toolbar

Cross-hatches or pattern-fills an enclosed area. The hatch can be associative in that it remembers its hatching parameters and can be updated dynamically. *bhatch* defines the boundary by creating its own polyline or region. You can choose to save this boundary or have it automatically erased, preview the hatch before making it a part of your drawing, and hatch other areas based on existing hatch patterns.

You lose most associativity features when you alter a boundary hatch pattern so that it is no longer "closed" (i.e., you separate the bhatch from the geometry it originally hatched). However, you can still use the Inherit Properties option when bhatching other objects. You can bypass the dialog box and answer all the prompts and options from the command line by typing a hyphen (-) before *bhatch*. Entering *hatch* or *-h* at the command line activates an older version of the *bhatch* command

Initiate Command By

    Command: **bhatch**
    Alias: **bh** or **h**
    Draw → Hatch

Options

The Boundary Hatch dialog contains the Quick tab and the Advanced tab.

The Quick Tab

The Quick Tab defines the appearance of the hatch pattern.

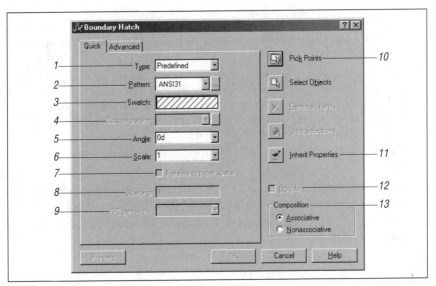

1. **Type**.

   Predefined

   > Sets the hatch pattern choices in the Pattern drop-down list to those defined in the *acad.pat* and *acadiso.pat* files.

   User-defined

   > Defaults to the current linetype setting and activates the Swatch and Spacing edit boxes.

   Custom

   > Sets the Custom Pattern drop-down list choices to those defined in customized hatch files. Custom hatch patterns files must be located in the AutoCAD search path defined in the *options* command. Customized hatch filenames end with *.pat*.

2. **Pattern**. Lists all the hatch patterns defined in the *acad.pat* and *acadiso.pat* files. The Pattern box is active when the hatch type is set to Predefined. It is directly linked to the small box containing three dots to the right and to the Swatch option. If you don't know the name of the hatch pattern, you can activate image tiles containing pictures of the hatch patterns by clicking on the small box or the Swatch box. Changing the pattern updates the Swatch box; changing the Swatch box updates the Pattern box. This value is maintained by the *hpname* variable.

3. **Swatch**. Opens the Hatch Pattern palette, which displays examples of the available patterns. Selecting one of the patterns updates the Pattern box.

4. **Custom pattern**. Displays a drop-down list of custom patterns when the hatch pattern type is set to Custom. This drop-down list is empty if there are no custom hatch patterns. Selecting the small box containing three dots to the right activates image tiles containing pictures of all the available hatch patterns. This value is maintained by the *hpname* variable.

5. **Angle**. Specifies a hatch pattern angle. This value is maintained by the *hpang* variable.

6. **Scale**. Sets a scaling factor for expanding or compressing the hatch pattern. A scale of 1 sets the pattern back to its original size. This value is maintained by the *hpscale* variable.

7. **Relative to paper space**. Automatically determines a scale factor that is relative to paper space units. *tilemode* must be set to 0 and model space must be active. You can always change the size before accepting the hatch pattern settings or by editing the hatch pattern with the *hatchedit* command. This value is maintained by the *hpspace* variable.

8. **Spacing**. Defines the spacing of lines when using the user-defined pattern type.

9. **ISO pen width**. This box is active only if one of the ISO patterns is selected. The pattern scaling is based on the selected ISO pattern pen width.

10. **Pick Points**. Allows you to pick a point in an enclosed area to define the intended hatch boundary.

11. **Inherit Properties**. Allows you to select an existing associative hatch pattern and then copies its pattern, angle, and scale values. Once you pick an existing associative hatch pattern, you can either select an internal point of the area to hatch or press Enter and return to the dialog box.

12. **Double**. Creates a perpendicular crosshatch for the user-defined hatch type. This value is maintained by the *hpdouble* variable.

13. **Composition**. Determines whether the hatch pattern remains flexible and can be edited dynamically. The default value is maintained by the *pickstyle* variable.

Associative

The hatch pattern is dynamically linked to its boundary and therefore changes its shape and size when the boundary is modified. Using grips to move the hatch automatically separates the hatch from the boundary, and it is no longer associative.

Nonassociative

The hatch pattern is not dynamically linked to its boundary and therefore will not change its shape and size when the boundary is modified.

The Advanced Tab

The Advanced tab lets you customize how AutoCAD creates and hatches boundaries. These options also help to speed up the hatching process when working with large or intricate drawings.

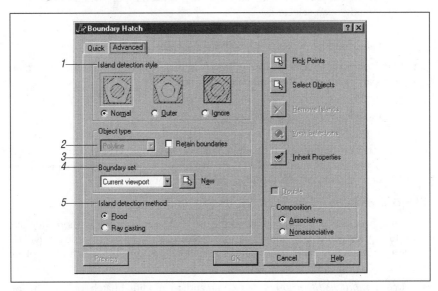

1. **Island detection style**. Determines whether objects inside the outermost boundary are part of the boundary or ignored. This value is maintained by the *hpname* variable.

Normal
> Hatch every other boundary.

Outer
> Hatch only the outermost boundary.

Ignore
> Hatch everything inside the outermost boundary.

2. **Object type.** Controls whether the boundary set is created with a polyline or region. This option is available only when Retain Boundaries is checked. This value is maintained by the *hpbound* variable.

3. **Retain boundaries.** Specifies whether the boundary set remains a part of the drawing or is removed at the end of the command. This value is maintained by the *delobj* variable.

4. **Boundary set.** Determines which objects AutoCAD calculates when defining a hatch boundary. It is directly linked to the option for picking a point in an enclosed boundary.

Current viewport
> Only the objects visible in the current viewport are taken into account when AutoCAD determines the boundary.

Existing set
> Defines the boundary set from objects already selected with the Select New Boundary Set icon. This option is available only when objects have already been selected.

New
> Select objects to create a new boundary set.

5. **Island detection method.** Determines whether objects inside the outermost boundary are part of the boundary or ignored.

Flood
> Includes islands as boundary objects.

Ray casting
> Defines the boundary by creating a line from the point you specify to the nearest object and then follows that object in a counterclockwise direction. Islands are not included as boundary objects.

Tips & Warnings

- *bhatch* is similar to the *hatch* command; however, *bhatch* is more flexible. Moving and stretching bhatch boundaries causes the bhatch to update dynamically. Boundary hatch lines are projected in the current construction plane defined by the UCS.

- Use the *hatchedit* or *properties* command to modify bhatch objects. If you need precise bhatch pattern placement, set *snapbase* to a point where you want the hatch pattern to originate. Be sure to reset *snapbase* when you are done with *bhatch*, because *snap* and *grid* also use it.

- Hatch patterns are invisible when *fill* is off. This is true only for hatch patterns created with Release 14 or 15.

Related Variables	fillmode, hpang, hpdouble, hpname, hpscale, hpspace, pickstyle, snapbase
Associated Commands	boundary, fill, hatch, hatchedit, properties

Example

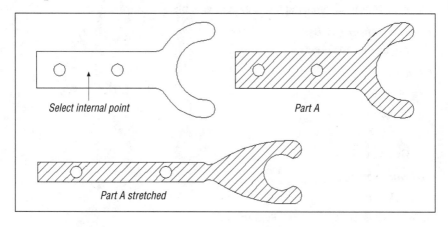

Select internal point

Part A

Part A stretched

'BINDTYPE 2000

Determines how named items (layers, linetypes, text styles, blocks, and dimension styles) of an external reference are saved when the external reference is permanently bound. Named items remain separate or they can merge with the drawing. If they remain separate, they retain their filename followed by *O*. If a drawing is externally referenced more than once, the *O* is sequentially incremented to the next number. *bindtype* is set when selecting the bind option from the Xref Manager.

Initiate Command By

Command: **bindtype**

Options

O   Binding an external reference causes named items to retain their filename followed by *O*.

1   Binding an external reference is equivalent to using the *insert* command.

Tips & Warnings

Layer 0 is special in that it is never prefaced by the filename followed by *O*.

Variable Settings

Initial default:	0
Subsequent default:	Initial default
Value:	Integer
Associated Commands	xref

'BLIPMODE `2000mod`

Controls the display of the small temporary blips or cross marks that appear when you enter points or select objects. *redraw*, or any command like *grid–on* or *grid– off* that automatically creates a redraw or regeneration, clears away blip marks. *blipmode* is both a command and a system variable.

Initiate Command By

Command: **blipmode**

Options

0 (off)

Suppresses blips.

1 (on)

Generates blips.

Variable Settings

Initial default:	0
Subsequent default:	Registry file
Value:	Integer
Associated Commands	setvar

-BLOCK `2000`   *see BLOCK*

BLOCK `2000mod`   Draw toolbar

Defines and fuses one or more objects as a single object within the current drawing. Each block is assigned a name and insertion point. The *insert* command or the AutoCAD DesignCenter (ADC) feature is used to place copies of blocks into a drawing. You can globally update all blocks in a drawing containing the same name by creating another block and assigning it the same name. You may have to regenerate your drawing to see the changes. You can also use *refedit*.

Blocks can include objects assigned to any layer, color, or linetype. Blocks created with objects on layer 0 take on the color and linetype of the layer on which they are inserted. Blocks created with objects that have color or linetype set to ByBlock take on the current explicit color or linetype setting. Blocks created with multiple layers may react unexpectedly when you freeze or turn off layers. Blocks can contain other blocks.

You also can create blocks by using *copyclip* or *copybase* and inserting those objects with *pasteblock*. AutoCAD automatically assigns a block name to those objects. You also can use the *-block* command, so all prompts and options appear on the command line.

If grips are enabled and *gripblock* is set to 1, only the grips assigned to individual objects making up the block are shown. If *gripblock* is set to 0, the only grip is the insertion point definition.

You can insert a block into other drawings by creating a wblock, using *copybase* and *pasteblock*, or by using the AutoCAD DesignCenter feature.

Initiate Command By

Command: **block** or **bmake**
Alias: **b**
Draw → Block → Make

Options

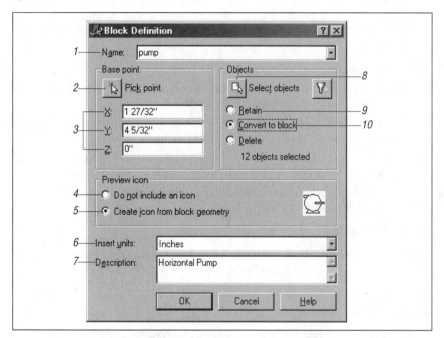

1. **Name.** Can contain up to 255 characters depending on the *extnames* setting. Rename blocks with the *rename* command.

2. **Pick point.** Allows you to specify the insertion base point by picking a point on the drawing. This value is maintained by the *insbase* variable.

3. **X, Y, Z.** Define the insertion or reference point of the block. You may find it easier to use the Pick Point button to select a point on the drawings.

4. **Do not include an icon.** Does not create a picture of the block for the AutoCAD DesignCenter feature to display. If you change your mind after the block is created, you can use the *blockicon* command to create the preview image.

5. **Create icon from block geometry.** Creates a picture of the block to display when using the AutoCAD DesignCenter for block insertion.

6. **Insert units**. Defines the units to which the block is scaled when you insert it into another drawing using the AutoCAD DesignCenter.

7. **Description**. Defines a description of the block. This is optional, but it is helpful when using the AutoCAD DesignCenter for block insertion.

8. **Select objects**. Lets you select objects through the normal selection set process by picking the button to the left; selecting the button to the right activates the Quick Select dialog box.

9. **Retain**. Preserves the selected objects in the drawing as they were before the *block* command was executed. If you forget to check the Retain Objects button and want to restore the original objects, use the *oops* command.

10. **Convert to block**. Converts selected objects to a block reference. They remain a part of the drawing but not as they were before executing the block command. You can always *explode* or *xplode* the block to revert it to its original state.

Tips & Warnings

- You can hatch blocks as though they were individual objects by using the Pick Points option of the *bhatch* command.

- The *group* command also fuses objects together, but each group name is unique and can be used only once, making global updates impossible.

- *bcount* lists the names of inserted blocks and the number of times each block was inserted. *xlist* provides information on a nested object in a block.

- You can create a boundary around a block to define how much of the block you want displayed with *xclip* and *clipit*.

Related Variables	extnames, insunits
Associated Commands	adcenter, bcount, blockicon, clipit, explode, grips, group, insert, refedit, wblock, xclip, xplode, xref

---

BLOCKICON 2000

Creates preview images of blocks, which are displayed when you use the AutoCAD DesignCenter feature and when you create blocks. This feature is unavailable for blocks created with earlier releases of AutoCAD. You can quickly update drawing files and create preview images. Wildcard characters can be used to specify the block names. See "Wildcard Characters" in Chapter 2, *Command Index and Global Topics*.

Initiate Command By

Command: **blockicon**

Associated Commands	adcenter, block

BMAKE 2000mod   *see BLOCK*

References A–C

BMOD	*see BLOCK*

BMPOUT	*see EXPORT*

-BOUNDARY	*see BOUNDARY*

BOUNDARY 2000mod

Converts lines, arcs, circles, ellipses, polylines, and splines into polylines or regions. The objects must form a closed border by sharing vertices or overlapping. Since the boundary is created on top of the original objects, you can easily edit it using the Previous selection set option.

You can achieve the same results using the *-boundary (-bo)* command, where all prompts and options appear on the command line.

Initiate Command By

> Command: **boundary**
> Alias: **bo**
> Draw → Boundary

Options

See the advanced options of the *bhatch* command since *boundary* is a subset of that command.

Tips & Warnings

splines can convert only to regions, not to polylines.

Related Variables	hpbound

Associated Commands	area, bhatch, explode, pline, region

Example

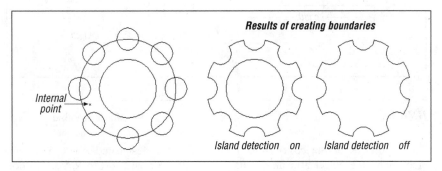

Results of creating boundaries

Internal point

Island detection   on   Island detection   off

BOX

Solids toolbar

Creates a 3D solid box. Use negative values when referencing the negative direction of the current UCS *X*, *Y*, and *Z* axes. Use the *rectang* command to create a 2D box and the *ai_box* command to create a 3D surface mesh box. Extruding a polyline creates a solid box with the option to include a taper.

Initiate Command By

Command: **box**
Draw → Solids

Options

```
Specify corner of box or [CEnter] <0,0,0>:
Specify corner or [Cube/Length]:
Specify height:
```

Cube

Determines the length, width, and height of equal value.

Tips & Warnings

Use the *ddvpoint*, *dview*, *vpoint*, and *3dorbit* commands to view the box at different angles and elevations. Use the *hide*, *render*, and *shademodec* commands to enhance the box's display.

Associated Commands   ai_box, extrude, rectang

Example

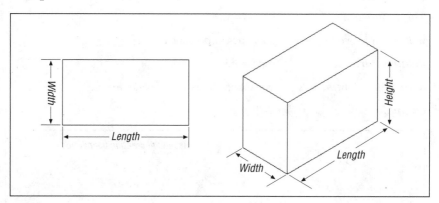

BREAK

Modify toolbar

Erases portions of objects or separates objects at a designated point. You can break only one object at a time. Once you pick the object to break, you do not need to select the object to show the actual break points. Instead, your pick points project onto the object you chose to break. Circles and ellipses (*pellipse* = 0) break counterclockwise. Closed splines break in the direction they were created. If you want to break or split an object without actually deleting any part of the object use the at character (@) at the "Specify second break point" prompt.

Breaking rays results in one line and one ray; breaking xlines creates two rays. You can't break multilines, solids, blocks, 3D solids, 3D meshes, or borders of viewport objects. Since you may get unexpected results when breaking polylines, try using the Edit Vertex → Break option of the *pedit* command.

Initiate Command By

Command: **break**
Alias: **br**
Modify → Break

Options

```
Select object:
Specify second break point or [First point]: F
Specify first break point:
Specify second break point:
```

Specify second break point
Breaks the object between two specified points. The "Select object" prompt determines the first point and then you pick the second point.

First point
Breaks the object between two specified points. After you select the object, pick two specific break points.

Tips & Warnings

• At times you can substitute *grips*, *trim*, or *lengthen* for the *break* command.

• To break between a first point and the end of an object, pick beyond the end of the object rather than trying to pick the exact endpoint. Once you pick the object to break, you do not need to select the object to show the actual break points. Instead, your pick points project onto the object you chose to break.

Associated Commands   lengthen, pedit, trim

Example

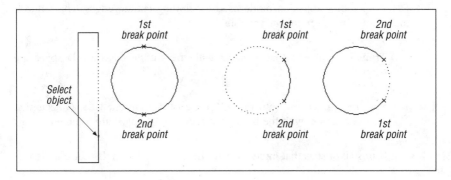

BROWSER

Web toolbar

Activates the default web browser defined in your system's registry. The default web browser must be Netscape Navigator 3.0 (or later) or Microsoft Internet Explorer 3.0 (or later). You can go directly to Autodesk web sites by using the "Autodesk on the Web" option of the Help pull-down menu.

Initiate Command By

Command: **browser**

Related Variables

inetlocation

BTRIM

Express Block toolbar

Clips portions of objects to the cutting edge or implied cutting edge of objects. These cutting edges can be individual objects or objects that are part of a block definition.

Initiate Command By

Command: **btrim**
Express → Blocks → Trim to Block Entities

Options

```
Select cutting edges:
Select objects:
Select object to trim or [Project/Edge/Undo]:
```

cutting edges
Enables you to pick one or more objects to trim, including the individual objects that are part of a block definition.

object to trim
Enables you to select multiple objects by using the fence selection set method.

Project
Determines the projection mode used for finding cutting edges. This value is maintained by the *projmode* variable.

None
Trims only objects that intersect with the cutting edge in 3D space are trimmed.

UCS
Specifies projection onto the *XY* plane of the current UCS. Objects that do not intersect with the boundary edges in 3D space are trimmed.

View
Trims all objects that intersect with the cutting edge in the current view.

Edge

Determines whether the object trims to the implied intersection or whether it must actually intersect the boundary edge. This value is maintained by the *edgemode* variable.

Extend

Trims to the cutting edge or to the implied cutting edge.

No extend

Trims only if it actually intersects the cutting edge.

Undo

Restores the last object trimmed.

Related Variables   edgemode, projmode

Associated Commands   block, expresstools, extend

BURST

Express Block toolbar

Explodes attributes and converts the attribute values to text.

Initiate Command By

Command: **burst**
Express → Blocks → Explode Attributes to Text

Associated Commands   explode, expresstools, xplode

'CAL

Functions as an online calculator for evaluating mathematical and geometric expressions. This command works with any command requesting points, vectors, or numbers. You can create expressions that access existing geometry using the object snap options, insert AutoLISP variables, and assign values to AutoLISP variables. See the online AutoCAD *Command Reference*, accessed from the *help* command, for more detailed information.

Initiate Command By

Command: **cal**

Example

Create a centerline by locating the midpoint between two endpoints.

```
Command: line
Specify first point: 'cal
>> Expression: MEE
>> Select one endpoint for MEE: Pick point 1
>> Select another endpoint for MEE: Pick point 2
(1.23422 7.16791 0.0)
Specify next point or [Undo]: Pick point 3
Specify next point or [Undo]: Pick point 4
```

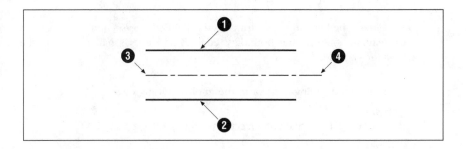

CAMERA 2000

View toolbar

Defines a camera location and target point for viewing a drawing in 3D. You can also use the *ddvpoint*, *dview*, and *vpoint*, and *3dorbit* commands to view the drawing in 3D. Use the *plan* command to return to the plan view.

Initiate Command By

Command: **camera**

Options

```
Specify new camera position <6,5,16>:
Specify new camera target <6,5,0>:
```

Tips & Warnings

Use the *hide*, *render*, and *shademode* commands to enhance the display of the 3D objects.

Related Variables target

Associated Commands 3dorbit, ddvpoint, dview, vpoint

Example

```
Command: CAMERA
Specify new camera position <7.7658,4.5000,21.3700>: -2.5,-2.5,6.5
Specify new camera target <7.7658,4.5000,0.0000>: 1.25,1.5,2.8
Regenerating model.
```

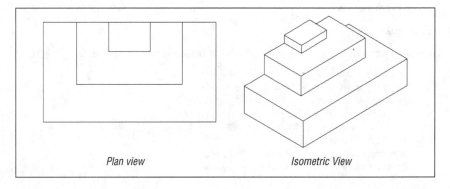

Plan view   Isometric View

'CDATE

Provides the current date and time in calendar and clock format.

Initiate Command By
Command: **cdate**

Variable Settings

Initial default:	System default, read-only
Subsequent default:	System default
Value:	Real

Tips & Warnings

cdate's value is taken from your computer's internal clock. Its value is only as accurate as your computer's date and time settings.

Related Variables	date, tdcreate, tdindwg, tdupdate, tdusrtimer
Associated Commands	time

'CECOLOR

Determines the color of new objects. Changing this value does not affect existing objects. This value is set with the *color* or *properties* command. You can change a color assigned to an object with the *change*, *chprop*, or *properties* command. See the *color* command for more detailed information.

Initiate Command By
Command: **cecolor**

Variable Settings

Initial default:	ByLayer
Subsequent default:	Last value used in the drawing
Value:	String
Related Variables	celtype, clayer
Associated Commands	color, layer

'CELTSCALE

Determines the current entity linetype scale factor for new objects. Changing this value does not affect existing objects. This value is set using the *linetype* or *properties* command. You can change a linetype scale assigned to an object with the *change*, *chprop*, or *properties* command.

Initiate Command By
Command: **celtscale**

Variable Settings

Initial default:	1.0000
Subsequent default:	Last value used in the drawing
Value:	Real

Tips & Warnings

Use the *ltscale* variable to set a global scale factor value. All objects are multiplied by this setting. Use *psltscale* to control paper space linetype scaling.

Related Variables	ltscale, psltscale
Associated Commands	linetype, properties

'CELTYPE

Determines the current entity linetype for new objects. Changing this value does not affect existing objects. This value is set using the *linetype* or *properties* command. You can change the linetype assigned to an object with the *change*, *chprop*, or *properties* command. See the *linetype* command for more detailed information.

Initiate Command By

Command: **celtype**

Variable Settings

Initial default:	ByLayer
Subsequent default:	Last value used in the drawing
Value:	String
Associated Commands	layer, linetype, properties

'CELWEIGHT 2000

Determines the current entity lineweight for new objects. Changing this value does not affect existing objects. This value is set with the *lweight* or *properties* command. You can change the lineweight assigned to an object with the *change*, *chprop*, or *properties* commands. Only polylines and traces that are set with a 0 width display the current lineweight setting. See the *lweight* command for more detailed information.

Initiate Command By

Command: **celweight**

Options

−1 The lineweight is set to ByLayer.

−2 The lineweight is set to ByBlock.

−3 The lineweight is set to default. The default value is defined by the *lwdefault* variable.

Variable Settings

Initial default:	ByLayer
Subsequent default:	Last value used in the drawing
Value:	Integer

Tips & Warnings

If you want lineweights to appear on your plotted drawing but you don't want them to appear on your screen, you may find that your plotter will let you set different lineweights based on the object's color assignment.

Related Variables   celweight, lwdefault, lwdisplay, lwunits

Associated Commands   layer, lweight, properties

CHAMFER
Modify toolbar

Creates a beveled edge from nonparallel lines, polylines, rays, and selected solid shapes.

Initiate Command By

Command: **chamfer**
Alias: **cha**
Modify → Chamfer

Options

```
(TRIM mode) Current chamfer Dist1 = 0.5000, Dist2 = 0.5000
Select first line or [Polyline/Distance/Angle/Trim/Method]:
```

Polyline
Chamfers all the intersections of a polyline. If you chamfer two line segments of a polyline with an arc in between the segments, the arc will be replaced by the chamfer line. To achieve this effect, you must use the polyline option.

Distance
Prompts you to enter first and second chamfer distances. These values are assigned to *chamfera* and *chamferb* variables. Set the chamfer distances equal to each other to create a 45-degree bevel; set different chamfer distances for A and B to create other angles.

If you chamfer a polyline with chamfer distances of different lengths, the chamfer is based on the direction in which the polyline was created.

Angle
Sets the chamfer distances using a chamfer distance for the first line and an angle for the second. Chamfer length is assigned to *chamferc*, and chamfer angle is assigned to *chamferd*.

Trim/Notrim

Determines whether to trim or extend the original lines to meet the chamfer edge or to leave the lines intact and add the chamfer in the appropriate spot. This value is assigned to the *trimmode* variable.

When Trim is active, chamfering a line with a polyline causes the line to convert and join or attach itself to the polyline. When No Trim is active, chamfering a line with a polyline lets those objects keep their original definition, and the chamfer object is defined as a line.

Method

Toggles between the distance and angle modes. This value is assigned to the *chammode* variable.

Solids

Enter surface selection option
Allows you to pick one of the surfaces that will be chamfered.

Specify base surface chamfer distance/Specify other surface chamfer distance
Allows you to enter the chamfer distances.

Select an edge
Allows you to pick the edge of the second (adjacent) base surface.

Loop
Chamfers all edges on the base surface.

Tips & Warnings

- The chamfered edge resides on the layer of the picked objects as long as the objects share the same layer; if the two objects are on different layers, the chamfered edge is placed on the current layer. The same rules apply to color and linetype.

- If you need the endpoints of two lines to meet, set the chamfer distance to 0 and set Trim on. You can achieve the same result with the *fillet* command.

- When offsetting a polyline, you can chamfer the new polyline by setting the *offsetgaptype* variable to 2. The chamfer angle is based on the distance the endpoints of the polylines are extended to fill the gap caused by the offset command.

- The *rectangle* command lets you define a chamfer during its construction. You can remove 3D solid chamfers with the face option of *solidedit*.

Related Variables	chamfera, chamferb, chamferc, chamferd, chammode, trimmode
Associated Commands	extend, fillet, pline, trim

Example

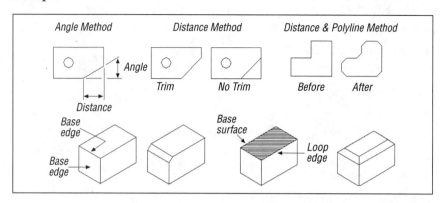

'CHAMFERA

Sets the first chamfer distance using the distance option of the *chamfer* command.

Initiate Command By

> Command: **chamfera**

Variable Settings

Initial default:	0.5000
Subsequent default:	Last value used in the drawing
Value:	Real

Related Variables	chamferb, chammode
Associated Commands	chamfer

'CHAMFERB

Sets the second chamfer distance using the distance option of the *chamfer* command.

Initiate Command By

> Command: **chamferb**

Variable Settings

Initial default:	0.5000
Subsequent default:	Last value used in the drawing
Value:	Real

Related Variables	chamfera, chammode
Associated Commands	chamfer

'CHAMFERC

Sets the chamfer length using the angle option of the *chamfer* command.

Initiate Command By
>   Command: **chamferc**

Variable Settings

Initial default:	1.0000
Subsequent default:	Last value used in the drawing
Value:	Real
Related Variables	chamferd, chammode
Associated Commands	chamfer

'CHAMFERD

Sets the chamfer angle using the angle option of the *chamfer* command.

Initiate Command By
>   Command: **chamferd**

Variable Settings

Initial default:	0
Subsequent default:	Last value used in the drawing
Value:	Real
Related Variables	chamferc, chammode
Associated Commands	chamfer

'CHAMMODE

Determines whether chamfers are created based on distances or by a specified length and angle using the method option of the *chamfer* command.

Initiate Command By
>   Command: **chammode**

Options

0   Uses *chamfera* and *chamferb* to set the chamfer distance.

1   Uses *chamferc* and *chamferd* to set the chamfer length and angle.

Variable Settings

Initial default:	0
Subsequent default:	Initial default
Value:	Integer

Related Variables	chamfera, chamferb, chamferc, chamferd
Associated Commands	chamfer

CHANGE 2000mod

Modifies objects and their properties. Once you have completed this command, you may have to regenerate the screen to see the revisions. You must press Enter one extra time to end the command. You can achieve the same results using *properties*.

Initiate Command By

Command: **change**
Alias: **-ch**

Options

```
Specify change point or [Properties]: p
Enter property to change [Color/Elev/LAyer/LType/ltScale/LWeight/
Thickness]:
```

change point

Lets you redefine the location (or size) of the following objects:

lines

You can relocate the endpoints of the lines closest to the new point you specify. Having *ortho* on forces the lines to be horizontal or vertical to the current UCS or snap rotation. If *ortho* is off, the lines converge to the designated change point. Alternatives to the change point option are *extend*, *grips*, *lengthen*, *stretch*, and *trim*.

circle

You can modify the radius by picking a point showing the new circumference.

block

You can relocate the block insertion point and determine a new rotation angle.

text (single line)

You can redefine the text style, height, rotation angle, and text string. It is easier and faster to use the *ddedit* command when modifying text strings.

attribute definition (attdef)

Same as the text option, but you can also change the attribute tag, prompt, and default value. If you modify an attribute definition, use the *attredef* routine to reblock; otherwise, existing attributes will not inherit the changes. It is easier and faster to use the *ddedit* command when modifying attribute definition text.

Properties

Lets you change the following properties:

Color

See *color* for more detailed information.

Elev

> When changing the elevation of a line, 3D polyline, or 3D face, all points must share the same Z value. You can move an object along the Z axis with the *move* command. See *elev* for more detailed information.

LAyer

> Moves an object from one layer to another. As an alternative, use *laymch*. See *layer* for more detailed information.

LType

> See *linetype* for more detailed information.

ltScale

> Assigns a linetype scale to an object.

LWeight

> Assigns a lineweight to an object.

Thickness

> Assigns an extrusion thickness to an object. Assigning a thickness to 3D solids, 3D faces, 3D polylines, polygon meshes, splines, multilines, multitext, and dimensions has no effect. You can assign a thickness to single line text (*text* and *dtext*) and attribute definitions (*attdef*). You can also use *properties* and *chprop* to achieve the same results.

Tips & Warnings

- An alternative to using the *change* command is to preset the values by using the individual commands *color, elevation, layer, linetype, lweight, ltscale, thickness, textstyle,* or the *properties* command.

- Use the *matchprop* command if you want an object to inherit one or more properties from another object.

- *chprop* and *properties* are alternatives to the *change* command. However, all three commands do not offer the elevation option, and *chprop* contains only the properties option.

Associated Commands   chprop, color, ddedit, extend, grips, layer, laymch, lengthen, linetype, lweight, matchprop, properties, style, thickness, trim

Example

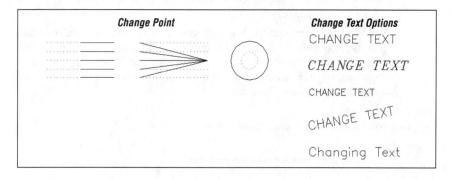

Change Point	Change Text Options
	CHANGE TEXT
	CHANGE TEXT
	CHANGE TEXT
	CHANGE TEXT
	Changing Text

CHPROP 2000mod

Modifies properties assigned to objects. It is a subset of the *change* and *properties* commands but does not include change point, elevation, and text modification options. Once you have completed this command, you may have to regenerate the screen to see the revisions.

Initiate Command By

Command: **chprop**

Options

    Enter property to change [Color/LAyer/LType/ltScale/LWeight/Thickness]:

Color

See *color* for more detailed information.

LAyer

As an alternative, use the *laymch* command. See *layer* for more detailed information.

LType

See *linetype* for more detailed information.

ltScale

Assigns a linetype scale to an object.

LWeight

Assigns a lineweight to an object.

Thickness

Assigns an extrusion thickness to an object. Assigning a thickness to 3D solids, 3D faces, 3D polylines, polygon meshes, splines, multilines, multitext, and dimensions has no effect. You can assign a thickness to single line text (*text* and *dtext*) and attribute definitions (*attdef*) You can also use *properties* and *change* to achieve the same results.

Tips & Warnings

An alternative to the *chprop* command is to preset the values by using the individual commands of *color, layer, linetype, ltscale (celtscale), lineweight,* and *thickness* or the *properties* command. You can also use the *matchprop* command if you want an object to inherit one or more properties from another object.

Associated Commands   change, color, layer, laymch, linetype, lweight, matchprop, properties, thickness

CHT (obsolete)

see FIND

CIRCLE

Draw toolbar

Draws circles. The default radius and diameter values are determined by the last circle drawn for the current session or by setting the *circlerad* value. Circles that are offset share the same center point, but their radii differ based on the offset distance. If grips are enabled, the circle's grip definition points are on the four quadrants and the center point. Selecting a quadrant lets you change the circle's size; selecting the center lets you move the circle. You also can change the size of circles using *properties, change,* or *scale.* Circles are treated as a solid face by the *shademode, render,* and *hide* commands when creating 3D displays.

Initiate Command By

Command: **circle**
Alias: **c**
Draw → Circle

Options

```
Specify center point for circle or [3P/2P/Ttr (tan tan radius)]:
Specify radius of circle or [Diameter]:
```

3P

Prompts you to specify three points on the circumference.

2P

Prompts you to specify two points to indicate the diameter.

Ttr

Prompts you to specify two points (on a line, circle, or arc) that you want tangent to the circle, then specify a radius.

Tips & Warnings

• To create a solid-filled circle use the *donut* command and set the inside radius to 0. To draw circles in an isometric plane, use the *ellipse* isocircle option.

• If circles look like polygons, this may be because of a low *viewres* setting. You can verify that the objects are circles by regenerating the display. In any case, the plotted output of the circles will be smooth.

• When using the *break* command, the deleted portion of a circle is determined by the order of your pick points. Circles break in a counterclockwise direction.

Related Variables

circlerad

Associated Commands

donut, ellipse

'CIRCLERAD

Sets the circle's radius and diameter default value for the current drawing. This value is changed every time you use the *circle* command. Setting the value to 0 removes any default value for the *circle* command.

Initiate Command By

Command: **circlerad**

Variable Settings

Initial default:	0.0000
Subsequent default:	Initial default
Value:	Real

Associated Commands   circle

'CLAYER

Determines the layer for new objects. The layer must already exist before it can become current. Changing this value does not affect existing objects. This value is typically set using the drop-down list on the Object Properties toolbar or with the *layer* or *properties* command. See the *layer* command for more detailed information.

Initiate Command By

Command: **clayer**

Tips & Warnings

You cannot set a frozen layer current.

Variable Settings

Initial default:	0
Subsequent default:	Last value used in the drawing
Value:	String

Related Variables   cecolor, celtype

Associated Commands   laycur, layer, properties

CLIPIT `2000mod`   Express Block toolbar

Hides parts of raster images, external references, and blocks that you don't want displayed or plotted. You do this by creating a boundary around the object. You also can use *imageclip* for raster images and *xclip* for external references and blocks. *clipit* provides a broader range of choices when you are defining the boundary for these objects. You also can use *wipeout* to create clipping boundaries for all objects.

Initiate Command By
Command: **clipit**
Express → Modify → Extended Clip

Options
Pick a POLYLINE, CIRCLE, ARC, ELLIPSE, or TEXT object for clipping edge..
Pick an IMAGE, a WIPEOUT, or an XREF/BLOCK to clip...
Enter maximum allowable error distance for resolution of arc segments
<24.0300>:

Pick a POLYLINE, CIRCLE, ARC, ELLIPSE, or TEXT object for clipping edge
Define the clipping boundary. The text can be single line (*text* or *dtext*),
multiline (*mtext*), or an attribute definition (*attdef*).

Pick an IMAGE, a WIPEOUT, or an XREF/BLOCK to clip
Select the image file, external reference, or block to clip.

Enter maximum allowable error distance for resolution of arc segments <24.0300>:
Determines how to convert arc segments to straight line segments. The error
distance defines the maximum distance from the midpoint of an arc to the
midpoint of the straight line segment. If the number is too small it will
decrease drawing and plotting performance.

Tips & Warnings
Remove the boundary of image files using the delete option of *imageclip* and the
boundary of blocks and external references using the delete option of *xclip*.

Related Variables	xclipframe
Associated Commands	block, expresstools, image, imageclip, vpclip, wipeout, xclip, xref

---

CLOSE 2000

Closes the current or active drawing file. You are prompted to save the drawing
file if you did not do this before issuing the *close* command. If you initiate the
close command and receive a message saying that the drawing is busy and it
cannot be closed, it is because you're still in a command. Once you end or cancel
that command, you can close the file. If the drawing is read-only and you want to
save any modifications, you will automatically activate the Save Drawing As
(*saveas*) dialog box.

Initiate Command By
Command: **close**
File → Close

Associated Commands	save, saveas

'CMDACTIVE

Lists the type of command or action that is active. This variable is available for people writing custom programs that interact with AutoCAD.

Initiate Command By

Command: **cmdactive**

Options

cmdactive is bit-coded, and its value is the sum of the following:

1   An ordinary command is active.

2   An ordinary and a transparent command are active.

4   A script is active.

8   A dialog box is active.

16 AutoLISP is active

Variable Settings

Initial default:	1, read-only
Subsequent default:	Initial default
Value:	Integer

'CMDECHO

Controls whether prompts and input are displayed on the command line during AutoLISP routines. This variable is available for people writing custom programs that interact with AutoCAD.

Initiate Command By

Command: **cmdecho**

Options

0   Prompts and variables are not written on the command line when LISP routines are active.

1   Prompts and variables are written on the command line when LISP routines are active.

Variable Settings

Initial default:	1
Subsequent default:	Initial default
Value:	Integer

'CMDNAMES

Displays the current command including any transparent command that is active. This variable is available for people writing custom programs that interact with AutoCAD.

Initiate Command By
    Command: **cmdnames**

Variable Settings

Initial default:	None, read-only
Subsequent default:	Initial default
Value:	String

'CMLJUST

Determines the justification for new multilines. Changing this value does not affect existing objects. This value is set with the *mline* command.

Initiate Command By
    Command: **cmljust**

Options

0   Top

1   zero (centerline)

2   Bottom

Variable Settings

Initial default:	0
Subsequent default:	Last value used in the drawing
Value:	Integer
Related Variables	cmlscale, cmlstyle
Associated Commands	mline, mlstyle

'CMLSCALE

Determines the scale (or width) for new multilines. Changing this value does not affect existing objects. This value is set with the *mline* command.

Initiate Command By
    Command: **cmlscale**

Options

0   The multiline is drawn as a single line.

any negative value
> Reverses the order of multilines. The smallest number is placed on top when drawing from left to right and top to bottom.

Variable Settings

Initial default:	1.0000
Subsequent default:	Last value used in the drawing
Value:	Real
Related Variables	cmljust, cmlstyle
Associated Commands	mline, mlstyle

'CMLSTYLE

Determines the style for new multilines. Changing this value does not affect existing objects. This value is set with the *mline* or *mlstyle* command.

Initiate Command By
Command: **cmlstyle**

Variable Settings

Initial default:	Standard
Subsequent default:	Last value used in the drawing
Value:	Text string
Related Variables	cmljust, cmlscale
Associated Commands	mline, mlstyle

-COLOR 2000
see COLOR

'COLOR 2000mod
Object Properties toolbar

Sets the color for new objects. You can reassign an object's color with the *properties, change, chprop,* or *matchprop* command. You also can preselect objects and then pick a layer name from the layer drop-down list located on the Object Properties toolbar. Depending on your graphics card and its configuration, you can have up to 255 colors defined in a drawing. The color's default value is maintained by the *cecolor* variable.

You can achieve the same results using the *-color* command, for which all prompts and options appear on the command line, or the *properties* command.

Initiate Command By
Command: **color**
Alias: **col**, **colour**, or **ddcolor**
Format → Color

Options

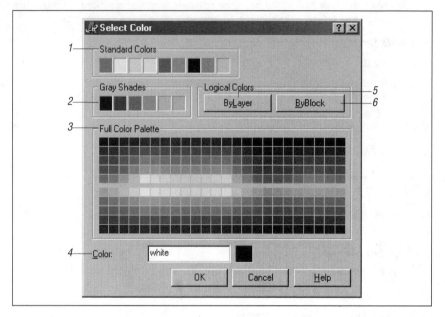

1. **Standard Colors.** Uses one of the colored boxes as the color setting. The first seven colors have a standard number assignment regardless of your graphics card.

2. **Gray Shades.** Represents gray shades assigned to objects. These are assigned to color numbers 250–255.

3. **Full Color Palette.** Represents color numbers 10–249.

4. **Color.** Displays your response to the previous options, or you can enter a color number or name directly in the text box. The value is maintained by the *cecolor* command.

5. **ByLayer.** New objects inherit the color assigned to the layer upon which they reside.

6. **ByBlock.** New objects are drawn in white (or black depending on your display screen's color setting) until they are saved as a block. When the block is inserted, it inherits the color value set by the *color* command.

Tips & Warnings

- You change the display screen colors using the *options* command. Layers and multiline styles have color options built into their commands.

- You can obtain multiple lineweights, linetypes, and color plots by assigning colors from your drawing to different pens on your plotter or printer, and you also can use the *lweight* (lineweight) and *plotstyle* commands.

- Mixing colors on a single layer can become confusing. Using the *layer* command to control color and setting the *color* command to ByLayer helps you identify an object's layer assignment. Changing the object's color is then a simple process of redefining the color with the *layer* command.

Related Variables   cecolor

Associated Commands   -color, layer, mlstyle, plot, properties

---

'COMPASS 2000

Tracks the visibility of the 3D compass in the current viewport when the 3D orbit feature is enabled. The compass is a visual aid and can be accessed with the shortcut menu.

Initiate Command By

Command: **compass**

Options

0   Turns the 3D compass off.

1   Turns the 3D compass on.

Variable Settings

Initial default: 0

Subsequent default: Initial default

Value: Integer

Associated Commands   3dclip, 3dorbit

Example

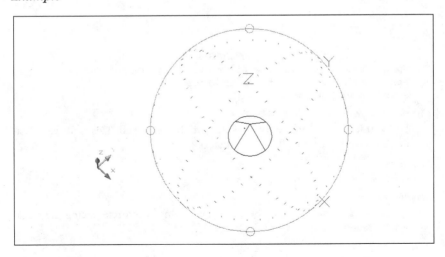

COMPILE

Compiles shape (*.shp*) files and postscript font (*.pfb*) files. Shape files must be compiled; compiling is optional with font files. Shape files can contain font or symbol definition information. Most people use the fonts supplied by Autodesk and Microsoft Windows and create their own symbols with the *block* command.

Initiate Command By

Command: **compile**

Options

Enter shape (.SHP) or PostScript font (.PFB) file name:

Tips & Warnings

If *filedia* is set to 1, a dialog box is activated; if *filedia* is set to 0, you are prompted on the command line. When *filedia* is set to 0, or off, entering a tilde (~) on the command line temporarily activates the dialog box.

Related Variables	filedia
Associated Commands	load, shape

CONE
Solids toolbar

Creates a 3D solid cone containing a circular or elliptical base. Use the *ai_cone* command to create a 3D surface mesh cone. Extruding a circle with a taper creates a solid truncated cone shape.

Initiate Command By

Command: **cone**
Draw → Solids → Cone

Options

    Current wire frame density: ISOLINES=4
    Specify center point for base of cone or [Elliptical] <0,0,0>:
    Specify radius for base of cone or [Diameter]:
    Specify height of cone or [Apex]:

Current wire frame density: ISOLINES=4
Lets you know the number of lines that will be displayed. This is for visualization only and does not affect the actual objects.

Elliptical
Creates a cone with an elliptical base.

height
Specifies the cone's height. Use a negative value when referencing the negative direction of the current UCS Z axis.

Apex
Specifies the height and orientation of the cone.

Tips & Warnings

Use the *ddvpoint*, *dview*, *vpoint*, and *3dorbit* commands to view the cone at different angles and elevations. Use the *hide*, *render*, and *shademode* commands to enhance the cone's display.

Related Variables	dispsilh, isolines
Associated Commands	ai_cone, extrude

Example

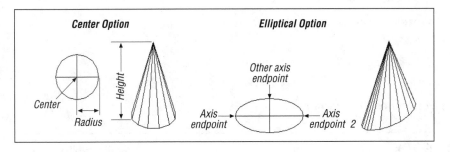

Center Option	Elliptical Option

CONFIG   *see OPTIONS*

CONVERT

Updates associative hatches and 2D polylines created in Release 13 or earlier to a more optimized format. You may get unexpected results when converting hatch patterns that were created with a different UCS rotation angle. Polylines are automatically updated if the *plinetype* variable is set to its initial default of 2. Polylines that are *pedited* with the fit or spline option and polylines that have extended entity data attached always retain the old format.

Initiate Command By

Command: **convert**

Options

```
Enter type of objects to convert [Hatch/Polyline/All] <All>:
Enter object selection preference [Select/All] <All>:
```

Related Variables   plinetype

CONVERTPLINES (obsolete)   *see CONVERT*

'COORDS `2000mod`

Tracks the *X*, *Y*, and *Z* coordinates as a three-way toggle on the status bar located on the lower-left side of your AutoCAD display. The coordinates represent the current units setting.

Initiate Command By
Command: **coords**, F6, or Ctrl-D
Status bar: Toggles coordinates among the three different modes

Options
0   Coordinate display is updated only when points are picked.

1   Display of absolute coordinates is constantly updated.

2   Distance and angle from the last point are displayed whenever a command requests a distance or angle.

Variable Settings
Initial default: 1

Subsequent default: Registry

Value: Integer

Associated Commands   units

COPY

Creates a replica of one or more objects. If *pickfirst* is set to 1, you can first select the objects and then issue the *copy* command.

Initiate Command By
Command: **copy**
Alias: **co** or **cp**
Modify → Copy

Options
```
Specify base point or displacement, or [Multiple]:
Specify second point of displacement or <use first point as displacement>:
```
Base point
Determine a point of reference. Think in terms of "from where." After locating your reference point, you can drag your object(s) to the new location at the "second point" prompt or enter the direct distance or absolute or relative coordinates.

Displacement
Enter the distance for *X,Y,Z* and press Enter at the "Specify second point of displacement" prompt. If you accidentally press Enter at the "Specify second point of displacement" prompt, your copy may end up out in outer space. This happens because it is using the *X,Y,Z* base point as the displacement.

Multiple
Copy an object more than one time by giving a designated reference point and responding to the "Specify second point of displacement" prompts.

Tips & Warnings

- You can copy objects from one drawing into another using *copybase*, *copyclip*, *wblock*, or the AutoCAD DesignCenter feature. Copy individual objects defined within blocks or external references with *ncopy*.

- For multiple copies of complex objects, first block the selection set, then insert and copy. This reduces the drawing size and gives greater flexibility for future global revisions.

- Use *array*, *grips*, *minsert*, or *3darray* for multiple copies of equally spaced objects. Use *offset* to make a copy of an object parallel to itself.

- Using grips, you have a copy option with the *mirror*, *move*, *rotate*, *scale*, and *stretch* features. The *mocoro* command lets you move, copy, rotate, and scale objects.

- See "Selection Sets" in Chapter 2, *Command Index and Global Topics*, for more information.

- You can also copy objects by dragging and dropping them to another location in the current drawing, to another drawing that is open in the same drawing session, to another drawing in another session, or to another application. You do this by first selecting the objects, making their grips active. Position the crosshairs over one of those objects (but not on a grip) and press the left mouse button without letting go. When an arrow with a small box appears, you can drag the selected objects to the new location. If you are copying in the same drawing, you must hold down the Ctrl key; otherwise, it will move the objects. As an alternative, pressing the right mouse button gives you the option to move, copy, paste as a block, or paste original coordinates. The options depend on whether you are in the same drawing or you select another open drawing file.

Related Variables	pickfirst
Associated Commands	array, block, copybase, copyclip, grips, minsert, mocoro, move, ncopy, offset

---

COPYBASE [2000]

Copies objects to the Windows clipboard and prompts you to specify a base point. You can paste those objects back into the current drawing or other drawings files using the base point as a reference. *copybase* is the same as *copyclip* except you have greater control since you cannot define a base point with the *copyclip* command. You can import the objects into most Windows programs using commands such as *paste* or *pastespec*. If you want to copy objects directly into another drawing that is active, use the *pasteblouk*, *pasteclip*, or *pasteorig* command.

Initiate Command By

Command: **copybase**
Edit → Copy with Base Point

Options

```
Specify base point:
```

Tips & Warnings

For multiple copies of complex objects, first *block* the selection set, then *insert* and *copy.* This reduces the drawing size and gives greater flexibility for future global revisions. If you need to use those objects in other drawing files then use the *wblock* command or use the block insertion method available with the *adcenter* command.

Associated Commands   adcenter, block, copyclip, wblock

COPYCLIP

Copies objects to the Windows clipboard. You can import the objects into most Windows programs using commands such as *paste* or *pastespec.* If you want to copy objects directly into another drawing that is active, use *pasteblock, pasteclip,* or the *pasteorig* command. You can copyclip a drawing with the AutoCAD Design-Center program. To do this, select the file and then activate the shortcut menu by right-clicking. Once you have sent the file to the Windows clipboard, return to the AutoCAD drawing and use *pasteclip.*

Initiate Command By

Command: **copyclip**
Alias: Ctrl-C
Edit → Copy
Shortcut menu: Copy

Tips & Warnings

You can also copy objects by dragging and dropping them to another location in the current drawing, to another drawing that is open in the same drawing session, to another drawing in another session, or to another application. You do this by first selecting the objects, making their grips active. Position the crosshairs over one of those objects (but not on a grip) and press the left mouse button without letting go. When an arrow with a small box appears, you can drag the selected objects to the new location. If you are copying in the same drawing, you must hold down the Ctrl key; otherwise, it will move the objects. As an alternative, pressing the right mouse button gives you the option to move, copy, paste as a block, or paste original coordinates. The options depend on whether you are in the same drawing or you select another open drawing file.

Associated Commands   copy, copybase, copyhist, copylink, cutclip, pasteclip

---

COPYHIST

Copies text from the current drawing's command line history window to the Windows clipboard. You can import that information into most Windows programs using commands such as *paste* or *pastespec. copyhist* is available through the shortcut menu when you are active in the AutoCAD Text Window. Press F2 to make the text active.

Initiate Command By
    Command: **copyhist**

Associated Commands   pasteclip, pastespec

COPYLINK

Copies the current drawing display to the Windows clipboard. This can be used to link to other Windows programs that also use OLE (Object Linking and Embedding) technology. Once you are in the other program, use *pastespec* to link to the AutoCAD file. Linked files are dynamic; editing linked files updates the original and the linked file.

Initiate Command By
    Command: **copylink**
    Edit → Copy Link

Associated Commands   cutclip, olelinks, pastespec

COUNT (renamed to BCOUNT)

'CPLOTSTYLE 2000

Maintains the current plot style setting for new objects.

Initiate Command By
    Command: **cplotstyle**

Variable Settings

Initial default:	ByColor, read-only
Subsequent default:	Last value used in the drawing
Value:	String

Associated Commands   options, plotstyle, preferences

'CPROFILE 2000

Stores the name of the current profile. Profiles retain some of the drawing environment settings found in the *options* command. These settings include pull-down menu structure, toolbar location, screen menu and scrollbar visibility, and default file locations. Profiles are extremely useful when you share a computer, work in a network environment, use different computer terminals, or work on multiple projects.

Initiate Command By
    Command: **cprofile**

Variable Settings

Initial default:	Unnamed profile, read-only
Subsequent default:	Registry file
Value:	String
Associated Commands	options, preferences

'CTAB 2000

Stores the name of the active tab: model or layout.

Initiate Command By
Command: **ctab**

Variable Settings

Initial default:	"Model," read-only
Subsequent default:	Last value used in the drawing
Value:	String
Related Variables	filedia
Associated Commands	layout

'CURSORSIZE

Stores the size of the crosshairs. The size is a percentage of the screen size, and valid sizes range from 1 to 100. This value is set when selecting the Crosshair Size option from the *options* Display tab.

Initiate Command By
Command: **cursorsize**

Variable Settings

Initial default:	5
Subsequent default:	Registry file
Value:	Integer
Associated Commands	options, preferences

CUTCLIP

Copies objects to the Windows clipboard and erases them from the drawing. These objects can be embedded into Windows programs that also use OLE (Object

Linking and Embedding) technology. Once you are in the Windows program, use *pastespec* to embed the AutoCAD file.

Initiate Command By

Command: **cutclip**
Alias: Ctrl-X
Edit → Cut
Shortcut menu: Cut

Tips & Warnings

Editing an embedded file updates only that file; the embedded file is not dynamically linked to the original file.

Associated Commands   erase

'CVPORT

Defines the viewport you want active. This is set by selecting the inside of a viewport. When paper space is active or Tablet mode is off, this variable cannot be set.

Initiate Command By

Command: **cvport**

Options

Enter new value for CVPORT <2>:

Variable Settings

Initial default: 2

Subsequent default: Last value used in the drawing

Value: Integer

Associated Commands   mview, viewport, vport

CYLINDER   Solids toolbar

Creates a 3D solid cylinder. Extruding a circle creates a solid cylinder with the option to include a taper.

Initiate Command By

Command: **cylinder**

Options

Current wire frame density: ISOLINES=4
Specify center point for base of cylinder or [Elliptical] <0,0,0>:
Specify radius for base of cylinder or [Diameter]:
Specify height of cylinder or [Center of other end]:

Tips & Warnings

Use the *ddvpoint*, *dview*, *vpoint*, and *3dorbit* commands to view the cylinder at different angles and elevations. Use the *hide*, *render*, and *shademode* commands to enhance the cylinder's display.

Related Variables	dispsilh, isolines
Associated Commands	extrude

Example

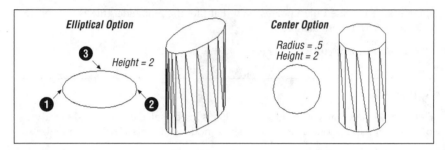

'DATE

Provides the current date and time. The date is represented in Julian format, and the time is shown as a fraction in a real number. The date's value is taken from your computer's internal clock.

Initiate Command By

Command: **date**

Variable Settings

Initial default:	System default, read-only
Subsequent default:	System default
Value:	Real

Related Variables	cdate, tdcreate, tdindwg, tdupdate, tdusrtimer
Associated Commands	time

DBCCLOSE [2000]   Standard toolbar

Closes the dbConnect Manager and removes the dbConnect pull-down menu.

Initiate Command By

Command: **dbcclose**
Alias: Ctrl-6

Associated Commands	dbconnect

DBCONNECT 2000

Standard toolbar

Activates the dbConnect Manager, an interface to external database programs, and adds the dbConnect pull-down menu.

Initiate Command By

Command: **dbconnect**
Alias: **dbc** or Ctrl-6
Tools → dbConnect

Associated Commands   dbcclose

DBLIST

Lists all the objects in a drawing, including information such as their coordinates, layer assignment, size, area, and so on. You should use the *list* command instead since its lets you selectively pick objects, making it easier to associate the description to the object.

Initiate Command By

Command: **dblist**

Associated Commands   list

'DBMOD

Database mode tracks the drawing's modification status.

Initiate Command By

Command: **dbmod**

Options

dbmod is bit-coded, and its value is the sum of the following:

1   Object database modified.

4   Database variable modified.

8   Window modified.

16 View modified.

Variable Settings

Initial default:	0, read-only
Subsequent default:	Initial default
Value:	Integer

'DCTCUST

Maintains the filename of the current custom spelling dictionary, including its location. This file maintains any words you add when using the spellcheck routine. The file is written in ASCII format and can be modified using the Windows Notepad program. The file's extension must be *.cus*.

Initiate Command By

Command: **dctcust**
Tools → Options → Files → Text Editor, Dictionary, and Font File Names →
Custom Dictionary File

Variable Settings

Initial default:	" " (none)
Subsequent default:	Registry file
Value:	String
Related Variables	dctmain
Associated Commands	options, preferences, spell

'DCTMAIN

Maintains the current dictionary filename. This value is set during the spellcheck routine. See the AutoCAD *Command Reference,* accessed through the *help* command, for a listing of the various choices.

Initiate Command By

Command: **dctmain**
Tools → Options → Files → Text Editor, Dictionary, and Font File Names →
Main Dictionary

Variable Settings

Initial default:	Varies by country
Subsequent default:	Registry file
Value:	String
Related Variables	dctcust
Associated Commands	options, preferences, spell

DDATTDEF (renamed to ATTDEF)

DDATTE
see ATTEDIT

DDATTEXT (renamed to ATTEXT)

DDCHPROP (obsolete)   *see PROPERTIES*

DDCOLOR (renamed to COLOR)

DDEDIT   Modify toolbar

Edits single-line, multiline, and attribute definition text. This command will not work for text contained in blocks, attributes, complex linetypes, external references, or text residing on locked layers. The text edit box varies depending on the type of object you are editing.

Initiate Command By

Command: **ddedit**
Alias: **ed**
Modify → Text

Options

Select an annotation object or [Undo]:

Undo

While in the *ddedit* command, you can undo the last modified text string and return to the previous value. Using the *undo* command immediately after you exit the command will undo every change you made while in *ddedit*.

Tips & Warnings

Although *ddedit* is the fastest way to edit single-line and attribute definition text you also can use the *properties* or *change* command. Use *properties* or *mtext* to edit multiline text. Use *attedit* to edit attribute text.

Associated Commands   attedit, change, mtprop, properties

DDEMODES (obsolete)   *see PROPERTIES*

'DDGRIPS 2000mod   *see OPTIONS*

DDIM 2000mod   *see DIMSTYLE*

DDINSERT 2000mod   *see INSERT*

DDLMODES (obsolete)   *see LAYER*

DDLTYPE (obsolete)   *see LINETYPE*

DDMODIFY (obsolete)   *see PROPERTIES*

DDOSNAP (obsolete)   *see OSNAP*

'DDPTYPE

Displays and sets the current point style and size. Points often are used as reference markers during the design phase of a project. You can locate the center of a point by using the node object snap.

Initiate Command By

Command: **ddptype**
Format → Point Style

Options

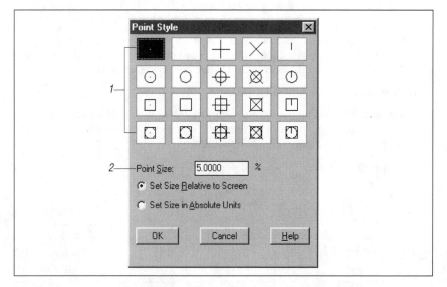

1. **Point Style.** Select a point style icon. This value is maintained by the *pdmode* variable.

2. **Point Size.** Set the point size either relative to the screen or in absolute units. This value is maintained by the *pdsize* variable.

Tips & Warnings

- You can have only one *pdmode* and *pdsize* setting at a time in a drawing. If you change the settings, the drawing will globally update at the next regeneration. Points that are placed on the Defpoints layer by associative dimensioning are not affected by *pdmode* and *pdsize* and are the only exceptions.

- Unlike blips, points are part of the drawing and will plot. If you do not want the points to plot, set *pdmode* to 1, erase the points, or set their layer to off, to freeze, or to the Do Not Plot mode.

Related Variables   pdmode, pdsize

Associated Commands   divide, measure, point

DDRENAME (obsolete)   *see RENAME*

DDRMODES (obsolete)   *see PROPERTIES*

'DDSELECT 2000mod   *see OPTIONS*

DDUCS 2000mod   *see UCSMAN*

DDUCSP 2000mod   *see UCSMAN*

'DDUNITS 2000mod   *see UNITS*

DDVIEW 2000mod   *see VIEW*

DDVPOINT

Specifies the direction and angle for viewing a drawing by selecting a 3D viewpoint. Issuing this command regenerates the drawing in parallel projection from the 3D point that you specify. Specify a viewpoint of 0,0,1 to return to plan view, or use the *plan* command. You cannot use the *ddvpoint* command in paper space. The *vpoint* (viewpoint) command achieves the same results but is mostly command line driven.

ddvpoint resizes the screen to include the entire drawing. Whenever possible, save the screen display with the *view* command. Use the *view* Restore option to bring back the different views. Since *ddvpoint* displays only parallel projection, use *dview* or *3dorbit* to generate perspectives.

Initiate Command By

Command: **ddvpoint**
Alias: **vp**
View → 3D Views → Viewpoint Presets

Options

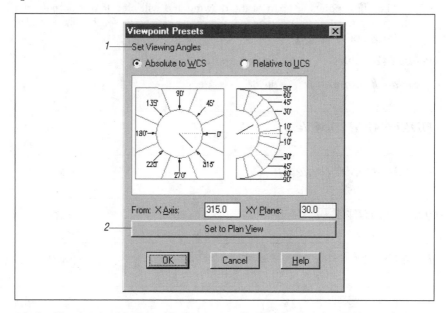

1. **Set Viewing Angles**. Sets the viewing angles absolute to the WCS or relative to the UCS. This value is maintained by the *worldview* system variable.

   From X Axis
   Enter the viewing angle in the text box or select the image tile. The solid line represents the new angle.

   XY Plane
   Enter the angle in the text box or select the image tile. The solid line represents the new angle.

2. **Set to Plan View**. Sets you to the plan view of the current UCS.

Tips & Warnings

You cannot control the distance from which you are viewing an object, only the orientation. To control the distance, use the *dview* or *3dorbit* command. You can also use the *camera, dview, vpoint,* and *3dorbit* commands to view the drawing in 3D. Use the *hide, render,* and *shademode* commands to enhance the display of the 3D objects.

Related Variables   viewdir, viewsize, vsmax, vsmin, worldview

Associated Commands   camera, plan, vpoint

Example

The settings shown in the previous dialog box would create the following view.

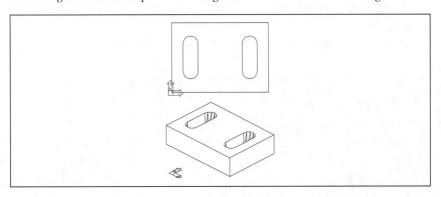

'DEFLPLSTYLE 2000

Maintains the default plot style for layer 0 for new drawings or drawings that were never saved with AutoCAD 2000. This variable is set by the "Default plot style for layer 0" option from the *options* Plotting tab. The "Use named plot styles" button must be active, or you can set *pstylepolicy* to 1. The various plot style choices depend on the default plot style table; however, Normal is always available.

Initiate Command By

Command: **deflplstyle**

Variable Settings

Initial default:	ByColor, read-only
Subsequent default:	Registry file
Value:	String
Related Variables	pstylepolicy
Associated Commands	options, plot, preferences

'DEFPLSTYLE 2000

Maintains the default plot style when creating new objects. This is for new drawings or drawings that were never saved with AutoCAD 2000. This variable is set when selecting the "Default plot style for objects" option from the *options* Plotting tab. The "Use named plot styles" button must be active, or you can set *pstylepolicy* to 1. The various plot style choices depend on the default plot style table; however, ByLayer, ByBlock, and Normal are always available.

Initiate Command By

Command: **defplstyle**

Options

ByLayer
    Based on its assigned layer.

ByBlock
    Based on the properties of the block that contains the object

Normal
    Based on the object's default properties

Variable Settings

Initial default:	ByColor, read-only
Subsequent default:	Registry file
Value:	String
Related Variables	pstylepolicy
Associated Commands	options, plot, preferences

'DELAY
see SCRIPT

'DELOBJ `2000mod`

Determines whether objects used to create new objects are saved or deleted from the drawing. Commands that can create new objects are *bhatch, boundary, extrude, region,* and *revolve*.

Initiate Command By
    Command: **delobj**

Options

0   Objects are retained.
1   Objects are deleted.

Variable Settings

Initial default:	1
Subsequent default:	Registry file
Value:	Integer
Associated Commands	boundary, extrude, region, revolve

'DEMANDLOAD

Determines how a third-party application is activated when opening or starting a new drawing. This value is set when selecting "Demand load object ARX apps" in the Open and Save tab from the *options* command.

Initiate Command By

Command: **demandload**

Options

0 (Disable load on demand)
Turns off demand loading.

1 (Custom object detect)
Loads the source application for drawings that contain custom objects.

2 (Command invoke)
Does not load the source application for drawings that contain custom objects except when one of the application's commands is issued.

3 (Object detect and command invoke)
Loads the source application for drawings that contain custom objects or when one of the application's commands is issued.

Variable Settings

Initial default:	3
Subsequent default:	Registry file
Value:	Integer

Associated Commands   options, preferences

'DIASTAT

(Dialog Status) Stores the way you exited the last dialog box.

Initiate Command By

Command: **diastat**

Options

0   Exited the last dialog box by selecting Cancel or by pressing Escape.

1   Exited the last dialog box by selecting OK or by pressing Enter.

Variable Settings

Initial default:	1, read-only
Subsequent default:	Initial default
Value:	Integer

DIM

Changes your command-line prompt to "Dim:" and allows only specific commands associated with dimensioning to be active. While in the dimensioning mode, you can use *redraw, undo,* and *transparency* commands. You return to the "Command:" prompt using the exit option or by pressing Escape.

Most of the *dim* options can be obtained directly from the command line. The *dim* command was left in this release to remain compatible with various third-party programs and routines. Only *leader* and *undo* are listed since they are different depending on whether they are options of the *dim* command or issued from the "Command:" prompt.

Initiate Command By

Command: **dim**

Options

Leader

l or *leader* is made up of an arrowhead, lines, and multiline text and is used to dimension complex areas or add reference notes. Leaders are drawn from the point of the arrowhead to where you want the dimension text or notes to be placed. To have no text present, press the Escape key at the "Dim:" prompt. You can use a *u* response to undo the last leader segment. If the leader length for the first segment is less than two arrow lengths, the arrowhead is not drawn.

You can enter only one line of text for a leader. Once the leader text has been placed in the drawing, you can edit it with *properties, ddedit,* or *mtprop* and add multiple lines of text. Dimension edit commands do not work for any dimensions entered by this leader method, because leaders are not associative.

Undo

Undo voids the latest dimensioning operation.

Tips & Warnings

• An *undo* executed during the "Dim:" prompt will not recognize the *redo* command.

• If you issue an *undo* at the "Command:" prompt, everything that was accomplished during a dimensioning session ("Dim:") will be undone. Issuing a *redo* will restore the dimensioning session.

• See Chapter 2, *Command Index and Global Topics,* for more information. The "Dimension" section lists the various variables associated with this command.

Associated Commands   dim1, dimstyle, leader

DIM1

Activates the "Dim:" prompt for a single command and returns you to the "Command:" prompt. See *dim* for more information.

'DIMADEC [2000mod]

Determines the decimal precision for angular dimension text. This variable is set with the Angular Dimensions → Precision option from the *dimstyle* Primary Units tab.

Initiate Command By

Command: **dimadec**

Options

−1

Sets angular dimensions to default to the *dimdec* value.

0−8

Specifies the number of places past the decimal that are displayed.

Variable Settings

Initial default:	0
Subsequent default:	Last value used in the drawing.
Value:	Integer

Related Variables	dimdec
Associated Commands	dimangular, dimstyle

DIMALIGNED

Dimension toolbar

Creates an aligned linear dimension by constructing the dimension line parallel to the origin points of the extension line or to a selected object.

Initiate Command By

Command: **dimaligned**
Alias: **dal** or **dimali**
Dimension → Aligned

Options

Specify first extension line origin or <select object>:
Specify second extension line origin:
Specify dimension line location or [Mtext/Text/Angle]:

select object

AutoCAD finds the endpoints for lines and arcs, the two nearest vertices for multilines and polylines, and the nearest quadrant for circles.

dimension line location

This option allows you to specify a dimension line location by dragging the dimension line and text to its destination.

Mtext/Text

Use these options to change the actual dimension value or to add text to the dimension. If you wish to enter text in addition to the default value, enter the text and include the angle brackets (< >). The brackets represent the actual dimension value.

Angle

Use this option to determine a text angle before specifying its location.

Tips & Warnings

See Chapter 2, *Command Index and Global Topics,* for more information. The "Dimension" section lists the various variables associated with this command.

Associated Commands   dimlinear, dimstyle

Example

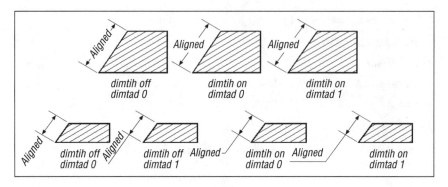

'DIMALT

Determines whether alternate units are visible. This variable is set by selecting the Display Alternate Units option from the *dimstyle* Alternate Units tab.

Initiate Command By

    Command: **dimalt**

Options

Off or 0
    Alternate units are invisible.

On or 1
    Alternate units are visible.

Variable Settings

Initial default:	Off
Subsequent default:	Last value used in the drawing
Value:	Switch

Related Variables   dimaltd, dimaltf, dimalttd, dimalttz, dimaltu, dimaltz, dimapost

Associated Commands   dimstyle

Example

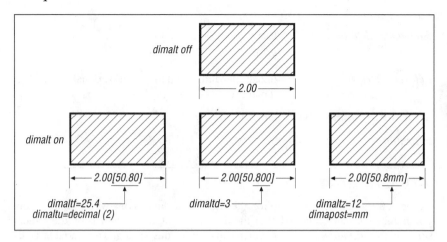

dimalt off

2.00

dimalt on

2.00[50.80]

dimaltf=25.4
dimaltu=decimal (2)

2.00[50.800]

dimaltd=3

2.00[50.8mm]

dimaltz=12
dimapost=mm

'DIMALTD

Sets the number of decimal places for alternate dimension units when *dimalt* is on. The first time this value is set using the *dimstyle* dialog box, *dimalttd* is automatically set to the same value. This variable is set with the Alternate Units → Precision option from the *dimstyle* Alternate Units tab.

Initiate Command By
ommand: **dimaltd**

Variable Settings

Initial default	2
Subsequent default:	Last value used in the drawing
Value:	Integer

Related Variables	dimalt, dimaltf, dimalttd, dimalttz, dimaltu, dimaltz, dimapost
Associated Commands	dimstyle
Example	See DIMALT.

'DIMALTF

Sets the scale factor or multiplier for alternate units when *dimalt* is on. This variable is set by selecting the Alternate Units → "Multiplier for all units" option from *dimstyle*'s Alternate Units tab.

Initiate Command By
Command: **dimaltf**

Variable Settings

Initial default:	25.4000
Subsequent default:	Last value used in the drawing
Value:	Real

Related Variables	dimalt, dimaltd, dimalttd, dimalttz, dimaltu, dimaltz, dimapost
Associated Commands	dimstyle
Example	See DIMALT.

'DIMALTRND 2000

Rounds off the dimension value for alternate linear dimensions when *dimalt* is on. The number of digits retained after the decimal point is determined by the dimension variable *dimadec*. Angular dimensions ignore this setting. This variable is set with the Alternate Units → Round Distances To option from the *dimstyle* Alternate Units tab.

Initiate Command By

Command: **dimaltrnd**

Variable Settings

Initial default:	0.0000
Subsequent default:	Last value used in the drawing
Value:	Real

Related Variables	dimadec, dimalt
Associated Commands	dimlinear, dimstyle

'DIMALTTD

Determines the number of decimal places for alternate tolerance dimension text. The first time the *dimaltd* value is set using the *dimstyle* dialog box, *dimalttd* is automatically set to the same value. *dimalttd* is displayed when *dimtol* and *dimalt* are on. This variable is set with the Alternate Unit Tolerance → Precision option of the *dimstyle* Tolerances tab.

Initiate Command By

Command: **dimalttd**

Variable Settings

Initial default:	2
Subsequent default:	Last value used in the drawing
Value:	Integer

| Related Variables | dimalt, dimaltd, dimaltf, dimalttz, dimaltu, dimaltz, dimapost, dimlim, dimtdec, dimtfac, dimtm, dimtol, dimtolj, dimtp, dimtzin |
| Associated Commands | dimstyle |

'DIMALTTZ

Controls the suppression of zeros for alternate tolerance dimension text when *dimalt* is on. *dimalttz* is displayed when *dimtol* and *dimalt* are on. This variable is set with the Alternate Unit Tolerance → Zero Suppression options of the *dimstyle* Tolerances tab.

Options

See *dimzin* for available options.

Initiate Command By
    Command: **dimalttz**

Variable Settings

Initial default:	0
Subsequent default:	Last value used in the drawing
Value:	Integer
Related Variables	dimalt, dimaltd, dimaltf, dimaltu, dimalttd, dimaltz, dimapost, dimlim, dimtdec, dimtfac, dimtm, dimtol, dimtolj, dimtp, dimtzin
Associated Commands	dimstyle

'DIMALTU

Defines the units format for alternate dimensions when *dimalt* is on. This variable is set with the Alternate Units → Unit Format option from the *dimstyle* Alternate Units tab.

Initiate Command By
    Command: **dimaltu**

Options

1 Scientific
2 Decimal
3 Engineering
4 Architectural (stacked)
5 Fractional (stacked)
6 Architectural

7   Fractional

8   Windows Desktop (the system defaults to the number settings defined in the Control Panel's Regional Settings)

Variable Settings

Initial default:	2
Subsequent default:	Last value used in the drawing
Value:	Integer

Related Variables	dimalt, dimaltd, dimaltf, dimalttd, dimalttz, dimaltz, dimapost
Associated Commands	dimstyle
Example	See DIMALT.

'DIMALTZ

Controls the suppression of zeros for alternate dimension text values when *dimalt* is on. This variable is set by selecting the Zero Suppression options from the *dimstyle* Alternate Units tab.

Initiate Command By

Command: **dimaltz**

Options

See *dimzin* for available options.

Variable Settings

Initial default:	0
Subsequent default:	Last value used in the drawing
Value:	Integer

Related Variables	dimalt, dimaltd, dimaltf, dimalttd, dimalttz, dimaltu, dimapost, dimzin
Associated Commands	dimstyle
Example	See DIMALT.

DIMANGULAR   Dimension toolbar

Creates angular dimensions.

Initiate Command By

Command: **dimangular**
Alias: **dan**, **dimang**
Dimension → Angular

Options

```
Select arc, circle, line, or <specify vertex>:
Specify dimension arc line location or [Mtext/Text/Angle]:
```

arc

The center of the arc is considered the angle vertex, and the endpoints become the origin points for the extension lines.

circle

The center of the circle is considered the vertex of the angle. The point used to pick the circle defines the origin of the first extension line.

line

Nonparallel lines or polyline segments can be selected. The angle vertex is the point at which the two lines intersect.

specify vertex

You determine the angle vertex and the angle's endpoints.

dimension arc line location

This option allows you to specify a dimension line location by dragging the dimension line and text to its destination.

Mtext/Text

Use these options to change the actual dimension value or to add text to the dimension. If you wish to enter text in addition to the default value, enter the text and include the angle brackets (< >). The brackets represent the actual dimension value.

Angle

This option determines a text angle before specifying its location.

Tips & Warnings

If ticks are enabled (*dimtsz*), you will still get arrowheads.

Related Variables   dimtix, dimtofl

Associated Commands   dimstyle

Example

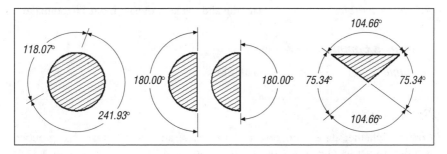

'DIMAPOST

Sets the prefix and/or suffix for alternate dimensions (except angular) when *dimalt* is on. This variable is set when selecting the Alternate Units → Prefix and/or Suffix options from the *dimstyle* Alternate Units tab.

Initiate Command By

Command: **dimapost**

Options

new value
    Sets a dimension text suffix. If tolerance dimensioning is enabled, the alternate dimension and each tolerance dimension receive the suffix.

< > new value
    Sets a dimension text suffix. If tolerance dimensioning is enabled, only the tolerances receive the suffix.

new value < >
    Sets a dimension text prefix.

new value < > new value
    Sets a dimension text prefix and suffix.

. (period)
    Resets and disables any prefix and suffix text.

Tips & Warnings

You can edit the dimension text and receive the same effect by using the new option of the *dimedit* command or by selecting Alternate Units → Alt suffix from the Properties window.

Variable Settings

Initial default:	None
Subsequent default:	Last value used in the drawing
Value:	String
Related Variables	dimalt, dimaltd, dimaltf, dimalttd, dimalttz, dimaltu, dimaltz
Associated Commands	dimstyle
Example	See DIMALT.

'DIMASO

Controls whether dimension objects (lines, arcs, arrows, and text) are grouped together to act as one object or are independent of one another. *dimaso* affects linear, angular, diameter, ordinate, and radius dimensioning. When dimension objects are grouped together, the dimension becomes associated with the dimensioned objects and automatically reflects size changes if the object is edited. New dimensions default to the current style's settings. If *dimaso* is on when dimensions are created, you can update them by changing their assigned dimension style or by changing individual dimension variables with the override function.

Placing your first associative dimension creates a layer named Defpoints (definition points). Defpoints are points that link the dimension to the object being dimensioned. Objects residing on the Defpoints layer are never plotted. If you want to plot objects on this layer, you must first rename the layer or move the objects to another layer.

Initiate Command By

Command: **dimaso**

Options

Off or 0

Dimension objects act individually. They cannot be updated when dimension variables or the objects they are referencing are modified.

On or 1

Dimension objects act as one object.

Variable Settings

Initial default:	On
Subsequent default:	Last value used in the drawing
Value:	Switch

Tips & Warnings

- For the greatest dimensioning flexibility, keep *dimaso* on. You can always *explode* the dimension and turn it into individual objects. Once the dimension is exploded, you cannot turn the objects back into a single dimension object.

- The following edit commands affect associative dimensions when used on dimensions and dimensioned objects: *trim* (only with linear dimensions), *extend* (only with linear dimensions), *stretch* (only with linear and angular dimensions), *array* (only with rotated polar arrays), *mirror, rotate,* and *scale.*

- You cannot assign *dimaso* to dimension styles. All styles read the current *dimaso* setting at the time of dimensioning.

- See Chapter 2, *Command Index and Global Topics,* for more information. The "Dimension" section lists the various variables associated with this command.

Associated Commands   dimaligned, dimangular, dimdiameter, dimlinear, dimordinate, dimradius, dimstyle, tolerance

'DIMASZ

Determines the size of the arrowheads placed at the end of dimension lines and leader lines. Multiples of this value (based on *dimscale*) help determine whether dimension lines and text fit between extension lines or are placed on the outside of the extension lines. *dimasz* determines the size of objects defined by *dimblk*, *dimblk1*, *dimblk2*, and *dimldrblk* variables. This variable is set with the Arrowheads → Arrow Size option from the *dimstyle* Lines and Arrows tab.

Initiate Command By

Command: **dimasz**

Variable Settings

Initial default:	0.1800
Subsequent default:	Last value used in the drawing
Value:	Real

Tips & Warnings

- To set the right arrowhead size for the finished plot, set *dimasz* to the size you want on the plotted drawing. Set *dimscale* to the appropriate scale factor. *dimscale* acts as a multiplier to the *dimasz* value.

- *dimasz* has no effect if *dimtsz* (tick size) is set to any number other than 0.

Related Variables	dimblk, dimblk1, dimblk2, dimgap, dimldrblk, dimscale, dimtsz
Associated Commands	dimstyle

'DIMATFIT 2000

Determines how arrowheads and text are displayed when there is not enough room for both within the dimension extension lines. This variable is set by selecting one of the radio buttons located in the Fit Options of the *dimstyle* Fit tab.

When *dimtix* is off, the dimension text automatically goes inside the dimension lines regardless of the *dimatfit* setting.

Initiate Command By

Command: **dimatfit**

Options

0 Text and arrowheads are placed outside the extension lines.

1 Arrowheads are moved outside the extension lines if there is not enough room to display arrowheads and text inside the extension lines. If there is still not enough room, the dimension text is also placed outside the extension lines.

2   Dimension text is moved outside the extension lines if there is not enough room to display arrowheads and text inside the extension lines. If there is still not enough room, the arrowheads are also placed outside the extension lines.

3   AutoCAD determines whether to move the arrowheads or dimension text outside the extension lines based on what it considers the best fit.

Variable Settings

Initial default:	3
Subsequent default:	Last value used in the drawing
Value:	Integer

Tips & Warnings

- *dimatfit*, along with *dimtmove*, replaces the *dimfit* variable.
- The dimension variables that determine the available space between extension lines are *dimasz*, *dimgap*, *dimscale*, *dimtxt*, and the *style* command.

Related Variables   dimasz, dimsoxd, dimtix, dimtmove, dimtxt

Associated Commands   dimstyle

Example

'DIMAUNIT

Specifies the angle format for angular dimensions. This variable is set by selecting the Angular Dimensions → Units Format option from the *dimstyle* Primary Units tab.

Initiate Command By

     Command: **dimaunit**

Options

0   Decimal degrees

1   Degrees, minutes, seconds

2	Grads
3	Radians
4	Surveyor's units

Variable Settings

Initial default:	0
Subsequent default:	Last value used in the drawing
Value:	Integer

| **Related Variables** | aunits |
| **Associated Commands** | dimangular, dimstyle |

'DIMAZIN 2000

Controls the zero display for angular dimension text. This variable is set when selecting the Angular Dimensions → Zero Suppression option from the *dimstyle* Primary Units tab.

Initiate Command By
Command: **dimazin**

Options

0	Display leading and trailing zeros.
1	Suppress leading zeros for decimal dimensions.
2	Suppress trailing decimal zeros for decimal dimensions.
3	Suppress leading and trailing zeros for decimal dimensions.

Variable Settings

Initial default:	0
Subsequent default:	Last value used in the drawing
Value:	Integer

| **Related Variables** | dimalttz, dimaltz, dimtzin, dimzin |
| **Associated Commands** | dimstyle |

DIMBASELINE   Dimension toolbar

Continues a linear (aligned, horizontal, ordinate, rotated, vertical) or angular dimension from the baseline of the previous or selected dimension. The dimension line offset distances are based on the *dimdli* value. Exit the command by pressing Enter twice or by using the Escape key. It is quicker to use *qdim* when you have more than one horizontal or vertical baseline dimension.

Initiate Command By

Command: **dimbaseline**
Alias: **dba**, **dimbase**
Dimension → Baseline

Options

Specify a second extension line origin or [Undo/Select] <Select>:

second extension line origin
Offsets each dimension from the last using the same first extension line.

Undo
Undoes the last extension line and returns you to the previous point.

Select
Allows you to create baseline dimensions from an existing dimension by picking the base dimension line from which to offset the rest of the dimensions.

Tips & Warnings

The Dim: *update* command will not modify existing baseline dimension offsets if *dimdli* is changed.

Related Variables	dimdli
Associated Commands	dimaligned, dimangular, dimcontinue, dimlinear, qdim

Example

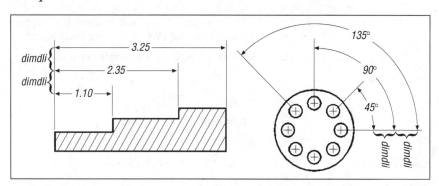

'DIMBLK

Defines your own symbols or blocks to place at the ends of dimensions, replacing the Autodesk-supplied symbols. The block must reside in the current drawing and *dimsah* must be off or set to 1. Return to the system default by entering a period (.) when asked for a new *dimblk* name.

The following dimension blocks are built into all drawing files:

►	.(period)	⇒	open	■	boxfilled
○	dot	→	open90	□	boxblank
·	dotsmall	⇒	open30	▷	closedblack
○	dotblank	▷	closed	◄	datumfilled
○	origin	○	small	◁	datumblank
◎	origin2		none	/	integral
		/	oblique	/	archtick

Initiate Command By
Command: **dimblk**

Tips & Warnings
- *dimasz* and *dimscale* values are multipliers to *dimblk*'s value.
- You can create dimension lines with different blocks on each end. Assign blocks to *dimblk1* and/or *dimblk2* and turn *dimsah* on. If *dimsah* is on and you have not defined *dimblk1* and/or *dimblk2*, *dimblk* becomes the default.
- Change the block assigned to leader lines with the *dimldrblk* variable.

Variable Settings
Initial default:	closedfilled
Subsequent default:	Last value used in the drawing
Value:	String
Related Variables	dimasz, dimblk1, dimblk2, dimsah
Associated Commands	block, dimstyle

'DIMBLK1 `2000mod`

Defines the symbol or block placed on the first end of the dimension line. There are 20 predefined options built into the software. If you create your own symbol, that block must reside in the current drawing, and *dimsah* must be on. Return to the system default by entering a period (.) when asked for a new *dimblk1* name. This variable is set by the Arrowheads → 1st option from the *dimstyle* Lines and Arrows tab. See the *dimblk* command for a listing of the various predefined choices.

Initiate Command By

Command: **dimblk1**

Tips & Warnings

dimasz and *dimscale* values are multipliers to *dimblk1*'s value.

Variable Settings

Initial default:	closedfilled
Subsequent default:	Last value used in the drawing
Value:	String
Related Variables	dimasz, dimblk, dimblk2, dimsah
Associated Commands	block, dimstyle

'DIMBLK2 `2000mod`

Defines the symbol or block placed on the second end of the dimension line. There are 20 predefined options built into the software. If you create your own symbol, that block must reside in the current drawing, and *dimsah* must be on. Return to the system default by entering a period (.) when asked for a new *dimblk2* name. This variable is set by the Arrowheads → 2nd option from the *dimstyle* Lines and Arrows tab. See the *dimblk* command for a listing of the various predefined choices.

Initiate Command By

Command: **dimblk2**

Variable Settings

Initial default:	closedfilled
Subsequent default:	Last value used in the drawing
Value:	String

Tips & Warnings

dimasz and *dimscale* values are multipliers to *dimblk2*'s value.

Related Variables	dimasz, dimblk, dimblk1, dimsah
Associated Commands	block, dimstyle

'DIMCEN

Sets the size of the center marks and center lines when you dimension circles and arcs with the *dimdiameter*, *dimcenter*, and *dimradius* commands. This variable is set by selecting the Center Marks for Circles → Type and Size options from the *dimstyle* Lines and Arrows tab.

Initiate Command By

Command: **dimcen**

Options

0
> Center marks and lines are not drawn.

Greater than 0
> Center marks are created.

Less than 0
> Center lines are created.

Variable Settings

Initial default:	0.9000
Subsequent default:	Last value used in the drawing
Value:	Real

Tips & Warnings

- The *dimscale* value is a multiplier to the value of *dimcen*.
- Changing *dimcen*'s value will not affect existing center marks and center lines.

Related Variables dimscale

Associated Commands dimcenter, dimdiameter, dimradius, dimstyle

Example See DIMCENTER, DIMDIAMETER, and DIMRADIUS.

DIMCENTER Dimension toolbar

Constructs center marks or center lines for circles and arcs. The size and type of mark are based on the *dimcen* setting.

Initiate Command By

> Command: **dimcenter**
> Alias: **dce**
> Dimension → Center Mark

Related Variables dimcen

Associated Commands dimradius

Example

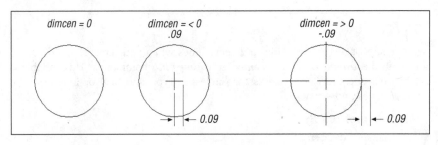

'DIMCLRD

Determines the color assigned to dimension lines, arrowheads, and leader lines. This variable is set when selecting the Dimension Lines → Color option of the *dimstyle* Lines and Arrows tab.

Initiate Command By
Command: **dimclrd**

Variable Settings

Initial default:	0
Subsequent default:	Last value used in the drawing
Value:	Integer

Tips & Warnings

If you set this variable at the command line, you must use the appropriate color number. You can set it to ByBlock by assigning the number 0 or to ByLayer with the number 256. If you set it at the "Dim:" prompt, you can use the color name, number or the words "ByLayer" or "ByBlock."

Related Variables	dimclre, dimclrt, dimlwd, dimlwe
Associated Commands	color, dimstyle

'DIMCLRE

Sets the color assigned to dimension extension lines. This variable is set by selecting the Extension Lines → Color option from the *dimstyle* Lines and Arrows tab.

Initiate Command By
Command: **dimclre**

Variable Settings

Initial default:	0
Subsequent default:	Last value used in the drawing
Value:	Integer

Tips & Warnings

If you set this variable at the command line, you must use the appropriate color number. You can set it to ByBlock by assigning the number 0 or to ByLayer with the number 256. If you set it at the "Dim:" prompt you can use the color name, number or the words "ByLayer" or "ByBlock."

Related Variables	dimclrd, dimclrt, dimlwd, dimlwe
Associated Commands	color, dimstyle

'DIMCLRT

Determines the color assigned to dimension text. This variable is set by selecting the Text Appearance → Text color option from the *dimstyle* Text tab.

Initiate Command By
Command: **dimclrt**

Variable Settings

Initial default:	0
Subsequent default:	Last value used in the drawing
Value:	Integer

Tips & Warnings

If you set this variable at the command line, you must use the appropriate color number. You can set it to ByBlock by assigning the number 0 or to ByLayer with the number 256. If you set it at the "Dim:" prompt you can use the color name, number or the words "ByLayer" or "ByBlock."

Related Variables	dimclrd, dimclre, dimlwd, dimlwe
Associated Commands	color, dimstyle

DIMCONTINUE

Dimension toolbar

Continues a linear (aligned, horizontal, ordinate, rotated, vertical) or angular dimension from the second extension line of the previous or a selected dimension. Exit the command by pressing Enter twice or by using the Escape key. It is quicker to use the *qdim* command when you have more than one horizontal or vertical continuous dimension.

Initiate Command By
Command: **dimcontinue**
Alias: **dco**, **dimcont**
Dimension → Continue

Options
Specify a second extension line origin or [Undo/Select] <Select>:

Specify a second extension line origin
Each dimension is drawn in line with the last.

Undo
Entering *U* (*undo*) undoes the last extension line and returns you to the previous point.

Select
Create continuous dimensions from an existing dimension by pressing Enter and picking the dimension line from which to continue.

Related Variables	dimdli
Associated Commands	dimaligned, dimangular, dimbaseline, dimlinear, dimordinate, qdim

Example

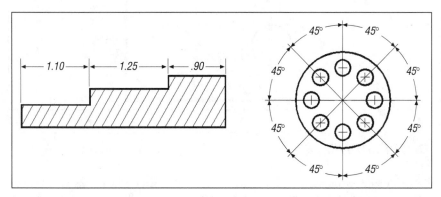

'DIMDEC

Determines the decimal precision for the primary units dimension. This variable is set by the Linear Dimensions → Precision option from the *dimstyle* Primary Units tab.

Initiate Command By

Command: **dimdec**

Options

0–8
Determines the number of places past the decimal that are displayed.

Variable Settings

Initial default:	4
Subsequent default:	Last value used in the drawing.
Value:	Integer
Related Variables	dimadec, dimlunit, dimzin
Associated Commands	dimaligned, dimdiameter, dimlinear, dimordinate, dimradius, dimstyle

Example

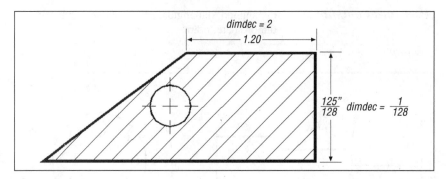

DIMDIAMETER

Dimension toolbar

Creates diameter dimensions for circles or arcs. Diameter dimensions take on the current dimension style and dimension variable settings. It is quicker to use the *qdim* command when you have more than one diameter to dimension.

Initiate Command By

Command: **dimdiameter**
Alias: **ddi**, **dimdia**
Dimension → Diameter

Options

Specify dimension line location or [Mtext/Text/Angle]:

Specify dimension line location
Allows you to specify a dimension line location by dragging the dimension line and text to its destination.

Mtext/Text
Changes the actual dimension value or adds text to the dimension. If you wish to enter text in addition to the default value, enter the text and include the angle brackets (< >). The brackets represent the actual dimension value.

Angle
Determines a text angle before specifying its location.

Tips & Warnings

- *dimtofl*, if on, draws a dimension line between the extension lines.

- If set to a positive value, *dimcen* creates center marks inside circles and arcs. A negative value constructs center lines that extend outside the diameter. A setting of 0 omits any marks. This variable is active only if the dimension line is placed outside the arc or circle.

- Leader lines are always at least the length of two arrowheads. If the angle of the leader line is greater than 15 degrees from the horizontal and the text is drawn horizontally, a short horizontal leader extension line (the length of an arrowhead) is drawn next to the dimension text.

Related Variables	dimatfit, dimcen, dimjust, dimtad, dimtih, dimtofl, dimtoh
Associated Commands	dimradius, qdim

Example

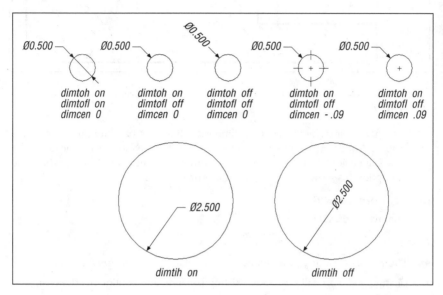

'DIMDLE

Maintains how far the dimension lines extend past the extension line. This variable takes effect only when oblique strokes instead of arrowheads are drawn. This variable is set with the Dimension Lines → Extend Beyond Ticks option from the *dimstyle* Lines and Arrows tab.

Initiate Command By
    Command: **dimdle**

Variable Settings

Initial default:	0.0000
Subsequent default:	Last value used in the drawing
Value:	Real

Tips & Warnings

The *dimscale* value is a multiplier to the default value of *dimdle*.

Related Variables	dimblk1, dimblk2, dimtsz
Associated Commands	dimaligned, dimangular, dimlinear, dimstyle

Example

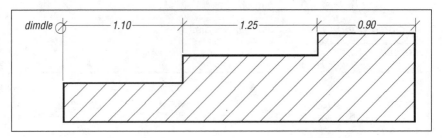

'DIMDLI

Sets the spacing increment between dimension lines for baseline and continuous dimensions. Continuous dimensions use this value to avoid writing on top of a previous dimension. This variable is set with the Dimension Lines → Baseline Spacing option from the *dimstyle* Lines and Arrows tab.

Initiate Command By

Command: **dimdli**

Tips & Warnings

- The *dimscale* value is a multiplier to the default value of *dimdli*.

- Changing *dimdli* will not affect existing baseline and continuous dimensions.

Variable Settings

Initial default:	0.3800
Subsequent default:	Last value used in the drawing
Value:	Real
Related Variables	dimscale
Associated Commands	dimbaseline, dimcontinue, dimstyle
Example	See DIMBASELINE.

'DIMDSEP 2000

Defines the character placed as a separator when you use decimal format. This variable is set with the Linear Dimensions → Decimal Separator option from the *dimstyle* Primary Units tab.

Initiate Command By

Command: **dimdsep**

Variable Settings

Initial default:	System variable
Subsequent default:	(Decimal point)

| *Value:* | Last value used in the drawing |

Tips & Warnings

You are offered only three choices when you set this variable using the *dimstyle* command. Setting this variable at the command line gives you greater flexibility since you can enter any character from your keyboard.

Related Variables   dimdec, dimlunit

Associated Commands   dimstyle

Example

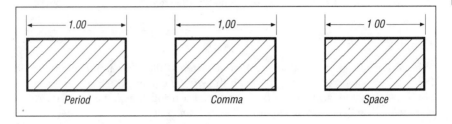

Period	Comma	Space

DIMEDIT

Dimension toolbar

Edits associative dimension text and extension lines.

Initiate Command By

Command: **dimedit**
Alias: **ded**, **dimed**
Dimension → Oblique
Dimension → Align Text → Home

Options

Enter type of dimension editing [Home/New/Rotate/Oblique] <Home>:

Home
Returns associative dimension text to its original location.

New–Dimension text <"<>">
Revises associative dimension text. The default < > returns any selected dimension text to its original value. If you wish to enter text in addition to the default value, enter the text and include angle brackets (< >) at the appropriate location.

Rotate
Rotates existing associative dimension text. You can also do this using the angle option of the *dimtedit* command. *dimedit* lets you modify one or more dimensions at a time; *dimtedit* lets you edit only one dimension at a time.

Oblique
Redefines the angle of existing associative dimension extension lines without altering the dimension value.

Tips & Warnings

- Using the *dimtedit* home option is the same as using the *dimedit* home option, and using the *dimtedit* angle option is the same as using the *dimedit* rotate option, except that *dimedit* can manipulate more than one dimension at a time, whereas *dimtedit* modifies only one dimension at a time.

- The Properties dialog box can be used as an alternative to the new and rotate options. You can use grips or stretch to relocate dimension text, dimension lines, and extension lines.

Related Variables	dimtad, dimtih, dimtoh, dimtvp
Associated Commands	ddedit, dimtedit, dimstyle

DIMEX

Exports dimension styles (dimstyles) to an external file. This information can be imported into another drawing file with the *dimim* command. Since the exported file is in ASCII format, you can open and read it using Notepad or another ASCII text editor. The extension of exported files is *.dim*.

Initiate Command By

Command: **dimex**
Express → Dimension → Dimstyle Export

Options

1. **Export Filename.** Determines the folder and filename to assign to the exported dimension style.

2. **Available Dimension Styles.** Allows you to select the dimension style(s) to export. Use the Shift and Ctrl keys to select the styles.

3. **Text Style Options.** Determines if only the name of text styles (*style, dimtxsty*) assigned to dimension styles are exported or if the text style name and all its properties are exported.

Tips & Warnings

The *adcenter* feature lets you drag and drop dimension styles from one drawing into another. However, if you need to constantly use the same dimension styles, it is more efficient to include those styles in a drawing template file.

Related Variables	dimtxsty
Associated Commands	dimim, dimstyle, expresstools, style

'DIMEXE

Maintains the distance the extension line extends beyond the dimension line. This variable is set with the Extension Lines → Extend Beyond Dim Lines option from the *dimstyle* Lines and Arrows tab.

Initiate Command By

Command: **dimexe**

Variable Settings

Initial default:	0.1800
Subsequent default:	Last value used in the drawing
Value:	Real

Tips & Warnings

The *dimscale* value is a multiplier to the value of *dimexe*.

Related Variables	dimscale
Associated Commands	dimstyle

Example

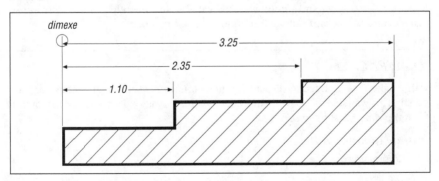

'DIMEXO

Specifies the offset distance for extension lines. This variable is set with the Extension Lines → Offset from Origin option from the *dimstyle* Lines and Arrows tab.

Initiate Command By

Command: **dimexo**

Tips & Warnings

The *dimscale* value is a multiplier to the *dimexo's* value.

Variable Settings

Initial default:	0.0625
Subsequent default:	Last value used in the drawing
Value:	Real

Related Variables	dimscale
Associated Commands	dimstyle

Example

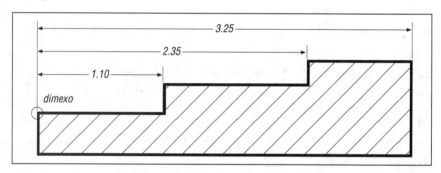

DIMFIT   *see DIMATFIT, DIMTMOVE*

Replaced by *dimatfit* and *dimtmove*. This variable has been left in the software so that existing scripts and AutoLISP routines can still function.

'DIMFRAC [2000]

Defines the type of fraction displayed when *dimlunit* is set to architectural or fractional. This variable is set with the Linear Dimensions → Fraction Format option from the *dimstyle* Primary Units tab.

Initiate Command By

Command: **dimfrac**

Options

0	Horizontal
1	Diagonal
2	Not stacked

Variable Settings

Initial default:	0
Subsequent default:	Last value used in the drawing
Value:	Integer
Related Variables	dimdec, dimlunit
Associated Commands	dimaligned, dimangular, dimlinear, dimstyle

Example

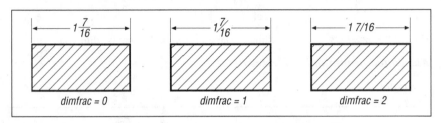

dimfrac = 0   dimfrac = 1   dimfrac = 2

'DIMGAP

Determines the space between the dimension line and text. It also determines the leader command's hook line and text. If *dimgap* is set with a negative number, a box is placed around the text.

dimgap is also used to calculate whether text defaults to the inside of the dimension line or is placed outside a dimension line. If text is placed outside a dimension line, its location is based on the second extension line pick point.

Dimension text is kept in the inside of the extension lines as long as the dimension line to both sides of the text is at least as long as the *dimgap* value. If text is set to go above or below a dimension line (*dimtad, dimtvp*), it is placed inside the extension lines as long as there is room for the arrowheads, dimension text, and a space between them at least the size of *dimgap*. The available space must be greater than or equal to 2 × (*dimasz* + *dimgap*).

dimgap is set with the Text Appearances → Draw Frame Around Text checkbox and Text Placement → Offset From Dim Line option from the *dimstyle* Text tab. This variable is also set when selecting the Tolerance Format → Basic Method option from the *dimstyle* Tolerances tab.

Initiate Command By

Command: **dimgap**

Options

Positive number
Determines the gap between the dimension lines and dimension text.

Negative number
> Determines the gap between the dimension lines and dimension text and places a box around the dimension text.

Tips & Warnings

The *dimscale* value is a multiplier to the value of *dimgap.*

Variable Settings

Initial default:	0.0900
Subsequent default:	Last value used in the drawing
Value:	Real

Related Variables   dimasz, dimatfit, dimscale, dimtix, dimtvp

Associated Commands   dimstyle

Example

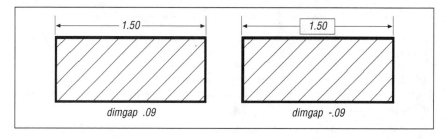

dimgap .09   dimgap -.09

DIMHORIZONTAL

see DIMLINEAR

DIMIM

Imports dimension styles created with *dimex* into the current drawing.

Initiate Command By

> Command: **dimim**
> Express → Dimension → Dimstyle Import

Options

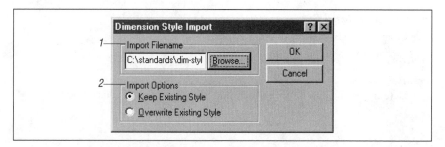

---

1. **Import Filename.** Specifies the folder and filename to import.

2. **Import Options.** Determines whether the imported dimension and text styles update existing dimension and text styles having the same name. You cannot individually determine the dimension and text styles to import. All the information is automatically imported into the drawing.

Tips & Warnings

The AutoCAD DesignCenter feature lets you drag and drop dimension styles from one drawing into another. However, if you need to constantly use the same dimension styles, it is more efficient to include those styles in a drawing template file.

Associated Commands   dimex, dimstyle, expresstools

'DIMJUST

Determines the horizontal dimension text location. This variable is set when selecting the Text Placement → Horizontal option from the *dimstyle* Text tab.

Initiate Command By

Command: **dimjust**

Options

0   Text is centered between the extension lines.

1   Text is placed next to the first extension line.

2   Text is placed next to the second extension line.

3   Text is placed above and aligned with the first extension line.

4   Text is placed above and aligned with the second extension line.

Variable Settings

Initial default:	0
Subsequent default:	Last value used in the drawing
Value:	Integer

Related Variables   dimatfit, dimtad

Associated Commands   dimstyle

Example

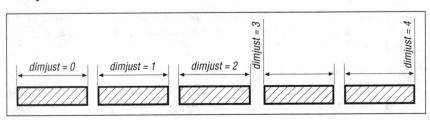

'DIMLDRBLK 2000

Defines the symbol or block placed on the end of leader lines. There are 20 predefined options built into the software. If you create your own symbol, that block must reside in the current drawing. Return to the system default by entering a period (.) when asked for a new leader block name. This variable is set with the Arrowheads → Leader option from the *dimstyle* Lines and Arrows tab or when setting drawing parameters with the *qleader* command.

Initiate Command By
Command: **dimldrblk**

Options

See the *dimblk* command for a listing of the various predefined choices.

Tips & Warnings

dimasz and *dimscale* values are multipliers to *dimldrblk*'s value.

Variable Settings

Initial default:	closedfilled
Subsequent default:	Last value used in the drawing
Value:	String
Related Variables	dimasz
Associated Commands	dim (leader), dimstyle, leader, qleader

'DIMLFAC

Defines a global scale factor used during linear dimensioning. Each dimension value is multiplied by the *dimlfac* value. This variable is set with the Measurement Scale → Scale Factor option from the *dimstyle* Primary Units tab.

Initiate Command By
Command: **dimlfac**

Options

current value
　　Sets the multiplier for each dimension text value.

Viewport
　　Calculates the scaling of model space to paper space, and the negative of this value is assigned to *dimlfac*. Use when dimensioning model space objects in paper space.

Tips & Warnings

• By using paper space viewports and the display command *zoom–xp*, you can depict different levels of drawing detail and you will not need to set *dimlfac*.

- *dimlfac* has no effect on angular dimensions and the variable settings *dimtm*, *dimtp*, and *dimrnd*.

Variable Settings

Initial default:	1.0000
Subsequent default:	Last value used in the drawing
Value:	Real

Associated Commands	dimstyle, pspace

'DIMLIM

Determines the visibility and display for dimension text tolerance limits (*dimtm* and *dimtp*). This variable is set with the Tolerance Format → Method option from the *dimstyle* Tolerances tab.

Initiate Command By

Command: **dimlim**

Options

Off or 0
Disables dimension text limits.

On or 1
Generates dimension text limits.

Variable Settings

Initial default:	Off or 0
Subsequent default:	Last value used in the drawing
Value:	Switch

Tips & Warnings

Setting *dimlim* on automatically turns *dimtol* off and vice versa.

Related Variables	dimgap, dimlim, dimtfac, dimtm, dimtol, dimtolj, dimtp
Associated Commands	dimaligned, dimangular, dimdiameter, dimlinear, dimordinate, dimradius, dimstyle

Example

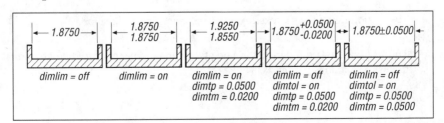

DIMLINEAR

Dimension toolbar

Creates linear (horizontal, vertical, and rotated) dimensions. The command is dynamic in that it will dimension horizontally or vertically, based on how you move your pointing device. You also can choose the angle of the extension lines and the angle of dimension text and change the default dimension text. Linear dimensions take on the current dimension style and dimension variable settings.

The horizontal and vertical options are similar to the rotated option. The dimension line for horizontal is rotated at an angle of 0 degrees; the dimension line for vertical is rotated at an angle of 90 degrees. If you select a circle, the diameter is dimensioned. The quadrants at 90 and 270 degrees are considered the two endpoints when moving vertically; the quadrants at 0 and 180 degrees are considered the two endpoints when moving horizontally. You can type *dimhorizontal*, *dimrotated*, or *dimvertical* at the command prompt to quickly define the dimension type.

Initiate Command By

Command: **dimlinear**
Alias: **dimlin, dli**
Dimension → Linear

Options

Specify first extension line origin or <select object>:
Specify dimension line location or
[Mtext/Text/Angle/Horizontal/Vertical/Rotated]:

Select object

AutoCAD finds the endpoints for lines and arcs, the two nearest vertices for multilines and polylines, and the nearest quadrant for circles.

dimension line location

This option allows you to specify a dimension line location by dragging the dimension line and text to its destination. Picking to the left or right of the object creates vertical dimensions; picking up or down creates horizontal dimensions.

Mtext/Text

Use these options to change the actual dimension value or add text to the dimension. If you wish to enter text in addition to the default value, enter the text and include the angle brackets (< >). The brackets represent the actual dimension value.

Angle

This option determines a text angle before specifying its location.

Rotated

This option draws the dimension line at any angle you specify while keeping the extension lines perpendicular.

Tips & Warnings

- If *dimupt* is off, the dimension text placement is based on the second extension line pick point. If you select an object to dimension, the dimension text is placed to the side farthest from the pick point. If *dimupt* is on, you can pick the side on which to place the dimension text.

- You can always change the text value and the angle by using the dimensioning edit commands *dimedit*, *dimtedit*, and *properties*. *ddedit* only lets you change the value.

- Dimensioning in model space gives you greater flexibility than dimensioning in paper space. Dimensions in paper space are not associative to objects created in model space.

- See Chapter 2, *Command Index and Global Topics*, for more information. The "Dimension" section lists the various variables associated with this command.

Associated Commands   dimhorizontal, dimrotated, dimvertical

Example

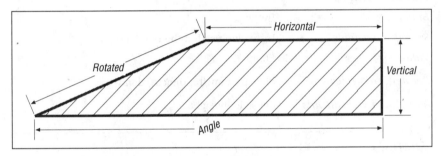

'DIMLUNIT 2000

Defines the units format for all dimensions (except angular). This variable is set with the Linear Dimensions → Unit Format option from the *dimstyle* Primary Units tab.

Initiate Command By

Command: **dimlunit**

Options

1 Scientific

2 Decimal

3 Engineering

4 Architectural

5 Fractional

6 Windows Desktop (the system defaults to the number settings defined in the Control Panel's Regional Settings)

Variable Settings

Initial default:	2
Subsequent default:	Last value used in the drawing
Value:	Integer
Related Variables	dimaltu, dimfrac
Associated Commands	dimstyle

'DIMLWD 2000

Determines the lineweight assigned to dimension lines. This variable is set with the Dimension Lines → Lineweight option from the *dimstyle* Lines and Arrows tab.

Initiate Command By

Command: **dimlwd**

Variable Settings

Initial default:	ByBlock
Subsequent default:	Last value used in the drawing
Value:	Enum
Related Variables	dimclrd, dimclre, dimclrt, dimlwe
Associated Commands	dimstyle, lweight

'DIMLWE 2000

Determines the lineweight assigned to extension lines. This variable is set with the Extension Lines → Lineweight option from the *dimstyle* Lines and Arrows tab.

Initiate Command By

Command: **dimlwe**

Variable Settings

Initial default:	ByBlock
Subsequent default:	Last value used in the drawing
Value:	Enum
Related Variables	dimclrd, dimclre, dimclrt, dimlwd
Associated Commands	dimstyle, lweight

DIMORDINATE

Dimension toolbar

Ordinate or datum dimensioning dimensions create individual *X* and *Y* distances from a common origin (0,0). The dimension text is automatically aligned with the leader line. Once you pick the feature to dimension, either point in the *X* or *Y* direction to indicate the type of dimension, or select Xdatum or Ydatum. Ordinate dimensions use the current UCS, dimension style, and dimension variable settings.

Initiate Command By

Command: **dimordinate**
Alias: **dor**, **dimord**
Dimension → Ordinate

Options

```
Specify feature location:
Specify leader endpoint or [Xdatum/Ydatum/Mtext/Text/Angle]:
```

feature location
Pick the location of the beginning point of the leader line or feature.

leader endpoint
When picking a point, the difference between the feature location and the leader endpoint is used to determine whether it is an *X* or *Y* dimension. If the difference in the *Y* axis is greatest, the dimension measures the *Y* coordinate; if not, it measures the *X*.

Xdatum
This option creates the *X* datum regardless of the length and location of the leader line.

Ydatum
This option creates the *Y* datum regardless of the length and location of the leader line.

Mtext/Text
These options change the actual dimension value or add text to the dimension. If you wish to enter text in addition to the default value, enter the text and include the angle brackets (< >). The brackets represent the actual dimension value.

Angle
Determines a text angle before specifying its location.

Tips & Warnings

• You can change the location of 0,0 by redefining the UCS.

• Keep *ortho* on for greater control of the feature line location.

Related Variables   dimtad, dimtvp

Associated Commands   dimstyle, qdim, ucs, ucsicon, ucsman

Example

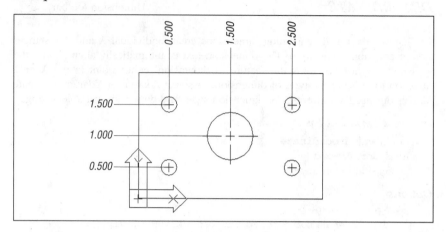

DIMOVERRIDE

Modifies individual dimension variables for existing dimensions without affecting the current dimension style. This command works only if the dimension you are editing is associative.

If you want to change a dimension variable for individual dimensions, it is far safer to use *dimoverride* than change the variable directly. *dimoverride* changes only associative dimensions you select during the command; it does not affect the current dimension style or any new dimensions you create. By directly changing dimension variables, you temporarily change the dimension style. This change remains active until you save the current dimension style with the modified dimension variable(s) or restore an existing dimension style.

Initiate Command By

> Command: **dimoverride**
> Alias: **dov, dimover**
> Dimension → Override

Options

> Enter dimension variable name to override or [Clear overrides]:
> Enter new value for dimension variable <default>:

dimension variable name to override
> Enter dimension variables you want to change on existing dimensions.

Clear overrides
> Reset a dimension to its original style settings.

Tips & Warnings

See Chapter 2, *Command Index and Global Topics*, for more information. The "Dimension" section lists the various variables associated with this command.

Associated Commands   dimstyle

'DIMPOST

Assigns a prefix and/or suffix text to dimension text. This variable is set with the Linear Dimensions → Prefix and/or Suffix options from the *dimstyle* Primary Units tab.

Initiate Command By

Command: **dimpost**

Options

new value
> Sets a dimension text suffix. If tolerance dimensioning is enabled, the main dimension and each tolerance dimension receive the suffix.

< > new value
> Sets a dimension text suffix. If tolerance dimensioning is enabled, only the tolerances receive the suffix.

new value < >
> Sets a dimension text prefix.

new value < > new value
> Sets a dimension text prefix and suffix.

. (period)
> Resets and disables any prefix and suffix text. If you change the value from the command line or "Dim:" prompt use the left and right angle brackets.

Tips & Warnings

You can edit the dimension text and receive the same effect by using the *ddedit*, *dimedit*, *dimtedit*, or *properties* command.

Variable Settings

Initial default:	" " (none)
Subsequent default:	Last value used in the drawing
Value:	String

Associated Commands   dimstyle

Example

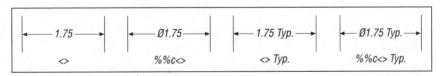

DIMRADIUS

Dimension toolbar

Creates radial dimensions for circles and arcs. Radius dimensions take on the current dimension style and dimension variable settings. *dimtofl*, if on, draws a dimension line between the extension lines. If set to a positive value, *dimcen* creates center marks inside circles and arcs. A negative value constructs center lines that extend outside the diameter. A setting of 0 omits any marks. This variable is active only if the dimension line is placed outside the arc or circle.

Initiate Command By

Command: **dimradius**
Alias: **dra, dimrad**
Dimension → Radius

Options

Specify dimension line location or [Mtext/Text/Angle]:

dimension line location
Enables you to pick the location by dragging the dimension line and text to their destination.

Mtext/Text
Changes the actual dimension value or adds text to the dimension. If you wish to enter text in addition to the default value, enter the text and include the angle brackets (< >). The brackets represent the actual dimension value.

Angle
Determines a text angle before specifying its location.

Tips & Warnings

- Leader lines are always at least the length of two arrowheads. If the angle of the leader line is greater than 15 degrees from the horizontal and the text is drawn horizontally, a short horizontal extension line (the length of an arrowhead) is drawn next to the dimension text.

- See Chapter 2, *Command Index and Global Topics*, for more information. The "Dimension" section lists the various variables associated with this command.

Associated Commands   dimdiameter, qdim

Example

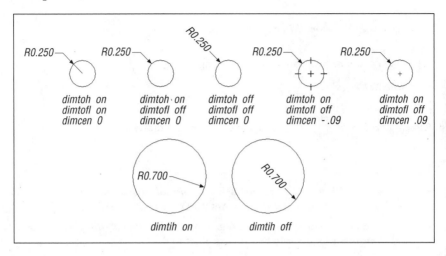

'DIMRND

Rounds the dimension value for linear dimensions. The number of digits retained after the decimal point is determined by the dimension variable *dimdec*. Angular dimensions ignore *dimrnd*. This variable is set by selecting the Linear Dimensions → Round Off option from the *dimstyle* Primary Units tab.

Initiate Command By
Command: **dimrnd**

Variable Settings

Initial default:	0.0000
Subsequent default:	Last value used in the drawing
Value:	Real
Related Variables	dimdec
Associated Commands	dimlinear, dimstyle

DIMROTATED   *see DIMLINEAR*

'DIMSAH

Displays separate arrowhead symbols for each dimension.

Initiate Command By
Command: **dimsah**

Options

Off or 0
> Suppresses the *dimblk1* and *dimblk2* settings.

On or 1
> Displays the *dimblk1* and *dimblk2* settings.

Variable Settings

Initial default:	Off or 0
Subsequent default:	Last value used in the drawing
Value:	Switch

Tips & Warnings

- If *dimblk1* and *dimblk2* are not defined, *dimsah* reads the *dimblk* value. If *dimblk* is not defined, *dimsah* uses AutoCAD's default arrowhead block.

- If you keep on getting tick marks regardless of the *dimblk, dimblk1, dimblk2,* and *dimsah* settings, verify that *dimtsz* is set to 0.

Related Variables	dimblk, dimblk1, dimblk2
Associated Commands	block, dimstyle

'DIMSCALE

Sets the overall dimensioning scale factor applied to most dimensioning variables related to sizes, distances, or offsets. *dimscale* does not alter the actual dimension value and tolerances. For best results, set the individual dimension variables to how you want them to appear on the plotted output, and set the *dimscale* value equal to the plot scale factor. *dimscale* is set by selecting the Scale for Dimension Features option from the *dimstyle* Fit tab.

Initiate Command By

> Command: **dimscale**

Variable Settings

Initial default:	1.0000
Subsequent default:	Last value used in the drawing
Value:	Real

Tips & Warnings

- If you decide to change the plot scale factor, remember to change *dimscale* and update the dimensions. If *dimaso* was off when the dimensions were created or if the dimensions were exploded, you may need to redimension your drawing.

- The size of the *revcloud*'s arcs are determined by the chord length multiplied by the *dimscale* variable.

Related Variables	dimasz, dimblk, dimblk1, dimblk2, dimcen, dimdle, dimdli, dimexe, dimexo, dimgap, dimtsz, dimtxt, revcloud
Associated Commands	dimstyle

'DIMSD1

Determines the visibility of the first dimension line and arrowhead. This variable is set by selecting the Dimension Lines → Suppress Dim Line 1 option from the *dimstyle* Lines and Arrows tab.

Initiate Command By

Command: **dimsd1**

Options

Off or 0

Displays the first dimension line and arrowhead.

On or 1

Suppresses the first dimension line and arrowhead.

Variable Settings

Initial default:	Off or 0
Subsequent default:	Last value used in the drawing
Value:	Switch
Related Variables	dimsd2
Associated Commands	dimstyle

Example

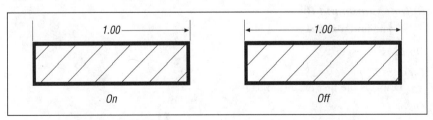

'DIMSD2

Determines the visibility of the second dimension line and arrowhead. This variable is set by selecting the Dimension Lines → Suppress Dim Line 2 option from the *dimstyle* Lines and Arrows tab.

Initiate Command By

Command: **dimsd2**

Options

Off or 0
Displays the second dimension line and arrowhead.

On or 1
Suppresses the second dimension line arrowhead.

Variable Settings

Initial default:	Off or 0
Subsequent default:	Last value used in the drawing
Value:	Switch

Related Variables   dimsd1

Associated Commands   dimstyle

Example

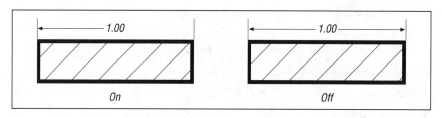

'DIMSE1

Determines the display of the first extension line. This variable is set by selecting the Extension Lines → Suppress Ext Line 1 option from the *dimstyle* Lines and Arrows tab.

Initiate Command By

Command: **dimse1**

Options

Off or 0
Displays the first extension line.

On or 1
Suppresses the first extension line.

Variable Settings

Initial default:	Off or 0
Subsequent default:	Last value used in the drawing
Value:	Switch

Related Variables   dimse2

Associated Commands   dimstyle

Example

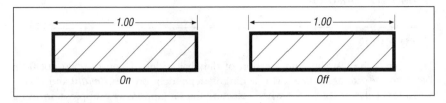

On   Off

'DIMSE2

Determines the display of the second extension line. This variable is set by selecting the Extension Lines → Suppress Ext Line 2 option from the *dimstyle* Lines and Arrows tab.

Initiate Command By

Command: **dimse2**

Options

Off or 0

Displays the second extension line.

On or 1

Suppresses the second extension line.

Variable Settings

Initial default:	Off or 0
Subsequent default:	Last value used in the drawing
Value:	Switch
Related Variables	dimse2
Associated Commands	dimstyle

Example

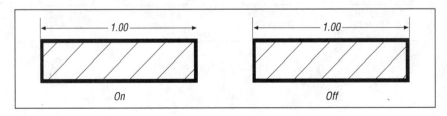

On   Off

'DIMSHO (obsolete)

'DIMSOXD

Determines the visibility and location of dimension lines when they do not fit in between the extension lines. This setting is dependent on the *dimatfit* and *dimtix* variables. This variable is set when selecting the Fit Options → "Suppress arrows if they don't fit inside the extension lines" option from the *dimstyle* Fit tab.

Initiate Command By

Command: **dimsoxd**

Options

Off or 0

Displays dimension lines outside extension lines if they do not fit inside the extension lines. *dimtix* must be on.

On or 1

Suppresses dimension lines if they do not fit inside the extension lines. *dimtix* must be on.

Variable Settings

Initial default:	Off or 0
Subsequent default:	Last value used in the drawing
Value:	Switch

Related Variables   dimatfit, dimtad, dimtix

Associated Commands   dimstyle

Example

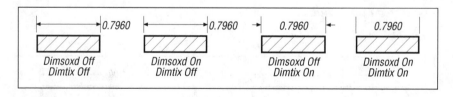

0.7960	0.7960	0.7960	0.7960
Dimsoxd Off Dimtix Off	Dimsoxd On Dimtix Off	Dimsoxd Off Dimtix On	Dimsoxd On Dimtix On

-DIMSTYLE 2000

see DIMSTYLE

DIMSTYLE 2000mod

Dimension toolbar

Enables you to create, save, restore, and modify dimension styles or to temporarily override the default style settings. Dimension styles define how you want dimensions displayed on your drawing. New dimensions inherit the settings of the current dimension style. Any changes made to that dimension style automatically update the dimensions assigned to that style. The exceptions are when using dimension overrides, for which associative dimensioning (*dimaso*) is turned off, and when the dimension was exploded.

To save time and maintain consistency among various drawing files, you can import dimension styles from one drawing into another. One method is to set up dimension styles in a template or prototype drawing; every time you start a new drawing using that template, the styles will already exist. Another method is to use the ADC (AutoCAD DesignCenter) feature. Selecting a drawing file in the ADC gives you access to that file's dimension styles. Once you find the desired style, you can drag and drop that style into your current drawing. Another method is to externally reference (*xref*) the file containing the existing dimension styles and then use *xbind* to import those styles. Once you have the styles imported, you can detach the external reference.

As an alternative, you can use the *-dimstyle* command, so all prompts and options appear at the command line. Using the *dimstyle* command is much easier because changes you make to any of the dialog box windows or tabs are reflected in the preview image tile.

Initiate Command By

Command: **dimstyle**
Alias: **ddim, dimsty**
Dimension → Style

Options

Making changes to any of the dialog box tabs affects one or more dimension variables. Refer to each variable's alphabetical listing for a more detailed description.

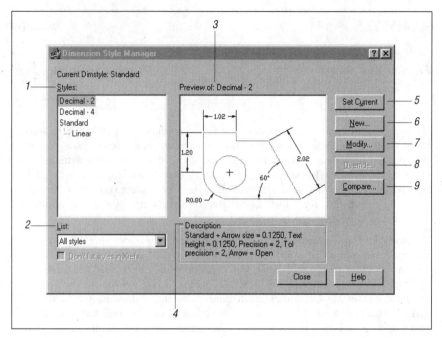

1. **Styles.** Lists all the styles currently defined in the drawing and highlights the current or active style. Although you can delete and rename styles using the shortcut menu, one style will always exist in each drawing. Once a style is referenced, it cannot be deleted. You can change the dimension styles assigned to objects with "Dim:" *update, properties,* or *matchprop.*

2. **List.** Determines which styles are displayed in the Styles window.

3. **Preview.** Displays the current dimension style settings in a graphical format.

4. **Description.** Lists the originating style name and the variables that were modified.

5. **Set Current.** Sets the current style to the style that is highlighted in the Styles window.

6. **New.** Creates new dimension styles. You assign a name and choose an existing style as a default. The variable settings assigned to that style become your starting point for making modifications. You also can define which types of dimensions receive the new settings: all dimensions, linear, angular, radius, diameter, ordinate, or leaders and tolerances. This activates the New Dimension Style dialog box consisting of six tabs. Each tab defines specific properties assigned to each dimension style. The same tabs are available when you modify an existing style or override an existing style's properties.

7. **Modify.** Makes changes to the dimension style highlighted in the Styles window. This activates the Modify Dimension Style dialog box consisting of six tabs. Each tab defines specific properties assigned to each dimension style. The same tabs are available when you create a new dimension style or override an existing style's properties.

8. **Override**. Sets dimension variable overrides to the style highlighted in the Styles window. This activates the Override Current Style dialog box consisting of six tabs. Each tab defines specific properties assigned to each dimension style. The same tabs are available when you create a new dimension style or you modify an existing style.

9. **Compare**. Compares the values assigned to two dimension styles or displays all the properties of one style. This information can be copied into the Windows clipboard.

The Modify Dimension Style Dialog Box

New, Modify, and Override Dimension styles display the following dialog box consisting of six tabs. Each tab is a different category and sets specific properties to the dimension style.

Lines and Arrows

Determines properties assigned to dimension lines, extension lines, and arrowheads, and determines how center marks for circles are displayed.

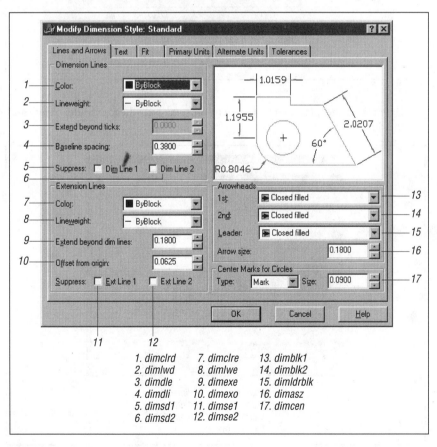

```
1. dimclrd      7. dimclre     13. dimblk1
2. dimlwd       8. dimlwe      14. dimblk2
3. dimdle       9. dimexe      15. dimldrblk
4. dimdli      10. dimexo      16. dimasz
5. dimsd1      11. dimse1      17. dimcen
6. dimsd2      12. dimse2
```

Text

Determines dimension text appearance, placement, and alignment.

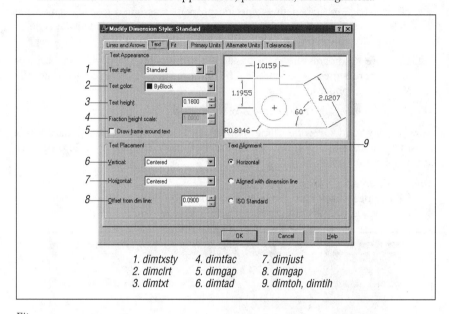

1. dimtxsty   4. dimtfac   7. dimjust
2. dimclrt   5. dimgap   8. dimgap
3. dimtxt   6. dimtad   9. dimtoh, dimtih

Fit

Determines the placement of dimension text, arrowheads, leader lines, and the dimension line.

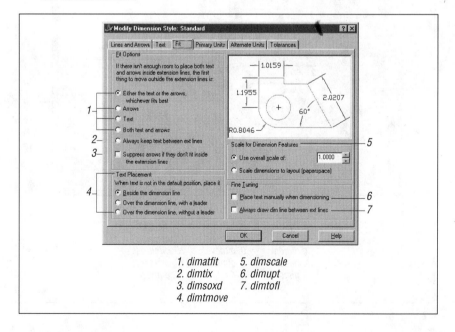

1. dimatfit   5. dimscale
2. dimtix   6. dimupt
3. dimsoxd   7. dimtofl
4. dimtmove

Primary Units

Controls the format of dimension units and sets prefixes and suffixes for dimension text.

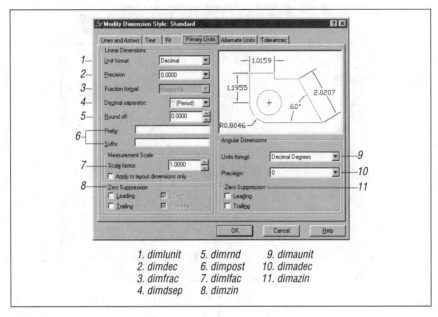

1. dimlunit	5. dimrnd	9. dimaunit
2. dimdec	6. dimpost	10. dimadec
3. dimfrac	7. dimlfac	11. dimazin
4. dimdsep	8. dimzin	

Alternate Units

Determines the format and precision units of alternate measurement units.

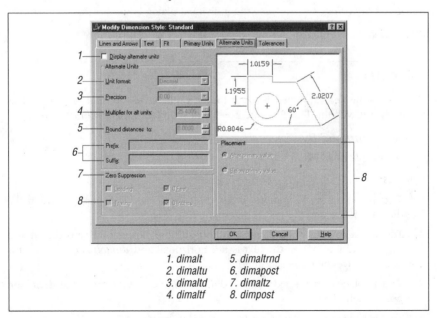

1. dimalt	5. dimaltrnd
2. dimaltu	6. dimapost
3. dimaltd	7. dimaltz
4. dimaltf	8. dimpost

Tolerances

Determines the display and format of dimension text tolerances.

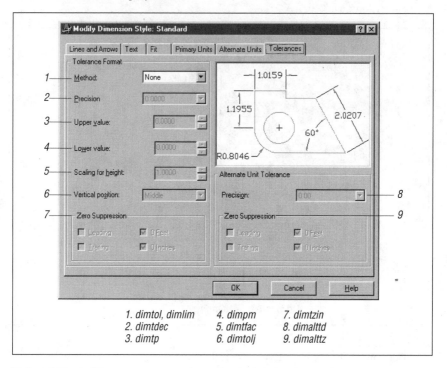

1. dimtol, dimlim   4. dimpm   7. dimtzin
2. dimtdec   5. dimtfac   8. dimalttd
3. dimtp   6. dimtolj   9. dimalttz

Related Variables   See the individual dialog boxes for this command.

Associated Commands   dim, dim1

'DIMTAD

Determines the vertical dimension text location relative to the dimension line. This variable is set with the Text Placement → Vertical option from the *dimstyle* Text tab.

Initiate Command By

Command: **dimtad**

Options

0   Text is placed in the middle of the dimension line. The space between the dimension line and the text is determined by *dimgap*.

1   Text is placed above the dimension line, and the dimension line is drawn as a single solid line. When the text is not horizontal and *dimtoh* is off, the text is placed above the dimension line.

2   Text is placed on the side of the dimension line furthest from the definition points (defpoints).

3   Text is based on JIS (Japanese Industrial Standards).

Variable Settings

Initial default:	0
Subsequent default:	Last value used in the drawing
Value:	Integer
Related Variables	dimgap, dimtih, dimtoh, dimtvp
Associated Commands	dimaligned, dimangular, dimdiameter, dimlinear, dimordinate, dimradius, dimstyle

Example

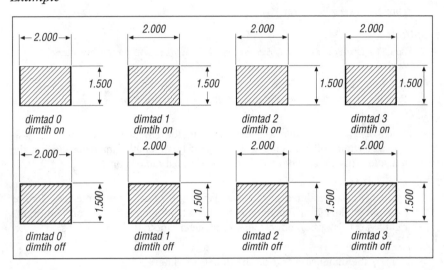

'DIMTDEC

(Dimension Tolerance Decimal) Determines the decimal precision for tolerance values for primary units in a dimension. This variable is set with the Tolerance Format → Precision option from the *dimstyle* Tolerances tab.

Initiate Command By

Command: **dimtdec**

Variable Settings

Initial default:	4
Subsequent default:	Last value used in the drawing
Value:	Integer
Related Variables	dimalttd, dimalttz, dimlim, dimtfac, dimtm, dimtol, dimtolj, dimtp, dimtzin
Associated Commands	dimstyle

DIMTEDIT

Dimension toolbar

Lets you change the location of associative dimension text. Depending on the *dimtmove* setting, the dimension and extension lines can move with the text or stay stationary. This command works only if the dimension you are editing is associative.

Initiate Command By

Command: **dimtedit**
Alias: **dimted**
Dimension → Align Text

Options

Specify new location for dimension text or [Left/Right/Center/Home/ Angle]:

new location for dimension text
Enables you to drag the dimension text to a new location.

Left
Places associative dimension text as far to the left of the dimension line as possible while still maintaining a two-arrowhead-length dimension line on the left side. This affects linear, diameter, and radial dimensions.

Right
Places associative dimension text as far to the right of the dimension line as possible while still maintaining a two-arrowhead-length dimension line on the right side. This option affects linear, diameter, and radial dimensions.

Center
Centers the dimension text on the dimension line.

Home
Places associative dimension text back at its original location.

Angle
Gives a new rotation angle for associative dimension text.

Tips & Warnings

- Using the *dimtedit* home option is the same as using the *dimedit* home option, and using the *dimtedit* angle option is the same as using the *dimedit* rotate option, except that *dimedit* can manipulate more than one dimension at a time, whereas *dimtedit* modifies only one dimension at a time.

- You can use grips or stretch to relocate dimension text, dimension lines, and extension lines.

Related Variables
dimtad, dimtih, dimtmove, dimtoh, dimtvp

Associated Commands
dimedit, dimstyle, properties

'DIMTFAC

Sets the scale factor used to determine the dimension text height of tolerance values and stacked fractions. This scale factor is relative to the dimension text height (*dimtxt*). This value is active when *dimtol* is on and *dimtm* is not equal to *dimtp* or when *dimlim* is on. *dimtfac* is set with the Tolerance Format → Scaling for Height option from the *dimstyle* Tolerances tab.

Initiate Command By
Command: **dimtfac**

Variable Settings

Initial default:	1.0000
Subsequent default:	Last value used in the drawing
Value:	Real
Related Variables	dimalttd, dimalttz, dimgap, dimlim, dimtdec, dimtm, dimtol, dimtolj, dimtp, dimtzin
Associated Commands	dimaligned, dimangular, dimdiameter, dimlinear, dimordinate, dimradius, dimstyle

'DIMTIH

Determines the text orientation for all dimensions (except ordinate) when the text fits between the extension lines. This variable is set by selecting one of the radio buttons located in the Text Alignment option of the *dimstyle* Text tab.

Initiate Command By
Command: **dimtih**

Options

Off or 0
Text is aligned with the dimension line.

On or 1
Text is displayed horizontally.

Variable Settings

Initial default:	On or 1
Subsequent default:	Last value used in the drawing
Value:	Switch
Related Variables	dimtad, dimtoh
Associated Commands	dimaligned, dimangular, dimdiameter, dimlinear, dimradius, dimstyle
Example	See DIMTAD, DIMTOH.

'DIMTIX

Defines whether text is placed inside the dimension lines even when it would fit better outside of the extension lines. This variable is set by selecting the Fit Options → "Always keep text between ext lines" option from the *dimstyle* Fit tab.

Initiate Command By
Command: **dimtix**

Options

Off or 0
Places dimension text inside the extension lines if there is enough room.

On or 1
Places dimension text inside extension lines regardless of the available space.

Variable Settings

Initial default:	Off or 0
Subsequent default:	Last value used in the drawing
Value:	Switch
Related Variables	dimatfit, dimgap, dimsoxd, dimtofl, dimupt
Associated Commands	dimlinear
Example	See DIMSOXD.

'DIMTM

Maintains the minimum tolerance limit for dimension text. This variable is set with the Tolerance Format → Lower Value option from the *dimstyle* Tolerances tab.

Initiate Command By
Command: **dimtm**

Variable Settings

Initial default:	0.0000
Subsequent default:	Last value used in the drawing
Value:	Real

Tips & Warnings

- *dimtm* is displayed as long as *dimtol* or *dimlim* is on.
- If *dimtol* is on and *dimtm* and *dimtp* have the same value, the ± symbol is listed next to that value.

Related Variables	dimalttd, dimalttz, dimgap, dimlim, dimtdec, dimtfac, dimtol, dimtolj, dimtp, dimtzin

Associated Commands	dimaligned, dimangular, dimdiameter, dimlinear, dimordinate, dimradius, dimstyle
Example	See DIMLIM.

'DIMTMOVE 2000

Determines how dimension text is displayed when it is moved from its default position.

Initiate Command By
Command: **dimtmove**

Options

0   The dimension line moves with dimension text.

1   A leader line is created when dimension text is moved.

2   Dimension text moves independently from the rest of the dimension objects.

Tips & Warnings

dimatfit, along with *dimtmove*, replaces the *dimfit* variable.

Variable Settings

Initial default:	0
Subsequent default:	Last value used in the drawing
Value:	Integer

Related Variables	dimatfit
Associated Commands	dimstyle, dimtedit, grips

Example

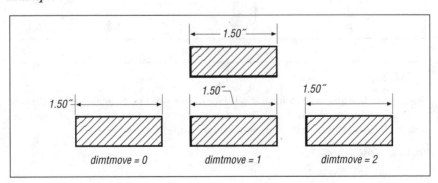

dimtmove = 0   dimtmove = 1   dimtmove = 2

'DIMTOFL

Controls the location of the dimension line. This variable is set by selecting the Fine Tuning → "Always draw dim line between ext lines" option from the *dimstyle* Fit tab.

Initiate Command By

Command: **dimtofl**

Options

Off or 0
Dimension lines are drawn on the inside of extension lines when they fit.

On or 1
Dimension lines are always drawn between extension lines.

Variable Settings

Initial default:	Off or 0
Subsequent default:	Last value used in the drawing
Value:	Switch
Related Variables	dimtix
Associated Commands	dimaligned, dimangular, dimdiameter, dimlinear, dimradius, dimstyle

Example

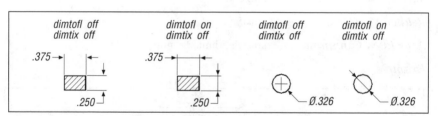

'DIMTOH

Determines the text orientation for all dimensions (except ordinate) when the text fits outside the extension lines. This variable is set by selecting one of the radio buttons located in the Text Alignment option of the *dimstyle* Text tab.

Initiate Command By

Command: **dimtoh**

Options

Off or 0
Text is aligned with the dimension line.

On or 1
　　Text is displayed horizontally.

Variable Settings

Initial default:	On or 1
Subsequent default:	Last value used in the drawing
Value:	Switch

Related Variables　　dimtad, dimtih

Associated Commands　　dimaligned, dimangular, dimdiameter, dimlinear, dimradius, dimstyle

Example

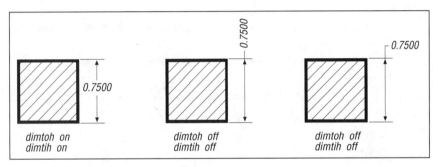

dimtoh on dimtih on	dimtoh off dimtih off	dimtoh off dimtih off

'DIMTOL

Determines the visibility and display of dimension tolerances to dimension text Setting *dimtol* on automatically turns *dimlim* off and vice versa. This variable is set with the Method option from the *dimstyle* Tolerances tab.

Initiate Command By

　　Command: **dimtol**

Options

Off or 0
　　Disables dimension text tolerances.

On or 1
　　Generates dimension text tolerances.

Variable Settings

Initial default:	Off or 0
Subsequent default:	Last value used in the drawing
Value:	Switch

Related Variables　　dimalttd, dimalttz, dimlim, dimtdec, dimtfac, dimtm, dimtolj, dimtp, dimtzin

Associated Commands	dimaligned, dimangular, dimdiameter, dimlinear, dimordinate, dimradius, dimstyle
Example	See DIMLIM.

'DIMTOLJ

Determines the text justification for nominal dimensions relative to the text's assigned tolerance values. This variable is set with the Tolerance Format → Vertical Position option from the *dimstyle* Tolerances tab.

Initiate Command By

Command: **dimtolj**

Options

0   The bottom of the nominal dimension is aligned with the bottom of the tolerance values.

1   The middle of the nominal dimension is aligned with the middle of the tolerance values.

2   The top of the nominal dimension is aligned with the top of the tolerance values.

Variable Settings

Initial default:	1
Subsequent default:	Last value used in the drawing
Value:	Integer
Related Variables	dimalttd, dimalttz, dimgap, dimlim, dimtdec, dimtfac, dimtm, dimtol, dimtp, dimtzin
Associated Commands	dimaligned, dimangular, dimdiameter, dimlinear, dimordinate, dimradius, dimstyle

Example

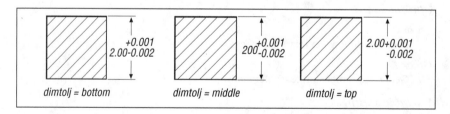

dimtolj = bottom   dimtolj = middle   dimtolj = top

'DIMTP

Maintains the maximum tolerance limit for dimension text. This variable is set with the Tolerance Format → Upper Value option from the *dimstyle* Tolerances tab.

Initiate Command By

Command: **dimtp**

Variable Settings

Initial default:	0.0000
Subsequent default:	Last value used in the drawing
Value:	Real

Tips & Warnings

- This is displayed only when *dimtol* or *dimlim* is on.

- If *dimtol* is on and *dimtm* and *dimtp* have the same value, the ± symbol is listed next to that value.

Related Variables   dimalttd, dimalttz, dimlim, dimtdec, dimtfac, dimtm, dimtol, dimtolj, dimtzin

Associated Commands   dimaligned, dimangular, dimdiameter, dimlinear, dimordinate, dimradius, dimstyle

Example   See DIMLIM.

'DIMTSZ

Controls the display of tick marks and tick size for linear, radius, and diameter dimensions.

Initiate Command By

Command: **dimtsz**

Options

0   Tick marks are disabled and arrowheads are displayed.

any value greater than 0
Determines the size of tick marks and makes them visible. *dimasz* becomes disabled.

Variable Settings

Initial default:	0
Subsequent default:	Last value used in the drawing
Value:	Real

Tips & Warnings

- The *dimscale* value is a multiplier to the default value of *dimtsz*.

- Regardless of the *dimtsz* value, angular dimensions are always drawn with arrows.

Related Variables   dimasz, dimscale

Associated Commands   dimstyle

Example

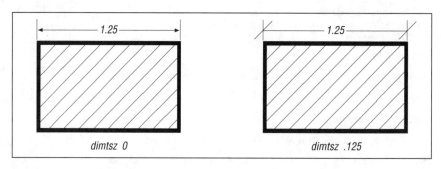

dimtsz 0   dimtsz .125

'DIMTVP

Sets the vertical position of dimension text in relation to the dimension line. This value is used when *dimtad* is off. The distance the text is offset from the dimension line is the product of the text height and *dimtvp*. Setting *dimtvp* to 1 is equivalent to setting *dimtad* on. The dimension line is broken to accommodate text only when *dimtvp*'s absolute value is less than 0.7.

Initiate Command By

Command: **dimtvp**

Variable Settings

Initial default:	0.0000
Subsequent default:	Last value used in the drawing
Value:	Real
Related Variables	dimtad
Associated Commands	dimaligned, dimangular, dimdiameter, dimlinear, dimordinate, dimradius, dimstyle

Example

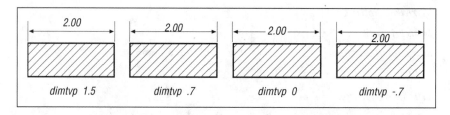

dimtvp 1.5   dimtvp .7   dimtvp 0   dimtvp -.7

'DIMTXSTY

Maintains the current dimension style setting. This variable is set with the Text Appearance → Text Style option from the *dimstyle* Text tab.

Initiate Command By

Command: **dimtxsty**

Variable Settings

Initial default:	Standard
Subsequent default:	Last value used in the drawing
Value:	String
Associated Commands	dimstyle

'DIMTXT

Sets the dimension text height. This variable is set with the Text Appearance →
Text Height option from the *dimstyle* Text tab.

Initiate Command By

Command: **dimtxt**

Variable Settings

Initial default:	0.1800
Subsequent default:	Last value used in the drawing
Value:	Real

Tips & Warnings

The *dimscale* value is a multiplier of the default value of *dimtxt*.

Related Variables	dimscale
Associated Commands	dimstyle, style

'DIMTZIN

Controls the zero display for tolerance values. This variable is set by selecting the
Tolerance Format → Zero Suppression option from the *dimstyle* Tolerances tab.

Initiate Command By

Command: **dimtzin**

Options

0   Suppresses zero feet and exactly zero inches (feet and inches only).

1   Displays zero feet and exactly zero inches (feet and inches only).

2   Displays zero feet and suppresses zero inches (feet and inches only).

3   Suppresses zero feet and displays zero inches (feet and inches only).

4   Suppresses leading zeros (decimal dimensions).

8   Suppresses trailing decimal zeros (decimal dimensions).

12 Suppresses leading and trailing zeros (decimal dimensions).

Variable Settings

Initial default:	0
Subsequent default:	Last value used in the drawing
Value:	Integer
Related Variables	dimalttd, dimlim, dimtdec, dimtfac, dimtm, dimtol, dimtolj, dimtp
Associated Commands	dimstyle

'DIMUNIT   *see DIMFRAC and DIMLUNIT*

Replaced by *dimfrac* and *dimlunit*. This variable has been left in the software so that existing scripts and AutoLISP routines can still function.

'DIMUPT

Determines the flexibility of locating dimension text during dimension creation. This variable is set by selecting the Fine Tuning → Place Text Manually When Dimensioning option from the *dimstyle* Fit tab.

Initiate Command By

Command: **dimupt**

Options

Off or 0
Dimension text is placed once you define a dimension line location.

On or 1
The dimension line is placed once you define a dimension text location.

Tips & Warnings

You can always send associative dimensioned text to its home location using the *dimedit* or *dimtedit* command.

Variable Settings

Initial default:	Off or 0
Subsequent default:	Last value used in the drawing
Value:	Switch
Associated Commands	dimedit, dimtedit

DIMVERTICAL   *see DIMLINEAR*

'DIMZIN

Controls the zero display for linear dimension text. This variable is set when selecting the Linear Dimensions → Zero Suppression option from the *dimstyle* Primary Units tab.

Initiate Command By
Command: **dimzin**

Options

0   Suppresses zero feet and exactly zero inches (feet and inches only).

1   Displays zero feet and exactly zero inches (feet and inches only).

2   Displays zero feet and suppresses zero inches (feet and inches only).

3   Suppresses zero feet and displays zero inches (feet and inches only).

4   Suppresses leading zeros (decimal dimensions).

8   Suppresses trailing decimal zeros (decimal dimensions).

12 Suppresses leading and trailing zeros (decimal dimensions).

Variable Settings

Initial default:	0
Subsequent default:	Last value used in the drawing
Value:	Integer
Related Variables	dimalttz, dimaltz, dimazin, dimtzin
Associated Commands	dimstyle

'DISPSILH

Controls the display of silhouette curves for 3D solid objects when using the *hide* command and *shademode* is set to 2D wireframe.

Initiate Command By
Command: **dispsilh**

Options

0   No silhouette is displayed for curved solids.

1   Silhouette is displayed for curved solids.

Variable Settings

Initial default:	0
Subsequent default:	Last value used in the drawing
Value:	Integer
Associated Commands	cone, cylinder, extrude, hide, revolve, shademode, sphere, torus

Example

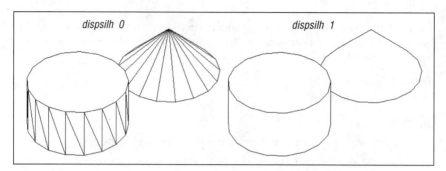

dispsilh 0   dispsilh 1

'DIST

Inquiry toolbar

Determines the distance between two points, the angle they form in the *XY* plane, the angle from the *XY* plane, and the delta *X*, *Y*, and *Z* values. The order in which you pick points determines the angle in the *XY* plane and positive or negative values for delta *X*, *Y*, *Z*. The current *units* setting determines the format for displaying coordinates, distances, and angles. Enter a number at the "Specify first point" prompt for an example of the current units format.

Initiate Command By

Command: **dist**
Alias: **di**
Tools → Inquiry → Distance

Options

```
Specify first point:
Specify second point:
```

Tips & Warnings

You can determine the distance between the endpoints of a line using the *lengthen*, *list*, or *properties* command.

Related Variables	distance
Associated Commands	list, properties, units

'DISTANCE

Retains the last computed distance resulting from the *dist* command.

Initiate Command By

Command: **distance**

Variable Settings

Initial default:	0.0000, read-only
Subsequent default:	Initial default
Value:	Real

Associated Commands   dist, units

DIVIDE

Marks an object at equal-length segments. The divided object is not physically separated; rather, points, blocks, or external references are placed as markers at each division point. You can object-snap to the points with the node option. You can divide arcs, circles, ellipses, lines, polylines, 3D polylines, and splines. You cannot divide multilines, rays, regions, traces, xlines, wireframes, and solid objects. You can divide only one object at a time.

When dividing circles, the first marker begins at the angle from the center based on the current snap rotation angle. The first marker location for closed polylines is placed on the beginning vertex. If you cannot see the points dividing an object, try adjusting *pdmode* and *pdsize* (you can use *ddptype*) and issue a *regen*.

Initiate Command By

Command: **divide**
Alias: **div**
Draw → Point → Divide

Options

```
Select object to divide:
Enter the number of segments or [Block]:
```

Block

Divides an object with a block or external reference currently defined in the drawing. After providing the block or external reference name, you are prompted for the alignment and number of segments. An aligned block is rotated around its insertion point and drawn parallel to the divided object. An unaligned block is drawn with a rotation angle to the object of 0. You cannot change the *X*, *Y*, and *Z* scale factor of a block or external reference.

Only blocks containing attributes defined as constant are displayed on the drawing. If you try editing the attribute, the message "That block has no editable attributes" appears.

Tips & Warnings

Divide markers are placed in the UCS of the object being divided. They are always placed on the object regardless of the current elevation setting.

Related Variables   pdmode, pdsize

Associated Commands   block, ddptype, measure, osnap, point, xref

Example

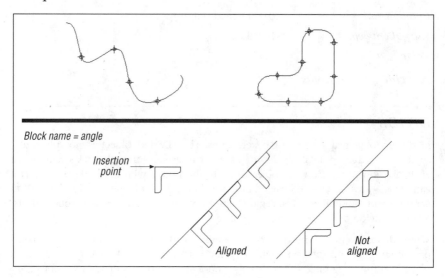

Block name = angle

Insertion
point

Aligned

Not
aligned

DONUT

Draws solid-filled rings and circles. Donut objects are constructed from closed polyline arc segments. You provide the inside and outside diameters and the center point location. Once you have located the first donut, the command repeats by asking for another center point location.

You can edit donuts with *pedit* because they are polyline arcs. If grips are enabled, the donut's grip definition points are defined by the two polyline arcs. Therefore, the grips are on the vertices and midpoints of the polyarcs. Rotating the donut offsets the grip location by the rotation angle.

Initiate Command By

    Command: **donut**
    Alias: **do**
    Draw → Donut

Options

    Specify inside diameter of donut <0.5000>:
    Specify outside diameter of donut <1.0000>:
    Specify center of donut or <exit>:

Tips & Warnings

- Convert donuts into cylinders by assigning a thickness, using the *change* or *extrude* command.

- Construct a solid-filled circle by setting the donut's inside diameter to 0.

- Donuts are wireframed if *fill* is off.

Related Variables	donutid, donutod, fillmode
Associated Commands	change, fill, grips, pedit, pline, properties

'DONUTID

Sets the inside diameter for donuts. If the value for *donutid* is greater than the value for *donutod*, the values are automatically swapped.

Initiate Command By
Command: **donutid**

Variable Settings

Initial default:	0.5000
Subsequent default:	Initial default
Value:	Real
Related Variables	donutod
Associated Commands	donut

'DONUTOD

Sets the outside diameter for donuts. If the value for *donutod* is less than the value for *donutid*, the values are automatically swapped.

Initiate Command By
Command: **donutod**

Variable Settings

Initial default:	1.0000
Subsequent default:	Initial default
Value:	Real
Related Variables	donutid
Associated Commands	donut

DOUGHNUT   *see DONUT*

'DRAGMODE 2000mod

Controls the way objects are displayed as they are dragged about the drawing. The system variable (*setvar*) that maintains this setting is also named *dragmode*. When using multiple viewports, you can see the objects drag only in the current viewport. If you pick objects in other viewports, you can watch them drag in the viewport from which they were chosen.

Initiate Command By

Command: **dragmode**

Options

Enter new value [ON/OFF/Auto] <Auto>:

ON

Enables dragging when requested. You must type **drag** at the appropriate command line option.

OFF

Ignores all dragging requests. Setting *dragmode* off may provide faster draw and edit operations.

Auto

Automatically enables drag for any command that supports dragging.

Related Variables	dragmode, dragp1, dragp2
Associated Commands	setvar

'DRAGP1 2000mod

Determines the regen-drag input sampling rate.

Initiate Command By

Command: **dragp1**

Variable Settings

Initial default:	10
Subsequent default:	Registry file
Value:	Integer
Related Variables	dragp2
Associated Commands	dragmode

'DRAGP2 2000mod

Determines the fast-drag input sampling rate.

Initiate Command By

Command: **dragp2**

Variable Settings

Initial default:	25
Subsequent default:	Registry file
Value:	Integer
Related Variables	dragp1
Associated Commands	dragmode

DRAWORDER

Modify II toolbar

Changes the display of objects and images so that you can send objects to the foreground or background or move them relative to other objects or images. You can change the display order of 2D objects residing on different elevations, but objects drawn in 3D may give you unexpected results.

Initiate Command By

Command: **draworder**
Alias: **dr**
Tools → Display Order

Options

Enter object ordering option [Above object/Under object/Front/Back]
<Back>:

Above object
Displays the object or image above another object or image. An additional prompt is given for you to select the reference object or image.

Under object
Displays the object or image under another object or image. An additional prompt is given for you to select the reference object or image.

Front
Displays the object or image in front of other objects and images.

Back
Displays the object or image behind other objects and images.

Tips & Warnings

All of the object sort methods are turned on when *draworder* is used, causing slower regenerations and redraws. You may want to reset the sorting options by activating the *options* command and selecting the User Preferences tab.

Related Variables   sortents

Associated Commands   image, options, preferences, wipeout

Example

'DSETTINGS 2000

Object Snap toolbar

Lets you access various drawing tools that help you work more efficiently and quickly. These settings include snap, grid, polar tracking, and object snap.

Initiate Command By

Command: **dsettings**
Aliases: **ds**, **se**
Tools → Drafting Settings

Options

The Snap and Grid Tab

snap restricts your crosshairs' movement to a specified increment. *grid* displays reference dots at any user-defined increment, helping you get a perspective of the space you are working in.

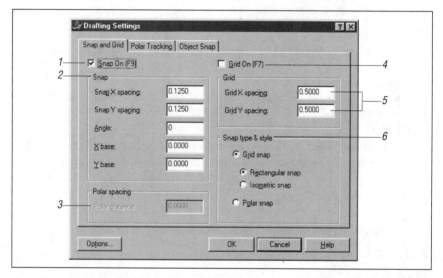

1. **Snap On (F9)**. Toggles *snap* on and off. You also can use the SNAP button on the status bar. This value is maintained by the *snapmode* system variable.

2. **Snap.** None of the following options are available when polar snap is enabled:

   Snap X spacing, Snap Y spacing
   Sets the *X* and *Y* snap increment. The value is maintained by the *snapunit* variable. When setting the *X* value, the *Y* defaults to that value. To create a different *Y* value, set the *Y* value and then set *X*.

   Angle
   Rotates the snap (and grid) by any specified angle. When working in isometric mode, you should use Isometric Snap setting. The Isometric Snap has greater functionality and more flexibility than setting the angle. This setting is maintained by the *snapang* variable.

   X base, Y base
   Specifies an X and Y base coordinate point for the grid. This setting is maintained by the *snapbase* variables.

3. **Polar distance.** Defines the snap increment when polar snap is enabled. This setting is maintained by the *polardist* variable. When the Grid Snap option is

---

on, this option is not available. When polar distance is set to 0, it inherits the value assigned to snap *X* spacing. Snap and polar tracking must be on for polar distance to take effect.

4. **Grid On (F7)** . Toggles grid on and off. You also can use the GRID button on the status bar. This value is maintained by the *gridmode* system variable.

5. **Grid X spacing, Grid Y spacing**. Sets the *X* and *Y* grid increment. This value is maintained by the *gridunit* variable. When setting the *X* value, the *Y* defaults to that value. To create a different *Y* value, set the *X* value and then set *Y*.

6. **Snap type & style**. Controls snap type and snap style settings. This value is maintained by the *snaptype* variable. When grid snap is active you can have the rectangular snap or isometric snap active. The *snapstyl* variable maintains this setting. See *isoplane* and *snap* for more detailed information about drawing in isometric mode.

The Polar Tracking Tab

The Polar Tracking tab enables you to preset absolute and relative distances and angles. When locating points with your cursor, temporary alignment paths and tooltips based on the polar distance and angle are displayed.

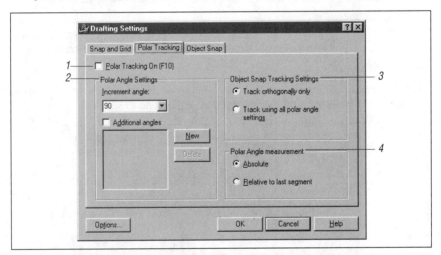

1. **Polar Tracking On (F10)**. Toggles polar tracking on and off. You also can use the POLAR button on the status bar. This value is maintained by the *autosnap* system variable. Turning *ortho* on automatically turns polar tracking off; turning polar tracking on automatically turns *ortho* off.

2. **Polar Angle Settings**.

   Increment angle

   Determines the polar increment angle when polar tracking is on. You can select a value from the drop-down list or enter an angle not provided in the list. If you want more than one setting, enter those values in the Additional Angles window. This value is maintained by the *polarang* system variable.

Additional angles

Defines additional polar increment angles when polar tracking is on. You can define up to 10 additional polar tracking angles. Press the New button to define additional angles; press the Delete button to remove additional angles. The *polarmode* variable determines if additional angles are being tracked, and the *polarddang* variable retains the additional angle settings.

3. **Object Snap Tracking Settings.**

Track orthogonally only

Sets only the horizontal and vertical object snap tracking paths for acquired object snap points to display when object snap tracking is enabled. This value is maintained by the *polarmode* variable.

Track using all polar angle settings

Lets the cursor track along any polar angle tracking path for acquired object snap points when object snap tracking is on while specifying points. This value is maintained by the *polarmode* variable.

4. **Polar Angle measurement.** Determines how polar tracking angles are measured. This value is maintained by the *polarmode* system variable.

Absolute/Relative to last segment

"Absolute" bases polar tracking on the current UCS; "Relative to last segment" bases polar tracking angles on the last object you created.

The Object Snap Tab

The Object Snap tab allows you to locate precise points on objects. You use these options as modifiers for most commands that require you to specify a point.

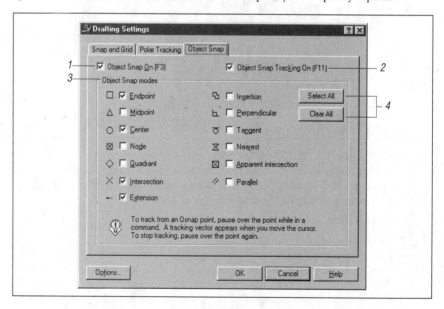

1. **Object Snap On (F3).** Toggles running object snap on and off. You also can use the OSNAP button on the status bar. This value is maintained by the *osmode* variable.

2. **Object Snap Tracking On (F11).** Toggles object snap tracking on and off. You also can use the OTRACK button on the status bar. Object snap tracking lets the cursor track along alignment paths based on other object snap points when specifying points in a command. This value is maintained by the *autosnap* system variable.

3. **Object Snap modes.** Snap to strategic points on objects. See *osnap* for more detailed information. This value is maintained by the *osmode* variable.

4. **Select All, Clear All.** Select All turns all the object snap settings on; Clear All turns all the object snap settings off.

Tips & Warnings

- If you activate the *dsettings* command transparently while in another command, some changes will not take place until you complete the initial command.

- See "Transparent Commands and Variables" in Chapter 2, *Command Index and Global Topics,* for more information.

Related Variables	fillmode, gridmode, gridunit, highlight, orthomode, pickstyle, qtextmode, snapang, snapbase, snapisopair, snapmode, snapstyl, snapunit
Associated Commands	blipmode, fill, grid, group, isoplane, keys/toggles, options, ortho, preferences, qtext, snap

---

'DSVIEWER

Activates the Aerial View window. The Aerial View window provides a way to quickly maneuver around your drawing using zoom and pan. This viewing tool can be accessed as long as your hardware is configured to use the Whip driver or the Windows accelerated display driver with the Display List option. Aerial View is not accessible if paper space or dynamic view (*dview*) is active or when fast zooms are disabled (*viewres*).

Initiate Command By

Command: **dsviewer**
Alias: **av**
View → Aerial View

Options

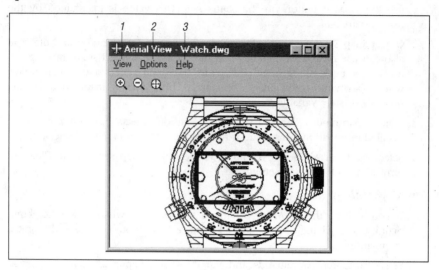

1. **View.**

   Zoom In

   Magnifies the drawing in the Aerial View window.

   Zoom Out

   Shrinks the drawing in the Aerial View window.

   Global

   Displays the entire drawing (zoom all) in the Aerial View window.

2. **Options.**

   Auto Viewport

   Determines whether the Aerial View automatically updates to match the display in the active viewport.

   Dynamic Update

   Determines whether the Aerial View window is updated as you edit the drawing.

   Realtime Zoom

   Equivalent to performing a real-time pan and zoom. As you move your pointer about the Aerial View, the drawing dynamically updates to that location. You also can resize the window by picking new points in the Aerial Window.

3. **Help.**

   Aerial View Help

   Activates the standard AutoCAD help screens

Associated Commands   pan, zoom

Example

This is the view you will see when the previous Aerial View window is active.

DTEXT/TEXT

dtext (dynamic text) creates one or more lines of text on your drawing. It is also known as single-line text since each line of text is considered a separate object. *mtext* (multiline text) is similar except that multiple lines of text are treated as one object. *rtext* (remote text) references the content of ASCII text files or the value of Diesel expressions. The *text* command also creates single lines of text, and the end results are the same as *dtext*.

When using *dtext*, the characters appear on the screen as they are being typed. You also can move the cursor to different parts of the drawing and enter more text without exiting the command. When using the *text* command, you do not see the text until you exit the command, and you must exit and reenter the command if you want to type more than one line at a time. With *dtext*, you press Enter once to enter a second line of text; with *text*, you must press Enter twice.

Initiate Command By

  Command: **dtext**
  Alias: **dt**
  Draw → Text → Single Line Text

Options

  Current text style: "Standard" Text height: 0.2000
  Specify start point of text or [Justify/Style]:
  Specify height <0.2000>:
  Specify rotation angle of text <0>:

start point of text
  Justifies text at the bottom left of the first character.

Justify

Specifies the text justification according to the following options:

Align

Specifies the beginning and ending point of a line of text. The text is adjusted to fit between these points.

Fit

Specifies the beginning and ending point of a line of text. You determine the height; the width is adjusted to fit between the two endpoints. You cannot use the fit option for text styles assigned a vertical orientation.

Center

Horizontally centers the text and vertically aligns it to the base of the text.

Middle

Aligns to the middle of the text horizontally and vertically.

Right

Justifies text to the bottom right of the last character for each line of text.

TL

Justifies text to the top left of the tallest character.

TC

Justifies text to the top center of the tallest character.

TR

Justifies text to the top right of the tallest character.

ML

Justifies text to the middle left, between the top of the tallest character and the bottom of the lowest descender.

MC

Justifies text to the middle center, between the top of the tallest character and the bottom of the lowest descender.

MR

Justifies text to the middle right, between the top of the tallest character and the bottom of the lowest descender.

BL

Justifies text to the bottom left of the lowest descender.

BC

Justifies text to the bottom center of the lowest descender.

BR

Justifies text to the bottom right of the lowest descender.

Style

Changes the current default style. See the *style* command for more detailed information.

pressing Enter

Causes new text to be placed directly below the last text already on the drawing. The new text acquires the existing text style, height, and rotation.

This works only if text was created during the current drawing session and the last text created was not erased. This will not work for mtext objects.

height

Assigns a text height. You are not prompted for this when using the align option or a text style with a predefined height.

rotation angle

Specifies the text angle.

special character codes

You can enter codes in your text string to obtain the following special characters in the following table.

Code	Description	Example	Result
%%o	Toggle overscore mode on/off	%%oOverscore	O̅v̅e̅r̅s̅c̅o̅r̅e̅
%%u	Toggle underscore mode on/off	%%uUnderscore	U̲n̲d̲e̲r̲s̲c̲o̲r̲e̲
%%d	Draw degrees symbol	30%%d	30°
%%p	Draw plus/minus tolerance symbol	30%%p	30±
%%c	Draw diameter symbol	%%c30	ø30

When entering dynamic text, the control characters appear in the drawing. Once you end the command, the appropriate characters replace the control codes.

Tips & Warnings

- Convert single line text into multiline text (*mtext*) using *txt2mtxt*.

- *mtext* creates paragraph text; *attdef* creates attribute text; *arctext* creates text along an arc; and *rtext* references the content of ASCII text files or the value of Diesel expressions.

- When using the same notes for multiple drawings, save time by write-blocking (*wblock*) the text and inserting it into the other drawings. You also can import ASCII text from a separate file by using the *mtext* command or the *copyclip* and *paste* options.

- You can import text by picking and dragging a text file (*.txt*) from the Windows Explorer program into your AutoCAD drawing session. This is brought in as multiline text.

- You can assign a thickness to text but only after the text is on the drawing. Do this with the *change, chprop,* or *properties* command.

- Edit text strings with the *ddedit, change,* or *properties* command.

- You can change the style assigned to text with *change, matchprop,* and *properties.*

- The object snap *insert* locates the insertion point of text.

- If all your text appears as empty boxes, you may have *qtext* turned on. To display your text, turn *qtext* off and regenerate the drawing.

- Text always appears to the right of the insertion point. Once you press Enter to end the command, the text adjusts itself to the correct justification.

- You must press Enter one extra time to end the *dtext* command.

- Check your spelling with the *spell* command. Use the *find* command to perform a search and replace on text strings.

- Base your text height on the scale with which you plan to plot the drawing. The text height you specify in AutoCAD should be the height of plotted text multiplied by the plot scale factor.

- You can assign a border or mask text with the *textmask* command.

Related Variables	texteval, textfill, textqlty, textsize, textstyle
Associated Commands	arctext, change, ddedit, grips, textmask, mtext, properties, qtext, rtext, spell, style, text, txt2mtxt

Example

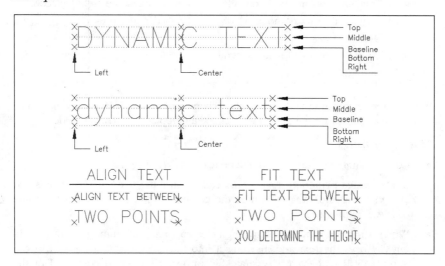

DVIEW

Provides better viewing of 3D models. Dynamic view is similar to *ddvpoint, vpoint,* and *3dorbit.* With *dview* you can dynamically drag and rotate all or part of a 3D model. You can display a perspective view of the model and toggle back and forth between parallel and perspective views. Using the *dview* command is similar to the concept of using a camera to view objects. You cannot use *dview* while in paper space.

Initiate Command By

Command: **dview**
Alias: **dv**

Options

```
Select objects:
[CAmera/TArget/Distance/POints/PAn/Zoom/TWist/CLip/Hide/Off/Undo]:
```

Select objects

Object selection is used to preview the results of the various *dview* options. If no objects are selected, a special 3D block named "dviewblock" is displayed as the preview image. Once you exit *dview*, the dviewblock is replaced by your actual drawing.

You can customize the dviewblock by creating your own 3D drawing with this name. Keep the geometry simple, but make sure the different sides are unique so that you can observe the dynamic movement of the symbol.

Enter direction and magnitude angles

Selecting a point on your screen activates the "Enter direction and magnitude angles" option. This option permits you to pick a target point and rotate your drawing about the screen, or you can enter angles between 0 and 360 degrees. If you enter the direction and magnitude angles from the keyboard, separate them with commas. The direction angle indicates the front of the view, and the magnitude angle determines how far the view rolls. The *X,Y* coordinates listed on the screen change to reflect the direction and magnitude.

CAmera

Enables you to pick a camera angle relative to the target. This is similar to the *vpoint* rotate option. You can move your camera point up, down, and around the target point.

TArget

Prompts you to specify a new target point relative to the camera.

Distance

Determines the distance from the camera to the target. This option turns perspective viewing on. During perspective viewing, the UCS icon is replaced by a special icon resembling a cube drawn in perspective. This is a reminder that perspective viewing is on, and only a subset of commands will work while perspective viewing is active.

When perspective viewing is enabled, you must use the zoom option of the *dview* command to change the viewing magnification or lens length. That is because the *zoom* command is disabled.

POints

Prompts you to specify a camera and target point.

PAn

Pans or scrolls around the screen.

Zoom

When perspective viewing is off, you can zoom in and out of the view with the zoom center option. If perspective viewing is on, you can zoom by changing the lens length of the camera. The default is a camera with a 50mm lens. Increasing the lens length is similar to using a telephoto lens; decreasing the lens length is similar to using a wide-angle lens.

TWist

Determines the view twist angle by rotating the camera around the line of sight.

CLip

Specifies the front and back clipping planes. A clipping plane is perpendicular to the line of sight between the camera and target.

Hide

Performs a hidden line removal on the current *dview* selection set.

Off

Turns perspective viewing off.

Undo

Reverses the last *dview* option.

eXit

Ends the command and regenerates the drawing to reflect any changes.

Tips & Warnings

- Use the *view* and *vports* save options to restore perspective views. Viewports retain all the *dview* display parameters.

- *zoom, pan, sketch,* and transparent *'zoom* and *'pan* commands, as well as many editing commands, do not work in perspective views.

- Once you initiate the *dview* command, you cannot move to another viewport to complete the command. You can cancel (Escape) the command, select another viewport, and then reissue the *dview* command.

- Issuing the *dview* command in a drawing containing rendered objects causes those objects to default to the latest *shademode* setting.

Related Variables   backz, frontz, lenslength, target, viewctr, viewdir, viewmode, viewsize, viewtwist, vsmax, vsmin, worldview

Associated Commands   ddvpoint, view, vpoint, vports/viewports, 3dorbit

Example

```
Command: Dview
Select objects or <use DVIEWBLOCK>: All
20 found
Select objects or <use DVIEWBLOCK>: Press Enter
Enter option
[CAmera/TArget/Distance/POints/PAn/Zoom/TWist/CLip/Hide/Off/Undo]: Ca
Specify camera location, or enter angle from XY plane,
or [Toggle (angle in)] <30.0000>: 30
Specify camera location, or enter angle in XY plane from X axis,
or [Toggle (angle from)] <30.00000>: -135
Enter option
[CAmera/TArget/Distance/POints/PAn/Zoom/TWist/CLip/Hide/Off/Undo]: X
Regenerating model.
```

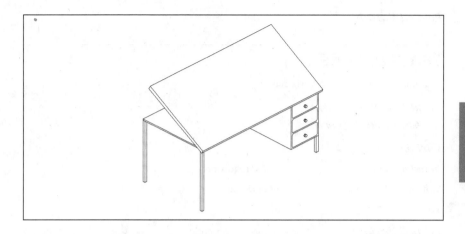

'DWGCHECK 2000

Determines whether a dialog box is displayed when you open a drawing that was last edited by a product other than AutoCAD.

Initiate Command By

Command: **dwgcheck**

Options

0 The Dwgcheck dialog box is suppressed.

1 When applicable, the Dwgcheck dialog box is displayed.

Variable Settings

Initial default:	0
Subsequent default:	Registry file
Value:	Integer
Associated Commands	open

'DWGCODEPAGE

Displays the code page of the drawing. *dwgcodepage* always has the same value as *syscodepage* and exists for compatibility purposes only.

Initiate Command By

Command: **dwgcodepage**

Variable Settings

Initial default:	Varies, read-only
Subsequent default:	Initial default
Value:	String

| *Related Variables* | syscodepage |

'DWGNAME 2000mod

Maintains the current drawing name.

Initiate Command By
Command: **dwgname**

Variable Settings

Initial default:	Varies, read-only
Subsequent default:	Initial default
Value:	String
Related Variables	dwgprefix, dwgtitled
Associated Commands	save, saveas

'DWGPREFIX

Maintains the drawings drive and/or folder prefix. If the drawing has not been assigned a drive and/or folder, it defaults to the current drive and folder.

Initiate Command By
Command: **dwgprefix**

Variable Settings

Initial default:	Varies, read-only
Subsequent default:	Initial default
Value:	String
Related Variables	dwgname
Associated Commands	save, saveas

DWGPROPS 2000

Tracks general drawing information and lets you create fields for data tracking. You can then search for this information using the AutoCAD DesignCenter or the Windows Explorer program. Right-clicking on a filename in Windows Explorer and selecting Properties will display the *dwgprops* dialog box.

Initiate Command By

Command: **dwgprops**
File → Drawing Properties

Options

The Drawing Properties dialog contains the following four tabs, which are detailed in this section: General, Summary, Statistics, and Custom.

The General Tab

The fields displayed in the General tab are read-only and are derived from your computer's operating system.

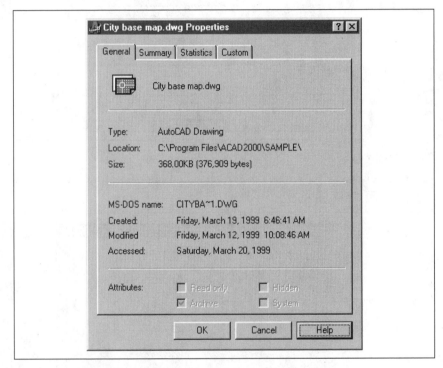

The Summary Tab

The fields in the Summary tab are manually entered and can be updated at any time. You can preset values in a template file and modify fields only when necessary. Keywords are directly linked to the Find option in the AutoCAD DesignCenter. By entering keywords, you can search for all files containing one or more of those words. Completing the Hyperlink Base box creates a default base path for all relative path hyperlinks in the current drawing.

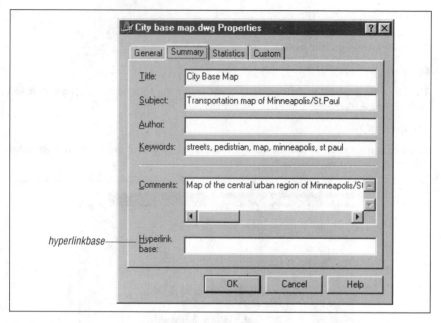

The Statistics Tab

The fields displayed in this tab are read-only and are derived from information AutoCAD has stored in the drawing file.

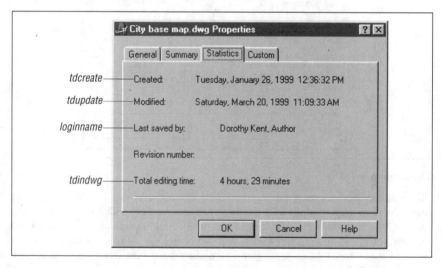

The Custom Tab

You can define up to 10 custom fields. These fields can be updated at any time. You can preset values in a template file and modify fields only when necessary. Since these fields are directly linked to the AutoCAD DesignCenter's Find option, you can search on any of the keywords to locate the drawing. These fields can be accessed through programming interfaces such as AutoLISP.

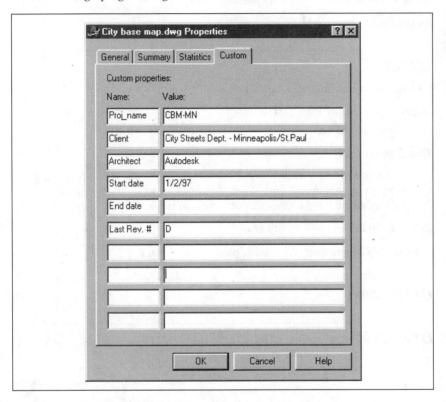

Related Variables	hyperlinkbase, loginname, tdcreate, tdindwg, tdupdate
Associated Commands	adcenter

'DWGTITLED

Maintains whether the current drawing has been assigned a name.

Initiate Command By

Command: **dwgtitled**

Options

0 The current drawing has no assigned name.

1 The current drawing has an assigned name.

Variable Settings

Initial default:	0, read-only
Subsequent default:	1 (set as soon as the drawing is saved)
Value:	Integer

Related Variables   dwgname

Associated Commands   save, saveas

DXBIN

Imports binary drawing exchange files (*.dxb*).

Initiate Command By

Command: **dxbin**

Tips & Warnings

If *filedia* is set to 1, a dialog box is activated; if *filedia* is set to 0, you are prompted on the command line. When *filedia* is set to 0, or off, entering a tilde (~) on the command line temporarily activates the dialog box.

Related Variables   filedia

Associated Commands   config, plot

DXFIN 2000mod   *see OPEN*

DXFOUT 2000mod   *see SAVEAS*

EDGE   Surfaces toolbar

Changes the visibility of 3D face edges. You can use the *properties* command to change the visibility of 3D face edges; however you must know which edge is considered edge 1, edge 2, and so on. This is based on how the 3D face was created. If edges overlap and are on the same plane, selecting one edge may make both edges invisible. You can make all edges visible by setting *splframe* to 1. You may have to update your display by regenerating the drawing to see the changes caused by the *edge* command.

Initiate Command By

Command: **edge**
Draw → Surfaces → Edge

Options

```
Specify edge of 3dface to toggle visibility or [Display]:
```

Specify edge

Select 3D face edges you want invisible.

Display

Gives you the following display options:

Select

Highlights the invisible edges of 3D face objects that you individually select. Selecting highlighted edges converts them back to being visible.

All

Highlights the invisible edges of all 3D face objects. Selecting highlighted edges converts them back to being visible.

Related Variables	splframe
Associated Commands	properties, 3dface

'EDGEMODE

Determines if an object selected for extending or trimming needs to find a physical boundary or if the boundary is based on the projected boundary of another object. This variable is set with *bextend, extend,* or *trim.*

Initiate Command By

Command: **edgemode**

Options

0 Uses the actual size of the boundary edge.

1 Extends or trims objects based on the actual or projected boundary.

Variable Settings

Initial default:	0
Subsequent default:	Registry file
Value:	Integer
Associated Commands	bextend, extend, trim

EDGESURF

Surfaces toolbar

Generates a 3D polygon mesh (surface) by approximating a Coons surface patch from four adjoining objects. The edges can be made up of lines, arcs, or open polylines anywhere in 3D space. The endpoints of each object must share the same vertices to form a closed path. You can pick the edges in any order. The first edge or object selected defines the *M* direction of the mesh. The two edges that intersect the *M* edge determine the *N* direction for the mesh.

Initiate Command By

Command: **edgesurf**
Draw → Surfaces → Edge Surface

Options

```
Current wire frame density:   SURFTAB1=6   SURFTAB2=6
Select object 1 for surface edge:
Select object 2 for surface edge:
Select object 3 for surface edge:
Select object 4 for surface edge:
```

Tips & Warnings

You can edit an *edgesurf* object with the *pedit* command.

Related Variables   surftab1, surftab2

Associated Commands   3dface, 3dmesh

Example

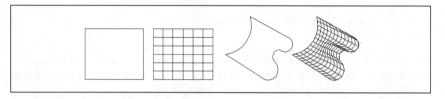

'ELEV

Sets the elevation and extrusion thickness of new objects. The *elev* is the object's location along the Z axis. The extrusion thickness (negative or positive) is its height above (or below) the Z elevation. The elevation setting affects only those objects whose Z value is not otherwise specified. Model space and layout space each have their own *elev* settings. When changing the UCS, the *elev* value automatically returns to 0.

Initiate Command By

Command: **elev**

Options

```
Specify new default elevation <0.0000>:
Specify new default thickness <0.0000>:
```

Tips & Warnings

* You can assign an elevation and thickness to existing objects, including text and attributes, by using the *change* or *chprop* command. You can provide only the thickness if you use the *properties* command.

* The combination of *elev* and *ucs* can be confusing. It is recommended that you use *ucs* and do not change the elevation.

Related Variables   elevation

Associated Commands   ucs, ucsman

'ELEVATION

Sets and maintains the value for the current *elev.*

Initiate Command By
Command: **elevation**

Variable Settings

Initial default:	0.0000
Subsequent default:	Last value used in the drawing
Value:	Real

Associated Commands   elev

ELLIPSE

Draw toolbar

Draws ellipses and elliptical arcs. There are two different types of ellipses you can construct. One is considered a true ellipse (the default) since it can be manipulated by its center point and the endpoints (quadrant) of its major and minor axes. The other is made up of 16 polyline arcs; therefore, you are unable to locate the center and endpoints. You can locate the center, endpoints, and midpoint of each polyline arc and use the *pedit* command to modify the arcs. You can assign a thickness to a polyline ellipse but not to a true ellipse. However, you can extrude both types of ellipses. The type of ellipse drawn is based on the *pellipse* variable setting.

Ellipses break in a counterclockwise direction. You can use *break* and *trim* on ellipses to create elliptical arcs. When you use *break*, the deleted portion of an ellipse is determined by the order of your pick points. You can request the area and perimeter/length of an ellipse by using the object option of the *area* command. The UCS object option does not let you use a true ellipse object to specify a User Coordinate System.

Initiate Command By
Command: **ellipse**
Alias: **el**
Draw → Ellipse

Options
```
Specify axis endpoint of ellipse or [Arc/Center]:
Specify other endpoint of axis:
Specify distance to other axis or [Rotation]:
```

Arc
Creates an elliptical arc. *pellipse* must be true (0) to work.

Rotation
Specifies the rotation around the major axis. The rotation angle must be between 0 and 89.4 degrees.

Isocircle

When isometric mode is enabled (see *snap*), the ellipse prompt includes an isocircle option. Isometric circles are drawn in the current isoplane. You provide the center point and the radius or diameter.

Related Variables   pellipse

Associated Commands   isoplane, pedit, pline, snap

Example

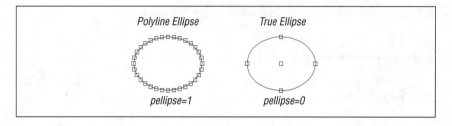

Polyline Ellipse   True Ellipse

pellipse=1   pellipse=0

END (obsolete)   see QUIT

ERASE   Modify toolbar

Deletes objects from the drawing. You can use the cut (*cutclip*) option found in the Edit pull-down menu. This places the deleted objects in the Windows clipboard. You also can use the Delete key to erase objects: first select the objects and then press the Delete key. Use the *purge* command to delete named layers, blocks, dimension styles, linetypes, plot styles, shapes, text styles, and multiline styles.

Initiate Command By

    Command: **erase**
    Alias: **e**
    Modify → Erase

Options

    Select objects:

Tips & Warnings

• Use *u, undo,* or *oops* to restore the last group of erased objects. If you executed commands after erasing objects, use *oops*.

• You can delete part of an object using *break, change, grips, lengthen, mledit* (multilines only), *stretch,* or *trim.*

Associated Commands   cutclip

EXCHPROP

see PROPERTIES

'EXPERT

Controls the frequency of some of the command-line messages such as "Are you sure?" Suppressing these messages and questions sets your response to "yes." Expert mode can also affect scripts, LISP routines, and macros.

Initiate Command By

Command: **expert**

Options

0   Issues all prompts.

1   Suppresses "About to regen, proceed?" and "Really want to turn the current layer off?"

2   Suppresses the prompts "Block already defined. Redefine it?" when a block by that name already exists and "A drawing with this name already exists. Over-write it?" when a file by that name already exists in the folder that you assigned to the write block or that you are trying to save.

3   Suppresses the preceding prompts and those issued by *-linetype–load* and *-linetype–create* if a linetype that is already loaded or created has the same name.

4   Suppresses the preceding prompts and those issued by *ucs* and *vport–save* if the name you provide already exists.

5   Suppresses the preceding prompts and those issued by *-dimstyle–save* if the dimension style name you provide already exists.

Variable Settings

Initial default:	0
Subsequent default:	Initial default
Value:	Integer

'EXPLMODE

Controls whether blocks with different *X*, *Y*, and *Z* values can be exploded.

Initiate Command By

Command: **explmode**

Options

0   Does not explode nonuniformly scaled blocks.

1   Explodes nonuniformly scaled blocks.

Variable Settings

Initial default:	1
Subsequent default:	Initial default
Value:	Integer

Associated Commands explode, xplode

EXPLODE

Modify toolbar

Converts complex objects into their individual components. Exploding some objects may result in a change in their color and linetype as they return to their original layer, color, and linetype definitions. Use the *xplode* command if you want to control the color, layer, and linetype of the exploded objects. The following table lists the different object types and the results of exploding them.

Object Type	Reverts to	Remarks
block	original objects	Blocks containing circles and arcs with unequal X, Y, and Z values become ellipses and elliptical arcs. Attributes lose their values and revert to their attribute definitions. Use *burst* to convert attribute values to text.
dimension	multiline text, solid, line	
hatch	line	
multiline	lines, arcs	
multiline text	text	
polyface	3D face	
polyline	lines, arcs	Polylines lose all tangent and width information.
region	lines, arcs	
remote text	multiline text	
3D mesh	3D face	
3D poly	line	
3D solid	planar surfaces become regions; nonplanar surfaces become bodies	

Initiate Command By

Command: **explode**
Alias: **x**
Modify → Explode

Tips & Warnings

- You can't *explode* a 3D face, complex linetype, ellipse (true), ray, revolved object, shape, solid, sphere, spline, tolerance dimension, torus, trace, or xline. You can explode groups by using the group explode option. You must bind an external reference before it can be exploded.

- You may have to *explode* a block more than once to break it down into its original components. This is referred to as "nested levels" of information. For example, blocks A, B, and C may make up a fourth block named D. Exploding D leaves you with the original blocks A, B, and C.

Related Variables	explmode
Associated Commands	burst, xplode

EXPORT

Saves drawings or parts of drawings to other file formats. The destination option of the *render* command lets you create *.tga*, *.tiff*, *.ps*, *.bmp*, and *.pcx* images. Create *.bmp*, *.tiff*, and *.tga* file formats by using the replay option. You can create *.tga* and *.tiff* files using the *saveimg* command. Not all programs can import AutoCAD files created with the *export* command. The code AutoCAD uses to create the export files may not be compatible with other programs even though they indicate that they can accept those file types.

Initiate Command By

Command: **export**
Alias: **exp**
File → Export

Options

Metafile (*.wmf)
Allows you to select the objects to export. This is the same as using *wmfout*.

ACIS (*.sat)
Converts regions, solids, and other objects representing NURBS (nonuniform rational B-spline) surfaces to ACIS files. This is the same as using *acisout*.

Lithography (*.stl)
Stores a solid in an ASCII or binary file.

Encapsulated PS (*.eps)
Gives you many options for defining the objects to export. Most are similar to the *plot* command. See also *psprolog* and *psfill*. This is the same as using *psout*.

DXX Extract (*.dxx)
Extracts data from drawings concerning block references, attribute information, and end-of-sequence objects. DXX files are a subset of the *dfx* command. This is the same as using *attext*.

Bitmap (.bmp)*
> This is the same as using the Save to File option of the *render* command or *bmpout.*

3D Studio (.3ds)*
> This is the same as using *3dsout.*

Block (.dwg)*
> Extracts a block defined in the current drawing to its own drawing file. This is similar to *-wblock.*

Tips & Warnings

If *filedia* is set to 1, a dialog box is activated; if *filedia* is set to 0, you are prompted on the command line. When *filedia* is set to 0, or off, entering a tilde (~) on the command line temporarily activates the dialog box.

Related Variables   filedia, psprolog

Associated Commands   acisout, attext, bmpout, dxbin, dxfout, import, psfill, psout, render, saveimg, wblock, wmfout, 3dsout

---

EXPRESSMENU   *see EXPRESSTOOLS*

EXPRESSTOOLS 2000

Loads the Express pull-down menu and readies the Express toolbars. The toolbars can be displayed on the screen with the menugroup option of the *toolbar* command. The express routines let you quickly access various AutoCAD routines that help you design and edit your drawings more efficiently. When the express tools are active, the folder location for these routines is placed in the support file search path.

Initiate Command By

> Command: **expresstools**

Tips & Warnings

The express tools are loaded onto your computer only if you installed AutoCAD with the Full option or if you chose the express tools feature with the Custom install. If you didn't load the express tools, you can rerun the AutoCAD installation program using the Add option and install them.

Associated Commands   menuload, toolbar

EXTEND

Lengthens an object to a boundary or implied boundary. Objects can be both a boundary and an object to extend. You can extend objects and define borders only for the space (model or layout) in which the objects were created. Use *bextend* if you want to use objects defined within blocks as boundaries.

The following table shows the capabilities of each object type.

Object	Object to Extend	Boundary	Object	Object to Extend	Boundary
arc	Yes	Yes	ray	Yes	Yes
associated dimension	Yes	No	region	No	Yes
block	No	No	shape	No	No
circle	No	Yes	solid	No	No
ellipse (polyline)	No	Yes	spline	No	Yes
ellipse (true)	No	Yes	text	No	Yes
leader	No	Yes	trace	No	No
line	Yes	Yes	viewport[a]	No	Yes
multiline	No	Yes	xline	No	Yes
3D face	No	No	multiline text	No	Yes
3D mesh	No	No	point	No	No
3D poly	Yes	Yes	polyface	No	No
3D solids	No	No	polyline	Yes	Yes

[a] Only when paper space is active.

Initiate Command By

> Command: **extend**
> Alias: **ex**
> Modify → Extend

Options

> Current settings: Projection=UCS Edge=None
> Select boundary edges ...
> Select object to extend or [Project/Edge/Undo]:

Select boundary edges

Allows you to determine the boundary location(s) for the extended object. All objects are selected if you press Enter for your response.

Select object to extend

Allows you to select the object(s) to lengthen. Pick closer to the endpoint being extended. You can select multiple objects by using the fence selection set method.

Project

Determines the projection mode used for finding boundary edges. This value is maintained by the *projmode* variable.

None

Specifies no projection. Only objects that intersect with the boundary edge in 3D space extend.

UCS
> Specifies projection onto the *XY* plane of the current UCS.

View
> Determines the projection based on the current view direction. All objects that intersect with the cutting edge in the current view are extended.

Edge
> Determines whether the object extends to the implied intersection or whether it must actually intersect the boundary edge. This value is maintained by the *edgemode* variable.

Extend
> Extends to the boundary edge or to the implied intersection.

No extend
> Extends only if it actually intersects the boundary edge.

Undo
> Restores the last object extended.

Tips & Warnings

- At times you can use *break, chamfer, change* (point), *fillet, grip* editing, *lengthen,* and *properties* to extend most objects. None of these commands require a boundary edge.

- Extending a linear associative dimension automatically updates the dimension.If an object will not extend, pick a new point on the object closer to the endpoint you are extending. Select the border of wide polylines and the centerline of objects assigned a lineweight.

Related Variables   edgemode, projmode

Associated Commands   bextend, change, grip, lengthen, stretch, trim

Example

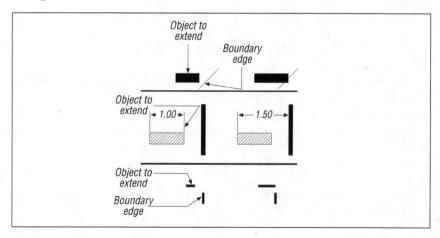

---

external reference   *see XREF*

'EXTMAX

(Extents Maximum) Tracks the upper-right drawing extents.

Initiate Command By
Command: **extmax**

Variable Settings

Initial default:	−1.0000E+20, −1.0000E+20, −1.0000E+20, read-only
Subsequent default:	Last value used in the drawing
Value:	3D point

Related Variables	extmin
Associated Commands	zoom

'EXTMIN

(Extents Minimum) Tracks the lower-left drawing extents.

Initiate Command By
Command: **extmin**

Variable Settings

Initial default:	1.0000E+20,1.0000E+20,1.0000E+20, read-only
Subsequent default:	Last value used in the drawing
Value:	3D Point

Related Variables	extmax
Associated Commands	zoom

'EXTNAMES 2000

Determines how many characters can be assigned to named objects. Named objects include attribute tag, block, dimension style, layer, layout name, linetype, page setup name, text style, UCS, view, and vports.

Initiate Command By
Command: **extnames**

Options

0 Name lengths are limited to 31 characters.

1 Name lengths are limited to 255 characters.

Variable Settings

Initial default:	1
Subsequent default:	Last value used in the drawing
Value:	Integer

Tips & Warnings

Multiline style and group are named objects, but their maximum name length is only 31 characters.

EXTRIM `2000mod`   Express Standard toolbar

Extended trim automatically trims objects crossing over the cutting edge of a polyline, line, circle, arc, ellipse, image, or text. Once you specify the cutting edge, you are asked to specify the side to trim. This is similar to the *trim* command except that when you use *trim*, you must specify each object to trim, and objects don't have to literally cross the cutting edge. See *trim* for a list of objects that can be trimmed.

Initiate Command By

Command: **extrim**
Express → Modify → Cookie Cutter Trim

Associated Commands   expresstools, trim

EXTRUDE   Solids toolbar

Generates solids by extruding 2D objects. The 2D objects can be closed polylines (including donuts, rectangles, and polygons), closed splines, planar 3D faces, circles, regions, and ellipses.

You can create 2D closed objects with lines, arcs, and polylines and then convert them into a closed polyline using the *pedit–join*, *pljoin*, or the *region* command. You cannot extrude blocks and multiline objects. You cannot assign a taper angle to splines. You cannot extrude polylines whose segments intersect. Defining a large taper angle can cause the object to be created before it reaches its extrusion height. Use the extrude option of the *solidedit* command when extruding 3D solids since it provides more flexibility than *extrude*.

Initiate Command By

Command: **extrude**
Alias: **ext**
Draw → Solids → Extrude

Options

```
Current wire frame density:  ISOLINES=4
Select objects:
Specify height of extrusion or [Path]:
Specify angle of taper for extrusion <0>:
```

---

height of extrusion

Defines the height along the Z axis. Use a negative value when referencing the negative direction of the current UCS Z axis.

Path

Defines the angle and length to extrude an object. The path can be a line, arc, circle, ellipse, elliptical arc, spline, 2D, or 3D polyline.

angle of taper for extrusion

Specifies the taper angle. Positive angles taper in from the base; negative angles taper out from the base. A zero (0) angle creates a top perpendicular to its base.

Related Variables   delobj, dispsilh, isolines

Associated Commands   dview, hide, render, shademode, ucs, vpoint, 3dorbit

Example

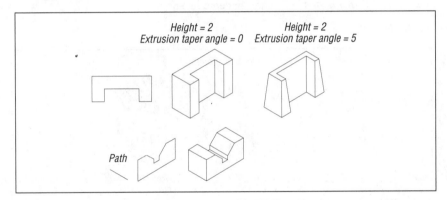

'FACETRATIO 2000mod

Determines the aspect ratio of faceting for cylindrical and conic ACIS solids.

Initiate Command By

Command: **facetratio**

Options

0   Creates an *N* by 1 mesh.

1   Creates an *N* by *M* mesh.

Variable Settings

Initial default: 0

Subsequent default: Initial default

Value: Integer

'FACETRES

Refines the smoothness of rendered and shaded curved solids. The *facetres* value can be between 0.01 and 10.0 and is directly linked to *viewres*. When *facetres* is set to 1, there is a 1-to-1 relationship between the *viewres* setting and how curved solids are displayed. When *facetres* is set to 2, its resolution is twice that of the *viewres* setting.

Initiate Command By
        Command: **facetres**

Variable Settings
Initial default:	0.5
Subsequent default:	Last value used in the drawing
Value:	Real

Associated Commands
hide, shademode, stlout, viewres

Example

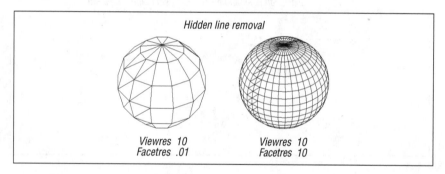

Hidden line removal

Viewres 10
Facetres .01

Viewres 10
Facetres 10

'FILEDIA

Determines whether a dialog box or the command line is activated for the following commands:

acisin	-lman (import, export)	psout
acisout	load	qsave
bmpout	menu	recover
compile	menuload	rtext
dxbin	menuunload	save
dxfin	mkltype	saveas
dxfout	mkshape	script
export	mslide	stlout
import	new	vslide
layout	open	wmfin
-linetype load	psin	wmfout

Initiate Command By

Command: **filedia**

Options

0   Disables dialog boxes.

1   Activates dialog boxes.

~   Entering a tilde (~) at the command line temporarily activates the dialog box when it is set to 0.

Tips & Warnings

- You can temporarily disable the dialog box for *attdef, attedit, attext, bhatch, block, boundary, color, group, image, insert, layer, linetype, mtext, osnap, rename, units, view, wblock, xbind,* and *xref* by typing a hyphen (-) before the command.

- Script and AutoLISP routines temporarily disable *filedia* if it is enabled.

Variable Settings

Initial default:	1
Subsequent default:	Registry file
Value:	Integer
Associated Commands	dialog boxes

'FILES (obsolete)

'FILL

Controls whether hatches, multilines, polylines, solids, and traces are displayed and plotted as filled or whether just the outline is displayed and plotted. Objects referencing a lineweight setting are not affected by the *fill* command. When you change the fill setting, you will not see the change until the drawing is regenerated. You can set this parameter using the Display tab of the *options* command. The *fillmode* variable stores this value.

Initiate Command By

Command: **fill**

Options

Enter mode [ON/OFF] <ON>:

ON

Hatches, multilines, polylines, solids, and traces are displayed and plotted as filled.

OFF

Only the outlines of hatches, multilines, polylines, solids, and traces are displayed and plotted.

Tips & Warnings

- The *shademode* and *render* commands fill in regardless of the *fill* setting.

- Use *textfill* to control the display of Bitstream, TrueType, and Adobe Type 1 fonts.

- Hatch patterns are invisible when *fill* is off. This is true only for hatch patterns that were created with Release 14 or 2000.

Related Variables   fillmode

Associated Commands   options, preferences

Example

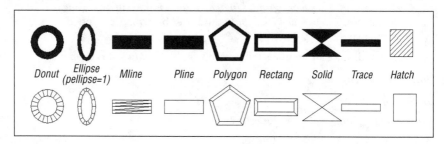

Donut | Ellipse (pellipse=1) | Mline | Pline | Polygon | Rectang | Solid | Trace | Hatch

---

FILLET

Modify toolbar

Creates an arc with a predefined radius between any two arcs, circles, lines, polylines, rays, splines, or selected solid shapes. If your selected objects do not meet or they extend past an intersecting point, *fillet* can extend or trim the objects until they intersect. The fillet arc is inserted based on the fillet radius value. The *filletrad* variable stores the value of the radius. When two parallel lines are filleted, an arc is placed starting from the endpoint closest to the first pick point. The radius is based on the distance between the two lines.

When Trim is active, *filleting* a line with a polyline causes the line to convert and join or attach itself to the polyline. When No Trim is active, *filleting* a line with a polyline lets those objects keep their original definitions, and the filleted object is defined as an arc. This arc resides on the current layer.

Initiate Command By

Command: **fillet**
Alias: **f**
Modify → Fillet

Options

Current settings: Mode = TRIM, Radius = 0.5000
Select first object or [Polyline/Radius/Trim]:

Select first object
Allows you to fillet arcs, circles, lines, polylines, rays, splines, or solid shapes.

3D solids

Prompts you to select an edge, chain, or radius once you pick one of the edges for filleting. If you press Enter without picking an edge, the adjacent edge fillets. Chaining lets you pick multiple edges for filleting; selecting one edge also selects the tangential sequence of edges. You can remove fillets with the face option of *solidedit*.

Polyline

Fillets all the intersections of a 2D polyline. The intersections must be contiguous segments.

Radius

Sets the fillet radius. Once you have set a radius, you are returned to the command line. Press Enter or reselect the *fillet* command for object selection. This value is maintained by the *filletrad* variable.

Trim/Notrim

Determines whether to trim or extend the original lines to meet the fillet edge or to leave the lines intact and add the fillet in the appropriate spot. This value is assigned to the variable *trimmode*.

Tips & Warnings

- Filleting a polyline containing two line segments separated by an arc causes the arc segment to be replaced with the results of the fillet command. Circles are not altered when they are filleted.

- The fillet resides on the layer of the picked objects as long as they share the same layer; if the two objects are on different layers, the fillet is placed on the current layer. The same rules apply to color, linetype, and lineweight. You cannot fillet borders of viewport objects or polyline segments from different polylines.

- If you need the endpoints of two lines to meet, set the *fillet* radius to 0 and set trim on. You can achieve the same result with the *chamfer* command. The *rectangle* command lets you define a fillet radius during its construction.

- When *offsetting* a polyline, you can have the new polyline filleted if you set *offsetgaptype* to 1. The fillet size is based on the distance the endpoints of polylines are extended to fill the gap caused by the *offset* command.

Related Variables   filletrad, trimmode

Associated Commands   chamfer, extend, pline, trim

Example

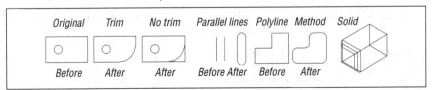

'FILLETRAD

Sets the current fillet radius value. This value is set using the *fillet* command.

Initiate Command By
Command: **filletrad**

Variable Settings

Initial default:	0.5000
Subsequent default:	Last value used in the drawing
Value:	Real
Associated Commands	fillet

'FILLMODE

Controls whether hatches, multilines, polylines, solids, and traces are displayed and plotted as filled or whether just the outline is displayed and plotted. This value is set using the Display tab of the *options* command.

Initiate Command By
Command: **fillmode**

Options

0 Only the outlines of hatches, multilines, polylines, solids, and traces are displayed and plotted.

1 Hatches, multilines, polylines, solids, and traces are displayed and plotted as filled.

Variable Settings

Initial default:	1
Subsequent default:	Last value used in the drawing
Value:	Integer

Tips & Warnings

- When you change the *fillmode* setting, you will not see the change until the drawing is *regenerated*.

- *shademode*, and *render* fill in regardless of the *fillmode* setting.

Associated Commands	bhatch, donut, fill, hatch, mline, options, pline, preferences, solid, trace
Example	See FILL.

FILTER   *see "Point Filter" in* Chapter 2, *Command Index and Global Topics*

'FILTER

Creates selection sets based on object properties. Some of these properties include location, color, object type, linetype, block name, text style, thickness, and layer. You can combine properties to make the filters very complex, and you can create multiple lists and retrieve them for future use. You use this in addition to or in place of the selection set options. You can activate the *filter* command at the command line or transparently while using another command. If you defined and located the filtered objects prior to a command, use Previous as your response to the "Select object" prompt. The *layer* command has its own variation of *filter*.

You also can select objects with the *qselect* command. *qselect* lets you select objects based on their object type, layer, color, lineweight, linetype, linetype scale, hyperlink, and plot style assignments. It is more user friendly than *filter* and has some different choices, but *filter* lets you save your search criteria for future use.

Initiate Command By

Command: **filter**
Alias: **fi**

Options

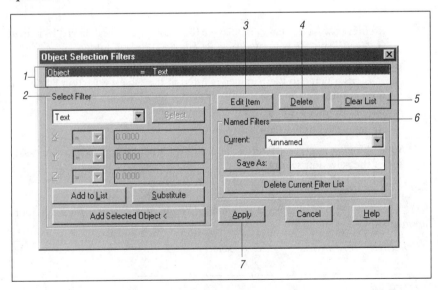

1. **Object Selection Filters list**. Lists the current search parameters. This list is created whenever the Add to List button is selected.

2. **Select Filter**. Lists all the possible categories for object selection.

   Select

   Lists named items located in the drawing. Named items include block names, dimension styles, layers, linetypes, and text styles. It also displays the Select Color dialog box for locating all objects assigned specific colors, ByLayer, or ByBlock.

X, Y, and Z
> List *X, Y,* and *Z* coordinates and the assignment of logical operators to each coordinate. When Attribute Tag, Block Name, Dimension Style, Hatch Pattern Name, Layer, Linetype, Multiline Style, Shape Name, Text Value, or Text Style Name is selected, you can enter the appropriate value in the *X* edit box or use the Select button.

Add to List
> Includes the latest object parameters in the Object Selection Filters list.

Substitute
> Replaces the highlighted item in the Object Selection Filters list with the current selected filter parameters.

Add Selected Object <
> Lets you pick objects directly from your drawing and adds them to the Object Selection Filters list.

3. **Edit Item.** Modifies items in the Object Selection Filters list.

4. **Delete.** Removes selected items from the Object Selection Filters list.

5. **Clear List.** Deletes all the items listed in the Object Selection Filters list.

6. **Named Filters.**

Current
> Retrieves a saved filter list. Saved filter lists are stored in a file named *filter.nfl.* This file is located in your AutoCAD default folder.

Save As
> Assigns a name to the parameters listed in the Object Selection Filters list. This creates or appends to a file named *filter.nfl* for future retrieval.

Delete Current Filter List
> Deletes the current filter list.

7. **Apply.** Takes the current filter list and applies it to the current drawing using any of the selection set options.

Tips & Warnings

See "Selection Sets" in Chapter 2, *Command Index and Global Topics,* for more information.

Associated Commands   qselect, select

FIND 2000   Standard toolbar

Locates, selects, replaces and zooms to text strings in the drawing. It finds single line text (*dtext, text*), multiline text (*mtext*), attributes, dimensions, hyperlink and hyperlink description text.

Initiate Command By
> Command: **find**
> Edit → Find

Options

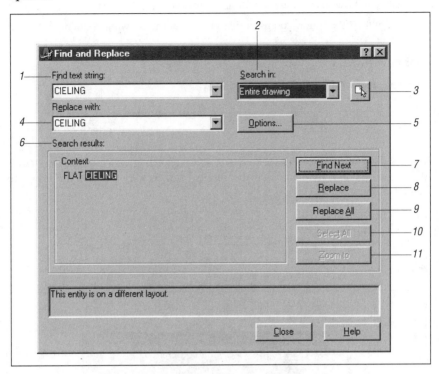

1. **Find text string**. Enter the text string for your search.

2. **Search in**. You can have the search look through the entire drawing or your current selection set. The current selection set can be defined by selecting the Select Objects icon located to the right or you can preselect objects before issuing the *find* command.

3. **Select Objects icon**. This will return to your drawing so you can select objects.

4. **Replace with**. Enter the replacement text.

5. **Options**. Define the type of text that will be included in the search. You can search for attributes, dimensions, single-line text (*text, dtext*), multiline text (*mtext*), hyperlink descriptions and hyperlinks. You also can refine the search by having it case sensitive, and you can have it look for whole words only.

6. **Search results**. The content box displays text found during the search, including any other text that is part of that object.

7. **Find Next**. This starts the search process.

8. **Replace**. Selecting this option substitutes the text matching the search criteria.

9. **Replace All**. Selecting this option substitutes all the text strings matching the search criteria.

10. **Select All**. This option is available only when you have defined the selection set as Current in the Search In edit box. Select All exits from the *find* dialog

box; locates, highlights, and grips every instance of the *find* text string; and tells you how many objects it found meeting the find criteria.

11. **Zoom to.** This option zooms to that portion of the drawing containing the text string.

Tips & Warnings

mtext has its own find and replace options.

FOG

Render toolbar

Defines the cue distance between objects and the current viewing direction. Once the *fog* is set, use *render* to see the results. You also can access *fog* from the *render* dialog window.

Initiate Command By

Command: **fog**
View → Render → Fog

Options

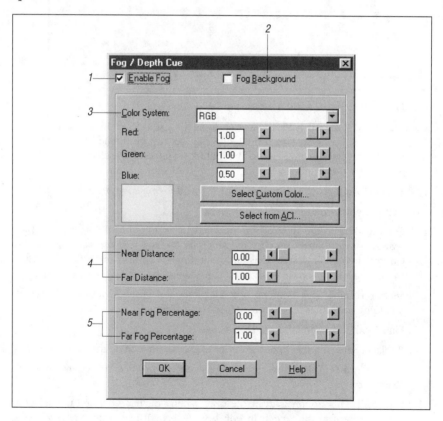

---

1. **Enable Fog**. Turns *fog* on and off.

2. **Fog Background**. Applies *fog* to the background of your drawing as well as to the objects.

3. **Color System**. Determines whether to use the red, green, blue (RGB) or the hue, lightness, saturation (HLS) color system. Once you determine the desired color system, you can manually set the colors by changing the slider bars or use the Select Custom Color or the Select from ACI button.

4. **Near Distance, Far Distance**. Determines the location where the fog starts and stops. The values are based on percentages of the distance from the camera to the back clipping plane.

5. **Near Fog Percentage, Far Fog Percentage**. Determines the fog's density at the near and far distances. Percentage values can be from 0 fog to 100 percent fog.

Tips & Warnings

This command takes effect when rendering the drawing.

Associated Commands   render, rpref

'FONTALT

Defines an alternate or default font when AutoCAD cannot locate font files assigned to drawings.

Initiate Command By

Command: **fontalt**
Tools → Options → Files → Text Editor, Dictionary, and Font File Names → Alternate Font File

Variable Settings

Initial default:	simplex.shx
Subsequent default:	Registry file
Value:	String
Related Variables	fontmap
Associated Commands	options, preferences

'FONTMAP

Directs AutoCAD to an ASCII file containing substitute font information. This file is used when AutoCAD is unable to locate fonts assigned to drawings. The file is named *acad.fmp* and is located in AutoCAD's support directory. If you plan to move a drawing file referencing the font map file to another computer or to a diskette, you need to include this file. Use *pack* to help you accomplish this.

Initiate Command By

Command: **fontmap**

Tools → Options → Files → Text Editor, Dictionary, and Font File Names → Font Mapping File

Variable Settings

Initial default:	acad.fmp
Subsequent default:	Registry file
Value:	String

Related Variables	fontalt
Associated Commands	options, pack, preferences

'FRONTZ

Retains the distance from the front clipping plane to the target plane when displaying objects in 3D. When the value is positive, it indicates that the front clipping plane is between the camera and target; when the value is negative, the front clipping plane is beyond the target. This value has meaning only if *viewmode*'s bits are set to 2 (front clipping on) and 16 (front clip not at eye). This value is set when using the clip option of the *dview* command or the *3dclip* command.

Initiate Command By

Command: **frontz**

Variable Settings

Initial default:	0.0000, read-only
Subsequent default:	Last value used in the drawing
Value:	Real

Related Variables	backz, viewmode
Associated Commands	dview, view, 3dclip

'FULLOPEN 2000

Tracks the current drawing as completely or partially opened.

Initiate Command By

Command: **fullopen**

Options

0   Partially opened drawing.

1   Fully opened drawing.

Variable Settings

Initial default:	1, read-only
Subsequent default:	Initial default
Value:	Integer

Associated Commands   open, partiaload

FULLSCREEN 2000

Toggles the AutoCAD display screen larger than the standard Windows maximize button and back to its previous setting. You can access the pull-down menus by moving your pointer to the top edge of the screen and pressing the first button on your pointing device.

Initiate Command By

Command: **fullscreen**
Express → Tools → Full Screen AutoCAD

Tips & Warnings

You also can gain more drawing space by turning off the scrollbars layout tabs and the menu on the right side of the screen. You do this through the *options* Display tab.

Associated Commands   expresstools

GATTE

Express Blocks toolbar

Edits attributes that share the same block and tag name.

Initiate Command By

Command: **gatte**
Express → Blocks → Global Attribute Edit

Options

```
Select block or attribute [Block name]:
Block: XXXX Attribute tag: XXXX
Enter new text:
Number of inserts in drawing = 4   Process all of them? [Yes/No] <Yes>:
```

Select block or attribute [Block name]

Select the attribute to modify or enter B for block name. If you select the attribute, the block and attribute tag name are displayed at the command line. If you enter the block name, you then are asked to select the attribute or enter the tag name within the block.

Enter new text

Enter the new text for the attribute value.

Number of inserts in drawing = 4 Process all of them? [Yes/No] <Yes>
Update all the attribute values assigned to the block and tag name automatically or use any of the selection set methods to determine which attributes to update.

Tips & Warnings

attedit and *-attedit* also edit attributes, but those attributes must all have the same value or text string. *gatte* edits any attribute value assigned to the same block and tag but their original value or text string can be different.

Related Variables   attmode

Associated Commands   -attedit, attedit, expresstools

GETSEL

Lets you quickly select objects that share the same layer and are assigned the same object type. These objects are retained and can be recalled when using the previous (P) selection set option. It often is used in macros, AutoLISP, and other programming routines.

You also can select objects with *select, filter,* or *qselect. select* lets you select the objects based on any of the selection set options. It is straightforward and not very sophisticated. *filter* and *qselect* let you select objects based on their object type, layer, color, linetype, linetype scale, location, and size. *qselect* also includes features such as lineweight, hyperlink, and plot style assignments.

Initiate Command By

Command: **getsel**
Express → Selection Tools → Get Selection Set

Tips & Warnings

You cannot select model space objects when working in paper space and vice versa.

Associated Commands   expresstools, filter, qselect, select, selection set

---

'GRAPHSCR/'TEXTSCR

graphscr and *textscr* flip your active window between graphics mode and text mode. The F2 key toggles between these two screens. Text mode enables you to review command prompts, your response, and often the result. Commands that generate information, such as *status, time, dblist,* and *list,* automatically activate the text screen. *graphscr* and *textscr* also are used to control the screen when working with macros, LISP, and script routines.

Initiate Command By

Command: **graphscr, textscr**, F2

Tips & Warnings

You can cut and paste information from the text screen into other programs that support Windows cutting and pasting features.

'GRID

Displays reference dots at any user-defined increment. It helps you get a perspective of the space in which you are working and the size of your drawing objects. You can modify the increment value and turn the setting on or off. Each model space viewport and layout space tab contains its own grid settings. You also can change your grid settings with *dsettings* and *3dorbit*.

If the grid is set to an increment that is too small to be shown on the screen, the message "Grid too dense to display" appears at the command line. Once you zoom into a portion of the drawing, you will be able to see the grid. Since the grid is a visual aid, the grid dots do not plot.

Initiate Command By

Command: **grid**, F7, or Ctrl-G
Tools → Drafting Settings → Snap and Grid tab
Status bar: GRID (left-clicking toggles *grid* on and off; right-clicking activates the *dsettings* Snap and Grid tab)

Options

Specify grid spacing(X) or [ON/OFF/Snap/Aspect] <0.5000>:

grid spacing (X)

Allows you to set the *X* and *Y* grid increments. If an *X* is placed after the number, it makes the grid a multiple of the current snap value. This value is maintained by the *gridunit* variable.

0 Sets the grid increment equal to the current snap increment.

ON

Grid is visible. This value is maintained by the *gridmode* variable.

OFF

Grid is invisible. This value is maintained by the *gridmode* variable.

Snap

Sets the grid increment equal to the current snap increment. This works the same as if you had set the grid equal to 0.

Aspect

Allows you to set individual horizontal and vertical grid increments. This value is maintained by the *gridunit* variable.

Tips & Warnings

• Regardless of the grid setting, it is the snap setting that helps you place objects accurately. In addition, use the style option of *snap* to set your grid to an isometric mode.

- If the grid does not appear the way you think it should, use any command (such as *redraw* or *regen*) that refreshes the current viewport. Editing commands such as *move* and *erase* may temporarily make it seem like grid dots have disappeared.

- If you are working in the WCS or a UCS that is the same as the WCS, the grid is displayed to the drawing limits. If you are working in a UCS different from the WCS, the grid extends to the edges of your viewport.

Related Variables   gridmode, gridunit, snapang

Associated Commands   dsettings, snap, 3dorbit

Example

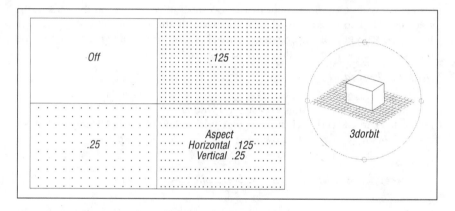

'GRIDMODE

Maintains grid visibility. This variable is set with *dsettings, grid, 3dorbit,* Ctrl-G, F7, or by picking the GRID button on the status bar at the bottom of your display screen.

Initiate Command By

Command: **gridmode**, Ctrl-G, or F7

Options

0   Grid is off (invisible) for the current viewport.

1   Grid is on (visible) for the current viewport.

Variable Settings

Initial default:	0
Subsequent default:	Last value used in the drawing
Value:	Integer

Related Variables	gridunit
Associated Commands	dsettings, grid, 3dorbit

'GRIDUNIT

Sets the *X,Y* grid increment for the current viewport. This value is set using *dsettings* or *grid*.

Initiate Command By
Command: **gridunit**

Variable Settings

Initial default:	0.5000,0.5000
Subsequent default:	Last value used in the drawing
Value:	2D point

Related Variables	gridmode
Associated Commands	dsettings, grid

'GRIPBLOCK

Determines whether the grip's location for a block is based on the block's insertion point or on the individual objects defining the block. This value is set from the Selection tab of the *options* command.

Initiate Command By
Command: **gripblock**

Options

0   Grip's location is based on the block's insertion point.

1   Grip's location is based on the individual objects that make up the block.

Variable Settings

Initial default:	0
Subsequent default:	Registry file
Value:	Integer

Related Variables	gripcolor, griphot, grips, gripsize
Associated Commands	grip, options, preferences

Example

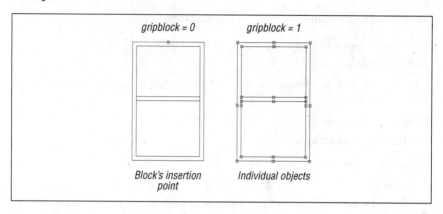

gripblock = 0   gripblock = 1

Block's insertion point   Individual objects

'GRIPCOLOR

Determines the color of nonselected, or cold, grips. Nonselected grips show the outline of the grip. This variable is set with the Unselected Grip Color drop-down list option from the *options* Selection tab.

Initiate Command By

Command: **gripcolor**

Variable Settings

Initial default:	5 (blue)
Subsequent default:	Registry file
Value:	Integer
Related Variables	gripblock, griphot, grips, gripsize
Associated Commands	options, preferences

'GRIPHOT

Determines the color of selected, or hot, grips. Selected grips are filled in. This variable is set with the Selected Grip Color drop-down list option from the *options* Selection tab.

Initiate Command By

Command: **griphot**

Tips & Warnings

You can unselect a hot grip by reselecting the grip.

Variable Settings

Initial default:	1
Subsequent default:	Registry file
Value:	Integer
Related Variables	gripblock, gripcolor, grips, gripsize
Associated Commands	options, preferences

'GRIPS

Determines whether grips are active or inactive. Grips provide a quick method of selecting objects and modifying them. When grips are on, you can select one or more objects if the command line is empty. This places grip boxes at predefined strategic positions on the objects. After selecting objects and activating their grips, you then select a grip box for further manipulation. The command line changes and the active *grip* command appears. You can either pick a new location that edits only that object, press the Shift key and pick multiple grip boxes, or press Enter and edit the group of objects. You can select any of the edit options by pressing the spacebar, typing ST (stretch), SC (scale), MO (move), MI (mirror), or RO (rotate). You also can use the shortcut menu. This variable is set when checking the Enable Grips box option from the *options* Selection tab.

Initiate Command By

Command: **grips**

Options

0 Turns grips off.

1 Turns grips on.

Variable Settings

Initial default:	1
Subsequent default:	Registry file
Value:	Integer

Tips & Warnings

- Exit grip mode by pressing Escape two or three times.

- You can create multiple copies with each of the grip edit commands.

- Stretching with grips does not require a crossing as does *stretch*.

- When grips are enabled, a box appears at the intersection of the crosshairs. This box also appears when *pickfirst* is on or when you are picking objects for object selection. You control the size of this box with *pickbox*.

- You can use ortho, snap, object snaps, and the normal point entry options when using the grips.

- When two objects' grip points overlap, picking the grip affects both objects.

| Related Variables | gripblock, gripcolor, griphot, gripsize |
| Associated Commands | options, preferences |

Example

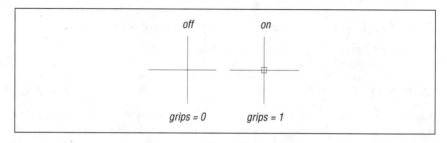

'GRIPSIZE

Determines the size of grip boxes. Since this size is based on pixel units, the value can be between 1 and 255. This variable is set when moving the Grip Size slider bar on the *options* Selection tab.

Initiate Command By

Command: **gripsize**

Variable Settings

Initial default:	3
Subsequent default:	Registry file
Value:	Integer
Related Variables	gripblock, gripcolor, griphot, grips
Associated Commands	options, preferences

-GROUP

see GROUP

GROUP

Creates a named selection set of objects. These grouped objects can be manipulated together or individually. At the "Select objects" prompt, you use the group selection method and then enter the group name assigned to the objects, or you can pick one of the objects with your pointing device.

At first glance, *group* and *block* seem to work similarly, but they are actually very different. They are similar in that you join objects together and have them act as one. However, in groups, you can edit individual objects without them losing their group membership. If you want to edit objects within a block, you must *explode* the block, causing the objects to permanently lose their block association. You can repeatedly use the same block definition in your drawing and globally update all instances of the block. Since each group has its own unique name, you cannot globally update groups.

You can achieve the same results using the *-group (-g)* command so all prompts and options appear on the command line.

Initiate Command By

Command: **group**
Alias: **g**

Options

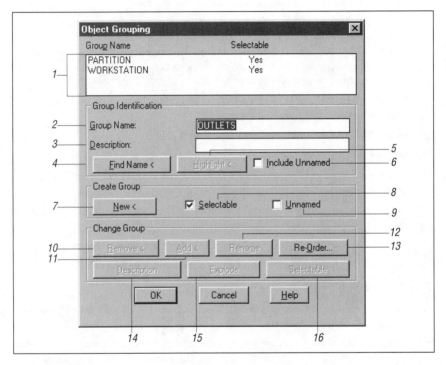

1. **Group Name/Selectable list**. Lists the groups defined in the current drawing and their status.

2. **Group Name**. Displays your selection from the Group Name list in the Group Name edit box, or you can enter a new group name when creating new groups. Group names can have up to 31 characters.

3. **Description**. Provides a description, if one was assigned, when a group from the Group Name list is selected.

4. **Find Name <**. Provides the group name in the Group Member List window assigned to a selected object.

5. **Highlight <**. Locates and highlights the objects belonging to the group selected from the Group Name list.

6. **Include Unnamed**. Determines whether unnamed groups are displayed in the Group Name list. Unnamed groups are created when you copy an existing group.

7. **New <**. Creates a new group by selecting objects. Unlike other named objects, the maximum number of characters you can use to name a group is 31 characters. Enter the new group name in the Group Name edit box before selecting New.

8. **Selectable**. Selectable groups are those that let you select any object defined in a group and the rest of the objects are automatically selected. Nonselectable lets you edit individual objects that are part of a group. Objects on locked layers are never selectable.

9. **Unnamed**. When creating new groups you can assign a name or let AutoCAD assign a group name to the objects. When AutoCAD assigns a group name, it begins with "*A" followed by a number. Unnamed groups also are created when you copy an existing group. *superhatch* and *textmask* objects are bound together as unnamed groups.

10. **Remove**. Removes objects assigned to a group. This does not delete the objects; it makes them independent.

11. **Add <**. Includes more objects into an existing group.

12. **Rename**. Renames the group highlighted in the Group Name list box.

13. **Re-Order....** Changes the order in which objects were selected and defined as group members.

14. **Description**. Assigns an optional description. This can be up to 255 characters long.

15. **Explode**. Removes the group definition but does not delete objects deleted.

16. **Selectable**. Specifies whether the selected group is selectable.

Tips & Warnings

- Groups saved as blocks lose their group definitions. Blocks saved as groups retain their block definitions.

- Removing all objects from a group does not remove the group name reference. Use the explode option to eliminate the name from the group list.

Related Variables	pickstyle
Associated Commands	select, superhatch

Example

```
Command: copy
Select objects: G
Enter group name: Workstation
4 found
Select objects: Press Enter
Specify base point or displacement, or [Multiple]: Pick point 1
Specify second point of displacement or <use first point as displacement>:
Pick point 2
```

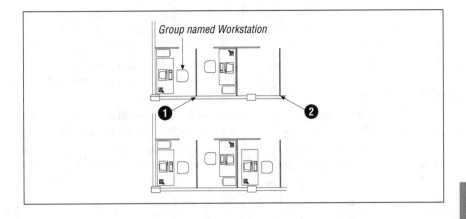

Group named Workstation

'HANDLES

AutoCAD assigns a unique label or *handle* to every drawing object. This label, in hexadecimal format, is permanently stored in the drawing and is used to access objects. Handles can be used by AutoLISP programs or to link objects to external database programs. Use *list* to determine an object's handle.

Initiate Command By
Command: **handles**

Variable Settings

Initial default:	1, read-only
Subsequent default:	Initial default
Value:	Integer
Associated Commands	list

HATCH

Cross-hatches, or pattern-fills, an area. For the most accurate results, the area should be enclosed and all object endpoints should intersect precisely. If there is an opening in the boundary, the hatch pattern may go beyond the boundary. You can use existing objects or create a temporary or permanent polyline boundary from within the *hatch* command. A hatch remembers its pattern name, scale, and angle as long as it has not been exploded.

Hatch lines are projected in the current construction plane defined by the UCS. If you need precise hatch pattern placement, set *snapbase* to a point at which you want the hatch pattern to originate. Be sure to reset *snapbase* after hatching since *snap* and *grid* also are affected by this variable. Use the *hatchedit* or *properties* command to modify hatch objects.

You should use *bhatch* as an alternative to the *hatch* command. Boundary hatch objects are more flexible since they can be defined as associative and therefore automatically adjust to most changes you make to their boundaries.

You can *hatch* a block. Blocks are processed as individual drawing objects. During object selection, you just need to pick the block you want to *hatch*. Hatch style defaults to normal, and every other boundary is hatched.

You can *explode* a hatch pattern and turn it back into individual drawing objects. The objects default to layer 0, and the color and linetype are set to ByLayer.

If you hatch an area containing text (attributes, text, and multiline text), you can draw the hatch pattern around the text as long as you include the text during object selection.

Initiate Command By

Command: **hatch**
Alias: **-h**

Options

```
Enter a pattern name or [?/Solid/User defined] <ANSI31>:
Specify a scale for the pattern <1.0000>:
Specify an angle for the pattern <0>:
Select objects to define hatch boundary or <direct hatch>,,
Select objects:
```

Enter a pattern name

Allows you to enter a hatch pattern name then asks you to enter the scale and angle for the pattern. When typing the hatch pattern, include an asterisk (*) before the name to pre-explode the hatch block. The default pattern is ANSI31 and is maintained by the *hpname* variable.

Specify the hatch style by appending a style code to the hatch pattern name, separated by a comma. Your choices are:

N (Normal)

Hatch every other boundary.

O (Outermost)

Hatch only outermost boundary.

I (Ignore)

Hatch everything inside outermost boundary.

? Lists one or all of the hatch pattern names including a short description. You can use wildcard characters to produce a specific list.

Solid

Creates a solid filled pattern.

User defined

Lets you create your own pattern by defining the spacing and angle for straight lines. You also can "double hatch" an area or create a perpendicular cross hatch. The variables *hpang*, *hpdouble*, and *hpspace* maintain the values for angle, spacing, and double hatch.

angle for the pattern <0>
Determines the angle of the hatch pattern. This value is maintained by the *hpang* variable.

objects to define hatch boundary
Allows you to select multiple objects that make up one boundary. Make sure that each object's endpoints share the exact coordinates of the adjoining object. You also can select multiple boundaries.

direct hatch
Lets you create a boundary from polylines and polyline arcs. You can trace over existing objects or create a new boundary. In addition, you can save the boundary or have it automatically deleted once you complete the command.

Tips & Warnings

- If you explode a hatch pattern, you may consider regrouping those objects into a block or a group. It will take up less drawing space and will be easier to manipulate.

- To speed up your drawing regenerate and redraw time, keep the hatches on their own layer, and freeze that layer until you are ready to plot.

- You may get unexpected results if your hatch pattern defaults to any linetype other than continuous. This is because hatch patterns use the current linetype, including its own line definition.

- Hatch patterns are invisible when *fill* is off. This is true only for hatch patterns created with Release 14 or Release 2000.

Related Variables   fillmode, hpang, hpdouble, hpname, hpscale, hpspace, snapbase

Associated Commands   bhatch, boundary, explode, properties, snap

Example

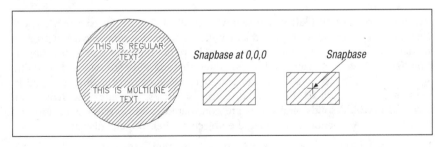

Snapbase at 0,0,0   Snapbase

-HATCHEDIT

see HATCHEDIT

HATCHEDIT

Modify II toolbar

Modifies hatch and boundary hatch objects by letting you change the pattern type, scale, angle, and style. This command does not work on exploded hatch patterns

---

or hatches created prior to Release 13. Since this command uses the same dialog box as *bhatch*, see the *bhatch* command for more detailed information.

You can achieve the same results using *properties* or *-hatchedit*, for which all prompts and options appear on the command line. *matchprop* lets you change a hatch pattern to match the properties of an existing hatch pattern.

Initiate Command By

Command: **hatchedit**
Alias: **he**
Modify → Hatch

Related Variables	hpang, hpdouble, hpname, hpscale, hpspace
Associated Commands	bhatch, hatch, matchprop, properties

'HELP

Standard toolbar

Provides information on commands and how they function, including cross references to the AutoCAD manuals. If you already started a command and enter 'help or ? on the command line or press F1, you will receive help for that particular command. Most dialog boxes provide a Help button, instantly providing information for that dialog box. You also can access the generic help options through these dialog Help buttons.

Initiate Command By

Command: **help**, F1, ?
Help → AutoCAD Help Topics

HIDE

Render toolbar

Performs a temporary hidden line removal on all objects in the current viewport. Normally, 3D objects are displayed as wireframe. *hide* determines what should be hidden from your viewpoint and temporarily removes those edges and objects from sight. *hide* evaluates circles, polylines that have been assigned a width, solids, traces, 3D faces, meshes, and extruded edges of objects assigned a thickness as opaque surfaces. In addition, extruded circles, polylines that have been assigned a width, solids, and traces are considered solid objects having top and bottom faces. A regeneration returns the objects to their original display.

If you want hidden lines suppressed during plotting, you must check the Plot Options → Hide Objects box under the *plot* Plot Settings tab. If you are using floating viewports (*tilemode* set to 0), use the hideplot option of the *mview* command.

Initiate Command By

Command: **hide**
Alias: **hi**
View → Hide

Tips & Warnings

- *hide* evaluates objects residing on layers that are turned off but does not evaluate objects on frozen layers.

- *render* automatically creates a hidden line removal.

- Text and dimensions are always displayed even if they are hidden by 3D objects. Turn off or freeze those layers containing text and dimensions if you don't want them to be displayed.

Related Variables   dispsilh, hideprecision

Associated Commands   ddvpoint, dview, vpoint, 3dorbit

Example

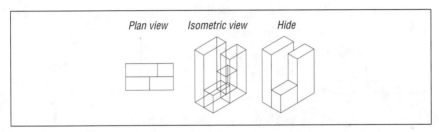

Plan view   Isometric view   Hide

'HIDEPRECISION 2000

Determines the precision of *shademode* and *hide*.

Initiate Command By
Command: **hideprecision**

Options

0   Single precision.

1   Double precision.

Variable Settings

Initial default:	0
Subsequent default:	Initial default
Value:	Integer

Associated Commands   hide, render, shademode

'HIGHLIGHT

Determines whether objects appear dotted (highlighted) during the selection set process or remain in their original format. When working with multiple viewports, objects are highlighted only in the viewport from which they were selected. The viewport from which you complete the command highlights all the selected objects.

You can save time during object selection by turning *highlight* off. This is because you do not have to wait for each object to be located before selecting the next object. Highlighting does not affect grips and noun/verb (*pickfirst* = 1) selection.

Initiate Command By

Command: **highlight**

Options

0   Disables highlighting.

1   Enables highlighting.

Variable Settings

Initial default:	1
Subsequent default:	Initial default
Value:	Integer
Related Variables	grips, pickfirst

'HPANG

Determines the angle for hatch patterns. This is set using *hatch* or *bhatch*. You can change the angle of existing hatches with *hatchedit* or *properties*.

Initiate Command By

Command: **hpang**

Variable Settings

Initial default:	0.0000
Subsequent default:	Initial default
Value:	Real
Related Variables	hpdouble, hpname, hpscale, hpspace
Associated Commands	bhatch, hatch, hatchedit, properties

'HPBOUND

Determines the type of object created with *boundary* and *bhatch*. This applies to *bhatch* only when Retain Boundaries is selected.

Initiate Command By

Command: **hpbound**

Options

0   Creates a region.

1   Creates a polyline.

Variable Settings

Initial default:	1
Subsequent default:	Initial default
Value:	Integer
Associated Commands	bhatch, boundary

'HPCONFIG (obsolete)

'HPDOUBLE

Determines whether user-defined hatches during *hatch* and *bhatch* have a second set of lines drawn perpendicular to the original line definition. You can change the hatch double option of existing hatches with *hatchedit* or *properties*.

Initiate Command By

Command: **hpdouble**

Options

0   Creates single-line hatch patterns.

1   Creates double-line hatch patterns.

Variable Settings

Initial default:	0
Subsequent default:	Initial default
Value:	Integer
Related Variables	hpang, hpname, hpscale, hpspace
Associated Commands	bhatch, hatch, hatchedit, properties

Example

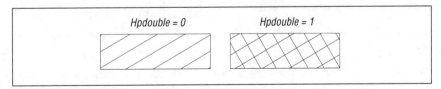

Hpdouble = 0   Hpdouble = 1

'HPMPLOT (obsolete)

'HPNAME

Remembers the last hatch pattern name used for the current session. This variable is set with *bhatch* or *hatch*. You can change the hatch pattern name of existing hatches with *hatchedit* or *properties*.

Initiate Command By
Command: **hpname**

Variable Settings

Initial default:	ANSI31
Subsequent default:	Initial default
Value:	String

Related Variables	hpang, hpdouble, hpscale, hpspace
Associated Commands	bhatch, hatch, hatchedit, properties

'HPSCALE

Determines the scale factor for hatch patterns. This variable is set with *bhatch* or *hatch*. You can change the hatch scale of existing hatches with *hatchedit* or *properties*.

Initiate Command By
Command: **hpscale**

Variable Settings

Initial default:	1.0000
Subsequent default:	Initial default
Value:	Real

Related Variables	hpang, hpdouble, hpname, hpspace
Associated Commands	bhatch, hatch, hatchedit, properties

'HPSPACE

Sets the line spacing for user-defined hatch patterns. This variable is set with *bhatch* or *hatch*. You can change the line spacing of existing hatches with *hatchedit* or *properties*.

Initiate Command By
Command: **hpspace**

Variable Settings

Initial default:	1.0000
Subsequent default:	Initial default

Value:	Real
Related Variables	hpang, hpdouble, hpname, hpscale
Associated Commands	bhatch, hatch, hatchedit, properties

-HYPERLINK 2000

see HYPERLINK

HYPERLINK 2000

Standard toolbar

Assigns and edits hyperlinks assigned to objects. Hyperlinked objects can be assigned to an Internet address or to another file. Moving your cursor over hyperlinked objects displays the hyperlink cursor along with the file or URL name. You can achieve the same results using *-hyperlink* so all prompts and options appear on the command line.

Initiate Command By

> Command: **hyperlink**
> Alias: Ctrl-K
> Insert → Hyperlink

Options

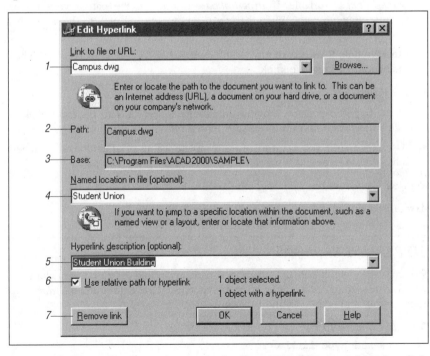

1. **Link to file or URL.** Enter the name of a file or URL (Internet address) to link with the selected objects. Be sure to include the file extension if appropriate.

The drop-down list remembers web site addresses you accessed and any document names you referenced during the AutoCAD drawing session. You also can pick the Browse button and find documents accessible from your computer.

2. **Path.** Displays the path associated to the hyperlinked file. When the "Use relative path for hyperlink" box is empty, the path defaults to the Base setting. When the box is checked, only the filename is listed. If the box is checked and you start entering a directory or folder name (i.e., `c:\`), the "Use relative path for hyperlink" box reverts to being unchecked.

3. **Base.** Maintains the default path for all relative path hyperlinks in the current drawing. The path default is based on the current drawing's location. Change the base with *dwgprops* or by resetting the *hyperlinkbase* variable.

4. **Named location in file.** Assigns a view or a bookmark (Microsoft Word) to objects. The view can exist in the current drawing or point to another drawing file if the file's name is listed in the "Link to file or URL" box.

5. **Hyperlink description.** Assigns a description. This is useful in cases in which you want a more detailed reminder about the purpose of the hyperlink. The description is displayed when you go to open the hyperlink. If a description and named location are not provided, the "Link to file or URL" is displayed.

6. **Use relative path for hyperlink.** When this is checked, the full path to the linked file is not stored with the hyperlink. The path is based on the *hyperlinkbase* variable. If *hyperlinkbase* is not set, the path reverts to the current drawing path. When the box is empty, the full path to the associated file is stored with the hyperlink.

7. **Remove link.** Removes the hyperlink association. This is available only when editing an existing hyperlink.

Tips & Warnings

- If the hyperlink cursor, tooltips, and shortcut menu fail to display, check to see if the *hyperlinkoptions* setting is turned off.

- Use *showurls* if you want to see a complete listing of all a drawing's hyperlinks, locate hyperlinks in a drawing, and edit the hyperlink name.

Related Variables   hyperlinkbase

Associated Commands   hyperlinkoptions, showurls

'HYPERLINKBASE 2000

Maintains the default path for all relative path hyperlinks in the current drawing. This variable is set by completing the Hyperlink Base field from the *dwgprops* Summary tab and is used by the *hyperlink* command.

Initiate Command By

Command: **hyperlinkbase**

Variable Settings

Initial default:	None
Subsequent default:	Last value used in the drawing
Value:	String

Associated Commands   dwgprops, hyperlink

HYPERLINKOPTIONS 2000

Controls the visibility of the hyperlink cursor, shortcut menu, and tooltips. If this feature is turned off, you can still create and edit hyperlinks. Since this setting is written to the registry file, all new drawings and drawing sessions take on the latest value.

Initiate Command By

Command: **hyperlinkoptions**

Options

```
Display hyperlink cursor and shortcut menu? [Yes/No] <Yes>:
Display hyperlink tooltip? [Yes/No] <Yes>:
```

Display hyperlink cursor and shortcut menu
Turns the hyperlink feature on and off.

Display hyperlink tooltip
Available when you answer "yes" to "Display the hyperlink cursor and shortcut menu." It lets you determine the visibility of the tooltip when the hyperlink cursor is enabled.

Associated Commands   hyperlink

'ID   Inquiry toolbar

Identifies the absolute *X, Y, Z* coordinates of any selected point. The point becomes the value for the *lastpoint* variable.

Initiate Command By

Command: **id**
Tools → Inquiry → Id Point

Tips & Warnings

Use the *id* command to establish a point for relative or polar coordinate input. Reference the *id* point by using the at symbol (@) for the next command that requests a point.

Related Variables   lastpoint

-IMAGE   *see IMAGE*

IMAGE
Reference and Insert toolbar

Loads the Image Manager dialog box, which manages the various images that can be imported into your drawing. Images include raster or bitmapped bitonal, 8-bit gray, 8-bit color, or 24-bit color files. You can achieve the same results using *-image* (*-im*) so all prompts and options appear on the command line. *properties* also offers much of the same functionality once the image is attached.

If you need to change the display order of images and even other objects, use *draworder*. This might happen when one image is sharing the same space as another image or other drawing objects.

You can change the name of an image by highlighting its name in the image name column and pressing F2. This doesn't alter the original filename, just the reference to that file. However, it may be confusing since you have more names to track and manage.

If you plan to move a drawing file containing images to another computer or to a diskette, you need to include any attached image files. Use *pack* to help you accomplish this.

Initiate Command By
Command: **image**
Alias: **im**
Insert → Image Manager

Options

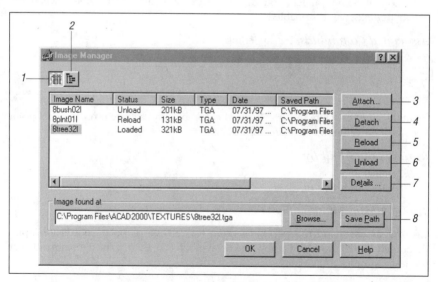

1. **List View.** Shows the images attached to the drawing. It provides the image name, status, size, type, date and time, and saved path. You can sort the list by selecting a column heading (Status, Size, Type, Date, or Saved Path). Each

time you press the same column heading, you change the listing from ascending to descending order.

The status column can have any of the following notations: Loaded, Reload, Unload, Unreferenced, or Not found. Loaded and Reload are directly related to the Reload and Unload buttons. Not found indicates that an attached image was erased from the drawing without using the Detach button. Unreferenced indicates the pathname no longer matches the file's location.

Change the size of each column by moving the cursor over the vertical bar and dragging the bar to the left (smaller) or to the right (larger). If you are in the Tree View and want to return to List View you can press F3.

2. **Tree View.** Shows the images attached to the drawing. It provides the filenames and their assigned folders. If you are in the List View and want to return to Tree View you can press F4.

3. **Attach.** Allows you to select image files to import into your drawing. You can attach *.bmp, .bil, .cal, .cg4, .dib, .flc, .fli, .gif, .gp4, .ig4, .igs, .jpg, .mil, .pct, .pcx, .png, .rlc, .rle, .rst, .tga,* and *.tif* files. The Attach dialog box gives you the option to preview the images before attaching them into your drawing. See *imageattach* for more detailed information. You also can attach images using the AutoCAD DesignCenter by dragging images onto your drawing.

4. **Detach.** Permanently removes attached images from your drawing. Although the reference to the file is removed, the actual image file isn't deleted.

5. **Reload.** Reloads images temporarily unloaded from the drawing. You also can reload images by clicking in the Status area on the word "Unload" associated with that image.

6. **Unload.** Temporarily removes the images or files from the drawing. This is one method of saving redraw and regeneration time. You also can unload images by clicking in the Status area on the word "Load" associated with that image.

7. **Details.** Provides status information for each image.

8. **Save Path.** Changes the path location of image files.

Tips & Warnings:

- Exploding an image converts the outline of the image box into lines, and the Image Manager status is marked as Unreferenced.

- *imageclip* and *clipit* hide part of the image; *imageadjust* modifies the brightness, contrast, and fade; *imageframe* controls the boundary's display.

- Save time while using the real-time pan and zoom by setting *rtdisplay* to 0.

Related Variables	imagehlt, rtdisplay
Associated Commands	adcenter, clipit, draworder, imageadjust, imageattach, imageclip, imageframe, imagequality, properties, transparency

-IMAGEADJUST   *see IMAGEADJUST*

IMAGEADJUST

Reference toolbar

Controls the brightness, contrast, and faded values for each image attached to the drawing. You can achieve the same results using *properties* or *-imageadjust*, for which all prompts and options appear on the command line.

Initiate Command By

Command: **imageadjust**
Alias: **iad**
Modify → Object → Image → Adjust

Options

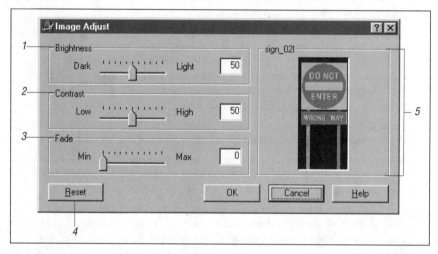

1. **Brightness.** Changing this value indirectly affects the contrast of the image. The brightness value range is from 0 to 100. The greater the value, the more white pixels the image displays.

2. **Contrast.** Changing this value indirectly affects the fading feature. The contrast value range is from 0 to 100. The greater the value, the more each pixel is forced to its primary or secondary color.

3. **Fade.** The fade value range is from 0 to 100. The greater the range, the more the image blends with the background color.

4. **Reset.** This changes the brightness, contrast, and fade values back to their original settings. The original settings for all images are brightness 50, contrast 50, and fade 0.

5. **Image preview.** This box displays the image file and dynamically updates when there is a change in the brightness, contrast, or fade value.

Tips & Warnings

Changing these settings has no effect on the original image file.

Associated Commands   image, imageattach, imageclip, imageframe, imagequality, properties, transparency

---

IMAGEATTACH 2000

Reference toolbar

Allows you to select image files to import into your drawing. Images include raster or bit-mapped bitonal, 8-bit gray, 8-bit color, or 24-bit color files. You can attach *.bmp, .bil, .cal, .cg4, .dib, .flc, .fli, .gif, .gp4, .ig4, .igs, .jpg, .mil, .pct, .pcx, .png, .rlc, .rle, .rst, .tga,* and *.tif* files. If you plan to attach more than one image you may want to use *image* so you can manipulate one or more images at a time. You also can attach images using the AutoCAD DesignCenter feature (*adcenter*).

Initiate Command By   Command: **imageattach**
    Alias: **iat**
    Insert → Raster Image

Related Variables   imagehlt

Associated Commands   adcenter, draworder, image, imageadjust, imageclip, imageframe, imagequality, properties, transparency

---

IMAGECLIP

Reference toolbar

Gives you the ability to hide parts of raster images that you don't want displayed or plotted. You also can use *clipit* which provides a wider range of boundary definitions.

Initiate Command By

    Command: **imageclip**
    Alias: **icl**
    Modify → Clip → Image

Options

    Enter image clipping option [ON/OFF/Delete/New boundary] <New>:
    Enter clipping type [Polygonal/Rectangular] <Rectangular>:

ON
    Displays only the portion of the image inside the clipping boundary.

OFF
    Displays the entire image.

Delete
    Deletes the clipping boundary.

New boundary
    Allows you to create a rectangular or polygonal boundary. You can define only one boundary per image. If an existing boundary is found, you are asked if you want to delete that boundary. Answering "no" exits the command; answering "yes" lets you create a boundary.

Polygonal
> Creates an irregular shaped polygon boundary.

Rectangular
> Creates a rectangular polygon boundary.

Tips & Warnings

- You can change size and shape of the clipping boundary with *grips* or *stretch*.

- Once you have defined a boundary, you can use *properties* to turn the clipping boundary on and off.

- Create clipping boundaries for external references with *xclip* and *clipit,* clipping boundaries for viewports with *vpclip,* and clipping boundaries for all objects with *wipeout.*

Associated Commands   draworder, image, imageadjust, imageattach, imageframe, imagequality, properties, transparency, wipeout

---

IMAGEFRAME

Reference toolbar

Controls the display of the borders of all the attached raster images. When the *imageframe* is off, you cannot select the images unless you use *qselect* or the selection set option All.

Initiate Command By

> Command: **imageframe**
> Modify → Object → Image → Frame

Options

ON
> The image frame is displayed.

OFF
> The image frame is invisible.

Associated Commands   draworder, image, imageadjust, imageattach, imageclip, imagequality, properties, transparency

---

'IMAGEHLT 2000

Determines whether the entire raster image or just the image's frame is highlighted when selected.

Initiate Command By

> Command: **imagehlt**

Options

0   The raster image frame is highlighted.

1   The entire raster image is highlighted.

Variable Settings

Initial default:	0
Subsequent default:	Registry file
Value:	Integer

Associated Commands draworder, image, imageadjust, imageattach, imageclip, imageframe, imagequality, properties, transparency

---

IMAGEQUALITY

Reference toolbar

Controls the display quality of raster images. Regardless of the *imagequality* setting, the drawing is always plotted using a high-quality display.

Initiate Command By

Command: **imagequality**
Modify → Object → Image → Quality

Options

Draft
Images are displayed at a lower quality but faster than a high-quality image.

High
Images are displayed at a higher quality but slower than a draft-quality image.

Associated Commands draworder, imageadjust, imageattach, imageclip, imageframe, properties, transparency

---

IMPORT

Insert toolbar

Brings different file formats into AutoCAD. These files are created by other computer programs. Although imported files can't be manipulated in the same way as AutoCAD objects, you can use commands such as *imageadjust*, *imageclip*, *imageframe*, and *imagequality* to change their appearance. You also can use the AutoCAD DesignCenter feature to import files.

Initiate Command By

Command: **import**
Alias: **imp**

Options

3D Studio (.3ds)*
These files contain the following rendering information: meshes, materials, mapping, lights, and cameras. This is the same as using *3dsin*.

ACIS (*.sat)

ACIS files are in ASCII format and are used to store solid and region geometric shapes. This is the same as using *acisin*.

Metafile (*.wmf)

Imported files are treated as blocks containing vector information. *wmfopts* presets import parameters. This is the same as using *wmfin*.

Encapsulated PS (*.eps)

This is the same as using *psin*. See also *psdrag* and *psquality*.

Tips & Warnings

• Import *dxb* files with *dxbin* and *dxf* files with *dxfin*.

• If *filedia* is set to 1, a dialog box is activated; if *filedia* is set to 0, you are prompted on the command line. When *filedia* is set to 0, or off, entering a tilde (~) on the command line temporarily activates the file dialog box.

Related Variables	filedia, psdrag, psquality
Associated Commands	acisin, adcenter, export, psout, replay, wmfin, wmfopts, 3dsin

---

'INDEXCTL

(Index Control) Determines whether layer and spatial indexes are created and saved in drawing files. These indexes are used to improve performance during demand loading (*partiaload, partialopen*). A spatial index organizes objects based on their location in 3D space. A layer index tracks which objects are on which layer. This variable is set with the Options button from *save* or *saveas*.

Initiate Command By

Command: **indexctl**

Options

0   No spatial and layer indexes are created when saving the drawing.

1   A layer index is created when saving the drawing.

2   A spatial index is created when saving the drawing.

3   Layer and spatial indexes are created when saving the drawing.

Variable Settings

Initial default:	0
Subsequent default:	Last value used in the drawing
Value:	Integer
Associated Commands	partiaload, partialopen, save, saveas

INETHELP (obsolete)

see HELP

'INETLOCATION

Stores the Internet location last used by the *browser* command.

Initiate Command By
Command: **inetlocation**

Variable Settings
Initial default:	www.autodesk.com/acaduser
Subsequent default:	Registry file
Value:	String

Associated Commands   browser

'INSBASE

Maintains the drawings' reference or base point. This value is set with the *base* command.

Initiate Command By
Command: **insbase**

Variable Settings
Initial default:	0.000,0.000,0.000
Subsequent default:	Last value used in the drawing
Value:	3D point

Tips & Warnings
- Drawing files that result from the *wblock* command have their *insbase* defined when selecting an insertion base point.
- When inserting or attaching external reference files, you can see the insertion base point because it is located at the intersection of the crosshairs.

Associated Commands   base, insert, wblock, xref

-INSERT 2000

see INSERT

INSERT 2000

Draw toolbar

Merges blocks and other drawing files (*.dwg*) including drawing interchange files (*.dxf*) into the current drawing. You can use *-insert* (*-i*), so all prompts and options appear at the command line.

You can globally update blocks in your drawing by reinserting the modified block as long as it has the same name. Exploded blocks cannot be updated.

A much more powerful alternative to using the *insert* command is to use the AutoCAD DesignCenter (*adcenter*) feature. Not only does it give you the ability to quickly search through folders accessible from your computer, you also can view the individual blocks existing in other drawing files.

If you redefine a block, the drawing must regenerate before you can see the changes. If you modify a block containing attribute definitions and insert the modified block into a drawing containing old attributes, any existing constant attributes are replaced by new constant attributes. If an attribute definition is removed, attributes will be removed from existing blocks. Variable attributes remain unchanged even if their definition is omitted in the new block. New variable attributes will be included in all new insertions but will not appear in previous block insertions. If you want existing attributes to be completely updated, you must replace the old blocks with new ones or use the *attredef* command.

Initiate Command By

Command: **insert**
Alias: **i** or **inserturl**
Insert → Block

Options

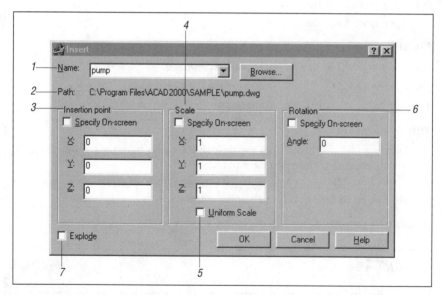

1. **Name.** Allows you to choose the block to insert. Only blocks already referenced in the drawing are valid. If you need to locate a drawing (*.dwg*) or drawing interchange file (*.dxf*) for insertion, use the Browse button.

2. **Path.** Displays the path and filename of the drawing or drawing interchange file selected with the Browse button.

3. **Insertion point.** Locates the insertion point. When the Specify On-screen box is checked, you drag the symbol around the screen until you pick an insertion

point. When this box is empty, you preset the *X*, *Y*, and *Z* coordinates for the insertion point.

4. **Scale**. Determines the *X*, *Y*, and *Z* scale factors. When the Specify On-screen box is checked, you use your pointing device. When this box is empty you preset the *X*, *Y*, and *Z* scale factors.

5. **Uniform Scale**. Allows you to specify only the *X* scale factor and sets *Y* and *Z* that value. Use this feature when inserting blocks containing the same *X*, *Y*, and *Z* scale factors. This feature is available only when the Specify On-screen box is not checked.

6. **Rotation**. Determines the rotation angle. When the Specify On-screen box is checked, you use your pointing device. When this box isn't checked, you preset rotation angle in the Angle box.

7. **Explode**. Determines whether to keep the block or file intact or insert it as individual objects. If you check this box, you can assign only one scale factor for *X*, *Y*, and *Z*, and it cannot be negative.

Tips & Warnings

- You can temporarily merge two or more drawings using the *xref–attach* or *xref–detach* commands. Use the *image* command to insert raster files.

- You can convert a block back to its original objects using the *explode* command. The only way to turn the objects back into blocks is to use the *insert* command (if a block by that name still exists) or create a new block. Inserted blocks reside on the layer that was current when they were inserted. Exploding blocks returns each object to its original layer.

- The variable *attreq*, if set to 0, lets you insert attributes without prompting and applies the attribute's default values. For normal prompting, set the variable to 1. The variable *attdia*, if set to 1, will cause a dialog box to appear when you insert blocks with attributes. The box displays the prompt and default value, which you can edit freely. A value of 0 causes attribute prompting at the command line.

- *bcount* lists the names of inserted blocks and the number of times each block was inserted.

Related Variables   attdia, attdisp, attreq, expert, insbase, insname

Associated Commands   adcenter, base, block, explode, -insert, minsert, wblock

---

INSERTOBJ
Insert toolbar

Inserts a linked or embedded object into the current drawing, using the Windows OLE (Object Linking and Embedding) technology. The other programs also must support OLE. Linked objects remain associated with their source file and application. Embedded objects lose their association to their source files but not to their application.

You can edit the OLE object by clicking twice on the object. This automatically activates the object's original program or application. You can move the OLE object with the pointing device by moving the crosshairs onto the picture. Clicking once on the object disables the crosshairs and changes the pointer to four arrows. Pick and drag the object to a new location. You can resize the object by manipulating its Windows handles.

Initiate Command By

Command: **insertobj**
Alias: **io**
Insert → OLE Object

Options

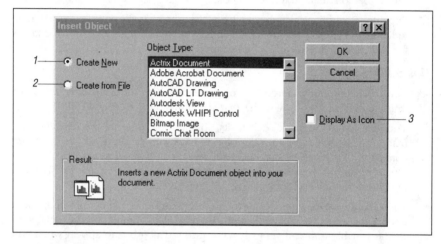

1. **Create New**. Create a new OLE object from any of the programs listed in the Object Type window. Once you exit that program that object is embedded in the current drawings.

2. **Create from File**. Select an existing file to link or embed into your current drawing.

3. **Display As Icon**. Your drawing can display the OLE object's content or an icon representing that object's source application. Regardless of this setting, you can quickly change to the other setting by using the shortcut menu.

Tips & Warnings

You cannot make slide files from OLE objects.

Associated Commands   copylink, pastespecial

'INSERTURL (obsolete)   *see HYPERLINK*

'INSNAME

Maintains the default block name for the *insert* command.

Initiate Command By
    Command: **insname**

Variable Settings

Initial default:	"" (none)
Subsequent default:	Initial default
Value:	String
Associated Commands	insert

'INSUNITS 2000

Defines the units automatically used when inserting an object from the AutoCAD DesignCenter into an open drawing file. This value is set with *units*.

Initiate Command By
    Command: **insunits**

Options

0	Unspecified unitless	7	Kilometers	14	Decimeters
1	Inches	8	Microinches	15	Decameters
2	Feet	9	Mils	16	Hectometers
3	Miles	10	Yards	17	Gigameters
4	Millimeters	11	Angstroms	18	Astronomical units
5	Centimeters	12	Nanometers	19	Light years
6	Meters	13	Microns	20	Parsecs

Variable Settings

Initial default:	0
Subsequent default:	Saved in drawing
Value:	Integer
Related Variables	insunitsdefsource, insunitsdeftarget
Associated Commands	adcenter, block, units, wblock

'INSUNITSDEFSOURCE 2000

Maintains the units value for source content. This value is set when selecting from the Source Content Units drop-down list from the *options* User Preferences tab. The value is automatically used for objects inserted into the current drawing when no insert units (*insunits*) are specified.

Initiate Command By

Command: **insunitsdefsource**

Options

0	Unspecified unitless	7	Kilometers	14	Decimeters
1	Inches	8	Microinches	15	Decameters
2	Feet	9	Mils	16	Hectometers
3	Miles	10	Yards	17	Gigameters
4	Millimeters	11	Angstroms	18	Astronomical units
5	Centimeters	12	Nanometers	19	Light years
6	Meters	13	Microns	20	Parsecs

Variable Settings

Initial default:	1
Subsequent default:	Registry file
Value:	Integer

Related Variables insunits, insunitsdeftarget

Associated Commands adcenter, options, preferences

'INSUNITSDEFTARGET 2000

Maintains the units setting for the target drawing content. This value is set when selecting from the Target Drawing Units drop-down list from the *options* User Preferences tab. The value is automatically used in the current drawing when no insert units (*insunits*) are specified.

Initiate Command By

Command: **insunitsdeftarget**

Options

0	Unspecified unitless	7	Kilometers	14	Decimeters
1	Inches	8	Microinches	15	Decameters
2	Feet	9	Mils	16	Hectometers
3	Miles	10	Yards	17	Gigameters
4	Millimeters	11	Angstroms	18	Astronomical units
5	Centimeters	12	Nanometers	19	Light years
6	Meters	13	Microns	20	Parsecs

Variable Settings

Initial default:	0
Subsequent default:	Registry file
Value:	Integer

Related Variables insunits, insunitsdefsource

Associated Commands adcenter, options, preferences

INTERFERE

Solids toolbar

Creates composite solids from two or more solids that overlap or interfere. The original objects remain unchanged.

Initiate Command By

Command: **interfere**
Alias: **inf**
Draw → Solids → Interference

Options

```
Select first set of solids:
Select objects:
Select objects:
Select second set of solids:
Select objects:
No solids selected.
Comparing 2 solids with each other.
Interfering solids: 2
Interfering pairs: 1
Create interference solids? [Yes/No] <N>:
```

Select first set of solids

If you have one selection set, all the solid objects are checked against one another.

Select second set of solids

If you have a second selection set, the first group of solids is compared to the solids in the second group. If a solid was selected for both groups, it defaults to the first group.

Create interference solids? [Yes/No] <N>

Answer "yes" if you want the composite solid objects highlighted and created from the selection sets.

Highlight pairs of interfering solids?

Answering "yes" highlights the new composite solids.

Next pair

If more than one composite solid is created, you can have AutoCAD highlight and cycle through each new composite solid.

Exit

Ends the command.

Tips & Warnings

Before using this command, you may want a different layer active from that of the original solids. Once you create the composite solids, you can freeze the layers from which the original solids reside. This will help you get a better look at the results.

Associated Commands intersect, subtract, union

Example

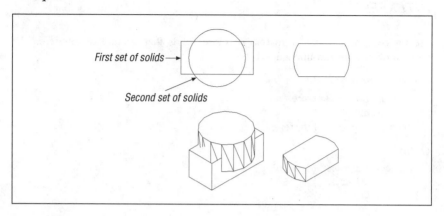

First set of solids →

Second set of solids

INTERSECT

Solids Editing toolbar

Creates composite solids or regions from two or more solids or regions that overlap or intersect by combining one set of solids with another set of solids or one set of regions with another set of regions. You can obtain detailed information about the intersect's result with *massprop*. Exploding intersects yields various results depending on the original objects and whether some of the objects were deleted due to the intersect process.

Initiate Command By

Command: **intersect**
Alias: **in**
Modify → Solids Editing → Intersect

Associated Commands   interfere, subtract, union

Example

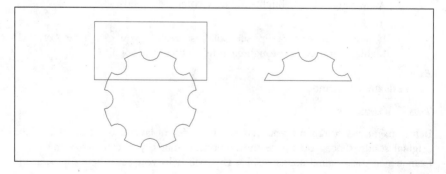

'ISAVEBAK

Determines whether incremental backup (*.bak*) files are created when drawings are saved. This value is typically saved when selecting "Create backup copy with each save" from the *options* Open and Save tab.

Initiate Command By

Command: **isavebak**

Options

0   Do not create backup (*.bak*) files.

1   Create backup (*.bak*) files.

Variable Settings

Initial default:	1
Subsequent default:	Registry file
Value:	Integer

Tips & Warnings

Setting this variable to 0 increases the speed if you periodically save during drawing sessions. However, you lose the ability of retrieving a backup (*.bak*) file if something happens to your drawing file.

Related Variables	isavepercent
Associated Commands	end, options, preferences, qsave, save

'ISAVEPERCENT

Defines the amount of wasted space (0–100) allowed in a drawing. It determines whether new drawing information is appended to the end of a drawing or whether a full save gets rid of the wasted space. Once a drawing reaches the *isavepercent* amount, it performs a full save as though it were set to 0. The lower the setting, the longer it takes to save. Setting *isavebak* to 0 and *rasterpreview* to 3 increases the speed of *isavepercent*. This value is set when selecting Incremental Save Percentage from the *options* Open and Save tab.

Initiate Command By

Command: **isavepercent**

Variable Settings

Initial default:	50
Subsequent default:	Registry file
Value:	Integer
Related Variables	isavebak, rasterpreview
Associated Commands	options, preferences, qsave, save

'ISOLINES

(Incremental Solid Lines) Determines the number of lines displayed on solids. You can set the value from 0 to 2,047. This is for visualization only and does not affect the actual solid objects. All solids are displayed with the current *isoline* setting. This setting has no bearing on *hide*, *render*, or *shademode*.

Initiate Command By
Command: **isolines**

Variable Settings

Initial default:	4
Subsequent default:	Last value used in the drawing
Value:	Integer

Associated Commands
cone, cylinder, extrude, revolve, sphere, torus

Example

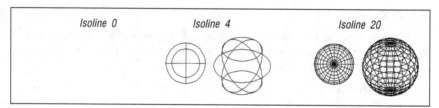

Isoline 0   Isoline 4   Isoline 20

'ISOPLANE

Defines which of the three isometric planes (top, left, right) you want to work in when isometric mode is enabled. You set the isometric mode with the isometric style option of *snap*. You also can set the isoplane by selecting the Isometric Snap radio button from the Snap and Grid tab of the *dsettings* dialog box. Pressing Ctrl-E or F5 is a shortcut to toggling between the three planes. Keep *ortho* on to help you draw in the correct plane. *isoplane*'s default value is maintained by the *snapisopair* variable.

Initiate Command By
Command: **isoplane**, Ctrl-E, or F5

Options
Enter isometric plane setting [Left/Top/Right] <Right>:

Left
Left isoplane is active in the 90-degree and 150-degree axis pair.

Top
Top isoplane is active in the 30-degree and 150-degree axis pair.

Right
Right isoplane is active in the 90-degree and 30-degree axis pair.

Tips & Warnings

You can draw isometric circles with the isocircle option of the *ellipse* command. It is recommended that you verify that *pellipse* is set to 0. This will give you greater flexibility when editing ellipses or isocircles.

Related Variables	lastpoint, snapisopair, snapstyl
Associated Commands	dsettings, ellipse, snap

Example

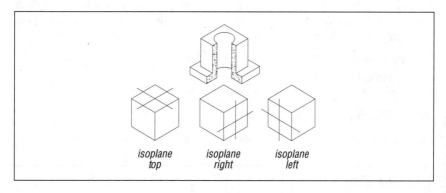

isoplane	isoplane	isoplane
top	right	left

'LASTANGLE

Maintains the location of the last angle of the last drawn arc.

Initiate Command By

Command: **lastangle**

Variable Settings

Initial default:	0, read-only
Subsequent default:	Initial default
System variable:	Real

Associated Commands	arc

'LASTPOINT

Maintains the location of the last point entered.

Initiate Command By

Command: **lastpoint**

Variable Settings

Initial default:	0.0000,0.0000,0.0000, read-only
Subsequent default:	Initial default
Value:	3D point

Tips & Warnings

When you need to reference the *lastpoint*, use the at symbol (@) for prompts such as "Specify first point" or "Specify insertion point."

Related Variables   lastangle

LAYCUR   Express Layer toolbar

Changes objects to the current layer. You also can use *properties, matchprop, change,* and *chgprop* to change objects to the current layer. However, those commands also provide other functions.

Initiate Command By
Command: **laycur**
Express → Layers → Change to Current Layer

Related Variables   clayer

Associated Commands   expresstools, layer

LAYDEL 2000

Permanently deletes layers and any objects residing on those layers. Blocks containing objects on multiple layers are affected by this command. The blocks are redefined, and the objects assigned to the layers chosen for deletion are removed. You are given a warning message and the chance to abort the command.

Initiate Command By
Command:**laydel**
Express → Layers → Layer Delete

Options
Select object on layer to delete or [Type-it/Undo]:

object on layer to delete
As you select objects to delete, their layer names appear on the command line. You cannot delete locked layers, the current layer, or layer 0. You can delete objects on external reference layers, but you are still required to unattach the external reference if you want to remove those layer names. Once the external reference is attached, use the *purge* or *layer* command to delete those layer names.

Type-it
Enter T to type the layer name to delete. This is helpful when there are no objects displayed on the screen that represent that layer. You can always use *layer* or *purge* and remove those layers as long as there are no objects assigned to those layers.

Undo
> Undo, one step at a time and in reverse order, whatever was chosen for deletion. Issuing a *u* (undo) once the command has completed restores the drawing back to its original state before *laydel* was issued.

Associated Commands   expresstools, layer, purge

'-LAYER `2000`   *see LAYER*

LAYER `2000mod`   Object Properties toolbar

Layers act as transparent drawing overlays. The Layer Properties Manager dialog box is used to control layer accessibility, status, color, visibility, linetype, lineweight, and plotting parameters. It also manages the *vplayer* command. You can selectively load layers or just portions of those layers displayed in views by using the Partial Open option of the *open* command. Once a drawing is partially opened, you can still selectively load layers and views using *partiaload*. The Object Properties toolbar also contains multiple icons (shown above) for controlling layers and is located next to the layers button.

You can achieve the same results using *-layer* (*-la*) so all prompts and options appear at the command line.

You can import layers used in other drawings using the AutoCAD DesignCenter feature. You can quickly select and unselect all the layers in the layer name list by using the short cut menu (right-click on your pointing device).

Objects on layers turned off are calculated during the *hide*, *render*, and *regen* commands. Objects on frozen layers are not calculated during those commands. Therefore, freezing layers provides better performance for many AutoCAD commands such as object selection, pan, and zoom. Layers that are turned off can still be assigned as the current layer but frozen layers cannot.

If you set color and linetype ByLayer, any objects you draw default to the color and linetype of the current layer. You can rename a layer by double-clicking on the layer name or by using *rename*. You cannot rename layer 0. Layer names can contain up to 255 characters.

Initiate Command By
> Command: **layer**
> Alias: **la** or **ddlmodes**
> Format → Layer

Options

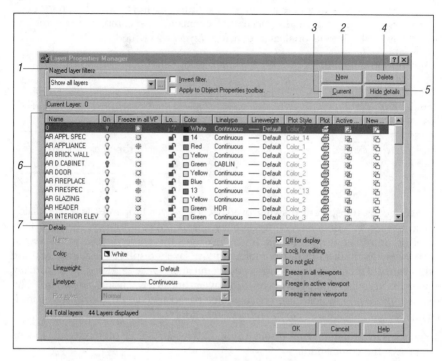

1. **Named layer filters.** Controls the layers listed in the layer name list. This drop-down list provides the options of displaying all the layers, only the used layers, all external-reference-dependent layers, or a saved filter that you select.

   Selecting the box with three periods (...) displays the Named Layer Filters list. This dialog box lets you refine the list of layers displayed using more detailed criteria. Once you set up the criteria, you can assign that group of settings with a filter name. This name becomes one of the options listed in the Named Layer Filters drop-down list.

   Invert filter

   Inverts or displays the opposite of your setting criteria defined in the Named Layer Filters list.

   Apply to Object Properties toolbar

   Displays the Named Layer Filters criteria in the Object Properties toolbar. If a filter criteria is active, the tooltip states Filter Applied when your cursor is placed on the layer name.

2. **New.** Creates new layers. A default layer name is provided, but you can enter your own layer name. If you want to create more than one layer, you can press Enter twice or type a comma (,) after each layer name. Typing a comma is shorter since it automatically creates a new layer entry. Depending on *extnames*, layer names can contain up to 255 characters.

You can create new layers based on the properties of an existing layer by first selecting that layer and then selecting the New button. If you want to create layers based on the layer default settings, make sure there are no active layers when selecting the New button. You can unselect all layers by using the shortcut menu.

3. **Current.** Makes the selected layer the default. Most new objects are automatically assigned to the current layer. This value is maintained by the *clayer* variable. You can quickly change objects to the current layer using *laycur*.

4. **Delete.** Removes the selected layer as long as there are no objects referencing that layer. Layer 0, the current layer, and external-reference-dependent layers can never be deleted. You cannot delete the layer named Defpoint as long as your drawing contains associative dimensions. However, you can *rename* that layer. You can also use *purge* to delete unreferenced layers. *laydel* lets you quickly delete layers and any objects referencing those layers.

5. **Hide details/Show details.** Displays or hides the Details section. This same information is provided in the layer name list discussed next.

6. **Name, On, Freeze in all VP, Lock, Color, Linetype, Lineweight, Plot Style, Plot, Active VP Freeze, New VP Freeze.** Displays the status and properties of each layer. You can select one or more of the layers and modify its accessibility, status, color, visibility, linetype, lineweight, and plotting parameters. Select multiple layers by using the Ctrl or Shift keys.

Selecting any of the headers automatically sorts the list by that property. Selecting the header a second time reverses the order. Once you exit the dialog box, the sort always defaults to the layer name in alphabetical order.

You can change the header length by moving the vertical line between each header name. If you see three periods (...), it means there is text hidden that can't be displayed because the header length is too short.

Name
Lists the layers based on the Named Layer Filters setting.

On
Turns layers on (visible) and off (invisible). You can turn off all the layers in the drawing except the layers assigned to selected objects with *layiso*. You can also turn layers off with *layoff*. *layoff* lets you select objects residing on the layers you want off. Both of these commands are helpful when you don't know the names of the layers where the objects reside. *layon* turns all layers on.

Freeze in all VP
Thaws (makes visible) and freezes (makes invisible) layers. You can quickly freeze layers with *layfrz*. *layfrz* lets you select objects residing on the layers you want frozen. This is helpful when you don't know the names of the layers on which the objects reside. *laythw* thaws all frozen layers.

Lock
Locks and unlocks layers. Unlocked layers can be edited; locked layers cannot be edited. You can lock layers with *laylck*. *laylck* lets you select

objects residing on the layers you want locked. This is helpful when you don't know the names of the layers you want locked.

Color

See *color* for more detailed information.

Linetype

See *linetype* for more detailed information.

Lineweight

See *lweight* for more detailed information.

Plot Style

See *plotstyle* for more detailed information.

Plot

Determines whether the layer is plotted. Regardless of this setting, if the layer is off or frozen, it will not plot.

Active VP Freeze

Allows you to set the layer visibility per viewport when *tilemode* is set to 0. See *vplayer* for more detailed information.

New VP Freeze

Allows you to preset the layer visibility per viewport for new layers when *tilemode* is set to 0. See *vplayer* for more detailed information.

7. **Details.** The Details section is visible when the Show Details button is selected. All of the options are available in the layer edit box previously discussed.

Tips & Warnings

- You may find it easier and quicker to stay on one layer while drawing new objects. Later, you can use *change, chprop, matchprop,* or *properties* and reassign objects to their proper layers.

- Blocks containing objects drawn on layer 0 adopt the current layer's properties upon insertion. Blocks created on multiple layers can display different results when some of those layers are off as opposed to frozen.

- You can change the layer settings for the way external reference drawings appear in the current drawing by setting *visretain* to 1.

- Issuing most of the rendering commands (*light, render, scene,* etc.) automatically creates a locked layer named Ashade. Even if you cancel out of the command, this layer is still created.

- Associative dimensioning creates a layer named Defpoints (definition points). This layer will not plot even when on and thawed. Renaming this layer will cause it to plot.

- See "Wildcard Characters" in Chapter 2, *Command Index and Global Topics,* for more information.

Related Variables   clayer, extnames, visretain

Associated Commands	change, chprop, color, laydel, layer, layfrz, layiso, laylck, layoff, layon, laythw, layulk, linetype, ltscale, lweight, matchprop, partiaload, partialopen, properties, purge, vplayer

LAYFRZ

Express Layer toolbar

Freezes layers of selected objects. You also can use *layer*, but you must know the layer names. You can thaw all frozen layers with *layer* and *laythw*.

Initiate Command By

Command: **layfrz**
Express → Layers → Layer Freeze

Options

Select an object on the layer to be frozen or [Options/Undo]:

object on the layer to be frozen
You cannot freeze the current layer.

Options
Lets you have more control of what layers are affected when you select objects that are part of nested blocks or external references.

Entity level nesting
Freezes the layer on which the object was created before it becomes part of a block or external reference.

No nesting
Freezes the layer on which the block or external reference was inserted.

Undo
Lets you undo one step at a time, and in reverse order, whatever layers were selected. Issuing a *u* (undo) once the command has completed restores the drawing to its original state before the *layfrz* command was issued.

Associated Commands   expresstools, layer, laythw

LAYISO

Express Layer toolbar

Turns off all the layers in the drawing except the layers assigned to selected objects. Use *layoff* when you want to select the objects residing on the layers to turn off. Use *layer* when you know the layer names to turn off. You can turn all layers on with *layer* and *layon*.

Initiate Command By

Command: **layiso**
Express → Layers → Layer Isolate

Associated Commands   expresstools, layer, layoff, layon

LAYLCK

Express Layer toolbar

Locks the layer of the selected object. You also can use *layer*, but you must know the layer name. *layulk* unlocks the layer of a selected object.

Initiate Command By
Command: **laylck**
Express → Layers → Layer Lock

Associated Commands   expresstools, layer, layulk

LAYMCH

Express Layer toolbar

Changes the layer assigned to objects based on another object's layer or by typing the destination layer name. *matchprop* lets you change the layer assignment of objects based on another object's layer. *properties*, *change*, and *chprop* let you change the object's layer assignment by selecting or typing the destination layer name.

Initiate Command By
Command: **laymch**
Express → Layers → Layer Match

Associated Commands   change, chprop, expresstools, matchprop, properties

LAYMRG 2000

Moves all the objects (including block references) residing on selected layers onto another layer. The layer that is merged with the target layer is then deleted.

Initiate Command By
Command: **laymrg**
Express → Layers → Layer Merge

Options
Select object on layer to merge or [Type-it/Undo]:
Select object on target layer or [Type-it]:

object on layer to merge
Layer 0 cannot be merged. Blocks referencing layers to merge are updated and modified to reference the target layer.

Type-it
Enter T to type the layer name to merge. This is helpful when there are no objects that represent the layer displayed on the screen.

Undo
Undo one step at a time, and in reverse order, the name of the layers to merge.

object on target layer
> Select an object representing the layer to which you want to merge.

> *Type-it*
>> Enter T to type the layer name of the target layer. This is helpful when there are no objects that represent that layer displayed on the screen.

Associated Commands   expresstools

LAYOFF
Express Layer toolbar

Turns layers of selected objects off. You also can use *layer*, but you must know the layer names. *layiso* turns off all the layers in the drawing except the layers assigned to selected objects. You can turn all layers on with *layer* and *layon*.

Initiate Command By
> Command: **layoff**
> Express → Layers → Layer Off

Options
> ```
> Select an object on the layer to be turned off or [Options/Undo]:
> ```

Options
> Lets you have more control of what layers are affected when selecting objects that are part of nested blocks or external references.

> *Entity level nesting*
>> Turns off the layer on which the object was created before becoming part of a block or external reference.

> *No nesting*
>> Turns off the layer on which the block or external reference was inserted.

Undo
> Lets you undo one step at a time, and, in reverse order, whatever layers were selected. Issuing a *u* (undo) once the command has completed restores the drawing to its original state before *layoff* was issued.

Associated Commands   expresstools, layer, layiso, layon

LAYON

Turns all layers on. You also can use *layer* to turn layers on. Use *layer* or *layoff* to turn layers off.

Initiate Command By
> Command: **layon**
> Express → Layers → Turn All Layers On

Associated Commands   expresstools, layer, layoff

LAYOUT 2000

Creates new layouts and copies, renames, saves, and deletes existing layouts. A layout is a way to display your model drawing for plotting. Each layout can contain model space and paper space objects and its own plotting parameters. Layouts can be developed to depict the different disciplines that might be represented on the model drawing.

If you don't see all the layout tabs listed for a drawing, use the arrow keys to the left of the tabs to scroll through the list. The first arrow takes you to the beginning of the list, which always starts with Model. The second arrow scrolls to the right. The third arrow scrolls to the left. The last arrows takes you the end of the list.

Selecting a layout tab for the first time activates the Page Setup dialog box. If you don't want the Page Setup dialog box displayed each time you begin a new drawing layout, you can deactivate it by unchecking the "Display when creating a new layout" box on the lower-left corner of the dialog box. You also can deactivate it by unchecking the "Show Page Setup dialog for new layouts" box located in the *options* Display tab.

Initiate Command By

Command: **layout, -layout**
Alias: **lo**
Insert → Layout → New Layout
Insert → Layout → Layout from Template

Options

Enter layout option [Copy/Delete/New/Template/Rename/SAveas/Set/?] <set>:
Enter layout to make current <Layout1>:

Copy

Copies an existing layout into a new layout. You are asked to assign a name to the new layout. If you don't enter a name, AutoCAD automatically assigns a name containing the name of the copied layout plus an incremental number in parentheses. You cannot copy the Model layout.

Delete

Removes layouts from your drawing. The default for removing a layout is based on the active layout. If a layout is active, that layout becomes the default for removal. If the Model is active, the last layout accessed becomes the default. You cannot delete the Model, and one layout is always present.

New

Creates a new layout. If you don't enter a name, AutoCAD automatically assigns a name of Layout1, Layout2, and so forth.

Template

Inserts a new layout based on the layout of another file. You can insert layouts from template files (*.dwt*), drawing files (*.dwg*), or drawing interchange files (*.dxf*). Since these files also may contain multiple layouts, you can select one or more layouts to insert into your drawing. You also can access the layouts defined in other files using the AutoCAD DesignCenter feature. Only the objects created on the layouts are merged with your drawing file. To create a template file from your current drawing, use the saveas option.

If *filedia* is set to 1, a dialog box is activated; if *filedia* is set to 0, you are prompted on the command line. When *filedia* is set to 0, or off, entering a tilde (~) on the command line temporarily activates the dialog box.

Rename

Renames a layout. You also can select the tab you want to rename and use the shortcut menu. Layout names can contain up to 255 characters, although only the first 32 characters are displayed. You cannot rename the Model tab.

SAveas

Lets you save a layout as a template file (*.dwt*), drawing file (*.dwg*), or drawing interchange file (*.dxf*). This file can be accessed by other drawing files using the template option.

If *filedia* is set to 1, a dialog box is activated; if *filedia* is set to 0, you are prompted on the command line. When *filedia* is set to 0, or off, entering a tilde (~) on the command line temporarily activates the dialog box.

Set

Makes a layout current. You also can select the tab with your pointing device.

?

Lists all the layouts in your drawing.

Tips & Warnings

*   Move and copy layouts by placing your pointing device on top of the layout tab and activating the shortcut menu. You cannot move or copy the Model layout.

*   Use *mview* to create viewports, *vplayer* to control layers in individual viewports, *pagesetup* to assign plot parameters, and *layoutwizard*, which automatically combines some of the *layout* and *pagesetup* commands.

*   When an AutoCAD 2000 drawing containing multiple layouts is saved to Release 14 format, only the last active layout is recognized. However, when that drawing is brought back into a Release 2000 format, all the other layouts are restored.

Related Variables   ctab, filedia

Associated Commands   adcenter, layoutwizard, pagesetup

Example

The paper background, margins, and shadow can be toggled on and off from *options* Display tab.

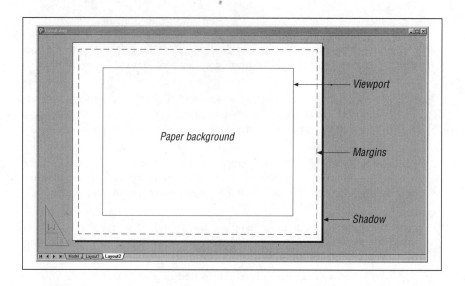

LAYOUTWIZARD 2000

layoutwizard is a combination of the commands that let you set up a page layout for printing. It lets you create a new layout, assign a printer to the layout, define the paper size and drawing units, determine the paper's orientation, select a title-block, and create a viewport setup. See *layout, pagesetup,* and *mview* for more detailed information.

Initiate Command By

> Command: **layoutwizard**
> Insert → Layout → Layout Wizard
> Tools → Wizards → Create Layout

Associated Commands   layout, mview, mvsetup, pagesetup

LAYTHW

Thaws all layers. You also can use *layer* to thaw layers. Use *layer* or *layfrz* to freeze layers.

Initiate Command By

> Command: **laythw**
> Express → Layers → Thaw All Layers

Associated Commands   expresstools, layer, layfrz

LAYULK   Express Layer toolbar

Unlocks the layer of the selected object. You also can use *layer*, but you must know the layer name. *laylck* locks the layer of a selected object.

Initiate Command By

    Command: **layulk**

    Express → Layers → Layer Unlock

Associated Commands   expresstools, layer, laylck

LEADER

Creates leader lines that are used as a way to enter callouts on a drawing. Leaders are made up of the following: arrowheads, straight or splined (curved) line segments, multiline text, and dimension information. All of the parts making up the leader (except the annotation) are associative or dynamic in that they act as one object. *dim* has a leader option, but it is not as flexible, and each part of the leader is a separate object. *qleader* offers most of the same options, and it uses a dialog box for setting up the leader parameters.

Canceling out of *qleader* before completion, leaves that part of the leader that was already created. Canceling out of *leader* before completion, erases all the geometry associated with that leader.

Initiate Command By

    Command: **leader**

    Alias: **lead**

Options

    Specify leader start point:
    Specify next point:
    Specify next point or [Annotation/Format/Undo] <Annotation>:
    Enter first line of annotation text or <options>:
    Enter an annotation option [Tolerance/Copy/Block/None/Mtext] <Mtext>:

Annotation

    Lets you add text (*mtext*) or symbols (*blocks*) at the end of the leader.

    Tolerance

        Activates the Geometric Tolerance dialog box. See *tolerance* for more detailed information.

    Copy

        Copies existing text, multiline text, blocks, and tolerances and places them as the annotation. It does not work for associative dimensions.

    Block

        Inserts a block as the annotation. You can activate a dialog box if you use a tilde (~) when prompted for the block name. See *insert* for more detailed information.

    None

        Ends the leader command without placing anything at the end of the leader line.

    Mtext

        Lets you enter multiple lines of text using the Multiline Text Editor dialog box.

Format

Determines whether there is an arrowhead and whether the lines are straight or splined (curved line segments).

Spline/Straight

Automatically creates straight line segments unless you enter S for spline. As long as the format option is available on the command line, you can toggle between straight and splined lines. *qleader* lets you assign a maximum number of leader lines.

Arrow/None

Automatically places an arrowhead at the "Specify leader start point" prompt unless you enter N for none. As long as the format option is available on the command line, you can toggle between arrow and none. *qleader* lets you select any of the arrowheads that are available through the dimension style (*dimstyle*) command.

Exit

Leaves the format option and returns to the Specify Next Point prompt.

Undo

Lets you undo, one step at a time, whatever was accomplished up to the annotation option. Once you proceed to annotation, this option is no longer available. Issuing a *u* (undo), once the command is ended, erases whatever was accomplished by the *leader* command. This option is not available with the *qleader* command.

Tips & Warnings

• Hook lines are automatically created if the angle of the leader is greater than 15 degrees from the horizontal.

• Leaders use some of the default dimensioning style values such as *dimasz*, *dimclrd*, *dimgap*, *dimldrblk*, *dimscale*, *dimtad*, and *dimtob*.

• You can disassociate leaders and their annotation using *qldetachset*. You can reassociate leaders to annotation using *qlattach*.

Related Variables	dimasz, dimgap, dimldrblk, dimscale, dimtad
Associated Commands	dim, dimstyle, qleader, tolerance
Example	See QLEADER.

LENGTHEN

Modify toolbar

Changes the length of objects.

Initiate Command By

Command: **lengthen**
Alias: **len**
Modify → Lengthen

Options

```
Select an object or [DElta/Percent/Total/DYnamic]:
```

object
>Lists the object's length. If the object is an arc, it also provides the included angle.

DElta
>Increases or decreases the length of 2D and 3D polylines, arcs, elliptical arcs, and lines by the amount specified.

>*Angle*
>>Changes the angle of arcs and elliptical arcs by increasing or decreasing the arc's length by the amount specified.

Percent
>Changes the length of 2D and 3D polylines, arcs, elliptical arcs, lines, and splines based on a percentage of its current length. The percentage you enter defines the amount of the object you want to keep.

Total
>Allows you to specify the absolute length for 2D and 3D polylines, arcs, elliptical arcs, lines, and splines.

DYnamic
>Allows you to drag the endpoints of arcs, elliptical arcs, and lines to new locations.

Undo
>Undoes the last object lengthened.

Tips & Warnings

* The endpoint lengthened is based on the nearest endpoint found during object selection.

* *break, change, extend, grip, properties,* and *trim* editing let you change an object's length.

Related Variables   grips

Associated Commands   break, change, extend, properties, trim

Example

'LENSLENGTH

Maintains the camera's lens length (in millimeters) when perspective viewing is enabled. Using the *zoom* command while perspective viewing is enabled causes the *lenslength* variable to update.

Initiate Command By

Command: **lenslength**

Initial default:	50.0000, read-only
Subsequent default:	Last value used in the drawing
Value:	Real
Associated Commands	dview, view, 3dorbit

LIGHT

Render toolbar

Creates, modifies, and controls the lighting parameters for rendering. For each light you create, a block or light symbol is placed in the drawing. Each block retains that light's specific values. Once one or more light sources have been created, use *scene* and link the lights to predefined views.

Initiate Command By

Command: **light**

View → Render → Light

Options

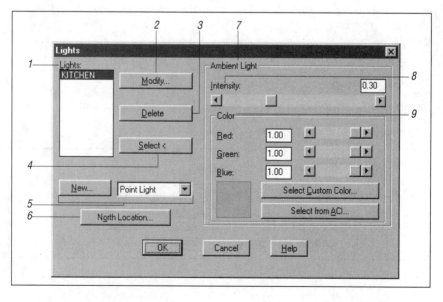

1. **Lights.** Lists the lights defined in the current drawing.

2. **Modify.** Modifies the light highlighted in the Lights list box. The dialog box this activates varies depending on whether the light is point, distant, or spotlight.

3. **Delete.** Removes the light highlighted in the Lights list box. You also can delete lights by erasing the light blocks from the drawing.

4. **Select <.** Lets you select an existing light block from the drawing and highlights its associated light name from the Lights list box.

5. **New.** Creates a new point light, distant light, or spotlight.

   Point Light
   > Point lights emit radiating beams of light. You specify either the intensity of the light to the distance traveled or the attenuation parameters. See the New Point Light dialog box.

   Distant Light
   > Distant lights emit parallel beams of light. There is no attenuation, so the light remains at a constant intensity. See the New Distant Light dialog box.

   Spotlight
   > Spotlights emit directional cones of light. You specify either the intensity of the light to the distance traveled or the attenuation parameters. See the New Spotlight dialog box.

6. **North Location.** Defines the north direction. The default north direction is based on the positive Y direction in the World Coordinate System (WCS). Any saved User Coordinate System (UCS) also can be used to define the north location. The Y axis in that UCS is used as the north direction.

7. **Ambient Light.** Maintains a constant or evenly distributed background light to all surfaces on the drawing. It is best to keep the light low so that it doesn't dull your image.

8. **Intensity.** Controls the intensity of the ambient light. The value can be between 0 and 1. No ambient light is 0; full brightness is 1. Enter the intensity value in the text box or use the slider bars.

9. **Color.** Sets the color for the ambient light. You can enter the color values in the Red, Green, and Blue text boxes, use the slider bars, or choose Select Custom Color or Select from ACI. The color box or swatch displays the current color. The custom color is based on the Windows operating software Color dialog box; the ACI is based on AutoCAD's color index.

The New Point Light Dialog Box

The dialog is accessed by selecting the New button on the Lights dialog with Point Light showing in the drop-down menu.

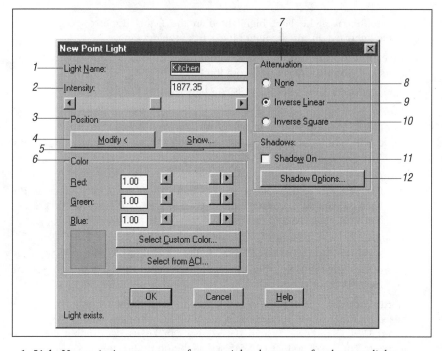

1. **Light Name.** Assigns a name, of up to eight characters, for the new light.

2. **Intensity.** Defines the light's brightness. Setting the value to 0 turns the light off. The maximum value you can assign is directly related to the attenuation setting and the drawing's extents.

3. **Position.** Shows you the current light coordinates and lets you relocate the light.

4. **Modify.** Temporarily brings up your drawing and lets you move the light to a different location.

5. **Show.** Shows the light location by providing the *X, Y,* and *Z* coordinates.

6. **Color.** Sets the color for the ambient light. You can enter the color values in the Red, Green, and Blue text boxes, use the slider bars, or choose Select Custom Color or Select from ACI. The color box or swatch displays the current color. The custom color is based on the Windows operating software Color dialog box; the ACI is based on AutoCAD's color index.

7. **Attenuation.** Determines the way light is diminished over distance. The further the object is from the point light, the darker it appears.

8. **None.** Assigns all objects the same brightness.

9. **Inverse Linear.** Decreases light intensity linearly as the distance from the light source to the center of the target face increases.

10. **Inverse Square.** Decreases light intensity as the square of the distance from the light source to the center of a target face increases.

11. **Shadow On.** Turns the point light shadow on. The type of shadow depends on the current renderer type and the settings defined in the Shadow Options dialog box.

12. **Shadow Options.** Defines the shadow map size, softness, and bounding box and specifies whether the shadow volumes or raytraced shadows are active.

The New Distant Light Dialog Box

The dialog is accessed by selecting the New button on the Lights dialog with Distant Light showing in the drop-down menu.

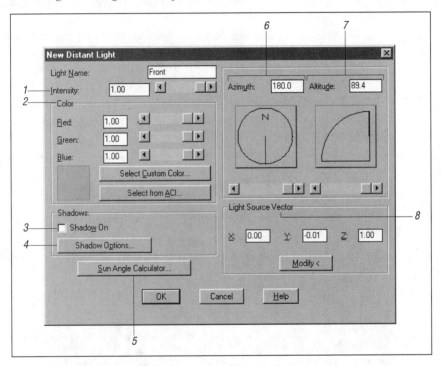

1. **Intensity.** Defines the light's brightness. The value for this setting ranges from 0 to 1. Setting the value to 0 turns the light off; setting the value to 1 gives the light full intensity.

2. **Color.** Sets the color for the ambient light. You can enter the color values in the Red, Green, and Blue text boxes, use the slider bars, or choose Select Custom Color or Select from ACI. The color box or swatch displays the current color. The custom color is based on the Windows operating software Color dialog box; the ACI is based on AutoCAD's color index.

3. **Shadow On.** Turns the point light shadow on. The type of shadow depends on the current renderer type and the settings defined in the Shadow Options dialog box.

4. **Shadow Options.** Defines the shadow map size, softness, and bounding box and specifies whether the shadow volumes or raytraced shadows are active.

5. **Sun Angle Calculator.** Defines the location and time so the rendering feature can calculate the sun's position.

6. **Azimuth.** Defines the location of the light by using site-based coordinates. The values range from −180 to 180 degrees. You can enter the values in the text box, click on the diagram, or use the slider bars. This value directly affects the light source vector.

7. **Altitude.** Defines the location of the light by using site-based coordinates. The values range from 0 to 90 degrees. You can enter the values in the text box, click on the diagram, or use the slider bars. This value directly affects the light source vector.

8. **Light Source Vector.** Displays the light source vector based on the azimuth and altitude settings. You can enter the values in the text box or use the Modify option. Modify lets you pick the light location directly from the drawing. Changing these values changes the azimuth and altitude settings.

The New Spotlight Dialog Box

The dialog is accessed by selecting the New button on the Lights dialog with Spotlight showing in the drop-down menu.

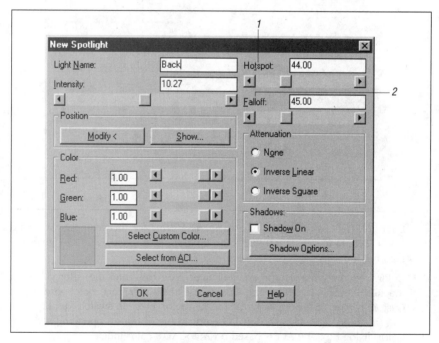

1. **Hotspot.** Determines the angle that defines the brightest cone of light. The value ranges from 0 to 160 degrees.

2. **Falloff.** Determines the angle that defines the full cone of light. The value ranges from 0 to 160 degrees.

LIMITS

Tips & Warnings

- You can modify lights by changing their location, scene assignment, color, and intensity, but you cannot change the type (i.e., point, distant, or spot) of light. If necessary, when locating lights, use the *X, Y, Z* filtering method since it helps you locate points more accurately.

- Light symbols (blocks) are placed on a locked layer named Ashade. These blocks are named Direct, Overhead, and Sh_spot. You can change the size of these lights with the light icon scale option of the *rpref* command.

- When creating scenes with no defined lights, AutoCAD assumes an "over-the-shoulder" distant light source intensity of 1 and an ambient light intensity of 0.

Related Variables   target

Associated Commands   render, rpref, scene, view

'LIMCHECK

Determines whether new objects can be created outside the limits. Model space and each layout space retain their own *limcheck* settings. This value is set with the *limits* command

Initiate Command By

Command: **limcheck**

Options

0   Creates objects at any location regardless of the limits setting.

1   Creates objects only within the defined limits setting.

Initial default:	0
Subsequent default:	Last value used in the drawing
Value:	Integer

Related Variables   limmax, limmin

Associated Commands   limits

'LIMITS   2000mod

Defines the drawing area. This area is defined by the absolute coordinates of the lower-left and upper-right corners. The *limits* command lets you modify these coordinates and turn limits checking on and off. Limits usually are set to represent the full size of the space you are working with. You may want to set the limits greater than your drawing size to include notes and dimensions.

There are no limits in the *Z* direction. If grid is on and you are in the World Coordinate System (WCS), grid dots are displayed to the drawing limits. The Create New Drawing wizard sets your limits based on your responses to its prompts.

Initiate Command By

Command: **limits**

Format → Drawing Limits

Options

```
Reset Model space limits:
Specify lower left corner or [ON/OFF] <0.0000,0.0000>:
Specify upper right corner <420.0000,297.0000>:
```

lower left corner

Changes the lower-left corner coordinates. This value is maintained by the *limmin* variable.

ON

Turns limits checking on; you cannot pick a point outside the limits. If you do try to edit or create objects that would go outside the limits, you will receive the message "**Outside limits," and your command will not complete. This value is maintained by the *limcheck* variable.

OFF

Turns limits checking off; you can pick a point outside the limits. This value is maintained by the *limcheck* variable.

upper right corner

Changes the upper-right corner coordinates. This value is maintained by the *limmax* variable.

Tips & Warnings

• If you change the limits, you must use *zoom–all* to readjust your drawing to the screen display. If you have objects outside the limits, the display will include those objects as well. *zoom–all* shows you the current limits or drawing extents, whichever is greater.

• *status* displays the drawing limits. You can *plot* to the drawing limits.

Related Variables   limcheck, limmax, limmin, vsmax, vsmin

Associated Commands   plot, status

'LIMMAX

Maintains the upper-right *X, Y* limit. Model space and each layout space retain their own *limmax* settings. This value is set with the *limits* command.

Initiate Command By

Command: **limmax**

Variable Settings

Initial default:	12.0000,9.0000
Subsequent default:	Last value used in the drawing
Value:	2D point

Related Variables	limcheck, limmin
Associated Commands	limits

'LIMMIN

Maintains the lower-left *X,Y* limit. Model space and each layout space retain their own *limmin* settings. This value is set with the *limits* command.

Initiate Command By
Command: **limmin**

Variable Settings

Initial default:	0.0000,0.0000
Subsequent default:	Last value used in the drawing
Value:	2D point

Related Variables	limcheck, limmax
Associated Commands	limits

LINE

Draw toolbar

Creates 2D (*X,Y*) or 3D (*X,Y,Z*) straight line segments. If the *Z* value is not given, it is assumed to be at the current elevation. You end the line command by canceling (Escape) or by pressing Enter. You can save time and draw lines more accurately by using snap and object snap or by entering the direct distance or absolute, relative, or polar coordinates of each point. Create construction lines using *xline* and *ray*.

You can construct lines with different linetypes by using the *linetype* or *layer* command. You can also assign plot styles to lines and achieve the same results.

If you want to draw lines with different lineweights, use the *lineweight, layer, pline*, or *trace* command or assign a plot style to the object or its layer.

If an arc is the last object drawn, you can draw a line tangent to the arc endpoint by using the continue option and specifying only the line length. The direction is determined by the endpoint of the arc.

Initiate Command By
Keyboard: **line**
Alias: **l**
Draw → Line

Options
```
Specify first point:
Specify next point or [Undo]:
Specify next point or [Undo]:
Specify next point or [Close/Undo]:
```

continue

At the "Specify first point" prompt, you can begin a line at the endpoint of the most recently drawn line or arc by pressing Enter.

Close

Entering C (close) at the "Specify next point" prompt closes the line segments created during the command by connecting the last endpoint to the start point. This option is available when at least two lines are created.

Undo

Entering u at the "Specify next point" prompt undoes the last line and returns you to the previous point.

Tips & Warnings

- Use *sketch* to construct freehand lines, *mline* to create parallel lines and arcs, *pline* to create lines and arcs connected by their vertices, and *spline* and *pline* to create curved lines.

- You can convert a line into a pline (see *pedit*), but you cannot convert a line into multiline, ray, spline, trace, or construction line (xline).

- If you turn *ortho* on, you can draw lines at 90-degree angles.

- Using the undo option while in the *line* command is different from issuing an *undo* at a command prompt. Using undo during the *line* command releases you to the previous point and lets you continue drawing lines. Using *undo* at a command prompt backsteps to the previous command.

- See "Point and Coordinate Entry" in Chapter 2, *Command Index and Global Topics*, for more information.

Related Variables   lastangle, lastpoint

Associated Commands   mline, pline, ray, spline, trace, xline

Example

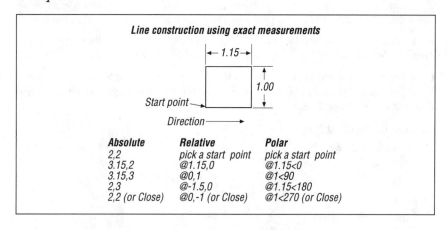

Line construction using exact measurements

Absolute	Relative	Polar
2,2	pick a start point	pick a start point
3.15,2	@1.15,0	@1.15<0
3.15,3	@0,1	@1<90
2,3	@-1.5,0	@1.15<180
2,2 (or Close)	@0,-1 (or Close)	@1<270 (or Close)

'-LINETYPE 2000

see LINETYPE

'LINETYPE 2000mod

Object Properties toolbar

Assigns a linetype for new objects and loads linetype definitions stored in library files. You can achieve the same results using the *-linetype* (*-lt* or *-ltype*) command so all prompts and options appear on the command line. The *-linetype* command has an added feature that lets you create new linetype definitions.

Two special linetypes are ByLayer and ByBlock. ByLayer means that new objects receive the linetype of the layers on which they reside; ByBlock means that new objects are drawn with the Continuous linetype until they are saved as a block. When the block is inserted, it inherits the current linetype setting.

You can rename a linetype by double-clicking on the linetype name or with the *rename* command. You cannot rename ByLayer, ByBlock, or Continuous. Linetype names can contain up to 255 characters.

Once a linetype is loaded, it does not need to access the library file from which it came. You must first load the different linetypes (except Continuous, ByLayer, and ByBlock) before they can be referenced by other commands. The only exception is when you use the *-layer* command.

Mixing linetypes on a single layer can become confusing. Using *layer* to control linetype and leaving linetype set ByLayer helps you identify the layer an object is on and makes changing linetypes a simple process of respecifying the linetype with the *layer* command.

Initiate Command By

Command: **linetype**
Alias: **lt**, **ltype**, or **ddltype**
Format → Linetype

Options

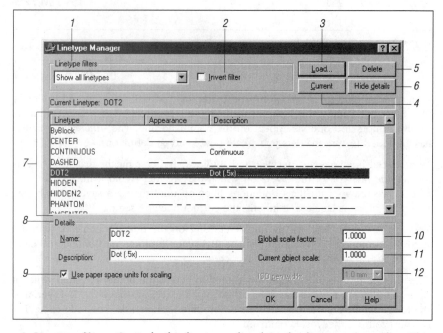

1. **Linetype filters.** Controls the linetypes listed in the linetype name list. This drop-down list provides the options of displaying all the linetypes, only the used linetypes, or all external-reference-dependent linetypes.

2. **Invert filter.** Inverts or displays the opposite of your setting criteria defined in the Linetype filters list.

3. **Load.** Loads linetypes by activating the Load or Reload Linetypes dialog box.

   File

   The files *acad.lin* and *acadiso.lin* supplied with AutoCAD are located in the AutoCAD support folder. Once the linetype definition file is located, you select one or more linetypes listed in the Available Linetypes list to load into your drawing.

4. **Current.** Makes the selected linetype the default. Most new objects are automatically assigned to the current linetype. This value is maintained by the *celtype* system variable

5. **Delete.** Purges or removes the selected linetype as long as there are no layers or objects referencing that linetype. Continuous, ByBlock, ByLayer, the current linetype, and external-reference-dependent linetypes can never be deleted. You also can use *purge* to delete unreferenced linetypes.

6. **Hide details/Show details.** Displays or hides the Details section. Some of the same information is provided in the linetype name list discussed next.

7. **Linetype, Appearance, Description.** Lists the loaded linetypes and describes their appearance. You can sort the list by linetype name or description by

picking the header name. Selecting the header a second time reverses the order. Once you exit the dialog box, the sort always defaults back to linetype names in alphabetical order.

You can change the header length by moving the vertical lines between header names. If you see three periods (...) in any of the linetype names, it means there is text that can't be displayed because the header length is too short.

Linetype
Lists the linetypes loaded in the drawing based on the Linetype Filters setting. ByLayer, ByBlock, and Continuous are always present although their names may not be displayed because of the filter setting.

Appearance
Illustrates the appearance of the linetype.

Description
Describes the linetype and may include how it looks graphically.

8. **Details**. Appears when the Show Details button is selected. The Name and Description are the same as what is displayed in the linetype edit box previously discussed.

9. **Use paper space units for scaling**. Determines whether a drawing using multiple viewports and paper space display the size of dashes, dots, spaces, and annotation in complex linetypes identically. This value is maintained by the *psltscale* system variable

10. **Global scale factor**. Determines the overall scale factor applied to all linetypes. This increases or decreases the size of dashes, dots, spaces, and annotation in complex linetypes. This value is maintained by the *ltscale* system variable

11. **Current object scale**. Determines the scale factor for new objects. This increases or decreases the size of dashes, dots, spaces, and annotation in complex linetypes. This value is maintained by the *celtscale* system variable

12. **ISO Pen Width**. Determines the pen width for ISO linetypes.

Tips & Warnings

- You can reassign an object's linetype with *change, chprop, matchprop*, or *properties*.

- Polylines offer more flexibility than lines by controlling the linetype pattern generation around the vertices. The linetype can be continuous in that all the inside vertices are ignored and do not reset the pattern. See *pedit* for more detailed information.

- You can import linetypes used in other drawings using the AutoCAD Design-Center (*adcenter*), *xbind*, and *xref–bind* features.

- Using noncontinuous linetypes can slow down redraws and regenerations. Use the Continuous linetype until you are ready to plot, and then use *change* or *chprop* to individually change an object's linetype, reset a layer's linetype assignment with *layer*, or assign a plot style to objects or layers.

- You can reassign and save an external reference layer's linetype by setting *visretain* to 1. This is saved only in the drawing referencing the external reference.

- If you change an object's linetype, the drawing must regenerate in order for you to see the results.

Related Variables   celtype, extnames, ltscale, plinegen, psltscale

Associated Commands   layer, ltscale, plot, plotstyle

Example

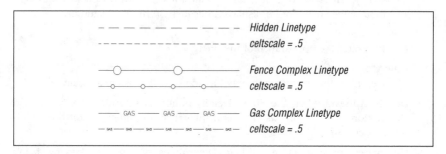

	Hidden Linetype
	celtscale = .5
	Fence Complex Linetype
	celtscale = .5
	Gas Complex Linetype
	celtscale = .5

'LISPINIT

Determines whether AutoLISP functions and variables are retained in the current drawing or whether they are preserved when a new or existing drawing is opened for editing. This assumes that *sdi* (single document interface) is enabled. When *sdi* is disabled, AutoLISP always sets the value of *lispinit* to 0.

Initiate Command By

Command: **lispinit**

Options

0   AutoLISP functions and variables are preserved when a new or existing drawing is opened for editing.

1   AutoLISP functions and variables are retained in the current drawing only.

Variable Settings

Initial default:	1
Subsequent default:	Registry file
Value:	Integer

Related Variables   sdi

Associated Commands   new, open

LIST

Inquiry toolbar

list provides detailed information on selected objects within a drawing; *dblist* (database list) provides information on all objects within a drawing; *xlist* provides information on a nested object in a block or external reference; and *xdlist* lists extended entity data attached to an object.

The *properties* dialog box provides the same information as the *list* command. However, use *list* if you want to save that information and copy it to a text editor or word processor. You can save a log file by checking the "Maintain a log file" box located in the *options* Open and Save tab.

Initiate Command By

Command: **list**
Alias: **li** or **ls**
Tools → Inquiry → List

Tips & Warnings

- If you pick too many objects to list, it is hard to tell which descriptions fit which objects.

- *list* automatically activates the AutoCAD Text Window. Pressing F2 toggles the display of this window between the front and back of your AutoCAD drawing.

Associated Commands   dblist, xdlist, xlist

-LMAN

see LMAN

LMAN 2000mod

Express Layer toolbar

Saves the current layer settings for future retrieval. You can achieve the same results using *-lman* so all prompts and options appear on the command line.

Initiate Command By

Command: **lman**
Express → Layers → Layer Manager

Options

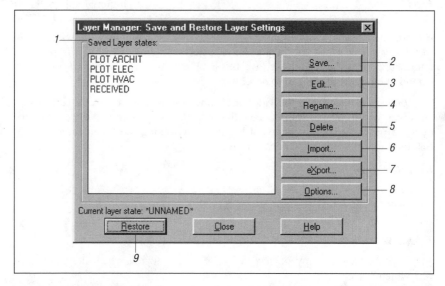

1. **Saved Layer states.** Lists the various layer states already saved. Double-clicking on a name restores those settings and exits out of the command. It combines the Restore and Close options.

2. **Save.** Saves the current layer settings. The default name is LAYER_STATE1, LAYER_STATE2, and so on. You can enter a more descriptive name. Any time you add more layers to the drawing, you may want to reselect this option.

3. **Edit.** Activates *layer* so you can make changes to the various layer properties.

4. **Rename.** Renames the layer state highlighted in the Saved Layer State box.

5. **Delete.** Removes the layer state highlighted in the Saved Layer State box.

6. **Import.** Imports a saved layer state that was saved to a file with the export option. The file's extension is *.lay.*

7. **eXport.** Saves a saved layer state to a file. The file's extension is *.lay.* This file can be imported into other drawings.

8. **Options.** Determines which layer properties are restored. The various choices are on/off, thaw/freeze, locked/unlocked, color status, linetype status, lineweight status, plot status, and plotstyle status. Any changes made to this list are retained until the next time the list is modified.

9. **Restore.** Restores the layer state highlighted in the Saved Layer States box and updates the current layer status. Local layers are automatically created if they do not exist in the drawing.

Tips & Warnings

- Make sure that *visretain* is set to 1 before you save settings for files containing external reference layers.

- There are some sample layer setting files located in Autodesk's *Express* sub-directory. These settings are based on AIA (American Institute of Architects) standards.

Related Variables   visretain

Associated Commands   expresstools, layer

LOAD

Makes shapes (*.shx*) available for the *shape* command. Shape files contain symbol definitions that are similar to blocks, but they are less flexible.

Using the *load* command when *filedia* is enabled lets you select any of your computers's drives, folders, and files. However, it does not display any of the shapes already defined in the current drawing. If you want to select shapes already defined in the current drawing, set *filedia* to 0.

Shape files must be compiled before they can loaded. After shape files are loaded, you can access them with the *shape* command.

Initiate Command By
   Command: **load**

Options
   Enter shape name or [?]:

?   Lists currently loaded shape files if *filedia* is enabled or set to 1.

~   Temporarily activates the file dialog box if *filedia* is disabled or set to 0.

Tips & Warnings

- If *filedia* is set to 1, a dialog box is activated; if *filedia* is set to 0, you are prompted on the command line. When *filedia* is set to 0, or off, entering a tilde (~) on the command line temporarily activates the dialog box.

- The shape files that are loaded contain symbol definitions and are different from the *.shx* files usually associated with fonts. Shapes placed on a drawing are directly linked to their shape file (*.shx*). If that shape file cannot be found when the drawing is opened for editing, the shape references are invisible. When sharing drawings with others, make sure you give them the shape files. For more flexibility and ease of use, consider using blocks.

Related Variables   filedia

Associated Commands   compile, shape

'LOCALE

Maintains the ISO (International Standards Organization) language code used by your version of AutoCAD.

Initiate Command By

Command: **locale**

Variable Settings

Initial default:	enu, read-only
Subsequent default:	Initial default
Value:	String

'LOGFILEMODE

Determines whether information written to the text window is saved in a log file. This variable is set by checking the "Maintain a log file" box located in the *options* Open and Save tab. The *logfilepath* determines the folder location for log files.

Initiate Command By

Command: **logfilemode**

Options

0   Log files are not created.

1   Log files are created.

Variable Settings

Initial default:	0
Subsequent default:	Registry file
Value:	Integer
Related Variables	logfilename, logfilepath
Associated Commands	logfileoff, logfileon, options, preferences

---

'LOGFILENAME 2000mod

Maintains the location and name of log files. See *logfileoff* for more detailed information.

Initiate Command By

Command: **logfilename**

Variable Settings

Initial default:	Varies, read-only
Subsequent default:	Last value used in the drawing
Value:	String
Related Variables	logfilemode, logfilepath
Associated Commands	logfileoff, logfileon, options, preferences

LOGFILEOFF/LOGFILEON

Log files are text files that record all the information displayed at the command line. You can open and write the contents of the AutoCAD text window to a file with *logfileon*. *logfileoff* turns that feature off. You can achieve the same result by checking the "Maintain a log file" box located in the *options* Open and Save tab. The variable that maintains this setting is *logfilemode*. Use a word processor or ASCII text editor (such as Notepad) if you want to read the file's contents. The first part of the log filename matches your drawing name; the second part is generated by AutoCAD. The file's extension is *.log*. The file's location is based on the *logfilepath* setting.

Initiate Command By

> Command: **logfileoff**, **logfileon**

| ***Related Variables*** | logfilemode, logfilename, logfilepath |
| ***Associated Commands*** | options, preferences |

LOGFILEON   *see LOGFILEOFF*

'LOGFILEPATH ⬛2000

Maintains the folder location or path for log files when that feature is enabled. The path is originally created during AutoCAD's installation procedure, but it can be modified by changing the Log File Location located in the *options* Files tab. The *logfilemode* setting determines whether log files are created and saved.

Initiate Command By

> Command: **logfilepath**

Variable Settings

Initial default:	Varies, read-only
Subsequent default:	Registry file
Value:	String
Related Variables	logfilemode, logfilename
Associated Commands	logfileoff, logfileon, options, preferences

---

'LOGINNAME

Maintains the user's login name. This variable is set during the initial AutoCAD configuration and can be up to 30 characters long. *loginname* is displayed when using *dwgprops* and *about*.

Initiate Command By

> Command: **loginname**

Variable Settings

Initial default:	Varies, read-only
Subsequent default:	Initial default
Value:	String

Associated Commands   about, dwgprops

LSEDIT

Render toolbar

Edits landscaped objects already placed in a drawing. Since the command options are the same as those provided in the *lsnew* dialog box, see that command for more detailed information.

Initiate Command By

Command: **lsedit**
View → Render → Landscape Edit

Associated Commands   lslib, lsnew, render, rmat

LSLIB

Render toolbar

Maintains library files containing objects or raster images. Each library file can contain multiple images. Library filenames have the extension *.lli*.

Initiate Command By

Command: **lslib**
View → Render → Landscape Library

Options

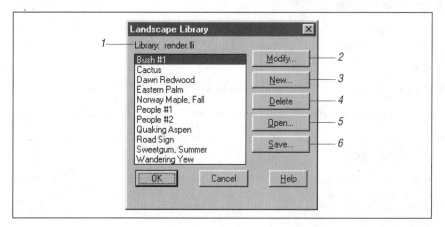

1. **Library**. Lists the objects stored in the current library.

2. **Modify**. Allows you to change the default geometry for objects listed in the Landscape Library. Once you select one of the objects, the Modify button is available. You also can double-click on one of the objects to activate the *modify* command.

   Single Face

   Single face objects appear as a triangle in the drawing when they are view aligned. These objects cannot be rotated with grip editing. Single face objects that are not view aligned appear as rectangles. These objects can be rotated with grip editing. Each object has a name tag that is rotated based on its orientation.

   Crossing Faces

   Crossing face objects appear as two triangles intersecting at right angles. When these objects are view aligned, they face the camera at a 45-degree angle. These objects cannot be rotated, but grip editing lets you change the object's size. When crossing face objects are not view aligned, they can be rotated with grip editing.

   View Aligned

   When checked, the object is always facing the camera. When unchecked, the object has a fixed orientation. Trees and bushes work well when View Aligned is checked. Road signs work better when View Aligned is unchecked.

   Preview

   Display the image.

   Name

   Change the description of the object.

   Image File

   Enter the name of the image file. The file types can be *.bmp*, *.png*, *.tga*, *.tif*, *.gif*, *.jpg*, and *.pcx*.

   Opacity Map File

   Enter the name of the image file. The file types can be *.bmp*, *.png*, *.tga*, *.tif*, *.gif*, *.jpg*, and *.pcx*.

3. **New**. Assigns the name of the new object you have entered to the current library. The options are the same as those described for the Modify button.

4. **Delete**. Removes the highlighted object from the current library.

5. **Open**. Activates the Open Landscape Library dialog box.

6. **Save**. Activates the Save Landscape Library dialog box. You can create a new library file by assigning a different name to the current library file.

Associated Commands   lsedit, lsnew, render, rmat

LSNEW

Render toolbar

Adds landscape objects to your drawing. A landscape object is an extended-entity objects with a bitmap image mapped to it.

Initiate Command By

Command: **lsnew**

View → Render → Landscape New

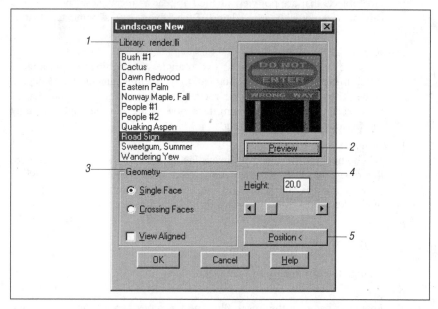

1. **Library**. Lists the objects stored in the current library. If you want to insert an image into the drawing, select the image, define the geometry, height, and position settings, and select OK.

2. **Preview**. Displays the image.

3. **Geometry**. Defines the geometry and alignment of the object.

   Single Face

   Single face objects appear as a triangle in the drawing when they are view aligned. These objects cannot be rotated with grip editing. Single face objects that are not view aligned appear as rectangles. These objects can be rotated with grip editing. Each object has a name tag that is rotated based on its orientation.

   Crossing Faces

   Crossing face objects appear as two triangles intersecting at right angles. When these objects are view aligned, they face the camera at a 45-degree angle. These objects cannot be rotated, but grip editing lets you change the object's size. When crossing face objects are not view aligned, they can be rotated with grip editing.

View Aligned

> When checked, the object is always facing the camera. When unchecked, the object has a fixed orientation. Trees and bushes work well when View Aligned is checked. Road signs work better when View Aligned is unchecked.

4. **Height.** Shows the height based on the positive *Z* direction of the current UCS. You can enter a value, use the slider bars, or use grip editing.

5. **Position.** Locates the image in the drawing. If this button isn't selected, the image is located at the origin of the UCS.

Tips & Warnings

Crossing face objects take longer to render than single face objects, but they look more realistic.

Associated Commands   lsedit, lslib, render, rmat

'LTSCALE

Assigns a global scale multiplier for all linetypes. This controls the spacing between linetypes that contain dashes and dots. The variable that maintains this value also is named *ltscale*. You can change this setting in the *linetype* dialog box by changing the value of Global Scale Factor. If you change your drawing's *ltscale*, you will not see a change until the drawing regenerates.

Initiate Command By

> Command: **ltscale**
> Alias: **lts**

Variable Settings

Initial default:	1
Subsequent default:	Last value used in the drawing
Value:	Real

Tips & Warnings

- A rule of thumb for determining a drawing's appropriate linetype scale is to set it to the drawing's scale factor. Once you have plotted the drawing, you can fine-tune its value.

- Use *psltscale* to control paper space linetype scaling. Use *celtscale* to control individual object linetype scaling. *change, chprop, matchprop,* and *properties* have options for linetype scale. However, this sets the *celtscale* and not the *ltscale*.

Related Variables   celtscale, ltscale, psltscale

Associated Commands   layer, linetype, setvar

'LUNITS

Sets the default for the type of units to display. This variable is set when you start a new drawing using the drawing setup wizards or with the *units* commands.

Initiate Command By

Command: **lunits**

Options

1   Scientific

2   Decimal

3   Engineering

4   Architectural

5   Fractional

Variable Settings

Initial default:	2
Subsequent default:	Last value used in the drawing
Value:	Integer

Related Variables   angbase, angdir, aunits, auprec, luprec

Associated Commands   units

'LUPREC

Sets the default for the number of digits to the right of the decimal point or smallest fraction to display. *area, dist, id, lengthen, list, properties,* and *units* all display the *luprec* setting. This is initially set when starting a new drawing using the drawing setup wizards or with the *units* command.

Initiate Command By

Command: **luprec**

Variable Settings

Initial default:	4
Subsequent default:	Last value used in the drawing
Value:	Integer

Related Variables   angbase, angdir, aunits, auprec, lunits

Associated Commands   units

'LWDEFAULT 2000

Maintains the default lineweight value in millimeters. Valid default values are 0, 5, 9, 13, 15, 18, 20, 25, 30, 35, 40, 50, 53, 60, 70, 80, 90, 100, 106, 120, 140, 158, 200, and 211.

Initiate Command By
Command: **lwdefault**

Variable Settings

Initial default:	25
Subsequent default:	Registry file
Value:	Enum
Related Variables	celweight, lwdisplay, lwunits
Associated Commands	lweight

'LWDISPLAY 2000

Defines the visibility of lineweights in model space. Paper space objects, True-Type fonts, raster images, points, and 2D solids cannot be displayed and plotted with lineweights. This value is set by clicking on the LWT option on the drawing status bar. It also can be set with the *properties* or *lweight* command.

Initiate Command By
Command: **lwdisplay**
Status bar: LWT (toggles *lwdisplay* on and off)

Options
On
  Lineweights are not displayed.
Off
  Lineweights are displayed.

Variable Settings

Initial default:	1
Subsequent default:	Last value used in the drawing
Value:	Integer
Related Variables	celweight, lwdefault, lwunits
Associated Commands	lweight

'-LWEIGHT   *see LWEIGHT*

'LWEIGHT `2000`

Object Properties toolbar

Lineweight can be assigned to objects and layers. Paper space objects, TrueType fonts, raster images, points, and 2D solids are not affected by this command. *lweight* is a quick way to define the units (millimeters or inches), set a lineweight, and control the display of lineweights.

If you want lineweights to appear on your plotted drawing but you don't want them to appear on your screen, you can set different lineweights based on an object's color assignment or assign plot styles to the objects.

You can achieve the same results using *-lweight* so all prompts and options appear on the command line.

Initiate Command By

Command: **lweight**
Alias: **lw** or **lineweight**
Format → Lineweight
Status bar: LWT (left-clicking toggles *lineweight* on and off; right-clicking activates the Lineweight Settings dialog box)

Options

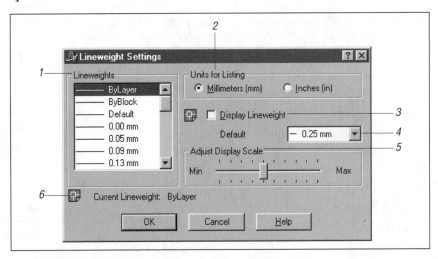

1. **Lineweights.** Displays the various lineweight values including ByLayer, ByBlock, and Default. Default is based on the value assigned to the *lwdefault* system variable. You also can access the lineweight listing with *properties*.

2. **Units for Listing.** Defines the lineweight units in either millimeters or inches. This value is maintained by the *lwunits* system variable.

3. **Display Lineweight.** Determines whether lineweights are displayed on the screen. You may save regeneration and redraw time by turning the line-weight display off. You can toggle this setting on and off by clicking on the

LWT button located on the AutoCAD status bar. This value is maintained by the *lwdisplay* system variable.

4. **Default.** Sets the value for the default lineweight option. This value is maintained by the *lwdefault* system variable.

5. **Adjust Display Scale.** Determines the display scale of lineweights. Since lineweights are displayed in pixels, this setting varies depending on the computer hardware being used. Changing this setting directly affects the Lineweights list.

6. **Current Lineweight.** Lists the current lineweight setting. This value is maintained by the *celweight* system Variable.

Tips & Warnings

- Traces and polylines have their own width settings. When they are assigned a 0 width, they assume the *lweight* setting. When they are assigned a width other than 0, they ignore the *lweight* setting.

- *change, chprop, matchprop,* and *properties* let you change the lineweights assigned to objects.

- When dimensioning, *dimlwd* assigns lineweights to dimension lines and *dmlwe* assigns lineweights to extension lines.

Related Variables   celweight, lwdefault, lwdisplay, lwunits

Associated Commands   layer

'LWUNITS 2000

Maintains the lineweight units in inches or millimeters. This value is set with the *lweight* command.

Initiate Command By

Command: **lwunits**

Options

0   Inches

1   Millimeters

Variable Settings

Initial default:	1
Subsequent default:	Registry file
Value:	Integer

Tips & Warnings

Related Variables   celweight, lwdefault, lwdisplay

Associated Commands   lweight

MAKEPREVIEW (obsolete)   *see RASTERPREVIEW*

MASSPROP   Inquiry toolbar

Evaluates region and solid objects and provides information such as mass, volume, moments of inertia, products of inertia, and radii of gyration.

Initiate Command By
Command: **massprop**
Tools → Inquiry → Mass Properties

Options
    Write analysis to a file? [Yes/No] <N>:

Write analysis to a file
If you answer "yes" an ASCII text file containing the mass properties data is created. The file extension *.mpr* is automatically assigned to that file. You can view this file with a text editor or word processing program. Double-clicking on the file will automatically bring up Notepad if you rename the file by changing its extension to *.txt*.

'MATCHPROP   Standard toolbar

Changes properties assigned to objects based on another object's properties. The properties include color, layer, linetype, linetype scale, lineweight, thickness, plot style, dimension, text, and hatch. *laymch* is a subset of *matchprop* in that it lets you change the layer assigned to objects based on another object's layer. *change*, *chprop*, *hatchedit*, *laycur*, and *properties* let you change an object's properties, but not based on the properties of any other object.

Initiate Command By
Command: **matchprop**
Alias: **ma**
Modify → Match Properties

Options
    Select source object:
    Current active settings: Color Layer Ltype Ltscale Lineweight Thickness
    PlotStyle Text Dim Hatch
    Select destination object(s) or [Settings]:

Select source object
The source object is the object containing the desired property or properties that you want the destination objects to mimic. The source object can reside on any open drawing. There can be only one source.

Current active settings

> The active settings are the settings currently checked in the Property Settings dialog box. All of the values assigned to the source object are acquired by the destination object(s).

Select destination object(s) or [Settings]

> Destination objects are the objects you want to change. The destination objects can reside on any open drawing. You can have one or more destination objects. Entering Settings activates the Property Settings dialog box and lets you decide which properties you want the destination object(s) to inherit from the source object.

The Match Property Settings Dialog Box

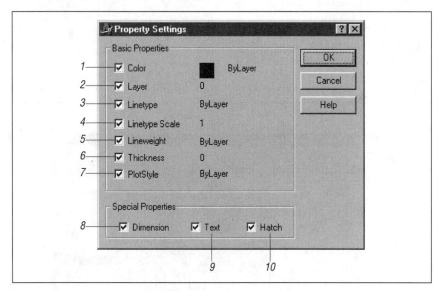

1. **Color.** Not available for OLE objects.

2. **Layer.** Not available for OLE objects.

3. **Linetype.** Not available for OLE objects, attributes, hatches, multiline text, points, and viewports.

4. **Linetype Scale.** Not available for OLE objects, attributes, hatches, multiline text, points, and viewports.

5. **Lineweight.** Available for all objects.

6. **Thickness.** Available for arcs, attributes, circles, lines, points, 2D polylines, regions, text, and traces.

7. **PlotStyle.** Not available for OLE objects and color-dependent (*pstylepolicy* = 1) plot styles.

8. **Dimension.** Available for dimension, leader, and tolerance objects.

9. **Text.** Available for single-line and multiline text objects.

10. **Hatch.** Available for hatch objects.

Tips & Warnings

Any changes made to the Property Settings dialog remain until you exit AutoCAD.

Associated Commands   change, chprop, hatchedit, laycur, laymch, properties

---

MATLIB

Render toolbar

Imports rendering materials from a library file to a drawing and exports rendering materials from the drawing to a library file. You also can access *matlib* from the *rmat* (render materials) dialog box.

Initiate Command By

Command: **matlib**
View → Render → Materials Library

Options

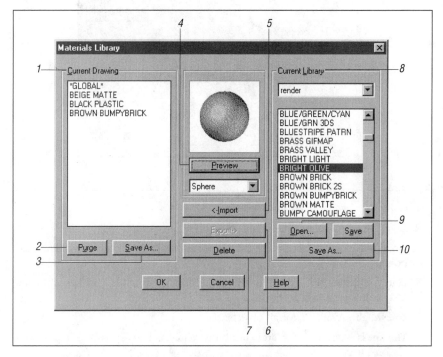

1. **Current Drawing.** Lists the materials currently defined in the drawing. *Global* is the default for objects with no materials attached.

2. **Purge.** Removes all the materials not assigned to objects.

3. **Save As.** Saves the group of materials from the Materials List box to an external file (*.mli*). This file can be read by another AutoCAD file, Auto-Vision, or 3D Studio.

---

4. **Preview**. Shows how materials will be displayed on objects. Only one material can be previewed at a time. Select the material from the Current Drawing list or the Current Library list. You can preview the material and see how it would display on a sphere or cube by selecting either option from the drop-down list located under the Preview button.

5. **<-Import**. Assigns material definitions from the current library to the current drawing.

6. **Export->**. Copies material definitions from the current drawing to the current library.

7. **Delete**. Removes selected materials from the Current Library list and Current Drawing list, including materials assigned to objects. If the material is currently assigned to an object, a warning message is issued. If that material is deleted, any objects assigned to that material default to *Global*. When materials are deleted from the current library and you select OK to exit, you are given one more chance to save changes, discard changes, or cancel from selecting the OK button.

8. **Current Library**. Lets you select a Render library file that has been opened for the drawing. The materials defined in the library file are listed underneath the drop-down list. The default file is *render.mli*.

9. **Open**. Activates the Library File dialog box, which lists any available material library files. *render.mli* is a sample library file that comes with AutoCAD.

10. **Save As**. Saves the Current Library list to a file. You may want to do this if you remove a material or if you import materials from a drawing into the library file. You should copy the *render.mli* file in case it accidentally gets edited.

Tips & Warnings

Once you import materials into your current drawing, you can assign those materials to a layer, to individual objects, or to colors using *rmat*. Use *render* to make sure the render option is set to select photo raytrace or photo real and the Apply Materials box is checked.

Associated Commands   render, rmat

'MAXACTVP 2000mod

Defines the maximum number of viewports that can be active and on.

Initiate Command By

Command: **maxactvp**

Variable Settings

Initial default:	64
Subsequent default:	Last value used in the drawing
Value:	Integer

Tips & Warnings

Regardless of this setting, all viewports will plot. If any viewports do not plot, make sure the viewports were not turned off with *mview* or frozen with *vplayer*.

Associated Commands   mview, viewports, vplayer, vports

'MAXSORT

Sets the maximum number of named items (blocks, dimension styles, layers, layouts, linetypes, text styles, and external references) that are listed alphanumerically or sorted. You can sort up to 200 named items. If you have more items than the *maxsort* value, sorting is disabled.

Initiate Command By

Command: **maxsort**

Variable Settings

Initial default:	200
Subsequent default:	Registry file
Value:	Integer

Tips & Warnings

See "Wildcard Characters" in Chapter 2, *Command Index and Global Topics*, for more information.

'MBUTTONPAN 2000

Determines the functionality of the third button or wheel on your mouse if it supports this feature.

Initiate Command By

Command: **mbuttonpan**

Options

0   Defaults to the AutoCAD menu file for its functionality. The default setting is the object snap shortcut menu.

1   Supports panning when pressing and dragging the third button or wheel of your mouse.

Variable Settings

Initial default:	1
Subsequent default:	Registry file
Value:	Integer

Associated Commands   pan

MEASURE

Marks an object at equal-length segments. The divided object is not physically separated; rather, points, blocks, or external references are placed as markers at each measured increment. You can object-snap to the points with *osnap–node*. You can measure arcs, circles, ellipses, lines, polylines, 3D polylines, and splines. You cannot measure multilines, rays, regions, traces, xlines, wireframes, or solid objects. You can measure only one object at a time.

When measuring circles, the first marker begins at the angle from the center based on the current snap rotation angle. The first marker location for closed polylines is placed on the beginning vertex. If you cannot see the points measuring an object, try adjusting *pdmode* and *pdsize* (you can use *ddptype*) and issuing a *regen.*

Initiate Command By

Command: **measure**
Alias: **me**
Draw → Point → Measure

Options

Select object to measure:
Specify length of segment or [Block]:

length of segment
Segments are measured starting with the endpoint of the object closest to the pick point you use to select the object.

Block
The object is measured with a block or external reference currently defined in the drawing. After providing the block or external reference name, you are prompted for the alignment and the length of each segment. An aligned block is rotated around its insertion point and drawn parallel to the measured object. An unaligned block is drawn with a rotation angle to the object of 0. You cannot change the *X, Y,* and *Z* scale factor of a block or external reference.

Only blocks containing attributes defined as constant are displayed on the drawing. If you try editing the attribute, the message "That block has no edit-able attributes" appears.

Tips & Warnings

Measure markers are placed in the UCS of the object being measured. They are always placed on the object regardless of the current elevation setting.

Related Variables　　　　pdmode, pdsize

Associated Commands　　　block, ddptype, divide, point, xref

Example

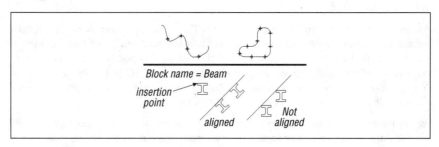

Block name = Beam
insertion point
aligned
Not aligned

'MEASUREINIT

Defines the default drawing units (English or metric), drawing template, hatch pattern and linetype files AutoCAD uses when starting new drawings. This value is set with the Default Settings option from the Startup dialog box. The *measurement* variable defaults to the same value as *measureinit*.

The drawing template is named *acad.dwt* when set to English and *acadiso.dwt* when set to metric. When set to English, the hatch pattern and linetype files are designated by the ANSIHatch and ANSILinetype registry settings; when set to metric, the hatch pattern and linetype files are designated by the ISOHatch and ISOLinetype registry settings.

Initiate Command By

Command: **measureinit**

Options

0   English (inches)

1   Metric (millimeters)

Variable Settings

Initial default:	Varies by country
Subsequent default:	Registry file
Value:	Integer
Related Variables	measurement
Associated Commands	new

'MEASUREMENT

Defines the drawing units (English or metric), hatch pattern, and linetype files AutoCAD uses for an existing drawing. Initially, this variable is set to the same value as *measureinit*. When set to English, the hatch pattern and linetype files are designated by the ANSIHatch and ANSILinetype registry settings; when set to metric, the hatch pattern and linetype files are designated by the ISOHatch and ISOLinetype registry settings.

Initiate Command By

Command: **measurement**

Options

0   English (inches)

1   Metric (millimeters)

Variable Settings

Initial default:	0
Subsequent default:	Last value used in the drawing
Value:	Integer

Related Variables	measureinit

MENU

Activates the Select Menu File dialog box and lets you load and display a menu file in the current drawing. Menu files define the pull-down, shortcut, screen, tablet, toolbar, tooltips, and menu groups. Regardless of your current menu file setting, you can always access all the commands by typing them on your keyboard.

Set the screen menu visibility by checking the Display Screen Menu box from the *options* Display tab. Changing this setting affects all drawings. You can have the screen menu change to match commands you type at the keyboard or have the menu remain unchanged until you select another command from the screen. You set this feature with the *menuctl* variable.

Initiate Command By

Command: **menu**

Tips & Warnings

- If you want to load the original default menu file, make sure you select *.mnu* for your Files of Type option and search for *acad.mnu*. Beware that loading this menu will overwrite any changes you made to your toolbar buttons and pull-down menus.

- If *filedia* is set to 1, a dialog box is activated; if *filedia* is set to 0, you are prompted on the command line. When *filedia* is set to 0, or off, entering a tilde (~) on the command line temporarily activates the dialog box. When *filedia* is set to 0, you can disable all menus by typing a period (.) at the command line.

Related Variables	filedia, menuctl, menuecho, menuname, tooltips
Associated Commands	expresstools, menuload, menuunload, shortcutmenu, tablet, toolbar

'MENUCTL

Determines whether the screen menu swaps to the same command screen entered from the keyboard.

Initiate Command By

Command: **menuctl**

Options

0   Screen menu does not follow commands entered from the keyboard.

1   Screen menu follows commands entered from the keyboard.

Variable Settings

Initial default:	1
Subsequent default:	Registry file
Value:	Integer
Associated Commands	menu

'MENUECHO

Controls the frequency and type of prompts provided at the command line. This is often used by programmers and third-party developers as a way to control the information displayed on the command line.

Initiate Command By

Command: **menuecho**

Options

Menuecho is bit-coded, and its value is the sum of the following:

0   Normal, all menu items and command prompts are shown.

1   Suppresses echo of menu items.

2   Suppresses printing of command prompts during menu use.

4   Disables ^P toggle of menu item echoing

8   Debugging aid for Diesel macros by displaying the input/output text Strings.

Variable Settings

Initial default:	0
Subsequent default:	Initial default
Value:	Integer
Associated Commands	menu

MENULOAD

see MENUUNLOAD

'MENUNAME

Maintains the current menu group name. If the current menu has no menu group name, then the base menu name and its location (drive/folder) are maintained by this variable. This variable is set with the *menu* and *menuload* commands.

Initiate Command By

    Command: **menuname**

Variable Settings

Initial default:	AutoCAD support folder, read-only
Subsequent default:	Application header
Value:	String
Associated Commands	menu, menuload

MENUUNLOAD/MENULOAD

menuunload unloads partial menu files from an existing base menu file. *menuload* loads partial menu files to an existing base menu file. Each base menu file and partial menu file has an associated menu group name. From each menu group you can retrieve the individual pull-down and toolbar menus residing in its associated menu file.

Initiate Command By

    Command: **menuunload** and **menuload**
    Tools → Customize Menus

Options

The Menu Customization dialog contains the Menu Groups and Menu Bar tabs, which are covered in detail in this section.

The Menu Groups Tab

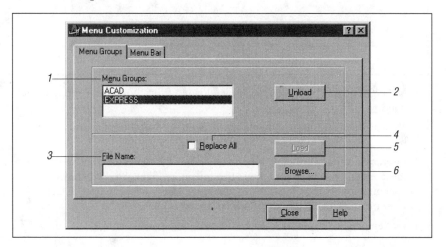

1. **Menu Groups**. Lists the menu groups currently loaded.

2. **Unload**. Removes the menu groups highlighted in the Menu Groups content window.

3. **File Name**. Allows you to enter the name of the menu file for loading with the Load button. When you want to load the original AutoCAD menu settings, make sure you select *.mnu* for your Files of Type option and search for *acad.mnu*, using the Select Menu File dialog box. Loading this menu will overwrite any changes you made to the toolbar buttons.

4. **Replace All**. Unloads all files listed in the Menu Groups content window when loading a new menu file.

5. **Load**. Retrieves the file listed in the File Name text box.

6. **Browse**. Lets you select a menu file to load using the Select Menu File dialog box.

The Menu Bar Tab

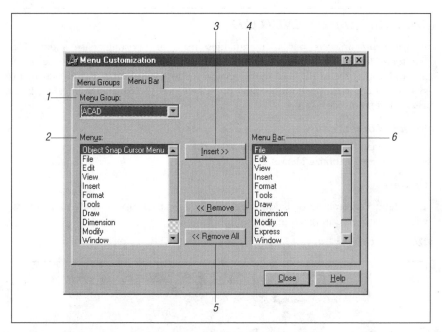

1. **Menu Group**. Displays the menu files loaded from the Menu Groups content window.

2. **Menus**. Lists the pull-down menus defined in the current Menu Group list box.

3. **Insert >>**. Imports a highlighted menu from the Menus content window into the Menu Bar content window. If a menu is highlighted in the Menu Bar content window then the inserted menu is placed before the highlighted item. If no menu is highlighted, the inserted menu is placed at the top of the list.

4. **<< Remove**. Removes selected items from the Menu Bar content window.

5. **<< Remove All**. Removes all items from the Menu Bar content window.

6. **Menu Bar**. Lists the pull-down menus currently loaded in AutoCAD.

Tips & Warnings

If *filedia* is set to 1, a dialog box is activated; if *filedia* is set to 0, you are prompted on the command line. When *filedia* is set to 0, or off, entering a tilde (~) on the command line temporarily activates the dialog box.

Related Variables filedia, tooltips

Associated Commands menu, toolbar

MINSERT

Inserts multiple copies of a block in a rectangular pattern. *minsert* is a combination of the *insert* and *array* (rectangular) commands, but it takes up less memory. All the blocks making up the array are considered one object, and they cannot be individually edited or exploded.

Initiate Command By

Command: **minsert**

Options

```
Enter block name or [?]:
Specify insertion point or [Scale/X/Y/Z/Rotate/PScale/PX/PY/PZ/PRotate]:
Enter X scale factor, specify opposite corner, or [Corner/XYZ] <1>:
Enter Y scale factor <use X scale factor>:
Specify rotation angle <0>:
Enter number of rows (---) <1>:
Enter number of columns (|||) <1>:
Enter distance between rows or specify unit cell (---):
Specify distance between columns (|||):
```

Enter block name
Allows you to enter the name of a block or the name of another drawing file.

? Lists the names of blocks defined in the current drawing. The default, an asterisk, displays a sorted listing of all named blocks. You can use any of the wildcard options to create a more specific list.

~ Displays the Select Drawing File dialog box. This method limits you to drawing files (*.dwg*) and drawing interchange (*.dxf*) files. It does not let you select blocks located in the current drawing.

After entering a block name, you receive the standard insert and array command prompts.

Tips & Warnings

You can array at an angle with the *minsert* command. In order to do this, you must change your snap rotation angle, define a UCS at the desired angle, or use the *rotate* command once the blocks have been *inserted*.

Associated Commands array, block, insert

MIRROR

Modify toolbar

Reflects a copy of selected objects. You can have text remain right side up if the variable *mirrtext* is set to 0. However, text and constant attributes assigned to blocks are always mirrored, and associative dimensions are never mirrored.

Initiate Command By

Command: **mirror**
Alias: **mi**
Modify → Mirror

Options

```
Select objects:
Specify first point of mirror line:
Specify second point of mirror line:
Delete source objects? [Yes/No] <N>:
```

Specify first point of mirror line
Designate the first point on an axis about which the objects are mirrored.

Specify second point of mirror line
Designate the second point on an axis about which the objects are mirrored.

Tips & Warnings

- Mirroring viewport objects in paper space has no effect on model space views or objects.

- The *grips* command has its own mirror routine that also lets you create multiple copies.

Related Variables   grips, mirrtext

Associated Commands   insert, mirror3d

Example

```
Command:  Mirror
Select objects:  Select objects
Specify first point of mirror line:  Pick point 1
Specify second point of mirror line:  Pick point 2
Delete source objects? [Yes/No] <N>:  Press Enter
```

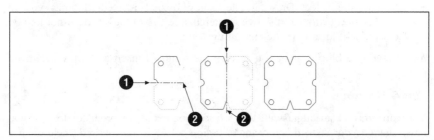

MIRROR3D

Mirror3d reflects objects about a specified plane.

Initiate Command By

Command: **mirror3d**
Modify → 3D Operation → Mirror 3D

Options

```
Specify first point of mirror plane (3 points) or
[Object/Last/Zaxis/View/XY/YZ/ZX/3points] <3points>:
Specify second point on mirror plane:
Specify third point on mirror plane:
Delete source objects? [Yes/No] <N>:
```

Object

The mirroring plane is the plane of an AutoCAD planar object. The planar object can be a polyline, arc, or circle.

Last

The object(s) are reflected using the last used mirroring plane.

Zaxis

The mirroring plane is defined by a point on the plane and a point on the *Z* axis of the plane.

View

The mirroring plane is aligned to the viewing plane of the current viewport through a point.

XY, YZ, ZX

The mirroring plane is aligned with one of the standard planes (*XY, YZ,* or *ZX*) through a specified point.

3points

The mirroring plane is defined by three points on a plane.

Related Variables	grips, mirrtext
Associated Commands	mirror

'MIRRTEXT

Determines whether mirrored text is reflected or retains the same text direction. Text and constant attributes assigned to blocks are always mirrored, and associative dimensions are never mirrored.

Initiate Command By

Command: **mirrtext**

Options

0   Text direction remains unchanged.

1   Text is mirrored.

Variable Settings

Initial default:	1
Subsequent default:	Last value used in the drawing
Value:	Integer

Related Variables	grips
Associated Commands	mirror

MKLTYPE 2000

Creates custom linetypes. Linetypes are a series of repeating lines, dots, spaces, shapes, and text objects. You create the first series of objects to make up the linetype, and once the linetype is created, it automatically repeats that pattern. When this command is completed, the linetype is automatically loaded into the drawing.

Initiate Command By

Command: **mkltype**
Express → Tools → Make Linetype

Options

```
Enter linetype name:
Enter linetype description:
Specify starting point for line definition:
Specify ending point for line definition:
Select objects:
Linetype "XXX" created and loaded.
```

MKLTYPE—Select Linetype File dialog box

Enter the name of a file and folder location that will contain the new linetype. The file's extension is *.lin*. One file can contain many linetype definitions. If you use the name of an existing linetype file, you will receive a warning that the file already exists and you are asked if you want to replace the file. If you answer "yes," you do not actually replace the file; instead, you append to the file. It is easier to manage one or just a few files containing your custom linetype definitions than to create a new linetype file for each customized linetype.

Enter linetype name; Enter linetype description

Depending on *extnames*, each linetype name and description can contain up to 255 characters.

Select objects:

Lines, polylines, points, shapes, and text can be used to create linetypes. Points are always shown as dots regardless of your *pdmode* setting. Shapes must reside in the current UCS plane and cannot be mirrored. Create shapes with *mkshape*. Linetypes cannot start with an empty space. If you define the beginning of a linetype with an empty space, a dot is automatically placed at the start point.

Tips & Warnings

- If *filedia* is set to 1 a dialog box is activated; if *filedia* is set to 0, you are prompted on the command line. Entering a tilde (~) on the command line temporarily activates the File dialog box when it is set to 0.

- Be careful when using shapes as part of the linetype definition. Shapes are external to the drawing file and must always accompany the drawing. If you are sharing files containing shapes with others, make sure they have access to the shape files.

Related Variables
filedia

Associated Commands
expresstools, linetype

Example

```
Command: Mkshape
Enter the name of the shape: Instr
Enter resolution <128>: Press Enter
Specify insertion base point: Pick point 1
Select objects: Select all of the objects
Select objects: Press Enter
Determining geometry extents...Done.
Building coord lists...Done.
Formating coords...Done.
Writing new shape...Done.
Compiling shape/font description file
Compilation successful.
Output file C:\Program Files\ACAD2000\P&ID.shx
contains 123 bytes.
Shape "INSTR" created.
Use the SHAPE command to place shapes in your drawing.
```

Insertion base point

```
Command: Mkltype
Enter linetype name: Instr
Enter linetype description: Instrumentation line
Specify starting point for line definition: Pick point 1
Specify ending point for line definition: Pick point 2
Select objects: Select the Instr shape
Select objects: Press Enter
Linetype "INSTR" created and loaded.
```

*References
M–N*

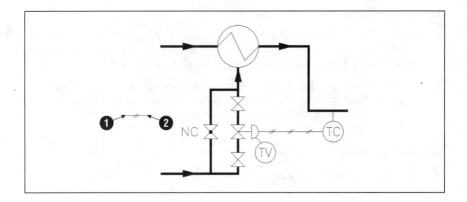

MKSHAPE 2000

Creates shape definitions that can be used as alternatives to blocks and can be part of a complex linetype definition. When this command is completed, the shape is automatically loaded into the drawing. Use the *shape* command to insert the shapes into your drawing. Shapes are external to the drawing file and must always accompany the drawing. If you are sharing files containing shapes with others, make sure they have access to the shape files.

Initiate Command By

Command: **mkshape**
Express → Tools → Make Shape

Options

```
Enter the name of the shape:
Enter resolution <128>:
Specify insertion base point:
Select objects:
Determining geometry extents...Done.
Building coord lists...Done.
Formating coords...-Done.
Writing new shape...Done.
Compiling shape/font description file
Compilation successful.
Output file C:\Program Files\ACAD2000\XXX.shx
contains 95 bytes.
Shape "XXX" created.
Use the SHAPE command to place shapes in your drawing.
```

MKSHAPE—Select Shape File dialog box

Enter the name of a file and folder location that will contain the new shape. The file's extension is *.shp*. One file can contain many shape definitions. If you use the name of an existing shape file, you will receive a warning that the file already exists and you will be asked if you want to replace the file. If you answer "yes," you do not actually replace the file; instead, you append to the file. It is easier to manage one or just a few files containing your custom shape definitions than to create a new shape file for each customized shape.

Enter resolution <128>:

    Define a resolution value for arcs, circles and ellipses. The larger the number, the more accurate the resolution, but it also can slow down the system's performance. Values range from 8 to 23,767.

Select objects:

    Lines, polylines, arcs, circles, and ellipses can be used to create shapes.

Tips & Warnings

- You can only perform an object-snap to the insertion point of shapes.

- If *filedia* is set to 1, a dialog box is activated; if *filedia* is set to 0, you are prompted on the command line. When *filedia* is set to 0, or off, entering a tilde (~) on the command line temporarily activates the dialog box.

Related Variables	filedia
Associated Commands	expresstools, mkshape, shape
Example	See MKLTYPE.

MLEDIT

Modify II toolbar

Edits multilines (mlines). *mledit* creates various cross and tee intersections, produces corner joints, adds and deletes vertices, creates a break in one or all elements of a multiline, and patches a multiline broken by one of the other *mledit* options. Create multilines with *mline*. Customize multilines with *mlstyle*. *explode* converts mlines to lines.

Initiate Command By

    Command: **mledit**
    Modify → Multiline

Options

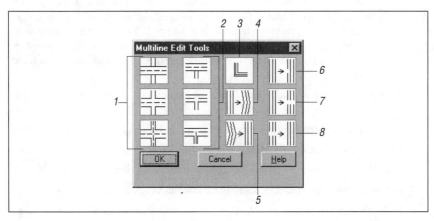

1. **Closed, Open, or Merged Cross.**

   Intersecting mlines

   Creates a closed, open, or merged cross intersection from two inter-secting mlines. For Closed, the first mline elements are broken to the exterior elements of the second mline; the second mline elements are left intact. For Open, the exterior elements of both mlines are broken; the first selected mline's interior elements are broken at the intersection; the interior elements of the second selected mline remain intact. For Merged, the exterior elements of both mlines are broken at their intersection; the interior elements of both mlines remain intact.

   Nonintersecting mlines

   For Closed, extends the first selected mline to the closest element of the second selected mline. Breaks all of the elements of the first selected mline based on the projection of the second selected mline. The second selected mline remains unmodified. For Open, extends the first selected mline to the closest element of the second selected mline. An opening is created on the exterior elements of the second selected mline. The first selected mline interior elements remain in their original location. For Merged, extends the first selected mline to the closest element of the second selected mline. An opening is created on the exterior elements of the second selected mline. The first selected mline interior elements remain in their original location.

2. **Closed, Open, or Merged Tee.**

   Intersecting mlines

   For Closed, Open, and Merged, trims the first selected mline to the exterior element of the second selected mline so that the two do not cross over. The first selected mline must be an open mline. For Open, an opening is created on the second selected mline exterior element.

   Nonintersecting mlines

   For Closed, Open, and Merged, extends the first selected mline to the closest element of the second selected mline. The first selected mline must be an open mline. For Open, an opening is created on the second selected mline exterior element. For Merged, an opening is created on the second selected mline exterior element. The interior elements of the first selected mline meet the interior elements of the second selected mline.

3. **Corner Joint.** Creates a corner joint by extending or trimming two open mlines.

4. **Add Vertex.** Creates new vertex points that can be modified with grip editing.

5. **Delete Vertex.** Removes vertex points.

6. **Cut Single.** Creates an opening on any element of an mline.

7. **Cut All.** Creates an opening on all the elements of an mline.

8. **Weld All.** Repairs openings created with the *mledit* command.

Associated Commands   mline, mlstyle

MLINE
Draw toolbar

Creates multiple parallel lines and arcs that are fused together and act as one object. Each mline is also known as an element. You can create your own mline definitions containing up to 16 parallel lines and arcs and preset the width (offset distance), color, linetype, and endcaps with *mlstyle*. Edit mlines with *mledit*.

Initiate Command By
Command: **mline**
Alias: **ml**
Draw → Multiline

Options
```
Current settings: Justification = Top, Scale = 1.00,
Style = STANDARD
Specify start point or [Justification/Scale/STyle]:
Specify next point:
Specify next point or [Undo]:
Specify next point or [Close/Undo]:
```

Justification
Determines the offset direction for the mlines. This value is maintained by the *cmljust* variable.

Top
Draws mlines to the right of your pick points.

Zero
Sets your pick points as the centerline for mlines.

Bottom
Draws mlines to the left of your pick points.

Scale
Determines the width of mlines and acts as a multiplier to the current *mlstyle* offset settings. This value is maintained by the *cmscale* variable.

Style
Changing this value changes the *mlstyle* default setting. You cannot change the *mlstyle* values assigned to existing mlines nor change them to another multiline style. See *mlstyle* for more detailed information. This value is maintained by the *cmlstyle* variable.

Undo
Entering U at the "Specify next point" prompt undoes the last mline segment and returns you to the previous point.

Close
Entering C at the "Specify next point" prompt closes the mline segments created during the command. It connects the last endpoint to the start point.

References M-N

Tips & Warnings

- You can create parallel lines, arcs, polylines, rays, and xlines with the *offset*, *copy*, and *grip* editing commands.

- You cannot convert lines to multilines, but you can convert multilines to lines using *explode*.

Related Variables	cmljust, cmlscale, cmlstyle
Associated Commands	mledit, mlstyle
Example	See MLSTYLE.

MLSTYLE

Lets you create your own multiline (*mline*) definitions. These definitions can contain up to 16 parallel lines, and you can preset the width (offset distance), color, linetype, and endcaps. The lines making up an *mlstyle* are called "elements." Multiline styles often are used to represent streets and walls. Since you can't use arcs (except as endcaps), their usage is limited.

Initiate Command By

Command: **mlstyle**
Format → Multiline Style

Options

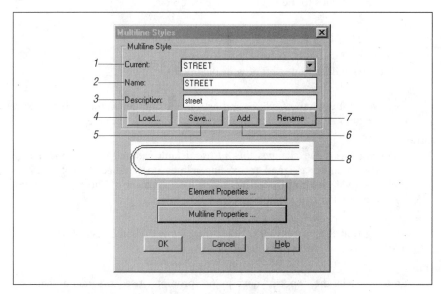

1. **Current.** Displays the current *mlstyle* default used when you construct a multi-line. Changing this value changes the mline style default setting. This value is maintained by the *cmlstyle* variable.

2. **Name.** Displays the current *mlstyle* default, which can be saved or renamed, or you can enter the name of a new mlstyle. Unlike other named objects, multiline style names cannot exceed 31 characters.

3. **Description.** Allows you to optionally assign a description to new mlstyles.

4. **Load.** Loads a file containing an mlstyle definition and makes it current. The file's extension is *.mln.*

5. **Save.** Saves the mlstyle definition listed in the Name text box to a file. The file's extension is *.mln.*

6. **Add.** Saves the Element Properties and the Multiline Properties settings to the mlstyle listed in the Name text box and adds the definition to the Current list box. Once you select Add, you cannot modify the mlstyle.

7. **Rename.** Renames the mlstyle listed in the Current list box to the name listed in the Name text box.

8. **Current mline display.** Graphically displays the mline style based on the element and multiline properties options.

The Element Properties Dialog Box

The Element Properties dialog box lets you define each of the mline elements, including offset distance, color, and linetype.

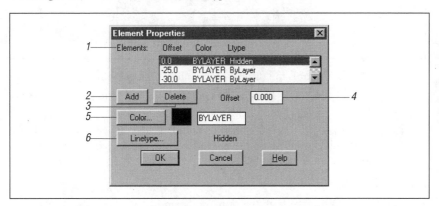

1. **Elements.** Lists all the elements defining the current mlstyle.

2. **Add.** Creates a new element based on the value displayed in the Offset edit box.

3. **Delete.** Deletes the element highlighted in the Elements list box. At least one element must be defined at all times.

4. **Offset.** Determines the offset for the elements. Entering a number and pressing Enter overwrites the highlighted element. Entering a number and picking Add creates a new element.

5. **Color.** Determines a color for the element highlighted in the Elements list box. For more detailed information, see the *color* command.

6. **Linetype.** Determines a linetype for the element highlighted in the Elements list box. Regardless of the linetype setting, all the lines appear continuous in

the current mline display box until you actually create the mline. If you draw mlines containing linetypes other than continuous and they aren't displayed, check your *ltscale* and *celtscale* variables settings. If you change those settings, make sure you regenerate the drawing to see any changes. For more detailed information, see the *linetype* command.

The Multiline Properties Dialog Box

The Multiline Properties dialog box lets you control the display of segment joints, endcaps, and background colors for all the elements of an mlstyle.

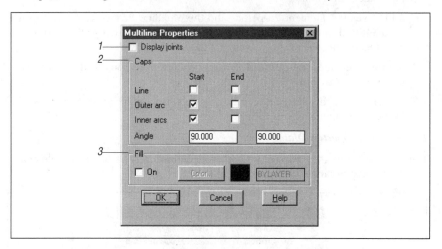

1. **Display joints.** Controls the display of the mline segment joints.

2. **Caps.** Controls the angle and type of endcaps assigned to the start and end of the mlstyle.

3. **Fill.** Determines whether multilines are solid filled and defines the color. If you set the fill on and it isn't displayed on the screen, check *fillmode* and make sure it is on.

Tips & Warnings

- Delete unused mlstyles with the *purge* command.

- You can't modify elements and properties in any existing mlstyle if your drawing has any multilines referencing that style. You can't change the mlstyle assigned to an existing mline with another mlstyle.

Related Variables   cmlstyle, fillmode

Associated Commands   mledit, mline

MOCORO   Express Standard toolbar

Lets you move, copy, rotate, and scale selected objects. To do only one of those functions, use the individual *move*, *copy*, *rotate*, or *scale* command. Grip editing lets you move, rotate, stretch, scale, and mirror, and create multiple copies simultaneously. Use *align* if you plan to move and rotate the same group of objects. If *pickfirst* is set to 1, you can first select the objects and then use this command, because that *pickfirst* setting suppresses the "Select objects" prompt. See *expresstools* if the Express pull-down menu and toolbars aren't available.

Initiate Command By
Command: **mocoro**
Express → Modify → Move Copy Rotate

Options
```
Base point:
[Move/Copy/Rotate/Scale/Base/Undo]<eXit>:
```

Base
Lets you define a reference point to which objects are copied, moved, rotated or scaled. You can change the base point as often as required.

Undo
Undoes only the last operation within the command. Using *u* (undo) after you end the command will undo every change you made.

Related Variables	pickfirst
Associated Commands	copy, expresstools, grips, move, rotate, scale

---

MODEL 2000

Returns you to model space when layout space is active. This is the same as selecting the MODEL button located on the status bar or setting *tilemode* to 1. Model space is where you create and dimension your drawing. Paper space is used to compose, add notes, and plot 2D and 3D drawings. When you are in model space, paper space objects are ignored and invisible. Model space and paper space each retain its own grid, limits, snap, UCS icon, and view settings.

Initiate Command By
Command: **model**

Related Variables	tilemode
Associated Commands	mspace, pspace

---

model space   *see MSPACE*

'MODEMACRO

Lets you enter text or special text strings, written in the Diesel macro language, on the status bar. If you want to remove the text, enter a period (.). For more detailed information, see AutoCAD's *Customization Guide*, found in the Help menu.

Initiate Command By
Command: **modemacro**

Variable Settings

Initial default:	None
Subsequent default:	Initial default
Value:	String

MOVE

Modify toolbar

Relocates objects anywhere in 2D or 3D space. If *pickfirst* is set to 1, you can first select the objects and then use the *move* command, because the *pickfirst* setting suppresses the "Select objects" prompt. Grip editing has its own move routine that lets you create multiple copies simultaneously; *align* lets you move and rotate the same group of objects; *mocoro* lets you move, copy, rotate, and scale objects.

Initiate Command By

Command: **move**
Alias: **m**
Modify → Move

Options

```
Select objects:
Specify base point or displacement:
Specify second point of displacement or <use first point as displacement>:
```

Specify base point/Specify second point of displacement

Specify a base point by defining a point on the drawing showing from where you want to move. Specify the second point by defining the destination. If you accidentally press Enter at the "Specify second point of displacement" prompt, your objects could end up out of view. This happens because *move* uses the *X*, *Y*, *Z* base point coordinates as displacement distances.

displacement/use first point as displacement

Enter the distance for *X*, *Y*, *Z* or press Enter at the "Use first point as displacement" prompt.

Tips & Warnings

• If you want to move objects to another layer, use *change*, *chprop*, *matchprop*, *properties*, or the drop-down layer list.

• Use the move option of *solidedit* if you want to move 3D solid planar faces.

Related Variables	grips, pickfirst
Associated Commands	align, mocoro

Example

```
Command: move
Select objects:  Select the circle
Select objects:  Press Enter
Specify base point or displacement:  Pick point 1
Specify second point of displacement or
<use first point as displacement>:  Pick point 2
```

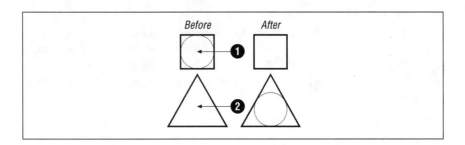

Before   After

MPEDIT

Lets you edit one or more polylines at the same time. This is similar to *pedit*, but *pedit* lets you edit only one polyline at a time and its individual vertices. See *pedit* for more detailed information.

Initiate Command By

Command: **mpedit**
Express → Modify → Multiple Pedit

Options

```
Convert Lines and Arcs to polylines? [Yes/No] <Yes>:
Enter an option [Open/Close/Join/Width/Fit/Spline/
Decurve/Ltype gen/eXit] <eXit>:
```

Convert Lines and Arcs to polylines? [Yes/No] <Yes>:
If lines, arcs, and polylines are all part of the selection set, you could have all the lines and arcs remain as they were created or convert them to polylines. Even if your selection set contained only polylines, you will still receive this message.

Enter an option [Open/Close/Join/Width/Fit/Spline/Decurve/Ltype gen/eXit] <eXit>:
See the *pedit* command for explanations of these options.

Related Variables   plinegen, splframe, splinesegs, splinetype, surftype

Associated Commands   expresstools, pedit, pline

MSLIDE

Creates a snapshot of your current screen display. This snapshot becomes a new file with the extension *.sld*. The slide is of the current viewport and is independent of the drawing file from which it was created. You can view any slide file, regardless of the drawing you are currently editing, using the *vslide* command. Since slide files do not retain any object data, viewing slides occurs at *redraw* speed.

Initiate Command By

Command: **mslide**

Tips & Warnings

- If *filedia* is set to 1, a dialog box is activated; if *filedia* is set to 0, you are prompted on the command line. When *filedia* is set to 0, or off, entering a tilde (~) on the command line temporarily activates the dialog box.

- Making slides of shaded and rendered objects captures only the wireframe image.

Related Variables	filedia
Associated Commands	script, vslide

MSPACE

(Model Space) Switches from drawing in paper space to model space. This command is available when layout space is active and at least one viewport is available. Viewports are created with the *mview* command. Model space is used to create and dimension your model. Paper space is used to annotate, compose, and plot drawings. Model space and paper space each retain its own grid, limits, snap, UCS icon, and views. You cannot edit objects created in model space while in paper space and vice versa. Plotting in model space plots only the current viewport.

You access model space by creating floating viewports with the *mview* command. Within each of these viewports, you can assign a drawing scale factor and control layer visibility (*vplayer*). If you are in model space and you want to work in another viewport, you can double-click inside the viewport border. If you are in paper space and you want to activate a model space viewport, double-click inside the viewport border, type mspace at the command line, or click on the word "PAPER" located on the status bar.

Paper space allows you to move the viewports and position them for plotting. Titleblocks, legends, and notes generally are placed in paper space. If you are in model space and want to activate paper space, double-click outside of the view-port border, type pspace at the command line, or click on the word "MODEL" located on the status bar.

Initiate Command By

Command: **mspace**
Alias: **ms**
Status bar: MODEL (toggles model space on and off)

Tips & Warnings

Copy objects from model space to paper space by using *copyclip* or *copybase*, or by creating a block. Move objects using *cutclip*.

Related Variables	tilemode
Associated Commands	layout, mview, pspace, ucsicon, vplayer

MSTRETCH

Express Standard toolbar

Lets you stretch multiple objects by creating one or more crossing windows and crossing polygons. This is similar to *stretch* except that *stretch* lets you define only one crossing window or one crossing polygon. See *stretch* for more detailed information.

Initiate Command By

Command: **stretch**
Express → Modify → Multiple Entity Stretch

Associated Commands   expresstools, stretch

-MTEXT 2000   *see MTEXT*

MTEXT 2000mod   Draw toolbar

Creates multiple lines of text that are treated as one object. The text is placed inside a boundary where you specify the width and alignment. This command is similar to *text* and *dtext* except that you can assign different properties (height, color, fonts) to individual characters, multiple lines of text are treated as one object, you can control line spacing, and you have immediate access to the *find* (find and replace) command.

You can convert multiline text into single-line text using *explode*. Once text is exploded, each line of text is considered a separate object. You can convert single-line text into multiline text using *txt2mtxt*. Exploding multiline text on characters, words, or lines that contain various formatting features causes that text to break up into multiple objects. You can disable the dialog box by using the *-mtext* (*-t*) command, but only a portion of the *mtext* options are offered on the command line.

When using the same block of text for multiple drawings, save time by *wblocking* the text and *inserting* it into the other drawings. You also can import ASCII text from a separate file with the *mtext* command.

Base your text height on the scale in which you plan to plot the drawing. The text height you specify in AutoCAD should be the height of plotted text multiplied by the plot scale factor.

When creating macros or LISP routines that request text, make sure you use the *text* command. This is because you can evaluate text strings (*texteval*) with the *text* command but not with *mtext* or *dtext*.

When the Multiline Text Editor dialog box is active, you can globally change text case with the shortcut menu. Highlight the text, right-click, and choose Change Case.

text and *dtext* create single-line text; *attdef* creates attribute text; *arctext* creates text along an arc; and *rtext* creates remote text. You can assign a border or mask text with *masktext*.

Initiate Command By	Command: **mtext**
	Alias: **mt** or **t**
	Draw → Text → Multiline Text

Options

```
Current text style:  "Standard"  Text height:  0.2000
Specify first corner:
Specify opposite corner or [Height/Justify/Line spacing/Rotation/Style/
Width]:
```

Specify first corner, Specify opposite corner

Allows you to determine the first and second corners of the mtext boundary box. The width of the boundary box determines the text line length; the length of the boundary box is not used. Regardless of the location of the "opposite corner," text remains right side up.

Height

Determines the default text height. You also can define the text height once the Multiline Text Editor dialog box is active.

Justify

Determines how the mtext boundary box is aligned to the insertion point and determines text justification inside the boundary box. You also can define the justification once the Multiline Text Editor dialog box is active.

Line spacing

Determines the distance between each line of text. You also can define the line spacing once the Multiline Text Editor dialog box is active. This value is stored with the *tspacefac* variable.

Rotation

Determines the rotation of the mtext boundary box. You also can define the rotation once the Multiline Text Editor dialog box is active.

Style

Determines the default style (font and formatting characteristics) for new mtext. Text styles are created with the *style* command. You also can define the style once the Multiline Text Editor dialog box is active.

Width

Defines the width of the boundary box. You also can determine the width by selecting a second corner point. You can redefine the width by using the Multiline Text Editor dialog box or by using the grip editing features when you have completed the *mtext* command.

The Multiline Text Editor Dialog Box

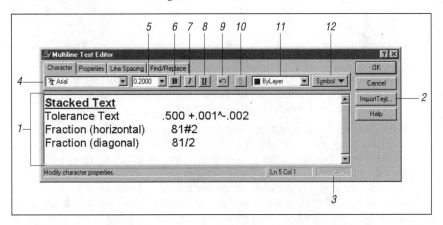

There are four tabs that help you set up the text height, font, color, and so on. Each of these tabs have the following features in common:

1. **Text box.** Displays the text. Entering and editing the text is similar to other word processor programs. If you want to change the number of characters that fit onto each line, wait until you end the command and then use *grips* to change the line length.

2. **Import Text.** Imports ASCII text files and Rich Text Format (RTF) files. These files usually have the file extension *.txt* and *.rtf.* Most programs let you save text in either of those two formats with the Save As option. You also can import text by picking and dragging a text file (*.txt*) from the Windows Explorer program into your AutoCAD drawing session. Make sure that the command line is empty when using this method.

3. **AutoCAPS.** Toggles the caps lock on and off.

The Character Tab

The options available from the Character tab let you assign different properties or characteristics to each letter, word, or line of text.

4. **Font drop-down list.** Determines the font for new text or highlighted text. You can first select the font and then enter the text, or you can highlight existing text and select a font. The default font is based on the current *style* setting.

5. **Height.** Determines the height for new text or highlighted text. You can first define the height and then enter the text, or you can highlight existing text and enter a text height. Initially the drop-down list shows only the default height. Once you enter different heights, they also appear in the drop-down list. The default height is based on the current *style* setting. If that style's text height is set to 0, the default height is based on the *textsize* variable.

6. **B.** Determines whether new or highlighted text is bold. This is a toggle button and it is available for only some of the TrueType fonts. When the B is light gray, it is unavailable.

7. **I.** Determines whether new or highlighted text is italic. This is a toggle button and is only available for some of the TrueType fonts. When the I is light gray it is unavailable.

8. **U.** Determines whether new or highlighted text is underlined. This is a toggle button and is available for all fonts.

9. **Undo/Redo.** Undoes or redoes previous commands. Clicking once on the button reverses the effects of the last command, and clicking a second time reverses that action. You also can press Ctrl-Z.

10. **Stack.** Creates stacked text. Stacked text is often used for fractions or for text that you want vertically aligned. There are three different ways to display stacked text. Use the caret (^) symbol if you want text representing left-justified tolerance values; use the forward slash (/) if you want center-justified text separated by a horizontal bar; or use the pound sign (#) if you want text displayed as a fraction separated by a diagonal bar. Once one of these symbols is placed within your text, select the text you want stacked and pick the Stack button. Unstack text by selecting the text you want unstacked and pick the Stack button again. *tstackalign* controls the vertical alignment of stacked text. You can edit stacked text with the Stack Properties dialog box. Activate this dialog box from within the Multiline Text Editor by right-clicking on the stacked text.

11. **Color.** Determines the color for new text or highlighted text. You can first select the color and then enter the text, or you can highlight existing text and select a color.

12. **Symbol.** Enters special symbols or a nonbreaking space at the cursor position. These symbols include the degree symbol (°), diameter symbol (Ø), and plus/minus tolerance symbol (±). Choosing Other displays the Character Map dialog box. This dialog box displays the entire character set for each font. To display one or more of these characters with your text, double-click on each character or click once on each character and pick the Select button. This places the character on the Characters to Copy edit box. Highlight the characters listed in the edit box and pick the Copy button. Close the dialog box, pick an insertion point in your mtext dialog box, right-click, and select Paste.

The Properties Tab

The options available from the Properties tab let you assign the same properties or characteristics to all the text.

Style

Assigns a style to all of the text. See *style* for more detailed information.

Justification

Determines how the mtext boundary box is aligned to the insertion point and determines text justification inside the boundary box.

Width

Defines the width or length of the boundary box. An easier method is to use the grip editing features once you have completed the *mtext* command.

Rotation

Determines the rotation of the mtext boundary.

The Line Spacing Tab

This tab determine the distance between lines of text. This value is stored with the *tspacefac* variable.

Tips & Warnings

- Edit mtext strings with *ddedit, mtprop,* and *properties.* Edit properties assigned to mtext with *matchprop, mtprop,* or *properties.*

- You can assign your own text editor to the *mtext* command by modifying the *mtexted* variable, and you can use the standard Windows control keys for cutting and pasting text to and from the clipboard. Check your spelling with the *spell* command.

- If all your text appears as empty boxes, *qtext* may be turned on. To change this, turn *qtext* off and regenerate the drawing.

Related Variables	mtexted, textfill, textqlty, textsize, textstyle, tspacefac, tspacetype, tstackalign, tstacksize
Associated Commands	arctext, dtext, mtprop, rtext, spell, style, text, txt2mtxt

Example

The text shown in the previous dialog box would create the following text.

Stacked Text	
Tolerance Text	$.500\ ^{+.001}_{-.002}$
Fraction (horizontal)	$8\frac{1}{2}$
Fraction (diagonal)	$8\frac{1}{2}$

'MTEXTED

Assigns a text editor to any command that creates or editing multiline text objects. You can change the text editor by selecting the "Text editor, dictionary, and font file names" option from the *options* Files tab.

Initiate Command By

Command: **mtexted**

Variable Settings

Initial default:	Internal text editor
Subsequent default:	Registry file
Value:	String
Associated Commands	ddedit, mtext, options, preferences

MTPROP

Allows you to edit multiline text objects by activating the Multiline Text Editor dialog box. You also can access this dialog box using *ddedit* and *propterties*. See *mtext* for more detailed information.

Initiate Command By
Command: **mtprop**

Associated Commands
ddedit, mtext, properties

MULTIPLE

Causes most commands to repeat. Type the word **multiple** before a command. To end the command, press Escape. *multiple* remembers and repeats the main command, but it does not retain command parameters or options. Use this when you have to repeatedly insert the same block, but with different scale or rotation values.

Initiate Command By
Command: **multiple**

Tips & Warnings

Be careful of using *multiple* before commands like *regen* or *redraw*. This causes the command to loop without stopping. You can type Escape to cancel.

MVIEW

Creates and restores viewports, controls viewport visibility, and performs hidden line removal during plotting when paper space is active. You also can use *vports* to create viewports, but *mview* has additional options. Control layer visibility per viewport with *vplayer* and preset the scale factor with the *psvpscale* variable. This command is accessible only when layout space is active.

Initiate Command By
Command: **mview**
Alias: **mv**

Options
```
Specify corner of viewport or
[ON/OFF/Fit/Hideplot/Lock/Object/Polygonal/Restore/2/3/4] <Fit>:
```
Specify corner of viewport/Specify opposite corner
Allows you to create a viewport by picking two diagonal points.

ON
Turns all objects in the selected viewports visible.

OFF

Turns all objects in the selected viewports invisible. You can save time if you turn off viewports that you are not using so you don't have to wait for those viewports to redraw or regenerate.

Fit

Creates a viewport that matches the edges of the paper margins. If the paper background is turned off, the viewport matches the size of your current display area.

Hideplot

Creates hidden line removal for selected viewports when plotting from paper space.

Lock

Lets you control whether the scale factor (*zoom–xp*) assigned to a viewport can be modified. When a viewport is locked, you cannot use any commands that change the scale factor (except for *3dorbit*). This includes *zoom, pan, dview, view,* and *vpoint*. Issuing the *pan* or *zoom* command automatically switches you to paper space.

Object

Converts a circle, ellipse, closed polyline, spline, or region to a viewport. These objects must reside in paper space.

Polygonal

Creates an irregularly shaped polyline viewport that can contain arcs as well as line segments.

Restore

Restores viewport configurations saved with *vports* or *viewports*.

2/3/4

Creates viewport configurations of two, three, or four viewports.

Tips & Warnings

- Invoking *mview* while a model space viewport is active causes paper space to temporarily become active. Once you have completed the command, you are returned to model space.

- The number of viewports displayed is based on the value of *maxactvp*.

- *redraw* and *regen* affect only the current viewport. *redrawall* and *regenall* affect all viewports.

Related Variables   cvport, maxactvp, psvpscale, tilemode

Associated Commands   layoutwizard, viewports, vplayer, -vports, vports

MVSETUP

(Model Space Viewpoint Setup) Sets up some of the general drawing parameters. It combines commands such as *units, limits, viewports,* and *mview.* You can use this command as often as you like, or you can change any of the settings individually. It is similar to some of the options offered by the Startup wizard and the Layout wizard although it doesn't take advantage of some of the newer AutoCAD features. The options you're offered are based on whether you're active in model space or layout space.

Initiate Command By

Command: **mvsetup**

Options

```
Enable paper space? [No/Yes] <Y>:
Regenerating layout.
Regenerating model.
Creating the default file mvsetup.dfs
in the directory C:\PROGRAM FILES\ACAD2000\support\.
Enter an option [Align/Create/Scale viewports/Options/Title block/Undo]:
```

Enable paper space?

This option is available only when the model tab is active. If layout space is active you won't receive this prompt.

Yes

Turns *tilemode* off (0) making layout space active.

Align

Aligns paper space viewports by panning the view in a viewport to align it with a base point in another viewport.

Create

Deletes and create viewports.

Scale viewports

Sets the scale factor of objects displayed in individual viewports using the xp option of the *zoom* command.

Options

Determines layer, limits, units, and titleblock method (*insert* or *xref*) for the current drawing.

Title block

Lets you delete titleblocks, resets the origin point for inserting title-blocks, and creates a border and titleblock for the drawing.

Undo

Voids the latest *mvsetup* option. You can undo one step at a time until you reach the beginning of the current *mvsetup* command.

No

Model space remains active.

Units type
> Determines whether the units are set to scientific, decimal, engineering, architectural, or metric.

Enter the scale factor
> Allows you to enter the scale factor based on what scale you would like to display on your plotted drawing. Although you enter a scale factor value, you are always working in full size. The scale factor value helps determine the drawing size or limits. Use the *plot* command to actually tell the computer the scale you want the drawing to represent.

Enter the paper width
> Allows you to enter the width of the paper you plan to use when you plot.

Enter the paper height
> Places a polyline border around the drawing limits once you have entered the height.

This setup routine calculates the drawing's limits based on the following formula:

> scale factor × paper width = X value (upper right of limits)
> scale factor × paper height = Y value (upper right of limits)
> Limits = 0,0 (lower-left corner) and X,Y (upper-right corner of limits)

Related Variables   tilemode

Associated Commands   layer, layout, limits, mview, new, units

---

NCOPY

Express Block toolbar

Copies individual or nested objects that define blocks and external references. The copied objects do not retain their association to the block or external reference. See *copy* for more detailed information.

Initiate Command By
> Command: **ncopy**
> Express → Blocks → Copy Nested Entities

Associated Commands   copy, expresstools

NEW

Standard toolbar

Begins a new drawing. There are two ways you can begin a new drawing: the first is using the Startup wizard and the second is using the command line.

Initiate Command By
> Command: **new**, Ctrl-N
> File → New

Options

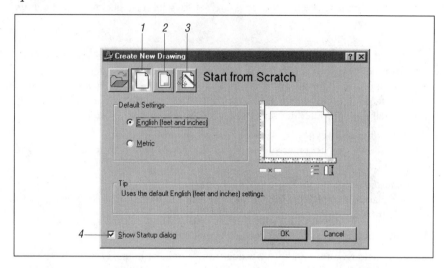

1. **Start from Scratch.** Lets you define the drawing as English (feet and inches) or metric (decimal). This value is maintained by the *measureinit* variable.

2. **Use a Template.** Allows you to select a drawing template or prototype file. These filenames have the extension *.dwt*. The default location for template files is defined with the "Drawing template file location" located in the *options* Files tab. If you have your own template files that have the extension *.dwg*, you can rename them using the Windows Explorer program and change their extension to *.dwt*. You also can open each *.dwg* file and save it as a template file using the *saveas* command.

3. **Use a Wizard.** Allows you choose either Advanced Setup or Quick Setup. Each of these options asks a series of questions and based on your responses sets up some of the key parameters for new drawing files.

    Advanced Setup
    Sets the drawing units and limits. You are asked detailed questions concerning the unit of measurement and precision, angle of measurement and precision angle, direction of angle measurement, orientation for angle measurement, and area of your drawing. See *limits* and *units* for more detailed information.

    Quick Setup
    Sets your units and limits. You are asked to define the unit of measurement and the area of your drawing. The rest of the values default to the template file, *acad.dwt*. See *limits* and *units* for more detailed information.

4. **Show Startup dialog.** Disables the Create New Drawing wizard when not checked. You turn this feature back on by selecting the Show Startup Dialog option from the *options* Open and Save tab.

Tips & Warnings

If *filedia* is set to 1, a dialog box is activated; if *filedia* is set to 0, you are prompted on the command line. When *filedia* is set to 0, or off, entering a tilde (~) on the command line temporarily activates the dialog box.

Related Variables   filedia, measureinit, sdi, tducreate

Associated Commands   saveas

NOMUTT 2000

(No Muttering) Determines whether most of the prompts and options displayed at the command line are visible or invisible. This is used by programmers writing scripts and AutoLISP routines who want to control the amount of information displayed at the command line during their routines.

Initiate Command By

Command: **nomutt**

Options

0   Activates normal muttering.

1   Disables muttering.

Variable Settings

Initial default:	0
Subsequent default:	Initial default
Value:	Short

OFFSET   Modify toolbar

Copies an arc, circle, line, spline, or 2D polyline parallel to itself by specifying a distance or a point through which the object will pass. You can offset only one object at a time. When offsetting joined polylines, you can automatically have the corners offset with a filleted arc or chamfer, or you can just have the ends extend by setting the *offsetgaptype* variable.

Initiate Command By

Command: **offset**
Alias: **o**
Modify → Offset

Options

```
Specify offset distance or [Through] <Through>:
Select object to offset or <exit>:
Specify point on side to offset:
```

Specify offset distance

> Allows you to enter the offset distance by typing a value or picking two points.

Through

> Allows you to pick a point through which the object will pass.

Tips & Warnings

- You can create parallel lines using *copy*, *array*, or *mline*.

- Offsetting splines may give you unexpected results. New splines contain more control points than the original object.

- Use the offset option of *solidedit* if you want to offset 3D solid planar faces.

Related Variables	offsetdist, offsetgaptype
Associated Commands	array, copy, mline

Example

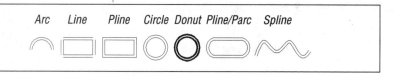

Arc   Line   Pline   Circle Donut Pline/Parc   Spline

'OFFSETDIST

Controls the default value for the *offset* command. This value is usually set with *offset*. Setting *offsetdist* to a negative number is considered the "through" option of the *offset* command.

Initiate Command By

> Command: **offsetdist**

Variable Settings

Initial default:	−1.0000
Subsequent default:	Initial default
Value:	Real
Related Variables	offsetgaptype
Associated Commands	offset

'OFFSETGAPTYPE 2000

Determines how two or more polylines, joined together, are offset when a gap is created at the endpoints due to the offset distance.

Initiate Command By

> Command: **offsetgaptype**

Options

0   The endpoints of polylines are extended to fill the gap.

1   A filleted arc is created to fill the gap.

2   A chamfer is created to fill the gap.

Variable Settings

Initial default:	0
Subsequent default:	Registry file
Value:	Integer

Related Variables   offsetdist

Associated Commands   offset, pline

Example

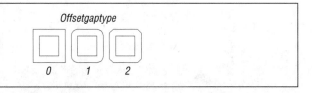

'OLEHIDE

Determines the visibility status of OLE objects. OLE objects are inserted into drawings with *pasteclip* and *pastespec*.

Initiate Command By

Command: **olehide**

Options

0   All OLE objects are visible.

1   Only OLE objects in paper space are visible.

2   Only OLE objects in model space are visible.

3   No OLE objects are visible.

Variable Settings

Initial default:	0
Subsequent default:	Registry file
Value:	Integer

Associated Commands   pasteclip, pastespec

OLELINKS

Updates, modifies, and removes existing OLE (Object Linking and Embedding) links. OLE objects come from other Windows programs that also support OLE. Linked files are inserted into AutoCAD with the Paste Link option of the *pastespec* command.

Initiate Command By

> Command: **olelinks**
> Edit → OLE Links

Options

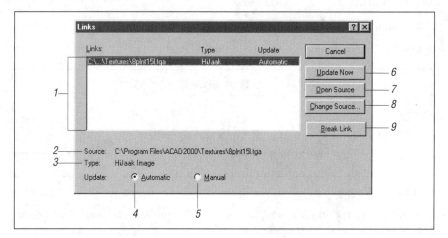

1. **Links.** Lists information about the linked files. The information varies depending on the link type.

2. **Source.** Lists the directory location and filename of the OLE object selected from the Links list. If more than one name is highlighted, this field is left blank.

3. **Type.** Displays the name of the application associated with the OLE object selected from the Links list. If more than one name is highlighted, and they are associated with different applications, this field is left blank.

4. **Automatic.** Updates the link whenever the source changes.

5. **Manual.** Prompts you to update links when there is a change in the source. This happens when you open up the AutoCAD file.

6. **Update Now.** Updates selected links.

7. **Open Source.** Activates the OLE object's application program.

8. **Change Source.** Changes the source file. If the same file is referenced more than once, you are given the option to change all references to the new source file.

9. **Break Link.** Removes the association of the linked file to its original location. The OLE object changes its status from linked to embedded.

Tips & Warnings

*   The *undo* command has no effect on *olelinks*.

*   This command will not display a dialog box if there are no linked files.

Associated Commands   copyclip, copylink, insertobj, pasteclip, pastespec

---

'OLEQUALITY 2000

Determines the default plot quality assigned to embedded OLE (Object Linking and Embedding) objects. This variable is set by selecting one of the choices in the OLE Plot Quality drop-down list from the *olescale* OLE Properties dialog box or by selecting the same drop-down list from the *options* Plotting tab. OLE objects are inserted into drawings with the *pasteclip* and *pastespec* commands.

Initiate Command By

Command: **olequality**

Options

0   Line art quality

1   Text quality

2   Graphics quality

3   Photograph quality

4   High quality photograph

Variable Settings

Initial default: 1

Subsequent default: Registry file

Value: Integer

Tips & Warnings

Most non-Windows print drivers do not support the printing of OLE objects. OLE raster objects will not plot with pen plotters.

Associated Commands   olescale, options, pasteclip, pastespec, preferences

---

OLESCALE 2000

Controls the size of OLE (Object Linking and Embedding) objects and determines the OLE plot quality. You must select an OLE object before using this command. OLE objects are inserted into drawings with the *pasteclip* and *pastespec* commands.

Initiate Command By

Command: **olescale**

Options

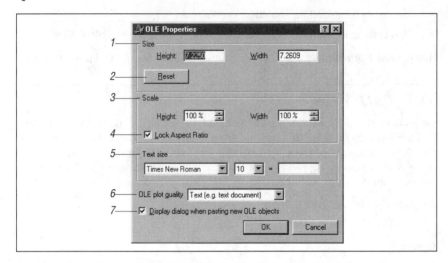

1. **Size.** Sets the height and width of the OLE object based on the current drawing units. When the Lock Aspect Ratio box is checked, changing the height causes the width to change proportionately so that they maintain their original ratio. You also can change the width and have the height change proportionately. Changing the size also changes the scale.

2. **Reset.** Returns the height and width of the size and scale to their original values.

3. **Scale.** Sets the height and width of the OLE object as a percentage of the current height and width. When the Lock Aspect Ratio box is checked, changing the height causes the width to change proportionately so that they maintain their original ratio. You also can change the width and have the height change proportionately. Changing the scale also changes the size. You also can use grips to change the scale of the OLE object.

4. **Lock Aspect Ratio.** Maintains the ratio of the height and width when changing either of those values. This applies to changing the size and scale values.

5. **Text size.** Changes the text size of OLE objects based on their assigned font and text height. Changing the height causes the other OLE text objects to adjust proportionately in size maintaining the same aspect ratio.

6. **OLE plot quality.** Determines the default plot quality assigned to embedded OLE objects This value is maintained by the *olequality* system variable.

7. **Display dialog when pasting new OLE objects.** Determines whether this dialog box is activated every time an OLE object is inserted into a drawing file. You also can change this setting when checking the "Display OLE properties dialog" box from the *options* System tab.

Tips & Warnings

The *undo* command does not work for changes you made in the OLE Properties dialog box. If you need to undo, right-click over the OLE object and choose the undo option from the shortcut menu.

Related Variables	olequality
Associated Commands	options, pasteclip, pastespec, preferences

---

'OLESTARTUP [2000]

Determines whether the source application of an embedded OLE (Object Linking and Embedding) object loads when the object is plotted. Loading the source application during plotting may improve the plot quality. This value is set by checking the "Use OLE application when plotting OLE objects" box from the *options* Plotting tab. OLE objects are inserted into drawings with the *pasteclip* and *pastespec* commands.

Initiate Command By

Command: **olestartup**

Options

0   The OLE source application is not loaded when plotting.

1   The OLE source application is loaded when plotting.

Variable Settings

Initial default:	0
Subsequent default:	Last value used in the drawing
Value:	Integer
Associated Commands	options, pasteclip, pastespec, preferences

References O-P

OOPS

Restores the last object or group of objects that were deleted by the most recent *block, erase,* or *wblock* command. This applies only to the current drawing session.

Initiate Command By

Command: **oops**

Tips & Warnings

oops will not restore objects removed with the *undo* or *u* commands. It only works with objects that were erased.

Associated Commands   undo

OPEN

Object Properties toolbar

Edits existing drawing (*.dwg*), template (*.dwt*), and drawing interchange (*.dxf*) files. You can open multiple drawings in a drawing session and run multiple AutoCAD sessions concurrently. When AutoCAD DesignCenter is active, you can open drawings by dragging the selected file into an empty drawing area. Dragging it into an active drawing is the same as using *insert*.

Initiate Command By

    Command: **open**, Ctrl-O
    File → Open

Options

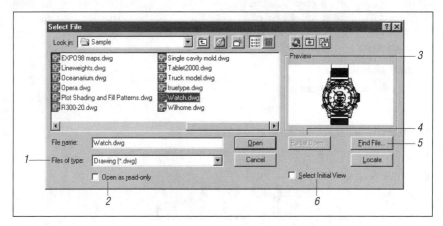

1. **Files of type.** Opens drawing (*.dwg*), template (*.dwt*), or drawing interchange (*.dxf*) files.

2. **Open as read-only.** Write-protects the drawing file. The drawing can be viewed, but any changes to it cannot be saved to that drawing. The *writestat* variable maintains the read-only setting. If you make any changes, use *saveas* and assign a different name to the filename.

3. **Preview.** Displays a bitmapped image of the file highlighted in the filename list. Preview is empty if no file is selected, if the selected file has never been saved with a version past Release 12, or if *rasterpreview* was set to 0 when the drawing was last saved.

4. **Partial Open.** Opens and loads only a portion of the drawing. You can limit the portion to only objects located on specific layers or to only those objects located within a view. The views include the ones created with the *view* command as well as drawing extents and what was displayed on your screen the last time the drawing was saved. If you want to view more layers and views once the drawing is open, use *partialload*.

5. **Find File.** Lets you search and browse through multiple paths and drives for drawing files. Browsing displays bitmap images of drawings from a designated

drive and folder. Searching lets you locate drawings from any of the drives and folders accessed by your computer. See the following Search and Browse dialog boxes for more detailed information.

6. **Select Initial View.** Displays the Select Initial View dialog box. This dialog box lets you select any views saved in the drawing or the "last view" used in the drawing and opens the drawing to that view. The "last view" option brings up the drawing as it was displayed at its last save. The *fullopen* variable maintains this setting.

The Search Tab

The Search tab lets you preview files and search for files based on a specified date and time, and the dialog is activated by selecting the Find File button on the Select File dialog.

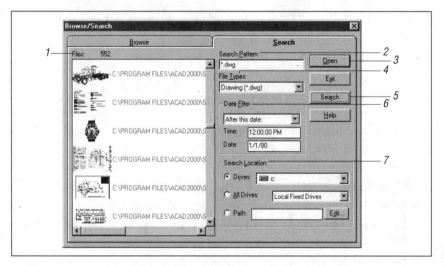

1. **Files.** Lists the number of files that meet the search criteria and displays a bitmap image (when possible) folder, path, and filename for each file.

2. **Search Pattern.** Specifies the files to search. You can use the DOS wildcard characters question mark (?) and asterisk (*).

3. **Open.** Opens the drawing, template, or drawing interchange file for editing.

4. **File Types.** Determines the file extension of files listed in the Search Pattern text box. The file extension options are *.dwg* (drawing), *.dwt* (template), or *.dxf* (drawing interchange) files.

5. **Search/Stop Search.** Begins the search based on the Search Pattern, File Types, Date Filter, and Search Location. Once the search has begun, the button changes to "Stop Search." You can stop the search at any time.

6. **Date Filter.** Determines whether the files being searched were created or modified before or after the time and date specified.

7. **Search Location.** Determines the drives and paths used to locate files.

References O–P

The Browse Tab

The Browse tab lets you preview files in a specified directories or folders, and this dialog is activated by selecting the Find File button on the Select File dialog.

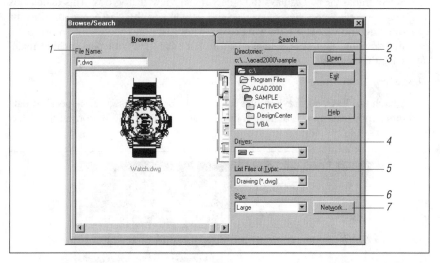

1. **File Name.** Displays the name of the currently selected file. If no file is selected, the asterisk (*) wildcard is displayed.

2. **Directories.** Lists the names of folders on the current drive.

3. **Open.** Opens the drawing listed in the File Name text box for editing.

4. **Drives.** Lists the names of the drives connected to your computer.

5. **List Files of Type.** Determines the type of file displayed in the File Name text box.

6. **Size.** Determines the size of the drawing images (small, medium, or large) displayed in the File Name display box.

7. **Network.** Connects to network drives.

Tips & Warnings

• If *filedia* is set to 1, a dialog box is activated; if *filedia* is set to 0, you are prompted on the command line. When *filedia* is set to 0, or off, entering a tilde (~) on the command line temporarily activates the dialog box.

• When *filedia* is disabled, you can still display the drawing in an existing view. You do this by typing the filename followed by a comma (,) and the view name.

• You can open a drawing using the AutoCAD DesignCenter. You do this by selecting the file and right-clicking to activate the shortcut menu or by picking and dragging the file onto the AutoCAD screen.

• If you can't open more than one drawing at a time, check the status of the "Single-drawing compatibility mode" box located in the *options* System tab or verify the value of the *sdi* variable.

Related Variables	dwgcheck, filedia, fullopen, lispinit, rasterpreview, sdi, writestat
Associated Commands	options, partiaload, preferences

OPTIONS 2000

Sets default values for many of the AutoCAD commands. Some of these values are set until you change them and others are set only for the current AutoCAD session. You can quickly activate this command by right-clicking in the command-line area when no other command is active or in the drawing area.

Initiate Command By

Command: **options**, **preferences**, or **config**
Alias: **pr** or **op**
Tools → Options

Options

The Options dialog contains many tabs, which are described in the following sections.

The Files Tab

The Files tab defines the search path AutoCAD uses when looking for various support files. It also lets you define some miscellaneous optional settings.

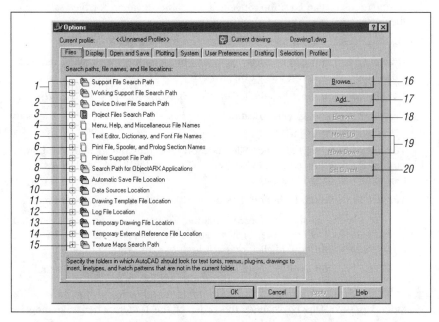

1. **Support File Search Path** and **Working Support File Search Path**. Specifies the location for support files. These support files are text fonts, customized menu files, insert and external reference files, linetypes, help files, and hatch

patterns. The first folder AutoCAD searches is always the folder of the current drawing. This value is maintained by the *acadprefix* system variable.

2. **Device Driver File Search Path**. Specifies the location for video display drivers, pointing devices, and printers.

3. **Project Files Search Path**. Specifies the location for external reference files. This value is maintained by the *projectname* system variable.

4. **Menu, Help, and Miscellaneous File Names**. Specifies the location for the main menu file, help files, default Internet location (*inetlocation*), configuration files, and license server location (*acadserver*).

5. **Text Editor, Dictionary, and Font File Names**. Specifies the location and file-name for multiline text's internal text editor (*mtexted*), the current spelling dictionary (*dctmain*), the location and filename for the custom spelling dictio-nary (*dctcust*), the location and filename of the alternate font (*fontalt*), and the location and name of the alternate font mapping file (*fontmap*).

6. **Print File, Spooler, and Prolog Section Names**. Specifies the default names for the print file for legacy plotting scripts, the print spooler program, and the prolog section to read when using the *psout* command (*psprolog*).

7. **Printer Support File Path**. Specifies the location for print spool files, configura-tion files, description files, and style tables.

8. **Search Path for ObjectARX Applications**. Specifies the location of ObjectARX applications.

9. **Automatic Save File Location**. Specifies the folder location for files saved with the automatic save feature (*savefilepath*).

10. **Data Sources Location**. Specifies the location for database source files.

11. **Drawing Template File Location**. Specifies the location for drawing templates (*.dwt*) files when using the Startup wizard.

12. **Log File Location**. Specifies the location for drawing log files (*logfilepath*).

13. **Temporary Drawing File Location**. Specifies the location for temporary drawing files (*tempprefix*).

14. **Temporary External Reference File Location**. Specifies the location for tempo-rary external reference files (*xloadpath*). If this is left blank, it defaults to the temporary drawing file location.

15. **Texture Maps Search Path**. Specifies the location for rendering texture maps.

16. **Browse**. Opens up the support information for each heading that is selected. If you select a folder or file, Browse opens the standard Select a File dialog box. You also can double-click on each item to achieve the same results.

17. **Add**. Lets you add another support folder location for the system to search.

18. **Remove**. Removes a highlighted search folder.

19. **Move Up/Move Down**. Changes the order of the folders when searching for information.

20. **Set Current**. Determines the default setting for the selected project or spelling dictionary since only one option can be active at a time.

The Display Tab

The Display tab specifies the screen appearance and performance.

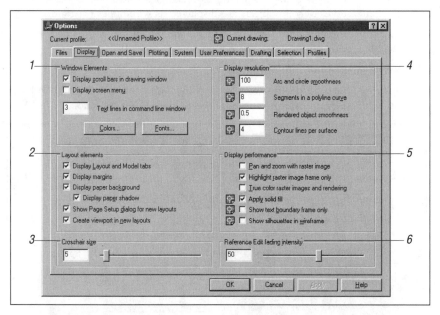

1. **Window Elements**. Toggles the horizontal and vertical scrollbars and the screen menu on the righthand side on and off. You also can set the number of command lines to display. The Colors button lets you change the screen background for model and layout space, text on the model and layout tabs, command-line text, command line background, and AutoTrack vector color. You can change some of the other color assignments using the Windows System icon located in the Control Panel. The Fonts button lets you change the font, font style, and font size that appears on the command line and screen menu.

2. **Layout elements**. Toggles the display of model and layout tabs, paper space display margins, paper background, and shadows. It also determines whether the Page Setup (*pagesetup*) dialog box and a viewport (*viewports, vports, mview*) are automatically activated when a new layout is created.

3. **Crosshair size**. Specifies the size of the cursor crosshairs (*cursorsize*). The size is a percentage of the screen pointing area.

4. **Display resolution**. Determines how objects are displayed. Setting the values to a high resolution impacts the program's performance. You can determine the smoothness of arcs and circles (*viewres*), segments in a polyline curve (*splinesegs*), rendered and shaded object smoothness (*facetres*), and the number of lines displayed on solids (*isolines*).

5. **Display performance**. Determines how raster images are displayed during realtime pan and zoom commands (*rdisplay, dragmode*), how raster image frames are highlighted during object selection (*imagehlt*), the quality of raster

images and rendered objects, whether solid filled objects (multilines, traces, wide polylines, hatches, and solids) are displayed as solid or wireframe (*fillmode*), whether text is displayed as rectangles (*qtextmode*), and whether silhouette curves of solid objects are displayed as wireframes (*dispsilh*).

6. **Reference Edit fading intensity.** Determines the fading intensity value for reference files being edited in the current drawing (*xfadectl*).

The Open and Save Tab

The Open and Save tab determines how drawings are opened and saved and sets demand load values for external references and ObjectARX application.

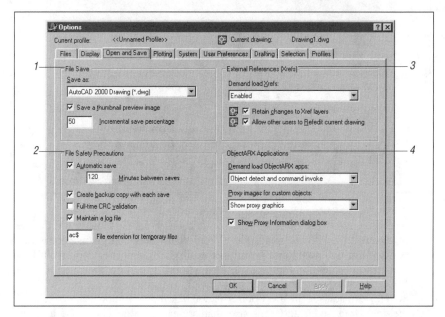

1. **File Save.** Determines the default format when saving files with the *save* and *saveas* commands. Drawings can be saved to earlier versions of AutoCAD, AutoCAD LT, drawing template files, and drawing interchange files. You can create a preview image (*rasterpreview*) that is displayed in the Preview area in the Select File dialog box. You can determine how often a drawing executes a full save based on an incremental save percentage (*isavepercent*).

2. **File Safety Precautions.** Sets the automatic save feature on and specifies the frequency of saves (*savetime*). Determines whether a *.bak* file (*isavebak*) is created each time a file is saved. Toggles error checking on and off. Maintains a log file (*logfilemode, logfilename*) to which all the information provided on the command line is written and determines the file extension for temporary files.

3. **External References (Xrefs).** Controls the demand loading of external references (*xloadctl*). You can have the current file retain any changes made to external reference layers (*visretain*) without altering the original file. Determines whether others referencing files can change the reference file (*xedit*).

4. **ObjectARX Applications**. Controls the demand loading of AutoCAD Runtime Extension (ObjectARX) applications (*demandload*) and the loading of proxy objects. You also can have a warning displayed (*proxynotice*) whenever a drawing that contains custom objects is brought up.

The Plotting Tab

The plotting tab determines default plot values for new drawings and lets you set some plotting parameters that affect existing drawings.

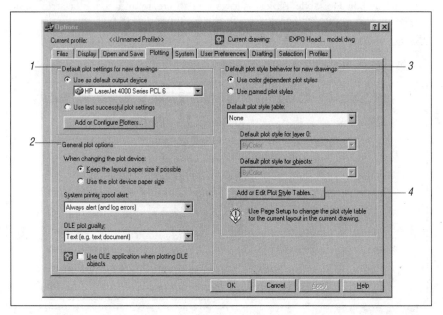

1. **Default plot settings for new drawings**. Determines the plotting device assigned to new drawings or drawings that have never been saved in AutoCAD 2000 format. The drop-down list displays plotters and printers that have been configured using the Add or Configure Plotters button. As an alternative, you can have new drawings or drawings never saved in AutoCAD 2000 format default to the last successful plot settings. Using the Add or Configure Plotters button is the same as using the *plottermanager* command, which lets you define the plotters and system printers.

2. **General plot options**. When changing the plotting device, allows you to keep the paper size defined on the Layout Settings tab as long as the plotting device can handle that sheet size. If the plotting device can't handle that sheet size, the system reverts to a plotter configuration file (*.pc3*) or the default system settings if the plotter device is a system printer. This is maintained by the *paperupdate* variable.

You can control the frequency with which you are alerted to plotting problems by selecting from the System Printer Spool Alert drop-down list. Selecting from the OLE (Object Linking and Embedding) Plot Quality list lets you determine the plot quality of OLE objects (*olequality*). Checking "Use

OLE application when plotting OLE objects" (*olestartup*) determines whether the OLE's source application is activated.

3. **Default plot style behavior for new drawings**. Determines if new drawings or drawings that were never saved in AutoCAD 2000 format are color dependent or use named plot styles (*pstylepolicy*). If drawings use named plot styles, you can select the plot style table, the default plot style for layer 0 (*defplstyle*), or the default plot style for objects (*defplstyle*).

4. **Add or Edit Plot Style Tables**. Allows you to create and edit plot style tables using *stylesmanager*. See *stylesmanager* for more detailed information.

The System Tab

The System tab maintains system settings.

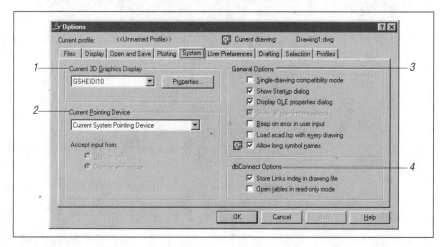

1. **Current 3D Graphics Display**. Lists the 3D graphics display systems that are available. The default is the Heidi graphics display system developed by Autodesk. Depending on your hardware, you may have other options. The Properties button offers various settings that affect the way objects are viewed and how various system resources are utilized when the *3dorbit* command is active. These options also affect how objects are shaded with *shademode*

2. **Current Pointing Device**. Assigns the pointing device used during the AutoCAD session. Typically most people use the system pointing device, which is a mouse.

3. **General Options**. Assigns general system parameters such as the ability to have two or more drawings open at the same time (*sdi*), display a Startup dialog box, display the OLE properties dialog box, and display all warning messages. You also can have AutoCAD beep when an invalid entry is detected, reload the *acad.lsp* file (*acadlspasdoc*) when starting or opening a drawing, and allow long names (*extnames*) for named items.

4. **dbConnect Options**. Defines some parameters associated with database connectivity. You can store the database index in the drawing file and determine whether database tables inside the drawing are read-only.

The User Preferences Tab

The User Preferences tab defines settings that increase productivity by the way you interact with AutoCAD.

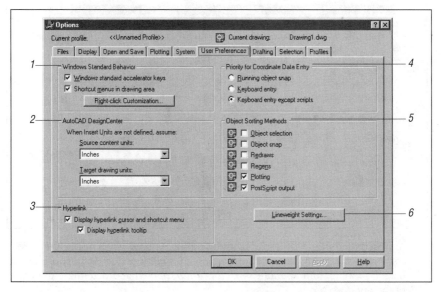

1. **Windows Standard Behavior.** Determines whether AutoCAD mimics Windows standards or reverts to some of its older methods. For example, you can have AutoCAD use its own definition of Ctrl-C (*cancel* instead of *copyclip*), and Ctrl-V (toggles to different paper space viewports instead of *paste*). You also can control the way the shortcut menus or the right mouse click behaves (*shortcutmenu*).

2. **AutoCAD DesignCenter.** Sets the default (*insunits*) or both source (*insunitsdefsource*) and target (*insunitsdeftarget*) drawing units when using *insert*.

3. **Hyperlink.** Controls the display of the hyperlink cursor, shortcut menu, and tooltips.

4. **Priority for Coordinate Data Entry.** Determines how coordinate entry and running object snaps interact (*osnapcoord*).

5. **Object Sorting Methods.** Determines the order in which objects are sorted (*sortents*) during selection set, object snap, redraws, regenerations, plotting, and PostScript output.

6. **Lineweight Settings.** Activates the *lineweight* command.

The Drafting Tab

The Drafting tab determines how some of the editing options appear on the screen.

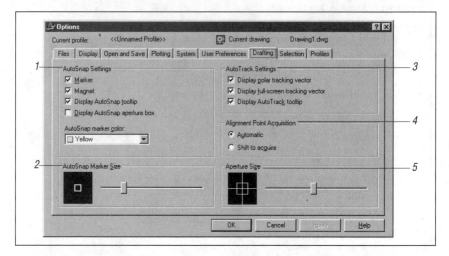

1. **AutoSnap Settings**. Sets some of the display features when using the object snap command. You can turn on and off visibility of the AutoSnap marker, magnet, tooltip, and aperture box (*autosnap, apbox*) and determine the color of the aperture box.

2. **AutoSnap Marker Size**. Sets the size of the AutoSnap marker in pixels.

3. **AutoTrack Settings**. Sets some of the display features such as the tracking vector (*trackpath*) and tooltips (*autosnap*) when polar tracking is active.

4. **Alignment Point Acquisition**. Determines whether tracking vectors appear automatically when the cursor moves over an object snap or whether you must press Shift to see the tracking vector (*polarmode*).

5. **Aperture Size**. Sets the size of the object snap aperture (*aperture*) box.

The Selection Tab

The Selection tab determines various settings that have to do with object selection. You also can access this dialog box with *ddselect.*

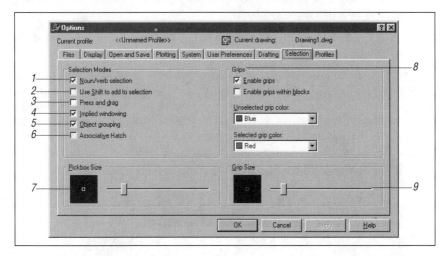

1. **Noun/verb selection.** When checked, allows you to select objects before activating a command and therefore bypass the "Select objects" prompt (*pickfirst*).

2. **Use Shift to add to selection.** Controls how objects are added or removed during the selection set process. This value is maintained by the *pickadd* variable. When this box is checked, each time you select an object to add to the selection set, it removes objects already selected. You can add objects by pressing the Shift key during the selection set process.

3. **Press and drag.** Determines the method used to define window or crossing during object selection. When the box is not checked, you are required to pick two diagonal points for the window and crossing methods. When the box is checked, you are required to hold down the pointing device button while defining the two points for the window and crossing options. Releasing your finger from the button defines the second diagonal point. This value is maintained by the *pickdrag* variable.

4. **Implied windowing.** Controls automatic windowing during "Select objects" prompts. If the pick fails to select an object, the selection method becomes a window or crossing. Moving the crosshairs to the right acts as a window, to the left as a crossing. This value is maintained by the *pickauto* variable.

5. **Object grouping.** Controls whether groups are temporarily treated as individual objects. This value is maintained by the *pickstyle* variable.

6. **Associative Hatch.** Determines if boundary hatch (bhatch) objects are linked to their boundaries. When this box is checked, selecting a bhatch object also selects its boundary. This value is maintained by the *pickstyle* variable.

7. **Pickbox Size.** Determines the size of the pick box (*pickbox*).

8. **Grips.** Determines whether grips are active or inactive (*grips*) and whether the grip's location for blocks is based on the block's insertion point or on the individual objects defining the block (*gripblock*). Unselected Grip Color determines the color of inactive grips (*gripcolor*); Selected Grip Color determines the color of active grips (*griphot*).

9. **Grip Size.** Determines the size of the grips (*gripsize*).

The Profiles Tab

The Profiles tab imports, exports, and renames profiles. Profiles store the various settings defined in the rest of the *options* tabs. Depending on your hardware configuration, how many people share workstations, and your different applications, you may have multiple profiles, each defining a different set of command and variable defaults. Issuing the *undo* command has no effect on the Profiles tab.

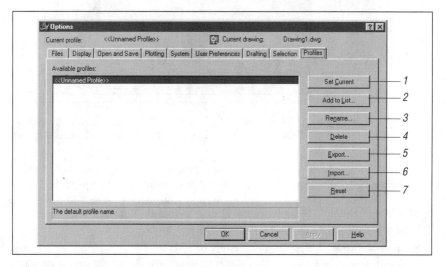

1. **Set Current.** Changes the current profile to the one highlighted on the Available Profiles list. Be careful because it also updates the profile highlighted in the Available Profiles window. This value is maintained by the *cprofile* variable.

2. **Add to List.** Creates a new profile by using the one highlighted on the Available Profiles list as a template. You also can add a description that is displayed on the bottom of the Available Profiles window.

3. **Rename.** Renames, adds, or changes the profile's description.

4. **Delete.** Removes profiles. The current profile cannot be deleted.

5. **Export.** Saves the profile to a file with the extension *.arg*. This file can be imported to the same computer (the original may have been altered by mistake) or to another AutoCAD workstation with the Import button.

6. **Import.** Imports a profile that was saved with the Export button.

7. **Reset.** Resets the highlighted profile to the original system settings.

'ORTHO

Constrains the construction of most objects (such as lines, multilines, polylines, and traces) to horizontal and vertical directions. *ortho* also controls the angle at which you pick the second point in many of the drawing and editing commands.

For most draw and edit commands, if *ortho* is on, your second pick point can be either horizontal or vertical, depending on how far your crosshairs are from the first point. The larger of these distances determines the direction.

Entering coordinates directly from the keyboard and using object snaps override the *ortho* setting.

You can toggle *ortho* on and off while in the middle of other commands. *ortho* has its own setting for model space and another for paper space. *orthomode* maintains the *ortho* setting.

Initiate Command By

> Command: **ortho**, F8
> Alias: Ctrl-L
> Status bar: ORTHO (toggles *ortho* on and off)

Options

On
> Enables ortho mode.

Off
> Disables ortho mode.

Tips & Warnings

- Turning *ortho* on automatically turns polar tracking off; turning polar tracking on automatically turns *ortho* off.

- Ortho angle is based on the snap rotation angle and current UCS.

Related Variables   orthomode, snapangle

'ORTHOMODE

Determines if your cursor movement is constrained horizontally and vertically or if you can move your cursor diagonally. This value is set by the *ortho* or by picking ORTHO from the status bar.

Initiate Command By

> Command: **orthomode**

Options

0   Turns orthogonal mode off.

1   Turns orthogonal mode on.

Variable Settings

Initial default:	0
Subsequent default:	Last value used in the drawing
Value:	Integer

Associated Commands   ortho

'OSMODE 2000mod

Maintains the current object snap settings. This value is set with the *dsettings* Object Snap tab.

Initiate Command By

Command: **osmode**

Options

osmode is bit-coded and its value is the sum of the following:

0 = None	32 = Intersection	2048 = Apparent intersection
1 = Endpoint	64 = Insertion	4096 = Extension
2 = Midpoint	128 = Perpendicular	8192 = Parallel
4 = Center	256 = Tangent	16383 = All object snaps
8 = Node	512 = Nearest	16384 = Toggles running
16 = Quadrant	1024 = Quick	object snaps on and off

Variable Settings

Initial default:	0
Subsequent default:	Registry file
Value:	Integer

Related Variables   apbox, aperture, autosnap

Associated Commands   dsettings, osnap

'-OSNAP 2000

see OSNAP

'OSNAP 2000mod

Standard toolbar

(Object Snap) Lets you locate precise points on objects. You use this as a modifier for most commands in which you are asked to specify a point. You can preset one or more object snaps and turn that setting on or off, or you can temporarily activate them during point selection. When you enable object snaps, the cursor displays an *aperture* box at its crosshairs. This box is sometimes confused with the *pickbox*. When your object snaps are preset and you want to temporarily turn

---

them off, use the object snap option on the status bar (OSNAP) or press F3. If you want to use an object snap (osnap) that is not preset, use the object snap toolbar, which is shown above.

When you are trying to locate a point with preset osnaps and the cursor keeps selecting the wrong location, you can use the Tab key to cycle through each of the available choices. Move your crosshairs near the location and press the Tab key until the appropriate point is located.

You can achieve the same results using -osnap (-os) so all prompts and options appear on the command line. You can preset more than one object snap by entering commas between options, omitting all spaces. You can override any presets by typing an object snap mode (only the first three characters are required) when a point is requested.

Initiate Command By

Command: **osnap**
Alias: **os**
F3 or Shift-right-click
Status bar: OSNAP (left-clicking toggles preset osnaps on and off; right-clicking activates the *dsettings* Object Snap tab)

Options

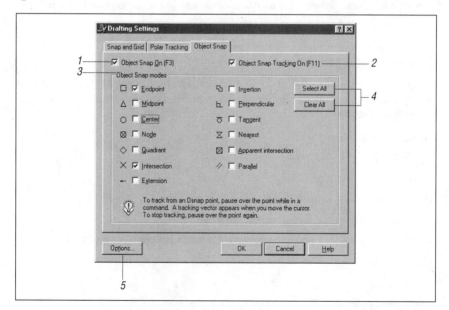

1. **Object Snap On (F3).** Toggles running *osnap* on and off. You also can use the OSNAP button on the status bar. This value is maintained by the *osmode* variable.

2. **Object Snap Tracking On (F11).** Toggles object snap tracking on and off. You also can use the OTRACK button on the status bar. Object snap tracking lets the cursor track along alignment paths based on other object snap points

when you specify points in a command. This value is maintained by the *autosnap* variable.

3. **Object Snap modes.** Lets you snap to strategic points on objects. The symbols to the right of each object snap name are AutoSnap markers. This value is maintained by the *osmode* variable.

4. **Select All/Clear All.** Select All turns all the *osnap* settings on; Clear All turns all the *osnap* settings off.

5. **Options.** Activates the Drafting tab from the *options* command. See *options* for more detailed information.

Tips & Warnings

- Grips and object snaps often share the same locations.

- When all of the object snaps are inactive, you may still see a box located at the intersection of the screen's crosshairs. This may be because the variables *grips* and *pickfirst* are active.

- See also "Point and Coordinate Entry" in Chapter 2, *Command Index & Global Topics* for more information.

Related Variables	apbox, aperture, grips, osmode, osnapcoord
Associated Commands	aperture, autosnap, dsettings, grip, options, point entry, preferences

---

'OSNAPCOORD

Determines if a keyboard entry overrides running object snaps. This variable is set when selecting one of the "Priority for coordinate data entry" radio buttons from the *options* User Preferences tab.

Initiate Command By

Command: **osnapcoord**

Options

0 Running object snaps override keyboard entry.

1 Keyboard entries override object snap settings.

2 Keyboard entries override object snap settings except during script routines.

Variable Settings

Initial default:	2
Subsequent default:	Registry file
Value:	Integer
Associated Commands	options, osnap, preferences

-PACK

see PACK

PACK [2000mod]   Express Standard toolbar

Gathers any external files (file dependencies) associated with the current file and copies those files, including the current file, to a user-specified location. The external files can include images, external references, fonts, shapes, plot styles, plotter configuration files, remote text, and the fontmap. You can achieve the same results using *-pack* so all prompts and options appear on the command line.

Initiate Command By

Command: **pack**
Express → Tools → Pack 'n Go

Options

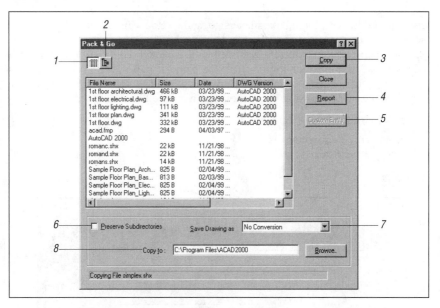

1. **List View.** Alphabetically lists the external files (including the current drawing file) that are directly associated to the current drawing. It provides the name, size, date, drawing version, and folder location. Unlike most of the dialog boxes, the list cannot be re-sorted; you can only change the column size.

2. **Tree View.** Lists by function the filenames that are directly associated with the current drawing, along with their locations. You can expand or collapse the list by picking the plus and minus signs located to the left of each name.

3. **Copy.** Copies the files listed in the tree or list view to the folder location displayed in the Copy To edit box. If any files with the same name already exist, you are warned and asked what to do.

4. **Report.** Provides a list, similar to the list and tree views, of the reference files. A Print button is available to send that information to the printer or to a file. A report is automatically generated and placed in the Copy To folder.

5. **Custom Entry**. Adds extra information about custom applications to the report.

6. **Preserve Subdirectories**. Maintains the file directory structure when using the Copy To directory.

7. **Save Drawing as**. Saves the drawing in its current format (no conversion) or as an AutoCAD 2000 or AutoCAD 14 file.

8. **Copy to**. Specifies the location for the copied files. Once the location is determined use the Copy button to complete the command.

Associated Commands   expresstools, image, plotstyle, rtext, shape, style, xref

---

PAGESETUP 2000   Layouts toolbar

Assigns and saves plotting parameters to a file. You can assign different page setups to model spaces and to each layout tab. The information retained with *pagesetup* includes parameters that define the plotter configuration, plot style tables, what to plot, plot location (file or plotter), paper size and paper units, drawing orientation, plot area, plot scale, and plot offset. Each page setup can be imported into other drawing files (*.dwg*) and template files (*.dwt*) with *psetupin*.

Initiate Command By
    Command: **pagesetup**
    File → Page Setup

Options

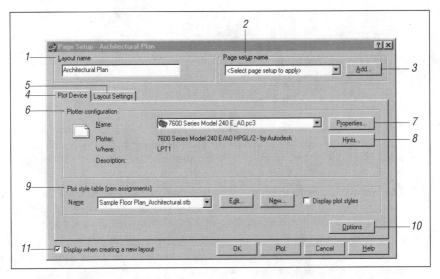

1. **Layout name**. Lists the tab name (model or layout) that will be plotted. This is based on the tab that was active before issuing the *plot* command. The What to Plot option of the *plot* Plot Device Tab lets you plot all the tabs, selected tabs, or the current tab.

---

2. **Page setup name.** Lets you choose a page setup name, containing predefined plotting parameters, and apply those settings to the selected layout tab. Page setup names are created with *pagesetup.*

3. **Add.** Lets you copy page setups defined in other drawing files (*.dwg*) and template files (*.dwt*) into the current drawing.

4. **Plot Device.** Specifies a plotting device and plot style table to assign to the current layout.

5. **Layout Settings.** Sets up plotting parameters for the layout name. It is the same as the *plot* command's Plot Settings tab. See *plot* for more information.

6. **Plotter configuration.** Determines the plotter device. Devices are defined with the Add-A-Plotter Wizard. Use *plottermanager* or the Add or Configure Plotters option from the *options* Plotting tab to access this wizard. Descriptive information, which is especially useful when you are networked and need to know the location of the plotting device, is provided.

7. **Properties.** Lets you edit a *.pc3* file. This file is created when using the Add-A-Plotter Wizard and contains specific information for each configured plotter. You may have more than one *.pc3* file for each plotter. You also can edit *.pc3* files with the *plottermanager* command.

8. **Hints.** Provides information about the current plotting device.

9. **Plot style table (pen assignments).** Sets the plot style table, edits plot style tables, and creates new plot style tables. Plot style tables contain plot styles that define color, lineweight, linetype, endcap, line fill, and screening. These styles are assigned to layouts and viewports. See *plotstyle* and *stylesmanager* for more detailed information.

10. **Options.** Activates the *options* Plotting tab.

11. **Display when creating a new layout.** Controls whether the Page Setup dialog is automatically activated whenever a layout tab is activated for the first time.

Tips & Warnings

• Depending on the *extnames* setting, a *pagesetup* name can contain up to 255 characters.

• *setupin* lets you copy a named page setup from one drawing into another.

Related Variables   extnames

Associated Commands   layout, layoutwizard, plot, psetupin

'-PAN

see PAN

'PAN

Standard toolbar

Lets you scroll around your drawing without altering the current zoom ratio. You do not physically move objects or change your drawing limits; you move your drawing display in the current viewport. While panning, you press the Pick button, defining from where you want to pan; without letting go, you drag your pointing device to define the direction and pan distance. Pans become part of the *zoom–previous* queue.

You can achieve the same results using *-pan* (*-p*) so all prompts and options appear on the command line. This method is not dynamic, in that you don't see the end result until you select two points to determine the displacement.

Initiate Command By

Command: **pan**
Alias: **p**
View → Pan

Options

Press Escape or Enter to exit, or right-click to display shortcut menu.

Tips & Warnings

- As an alternative, you can use the dynamic option of the *zoom* command or the *dsviewer* command. When working in 3D, use the *3dcorbit* and *3dorbit* commands to pan about the drawing in all directions.

- You can opt to only have at least one object displayed on the screen while panning. This will save time and may work better with your video display. You do this by using *3dpan*. Once you exit *3dpan*, the rest of the objects display appropriately. You do this by selecting your objects before issuing the command. *pickfirst* must be set to 1 in order to preselect objects. You cannot use *3dpan* while in paper space.

- Panning in a drawing that contains rendered objects causes those objects to default to the last *shademode* setting.

Related Variables	mbuttonpan, viewctr
Associated Commands	dsviewer, zoom, 3dpan

Example

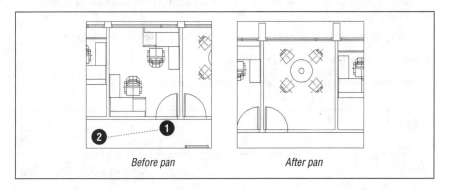

Before pan   After pan

---

paper space   *see PSPACE*

'PAPERUPDATE 2000

Controls the display of a warning message when the drawing layout paper size will not fit on the paper size defined by the plotter configuration file (.pc3) or the default system settings. This value is set when selecting one of the radio buttons from the General plot options from the *options* Plotting tab.

Initiate Command By

Command: **paperupdate**

Options

0   A warning message is given when the drawing layout paper size does not match the paper size defined by the plotter configuration file or the default system settings.

1 . This plots the drawing even when the drawing layout paper size does not match the paper size defined by the plotter configuration file or the default system settings. The paper size is based on the plotter configuration file.

Variable Settings

Initial default:	0
Subsequent default:	Registry file
Value:	Integer
Associated Commands	options, pagesetup, plot, preferences

PARTIALOAD 2000

Lets you load and view more objects in a partially opened (*partialopen*) drawing. You do this by selecting layers and/or views that already exist in the drawing. If a drawing was not partially opened during the *open* command, then *partiaload* is unavailable. A drawing must be saved at least once with AutoCAD 2000 in order to take advantage of this feature. You can achieve the same results using *-partiaload* so all prompts and options appear on the command line. See *-partialopen* for more detailed information.

Initiate Command By

Command: **partiaload**
File → Partial Load

Related Variables	fullopen, indexctl
Associated Commands	layer, open, -partialopen, view

-PARTIALOPEN 2000

Allows you to control the number of layers loaded and displayed. This command is available only when you *open* a drawing for editing. You also can load only those portions of layers residing within preselected views. Objects straddling a view are displayed in whole. Once the drawing is opened, you can load more layers and views with *partiaload*. The banner at the top of your AutoCAD window displays the filename followed by "(Partially loaded)" as a reminder that you are viewing only a portion of the entire drawing. You cannot partially open external references or objects and views residing in paper space.

When working with large drawings, such as maps and site plans, using *partialopen* will save you time whenever you need to regenerate, redraw, pan, and zoom. Although *-partialopen* is available at the command line, you may find it easier to click on the Partial Open button located on the *open* dialog box.

Initiate Command By

Command: **-partialopen**
Alias: **partialopen**

Options

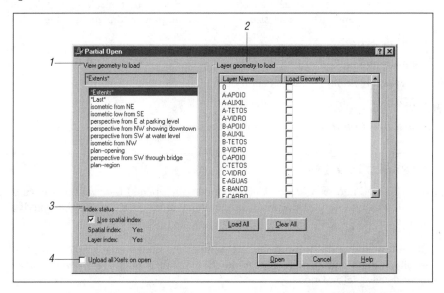

1. **View geometry to load**. Selects how you want your drawing displayed. The two options that are always listed are *Extents* and *Last*. *Extents* is similar to *zoom* extents, and *Last* refers to the way your drawing was displayed the last time it was saved. If you have other options, it is because your drawing contains views already defined with the *view* command. Although you can select only one view, you can load more views using *partiaload*.

2. **Layer geometry to load**. Selects the layers you want displayed. If you select a view other than *Extents*, you'll see only those objects residing on the selected layers that reside or straddle that view. Paper space objects are always displayed. You can always select more layers using *partiaload* once the drawing is opened.

Layers residing on external reference layers are also listed if *visretain* is set to 1. New layers added to an external reference file will not display until the next time the drawing containing the external reference is saved.

3. **Index status.** This option is available only for drawings in which *indexctl* is set to 1, 2, or 3. *indexctl* controls the creation of layer and spatial indexes. Spatial indexes track objects based on their location in space; layer indexes track objects and their layer assignment. Creating indexes minimizes the time it takes to open drawing files.

4. **Unload all Xrefs on open.** Defaults all external references to "unload" status. The external references are still attached to the drawing, but they are not loaded. Use the reload option of *xref* to view those objects.

Related Variables	filedia, indexctl
Associated Commands	layer, open, partiaload, view

PASTEBLOCK 2000

Inserts AutoCAD objects that were copied to the Windows clipboard as a block. Copy objects to the Windows clipboard using the *copybase, copyclip,* or *cutclip* command. The objects are automatically assigned a block name and an insertion base point. Individual drawing files are created for each block and are found in the Windows temporary folder. These files typically begin with *A$*.

Initiate Command By

Command: **pasteblock**
Edit → Paste as Block

Associated Commands	block, pasteclip, pasteorig, pastespec, wblock

---

PASTECLIP
Standard toolbar

Imports the contents of the Windows clipboard into the current drawing. The contents are OLE (Object Linking and Embedding) objects. Imported files are placed in the upper-lefthand corner of the drawing. If the object is from an ASCII text editor, such as Windows Notepad, it is converted to multiline text. Use *olehide* to control visibility, *olequality* and *olestartup* to control the plot quality, and *olescale* to control the size of OLE objects.

Initiate Command By

Command: **pasteclip**
Alias: Ctrl-V
Edit → Paste

Related Variables	olehide, olequality, olestartup
Associated Commands	copybase, copyclip, olescale, pasteorig, pastespec

PASTEORIG 2000

Imports AutoCAD objects that were copied to the Windows clipboard into the current drawing. You copy objects to the Windows clipboard using the *copybase*, *copyclip*, or *cutclip* command. The contents are inserted based on the object's location in the original file. Regardless of the current drawing's UCS setting, the objects are inserted based on the UCS in which they originated.

Initiate Command By

Command: **pasteorig**
Edit → Paste to Original Coordinates

Associated Commands   copybase, copyclip, pasteclip, pastespec

---

PASTESPEC

Imports the contents of the Windows clipboard into the current drawing. You determine the format and whether the file is embedded or linked.

Initiate Command By

Command: **pastespec**
Alias: **pa**
Edit → Paste Special

Options

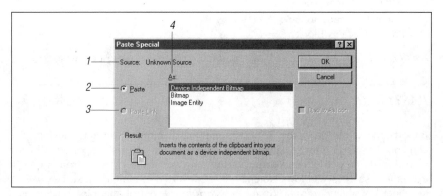

1. **Source.** Lists the name of the application that created the contents in the clipboard, including its file type.

2. **Paste.** Embeds the contents of the clipboard into the current drawing.

3. **Paste Link.** Links the contents of the clipboard into the current drawing.

4. **As.** Lists the various formats that you can use to paste the contents of the clipboard into the drawing.

Tips & Warnings

Use *olehide* to control visibility, *olequality* and *olestartup* to control the plot quality, and *olescale* to control the size of OLE (Object Linking and Embedding) objects.

Related Variables   olehide, olequality, olestartup

Associated Commands   copyclip, copylink, cutclip, insertobj, pasteclip

---

PCINWIZARD 2000

(Plot Configuration Information Wizard) Activates a wizard that takes you through a process of translating plot files (*.pcp* and *.pc2*) created from AutoCAD Release 13 and 14 into AutoCAD 2000. The settings are applied to the current model or layout space. These files contain settings for paper size, plot area, plot rotation, plot optimization, pen mapping, plot to file, plot scale, plot origin, and plot offset. You can modify these settings with *pagesetup* and *plot*.

Initiate Command By
> Command: **pcinwizard**
> Tools → Wizards → Import R14 Plot Settings

Associated Commands   pagesetup, plot

'PDMODE

Determines the shape of points. Points are used as reference markers. This variable is set with the *ddptype* command.

Initiate Command By
> Command: **pdmode**

Options

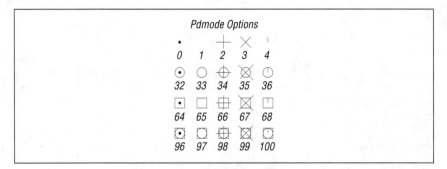

Tips & Warnings

- *pdsize* has no effect on points set to a *pdmode* of 0 or 1.

- You can have only one *pdmode* setting in a drawing at a time. If you change the setting, the drawing will globally update at the next regeneration. Points that are placed on the Defpoints layer by associative dimensioning are not affected by *pdmode* and are the only exception.

Variable Settings

Initial default:	0
Subsequent default:	Last value used in the drawing
Value:	Integer
Related Variables	pdsize
Associated Commands	ddptype, divide, grips, measure, point

'PDSIZE

Determines the size of points. Points are often used as reference markers. This variable is set with *ddptype*.

Initiate Command By

Command: **pdsize**

Options

0

Points are displayed at 5% of the graphics area height.

Less than 0

Points are displayed as a percentage of the viewport size.

Greater than 0

Points are displayed as an absolute size.

Tips & Warnings

- *pdsize* has no effect on points set to a *pdmode* of 0 or 1.

- You can have only one *pdsize* setting in a drawing at a time. If you change the setting, the drawing globally updates at the next regeneration. Points that are placed on the Defpoints layer by associative dimensioning are not affected by *pdsize* and are the only exception.

Variable Settings

Initial default:	0.0000
Subsequent default:	Last value used in the drawing
Value:	Real
Related Variables	pdmode
Associated Commands	ddptype, divide, grips, measure, point

PEDIT

Modify II toolbar

Edits 2D and 3D polylines and 3D polygon meshes. The editing options are based on the type of polyline you choose to edit. There are two basic sets of editing functions. The first set operates on the entire polyline; the second set lets you edit individual vertices. You can edit only one object at a time. *mpedit* allows you to edit more than one polyline at a time; however, it does not let you edit individual vertices.

Initiate Command By

>   Command: **pedit**
>   Alias: **pe**
>   Modify → Polyline

Options

```
Select polyline:
Enter an option [Close/Join/Width/Edit vertex/Fit/Spline/
Decurve/Ltype gen/Undo]:
```

The following list shows the editing options for the three types of polyline objects: 2D, 3D, and 3D polygon meshes. *pedit* automatically identifies the type of polyline that is being edited and adjusts its prompts accordingly.

Select polyline

>   Select a 2D or 3D polyline or a 3D polygon mesh. If you select a line or arc, you are given the opportunity to convert it into a polyline.

Close/Open

>   Closes an open polyline by drawing a polyline segment from the first point of the first polyline segment to the endpoint of the last polyline segment, or removes the closing segment of a closed polyline.

Join

>   Takes individual 2D polylines, lines, and arcs and combines them into one 2D polyline. In order for objects to be joined, they must be contiguous. That is, their endpoints must meet at the same coordinates. When using the join option, you can use any of the selection set methods to pick the items to join. Your selection may include objects you do not want included in the selection set. As long as these objects are not contiguous with another object, they will not join. You cannot join to a closed polyline. If the endpoints are not contiguous, use *pljoin* to quickly join polylines, lines, and arcs.

Width

>   Redefines the width of an entire 2D polyline. You cannot specify tapers with this option. You can assign only one width to the entire polyline segment. If you want different widths between vertices, use the width option of edit vertex.

Edit vertex

>   Individually edits the vertices that make up a polyline segment. An X appears at the first vertex for editing. If any of the segments were drawn with a specified tangent direction, an arrow is drawn in that direction.

References O–P

Next

    Moves the X or arrow marker to the next vertex. The order is based on the initial construction of the polyline.

Previous

    Moves the X or arrow marker to the previous vertex.

Break

    Removes a polyline between two vertices. When you break a closed polyline segment, it becomes open, and the closing segment is removed.

Insert

    Inserts a new vertex ahead of the X marker.

Move

    Moves the vertex marked with an X to a new location.

Straighten

    Creates a single segment between two vertices. Any vertices that are between the two you pick are deleted.

Tangent

    Attaches a tangent direction for curve fitting to the vertex marked with the X.

Width

    Edits the width between two vertices. You specify a starting and an ending width. The current polyline segment is considered to be between the X marker and the vertex found with the next option. The polyline must be regenerated before you will see the results.

Undo

    Undoes, one step at a time, the most recent edit vertex commands.

Go

    Used during the break and straighten options to tell the system you are ready to break or straighten the segments between two vertices.

Left

    For 3D mesh, moves left to a previous vertex in the *N* direction.

Right

    For 3D mesh, moves right to the next vertex in the *N* direction.

Up

    For 3D mesh, moves up to the next vertex in the *M* direction.

Down

    For 3D mesh, moves down to the previous vertex in the *M* direction.

Fit

    Places two arc segments between vertices. You can decurve a fit. If you edit a fit-curve polyline with *break, explode,* or *trim,* the decurve option is no longer available.

Spline

    Uses the polyline vertices as control points for a B-spline curve. The spline passes through the beginning and ending points of the polyline and is pulled toward the other vertices but does not pass through them. View the spline's frame by turning *splframe* on; use *splinesegs* to set the number of spline segments between vertices; determine the spline type by setting the variable *splinetype*. You can decurve a spline curve. If you edit a spline-curve polyline with *break*, *explode*, or *trim*, the decurve option is no longer available.

The greater the value for *splinesegs*, the more precise the curve will be and the closer to the control points. If you enter a negative number, you end up with a smoother curve. Setting *splinesegs* to a negative number is not allowed for 3D polylines. If the polyline is defined with arcs, the arcs are straightened when viewing the spline (*splframe* set to 1). If a polyline is made up of multiple widths, the spline tapers from the beginning width definition to the ending width definition.

Decurve

Removes the curves from any polyline that was either fit or splined and returns it to its original state.

Ltype gen

Determines whether the linetype pattern (other than Continuous) begins anew at every vertex point or whether the linetype ignores all vertices but the first and last. This value is maintained by the *plinegen* variable.

Undo

Takes you back, one *pedit* option at a time. This is different from the *undo* command, which backsteps to the previous command.

Smooth surface/Desmooth

Smooth replaces a 3D mesh with a smooth surface. Desmooth returns a smooth 3D mesh to its original state. Meshes that contain more than 11 vertices in either the *M* or *N* direction cannot be changed into a Bezier surface. Cubic B-spline surfaces require a minimum control point mesh size of 4 × 4. Quadratic B-spline surfaces require a minimum control point mesh size of 3 × 3. The type of surface is based on the *surftype* variable.

Mopen/Mclose, Nopen/Nclose

Mopen/Mclose opens or closes a 3D mesh in the *M* direction. Nopen/Nclose opens or closes a 3D mesh in the *N* direction.

Tips & Warnings

properties offers some of the *pedit* options depending on the individual object.

Related Variables   plinegen, splframe, splinesegs, splinetype, surftype

Associated Commands   mpedit, pline, pljoin, 3dmesh, 3dpoly

Example

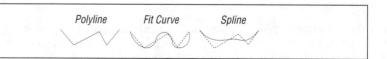

Polyline   Fit Curve   Spline

'PELLIPSE

Determines the type of ellipse created with the *ellipse* command. When *pellipse* is set to 0, you can locate the center and major and minor axes using object snap's center and quadrant options. When *pellipse* is set to 1, you can locate only the endpoint, center, and midpoint of each individual polyline arc.

Initiate Command By

Command: **pellipse**

Options

0   Creates a true ellipse object.

1   Creates an ellipse using polyline arcs.

Variable Settings

Initial default:	0
Subsequent default:	Last value used in the drawing
Value:	Integer
Associated Commands	ellipse
Example	See ELLIPSE.

'PERIMETER

Maintains the last perimeter value set by *area*, *list*, or *dblist*. Regardless of whether you are beginning a new drawing or editing an existing drawing, *perimeter* retains the last computed value until you end the AutoCAD session.

Initiate Command By

Command: **perimeter**

Variable Settings

Initial default:	0.0000, read-only
Subsequent default:	Initial default
Value:	Real
Related Variables	area
Associated Commands	area, list

PFACE

Creates arbitrary polyface meshes. The mesh, composed of vertices and faces, is used mainly by software developers writing programs for third-party applications.

You can enter the vertices as 2D or 3D points. You must keep track of each vertex and its number assignment in order to define the faces. If you press Escape before exiting the command, you must start over. You can make the edges of the poly-face mesh invisible by entering a negative vertex number for the beginning vertex of the edge. *splframe* controls the visibility of the invisible edges. You can use the *layer* and *color* commands when defining faces. Enter L or Layer and C or Color when prompted to define a face. Changing the layer and color does not affect any new objects you create for subsequent commands. Only part of the mesh becomes invisible when you assign that part of the mesh to a layer that is off or frozen.

Initiate Command By

Command: **pface**

Options

```
Vertex 1:
Face 1, vertex 1:
```

vertex

Specifies the location for each vertex

face

Specifies the vertex numbers that define each face

Tips & Warnings

Since you cannot use *pedit*, try manipulating the vertices with *grips*.

Related Variables

pfacevmax, splframe

Associated Commands

grips, 3dface

Example

```
Command: pface
Specify location for vertex 1: 3,2
Specify location for vertex 2 or <define faces>: 9,2
Specify location for vertex 3 or <define faces>: 9,6
Specify location for vertex 4 or <define faces>: 3,6
Specify location for vertex 5 or <define faces>: 6,4,9
Specify location for vertex 6 or <define faces>: Press Enter
Face 1, vertex 1: Enter a vertex number or [Color/Layer]: Layer
Enter a layer name <0>: Front
Face 1, vertex 1: Enter a vertex number or [Color/Layer]: 1
Face 1, vertex 2: Enter a vertex number or [Color/Layer] <next face>: 2
Face 1, vertex 3: Enter a vertex number or [Color/Layer] <next face>: 5
Face 1, vertex 4: Enter a vertex number or [Color/Layer] <next face>:
Press Enter
Face 2, vertex 1: Enter a vertex number or [Color/Layer]: Layer
Enter a layer name <front>: Back
Face 2, vertex 1: Enter a vertex number or [Color/Layer]: 3
Face 2, vertex 2: Enter a vertex number or [Color/Layer] <next face>: 4
Face 2, vertex 3: Enter a vertex number or [Color/Layer] <next face>: 5
Face 2, vertex 4: Enter a vertex number or [Color/Layer] <next face>:
Press Enter
Face 3, vertex 1: Enter a vertex number or [Color/Layer]: Press Enter
```

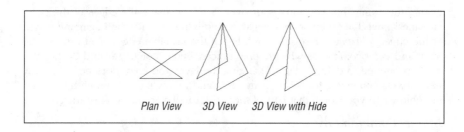

Plan View   3D View   3D View with Hide

'PFACEVMAX

Maintains the maximum number of vertices per polyface meshes. This variable is used by software developers writing specific customized AutoCAD routines.

Initiate Command By
Command: **pfacevmax**

Variable Settings

Initial default:	4, read-only
Subsequent default:	Initial default
Value:	Integer

Associated Commands   pface

'PICKADD

Controls how objects are added or removed during the selection set process. This variable is set when checking the "Use shift to add to selection" box from the *options* Selection tab.

Initiate Command By
Command: **pickadd**

Options

0   During object selection, picking objects releases those already chosen, and the selection process begins anew.

1   During object selection, picking objects adds to those already selected.

Tips & Warnings

- When *pickadd* is 0, you can add and remove objects from the selection set by pressing Shift when you select objects.

- When *pickadd* is 1, you can remove objects from the selection set by pressing Shift or by using the remove option of the selection set modes when selecting objects.

- See "Selection Sets" in Chapter 2, *Command Index and Global Topics,* for more information.

Variable Settings

Initial default:	1
Subsequent default:	Registry file
Value:	Integer
Related Variables	pickauto, pickbox, pickdrag, pickfirst
Associated Commands	options, preferences

'PICKAUTO

Controls automatic windowing during "Select objects" prompts. If the pick fails to select an object, the selection method becomes a window or crossing. Moving the crosshairs to the right creates a window, to the left a crossing. This variable is set when checking the Implied Windowing box from the *options* Selection tab.

Initiate Command By

Command: **pickauto**

Tips & Warnings

See "Selection Sets" in Chapter 2, *Command Index and Global Topics*, for more information.

Options

0   *pickauto* is disabled during object selection.

1   *pickauto* is enabled during object selection.

Variable Settings

Initial default:	1
Subsequent default:	Registry file
Value:	Integer
Related Variables	pickadd, pickbox, pickdrag, pickfirst
Associated Commands	options, preferences

'PICKBOX

Determines the size of the target box at the intersection of the crosshairs. This box is visible during object selection and when *pickfirst* and *grips* are enabled. This variable changes when moving the slider bar for Pickbox Size from the *options* Selection tab. Changing the value for *pickbox* using the slider bar cannot be undone with the *undo* command.

Initiate Command By

Command: **pickbox**

Tips & Warnings

- This box is sometimes confused with the aperture box used during object snap. For less confusion, set the *aperture* and *pickbox* to different sizes.

- Do not make the aperture setting so large or so small that it is difficult to pick objects. The maximum value you can use for the pickbox size when using the *options* dialog box is 20. If you set this value at the command line, the maximum value you can reference is 50.

- See "Selection Sets" in Chapter 2, *Command Index and Global Topics*, for more information.

Variable Settings

Initial default:	3
Subsequent default:	Registry file
Value:	Integer

Related Variables	aperture, grips, pickfirst
Associated Commands	options, preferences

'PICKDRAG

Determines the method used to define windows or crossings during object selection. This variable is set when checking the Press and Drag box from the *options* Selection tab. Using the *options* command to change the value for *pickdrag* cannot by undone with the *undo* command.

Initiate Command By

Command: **pickdrag**

Options

- *0* During object selection, you are required to pick two diagonal points for the window and crossing methods.

- *1* During object selection, you are required to hold down the pointing device button while defining the two points for the window and crossing options. Releasing your finger from the button defines the second diagonal point.

Tips & Warnings

See "Selection Sets" in Chapter 2, *Command Index and Global Topics*, for more information.

Variable Settings

Initial default:	0
Subsequent default:	Registry file
Value:	Integer

Related Variables	pickadd, pickauto, pickbox, pickfirst
Associated Commands	options, preferences

'PICKFIRST

Determines the order of execution of certain commands. When *pickfirst* is enabled, you can first select objects before issuing commands; when disabled, you must first begin the command before selecting objects. The following commands are affected:

array	copy	hatch	move	scale
block	dview	list	plotstyle	stretch
change	erase	mirror	properties	transparency
chprop	explode	mocoro	rotate	wblock

When *pickfirst* is enabled, you will see the pickbox located at the intersection of the screen's crosshairs. This value is set by checking the Noun/Verb Selection box from the *options* Selection tab.

Initiate Command By

Command: **pickfirst**

Options

0   Creates your selection set after activating commands.

1   Creates your selection set before (or after) activating commands.

Tips & Warnings

- When *pickfirst* is active (1), you will see a small box located at the intersection of the screen's crosshairs. If you disable *pickfirst* (0) and the box still appears, check the grips and object snap settings from the *options* command. These commands also enable a box to appear at the intersection of the screen's crosshairs.

- You can quickly change the layer, linetype, and lineweight settings of objects using the Object Properties toolbar. First select the objects and then pick the desired drop-down list for layer, color, or lineweight.

- Regardless of the *pickfirst* setting, you can always change the properties of objects using *properties*.

- See "Selection Sets" in Chapter 2, *Command Index and Global Topics*, for more information.

Variable Settings

Initial default:	1
Subsequent default:	Registry file
Value:	Integer
Related Variables	pickadd, pickauto, pickbox, pickdrag
Associated Commands	grips, options, preferences

'PICKSTYLE

Controls whether *groups* are temporarily treated as individual objects and how -*bhatch* objects are linked to their boundaries. This value is set by checking the Object Grouping and Associative Hatch boxes from the *options* Selection tab.

Initiate Command By

Command: **pickstyle**

Options

0   No group or associative hatch selection.

1   Group selection.

2   Associative hatch selection.

3   Group and associative hatch selection.

Variable Settings

Initial default:	1
Subsequent default:	Registry file
Value:	Integer

Tips & Warnings

- You can quickly toggle *pickstyle*'s 0 and 1 settings by pressing Ctrl-A.

- The *pickstyle* setting affects only -*bhatch*. *hatch* is always nonassociative, and *bhatch* defaults to associative. You can temporarily set *bhatch* to nonassociative as an option within that command.

Associated Commands   -bhatch, group, options, preferences

PLAN

Displays the plan view of the current UCS (User Coordinate System), defined UCS, or WCS (World Coordinate System). A plan view is defined as having a viewpoint of 0,0,1. *plan* affects only the current viewport and turns perspective and clipping plane viewing off.

Initiate Command By

Command: **plan**
View → 3D Views → Plan View

Options

Enter an option [Current ucs/Ucs/World] <Current>:

Current ucs
Restores the plan view of the current UCS.

UCS
Restores the plan view of a previously defined UCS.

World
> Restores the plan view of the WCS.

Related Variables   ucsfollow

Associated Commands   ucs, vpoint

Example

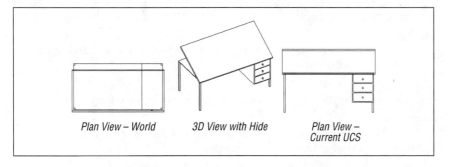

Plan View – World   3D View with Hide   Plan View – Current UCS

'PLATFORM

Stores the name of the AutoCAD platform in use. This information varies based on the combination of hardware and software on your system. The platforms are Microsoft Windows NT Version 4.00 (x86) or Microsoft Windows Version 4.00 (x86).

Initiate Command By
> Command: **platform**

Variable Settings

Initial default:	Varies, read-only
Subsequent default:	Initial default
Value:	String

PLINE   Draw toolbar

A polyline is a series of 2D lines and arc segments that share the same vertices and are processed as a single object. It has a line mode and an arc mode, each with different prompts. You start both modes by specifying a start point. To edit polylines, you can use *pedit, properties,* and most of the regular edit commands.

Donuts, ellipses (*pellipse* = 1), rectangles, and polygons are created from polylines. Therefore, you can assign widths to ellipses and polygons with the *pedit* command. If your polylines' assigned widths are not filled, it may be because *fill* is off. Convert polylines into lines using *explode.* You can convert lines into polylines using the join option of the *pedit* command.

Initiate Command By

Command: **pline**
Alias: **pl**
Draw → Polyline

Options

```
Specify start point:
Current line-width is 0.0000
Specify next point or [Arc/Close/Halfwidth/Length/Undo/Width]:
```

Arc

Switches from drawing straight line segments to drawing arcs and activates a submenu for the arc options.

Close

Closes the polyline segments connecting the start point to the end point.

Halfwidth

Specifies the width from the center of a polyline to one of its edges. The number is doubled for the actual width.

Length

Lets you specify the length of a new polyline segment at the same angle as the last polyline segment. If you use this option after constructing a polyline arc, the polyline will be tangent to the arc.

Undo

Undoes the last arc segment and returns you to the previous point when you enter u at the "Specify endpoint of arc" prompt.

Width

Creates polylines with width and mitered intersections. You can even construct polyline segments with tapers by defining different starting and ending widths. Once you have drawn a tapered line segment, the next segment defaults to the ending width of the previous segment. The default width is 0. This value is maintained by the *plinewid* variable. When a polyline's width is set to 0, it takes on the current lineweight setting; when a polyline's width is set to a number other than 0, it ignores the lineweight setting.

Tips & Warnings

- When offsetting joined polylines, you can automatically have the corners offset with a filleted arc or chamfer or have the ends extend by setting the *offsetgaptype* variable. This works only when a gap would be created to the endpoint due to the offset distance.

- *chamfer* and *fillet* have special options for polylines. *sketch* lets you define the objects as being plines or lines.

- You can request the area and perimeter/length of a polyline by using the object option of the *area* command. *list* also provides this information.

- *plinegen* determines whether a polyline's linetype pattern begins anew at every vertex or whether the linetype ignores all vertices but the first and last.

| *Related Variables* | fillmode, lastangle, lastpoint, offsetgaptype, plinegen, plinetype, plinewid, skpoly |
| *Associated Commands* | bhatch, boundary, convert, fill, pedit, 3dpoly |

Example

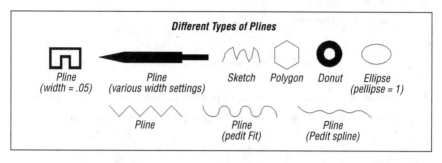

Different Types of Plines

Pline (width = .05)   Pline (various width settings)   Sketch   Polygon   Donut   Ellipse (pellipse = 1)

Pline   Pline (pedit Fit)   Pline (Pedit spline)

'PLINEGEN

Determines whether a polyline's linetype pattern begins anew at every vertex or whether the linetype ignores all vertices but the first and last.

Initiate Command By

Command: **plinegen**

Options

0   Linetype pattern begins anew at every vertex.

1   Linetype pattern ignores all vertices but the first and last.

Variable Settings

Initial default:	0
Subsequent default:	Last value used in the drawing
Value:	Integer

Tips & Warnings

- You can change the value assigned to polylines using *pedit* and *properties*.

- *plinegen* does not apply to polylines with tapered segments nor to 3D polylines.

| *Associated Commands* | mpedit, pedit, pline, properties |

Example

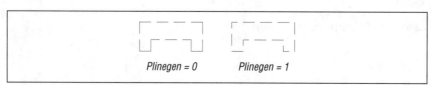

Plinegen = 0   Plinegen = 1

References O–P

'PLINETYPE

Determines whether 2D polylines created in Release 13 or earlier are converted to a more optimized format and whether new polylines are optimized.

Initiate Command By

Command: **plinetype**

Options

0   Polylines in older drawings are not updated, and new polylines retain the old format.

1   Polylines in older drawings are not updated, but new polylines are optimized.

2   Polylines in older drawings as well as new polylines are optimized.

Variable Settings

Initial default:	2
Subsequent default:	Registry file
Value:	Integer

Associated Commands   convert, pline

'PLINEWID

Determines the default width for new polylines. This value is set with the width option of the *pline* command.

Initiate Command By

Command: **plinewid**

Tips & Warnings

- You can create tapered polylines if you set the width while in the *pline* command.

- You can change the width assigned to polylines using the width option of the *pedit* command. However, all the polyline segments of the polyline take the new value. If you want different starting and ending widths, use the edit vertex option of the *pedit* command.

Variable Settings

Initial default:	0.0000
Subsequent default:	Last value used in the drawing
Value:	Real

Associated Commands   pedit, pline

PLJOIN 2000

Lets you join lines, arcs, and polylines into one polyline. This is similar to the join option of the *pedit* command except that *pedit* requires endpoints to be contiguous. The *pljoin* command cleans up endpoints so that they share the same coordinates and are contiguous.

Initiate Command By

Command: **pljoin**
Express → Modify → Polyline Join

Options

```
Select objects:
Join Type = Both (Fillet and Add)
Enter fuzz distance or [Jointype] <0.0000>:
```

Select objects

Allows you to select lines, arcs, and polylines. If the objects are lines or arcs, they are automatically converted into polylines.

fuzz distance

Determines the maximum distance the object's endpoints can be from one another and still be joined.

Jointype

Determines how the objects are connected.

Fillet

Automatically extends or trims the endpoints until they meet. This is equivalent to having the fillet radius set at 0.

Add

Adds a polyline connecting the endpoints.

Both

Combines the fillet and add options. If there is a gap between the objects, a polyline is added; if the lines overlap, a fillet is performed.

Associated Commands   expresstools, pedit

-PLOT 2000   *see PLOT*

PLOT 2000mod   Standard toolbar

Obtains an output, or hard copy, of your drawing file. *plot* directs your drawing to a plotter, printer, or plot file. *plot* activates a dialog box that also references the *pagesetup*, *preveiw*, and *psetupin* commands. You can use *-plot* so all prompts and options appear at the command line. Preset general plotting parameters using the *options* Plotting tab.

You can set the various plotting parameters with a dialog box or at the command prompt. It is recommended that you use the dialog box because of its added features. If you use the command line and make a mistake, you must cancel and begin the process again. With the dialog box, you just pick the error and make your correction.

Plan to spend time testing different plotting media. You may need to try several different combinations of papers, pens, pen speeds, and colors to get good results. In addition, room temperature and humidity will affect plotting quality.

Plot questions default to the current model space or layout space. In model space, the plot depends on the current viewport and the chosen plotting options. In layout space, the plot depends on how much of the drawing (including viewports) falls within the chosen plotting options. Viewports turned off with the *mview* command are not plotted.

Initiate Command By

Command: **plot**, Ctrl-P
Alias: **print**
File → Plot

Options

The Plot dialog contains two tabs. In this section, we start by covering the Plot Device tab and later cover the Plot Settings tab.

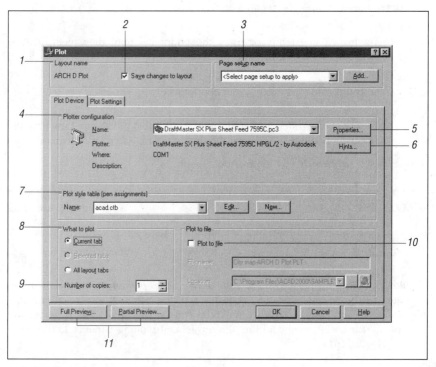

1. **Layout name.** Lists the tab name (model or layout) that will be plotted. This is based on the tab that was active before issuing the *plot* command. The section labeled "What to plot" lets you plot all the tabs, selected tabs, or the current tab.

2. **Save changes to layout.** Saves any changes you make with the *plot* command to the active tab. If multiple tabs are selected, this option is unavailable.

3. **Page setup name.** Lets you choose a page setup, containing predefined plotting parameters, and apply those settings to the selected layout tab. Page setup names are created with *pagesetup*. The information retained with *pagesetup* includes parameters that define the plotter configuration, plot style table, what to plot, plot location (file or plotter), paper size and paper units, drawing orientation, plot area, plot scale, and plot offset.

   Add

   Copies page setups (*pagesetup*) defined in other drawings (*.dwg*) and template files (*.dwt*) into the current drawing.

The Plot Device Tab

The Plot Device tab defines the plotter, plot style table, and layout of layouts to plot.

4. **Plotter configuration.** Determines the plotter device. Devices are defined with the Add-A-Plotter wizard. Use the *plottermanager* or the Add or Configure Plotters option from the *options* Plotting tab to access this wizard. Descriptive information is provided which is especially useful when you are networked and you need to know the location of the plotting device.

5. **Properties.** Lets you edit the *.pc3* file. This file is created when using the Add-A-Plotter wizard and contains specific information for each configured plotter. You may have more than one *.pc3* file for each plotter. You also can edit *.pc3* files with *plottermanager*.

6. **Hints.** Provides information about the current plotting device.

7. **Plot style table (pen assignments).** Sets the plot style table, edits plot style tables, and creates new plot style tables. Plot style tables contain plot styles that define color, lineweight, linetype, end cap, line fill, and screening. These styles are assigned to layouts and viewports. See *stylesmanager* and *plotstyle* for more detailed information.

8. **What to plot.** Determines if the current tab (*ctab*), selected tab, or all tabs are plotted. If you use selected tabs, you must preselect the tabs before issuing the *plot* command. Select multiple tabs by selecting tabs while holding down the Ctrl key.

9. **Number of copies.** When multiple layouts are selected, any layouts that are set to plot to a file or AutoSpool only produce a single copy.

10. **Plot to file.** Determines whether the plot is sent directly to the plotter or to a file. You cannot plot to a file when more than one tab is selected for plotting.

    File name

    The default filename is the name of the drawing, followed by a hyphen (-), and the tab or layout name. The file extension is *.plt*.

Location

Determines the location of the plot file.

11. **Full Preview**, **Partial Preview**. Displays how the plot will fit on the paper based on current plot settings. Exit out of this mode by using the shortcut menu.

Full

Displays a preview of the plot, showing how the actual drawing objects appear relative to the paper size. You can pan and zoom around the file using the shortcut menu.

Partial

Displays a quick preview of the plot showing the plotting area relative to the paper size. A triangular rotation icon portrays the plot rotation. A rotation of 0 places the icon in the lower-left corner. It also provides statistics listing the paper size, printable area, and effective area. Warnings are issued when the defined plotting area is greater than the paper size.

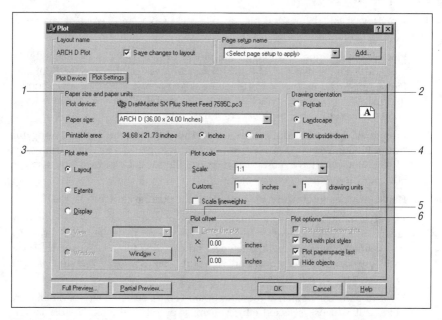

The Plot Settings Tab

The Plot Settings tab defines the paper size, drawing orientation, plot area, plot scale, plot offset, and some miscellaneous plotting parameters.

1. **Paper size and paper units**. The plot device is determined by the plotter configuration selected from the Plot Device tab. The paper size is based on the current plotting device. Standard sheet sizes are provided when the plotter is set to None. The printable area defines how much of the paper can actually be printed. The inches and mm radio buttons indicate whether the plotting units are based on inches or millimeters.

2. **Drawing orientation.** Defines how the plot is positioned on the paper. The plot can sit portrait or landscape, and it can rotate to sit upside down.

3. **Plot area.** Defines the portion of the drawing to plot.

   Layout

   Plots to the limits when the model tab is active or to everything within the margins of the specified paper size when a layout tab is active. When a layout tab is active and you are working inside a viewport (model space), you are automatically switched to paper space when activating *plot*. If the current viewport is not a plan view (0,0,1), the plot is based on zoom extents.

   Extents

   The plot is based on the drawing extents. It takes into account all drawing objects regardless of the limits setting. Objects on layers turned off and layers set to "Do not plot" also are calculated to determine the plot area, but they are not actually plotted.

   Display

   The plot is based on what is visible in the current viewport. Objects on layers set to "Do not plot" are not plotted.

   View

   Plots a previously saved view. Views are created with the *view* command. This option is available if one or more views are defined in the drawing. Select a view from the drop-down list located to the right of the View radio button.

   Window

   Plots the area you designate as a window by picking the Window button.

4. **Plot scale.** Determines what scale to plot the drawing. You do this by specifying how many plotted inches or millimeters equal how many drawing units. The drop-down list provides standard drawing scales. The first two choices, Scale and Custom, let you enter other scales in the custom boxes.

   Scale lineweights

   Determines if lineweights are plotted in proportion to the plot scale or if they are plotted to their actual size regardless of the plot scale.

5. **Plot offset.** Determines where the plot starts on the sheet of paper. You can center the plot or determine where the plot starts in relation to the lower-left corner of the paper.

6. **Plot options.** Lets you toggle some miscellaneous plotting parameters on or off. You can plot objects assigned a lineweight with or without their lineweight settings, plot with plot styles assigned to objects, plot model space objects first, and generate hidden line removal. Hidden line removal with the model tab active removes the hidden edges of 3D objects. When layout space is active, use the hideplot option of the *mview* command to have hidden edges removed.

Tips & Warnings

- If you see objects displayed on the drawing but not on the plot, it is probably because they are assigned to a layer is set to "Do not plot" or they are on the Defpoints layer. The Defpoints layer is created whenever you create an associative dimension, and objects on that layer will not plot.

- You cannot assign a specific scale factor value to a drawing plotted in perspective (*dview, 3dorbit*) view.

- Define plotting devices with *plottermanager*.

- When plotting in layout space, the variable *maxactvp* is ignored. So long as the viewport is on (*mview*), the viewport is plotted.

- Use the AutoCAD batch plotting utility to plot multiple drawings using the same plotting parameters. You can save the names of those drawings to a file and plot them out repeatedly with those same parameters.

Related Variables	maxactvp
Associated Commands	layout, layoutwizard, options, pagesetup, plottermanager, preferences, psetupin, stylesmanager

PLOTID (obsolete)

-PLOTSTYLE   *see PLOTSTYLE*

PLOTSTYLE 2000

Sets the current plot style for new xobjects and changes the plot style assigned to existing objects. If no objects are selected before issuing the command, the Current Plot Style dialog box is automatically activated; if objects are preselected the Select Plot Style dialog box is automatically activated.

Plot styles control how objects plot. You can change the color, dithering, grayscale, pen numbers, screening, linetype, lineweight, fill patterns, and line end definitions. Plot styles are stored in plot style tables. There are two types of plot styles: color-dependent mode and named plot style mode. The color-dependent mode plots objects based on their assigned color. The named plot style mode lets you assign a plot style to individual layers.

You can use *-plotstyle* so the prompts and options appear on the command line.

Initiate Command By

Command: **plotstyle**
Format → Plot Style

Options

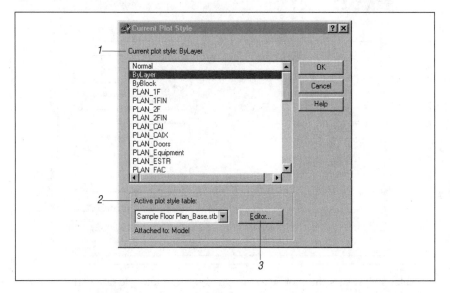

1. **Plot style list.** Lists the plot styles that can be assigned to objects. Plot styles define overrides for color, dithering, grayscale, pen assignments, screening, linetype, lineweight, end styles, join styles, and fill styles. The list is based on the active plot style table listed at the bottom of the dialog box. This value is maintained by the *cplotstyle* setting.

2. **Active plot style table.** Lists the plot style table attached to the current layout. You can change this by selecting other plot styles from the drop-down list.

3. **Editor.** Lets you modify the current plot styles assigned to the plot style table by activating the Plot Style Table Editor.

The Plot Style Editor

The Plot Style Table Editor has three tabs. The first tab, named General, provides some general information about the plot style table. The Table View and Form View tabs provide the same information but in a different format. The Form View tab is more commonly used because it is more graphically descriptive than the Table View.

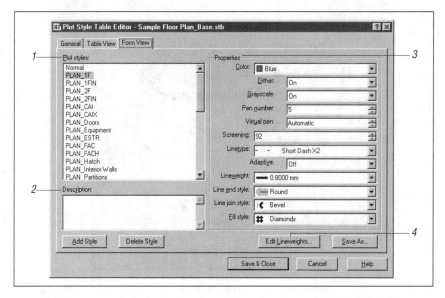

1. **Plot styles**. Lists the plot styles assigned to the plot style table. The plot style named Normal represents an object's default properties (no plot style applied). Highlighting a style causes the Properties section to display the values for that style. Plot styles in named plot style tables can be changed; plot styles in color-dependent plot style tables are tied to an object color and cannot be changed.

2. **Description**. Displays a description for each plot style.

3. **Properties**. Defines the properties assigned to the plot style highlighted in the Plot Styles list.

   Color

   Defines the plotted color for an object.

   Dither

   Toggles dithering on and off. Dithering is the method used by plotters to approximate colors by using dot patterns. Not all plotters support this feature. Dithering thin lines assigned a linetype other than Continuous can sometimes look distorted.

   Grayscale

   Toggles grayscale on and off. When grayscale is enabled, the object's colors are converted to grayscale. When disabled, the object's colors are based on RGB values. Not all plotters support this feature.

   Pen number

   Determines the pen to use. Available pens range from 1 to 32. This is for pen plotters only.

Virtual pen

Used by non-pen plotters that are configured for virtual pens. Available pen numbers range from 1 to 255. When this option is used, all the other style settings are ignored.

Screening

Determines a color intensity setting. Valid ranges are from 0 to 100. A setting of 0 reduces the color to white; a setting of 100 displays the color at its full intensity.

Linetype

Assigns a different linetype to objects regardless of their current setting.

Adaptive

Toggles adaptive on and off. Adaptive adjusts linetypes to determine if the linetype pattern is completed at its ending point or if it stops in the middle of a pattern.

Lineweight

Determines the lineweight of objects. If set to a value other than "Use object lineweight," it will override the object's lineweight setting. You can change the lineweight values by selecting the Edit Lineweights button at the bottom of the screen.

Line end style

Lets you assign line end styles. These include butt, square, round, diamond, and "Use object end style."

Line join style

Lets you assign line join styles. These include miter, bevel, round, diamond, and "Use object join style."

Fill style

Lets you assign fill styles. These include solid, checkerboard, crosshatch, diamonds, horizontal bars, slant left, slant right, square dots, vertical bar, and "Use object fill style."

4. **Edit Lineweights**. Lets you edit lineweight values. There are 28 lineweights that can be modified. Changing any of the values affects other plot styles referencing that lineweight.

Tips & Warnings

- You can change the plot style assigned to layouts using *properties*, to layers using the *layer* command, and to objects using *matchprop*.

- If you plan to move a drawing file containing plot styles to another computer or to a diskette, you need to include any referenced plot styles. Use *pack* to help you accomplish this.

Related Variables   defplstyle, deflplstyle, pstylemode, pstylepolicy

Associated Commands   layer, layout, pack, pagesetup

References O–P

PLOTTER (obsolete)   *see PLOT*

PLOTTERMANAGER 2000

Defines plotting devices with the Add-A-Plotter wizard and edits existing plotter configuration files. The information collected by *plottermanager* is stored in a file with the extension *.pc3*. The information stored in the *.pc3* file is the plotter configuration name, plotter type, driver type, port connections, media size, graphics resolution, and paper size.

Initiate Command By

> Command: **plottermanager**
> File → Plotter Manager

Associated Commands   plot

'PLQUIET 2000

Controls the display of nonfatal error messages and plot dialog boxes during *script* and batch plotting routines.

Initiate Command By

> Command: **plquiet**

Options

0   Nonfatal error messages and plot dialog boxes are displayed during *script* and batch plotting routines.

1   Nonfatal error messages and plot dialog boxes are suppressed during *script* and batch plotting routines.

Variable Settings

Initial default:	0
Subsequent default:	Registry file
Value:	Integer

Associated Commands   plot, script

POINT   Draw toolbar

Creates a point in *X, Y, Z* space. Place a point by absolute, relative, or polar coordinates, or pick a point in the drawing with your pointing device. (See "Point and Coordinate Entry" in Chapter 2, *Command Index and Global Topics.*) You can object-snap to points using the node option.

You can change the way points are displayed with the *ddptype* command or by individually setting the *pdmode* and *pdsize* variables. *pdmode* determines the shape; *pdsize* determines the size.

Initiate Command By
Command: **point**
Alias: **po**
Draw → Point

Options
```
Current point modes:  PDMODE=0  PDSIZE=0.0000
Specify a point:
```

Tips & Warnings

You can have only one *pdmode* and *pdsize* setting in a drawing at a time. If you change the settings, the drawing globally updates at the next regeneration. Points that are placed on the Defpoints layer by associative dimensioning are not affected by *pdmode* and *pdsize* and are the only exceptions.

Related Variables   pdmode, pdsize

Associated Commands   ddptype, divide, grips, measure

Example   See DDPTYPE.

'POLARADDANG 2000

Defines additional polar increment angles when polar tracking is on. You can define up to 10 additional polar tracking angles. Enter each angle followed with a semicolon (;). Each angle can contain up to 25 characters. You also can set the values by selecting the New button from the *dsettings* Polar Tracking tab. The *polarang* values (90, 45, 30, 22.5, 18, 15, 10, 5) are preset and cannot be changed, and only one value is active at a time. The *polarmode* variable determines if *polaraddang* is active. The *aunits* variable determines the angle format: decimal degrees; degrees, minutes, and seconds; gradients; radians; or surveyor's units.

Initiate Command By
Command: **polarddang**

Variable Settings

Initial default:	Null
Subsequent default:	Registry file
Value:	String

Related Variables   aunits, polarang, polarmode

Associated Commands   dsettings

'POLARANG 2000

Defines a polar increment angle when polar tracking is on. The *polarang* values (90, 45, 30, 22.5, 18, 15, 10, 5) are preset and can't be changed. You also can set the value by selecting the New button from the *dsettings* Polar Tracking tab. The *polarmode* variable determines if the *polaraddang* and *polarang* values are active. The *aunits* variable determines the angle format: decimal degrees; degrees, minutes, and seconds; gradients; radians; or surveyor's units.

Initiate Command By
Command: **polarang**

Variable Settings

Initial default:	90
Subsequent default:	Registry file
Value:	Real
Related Variables	aunits, polaraddang, polarmode
Associated Commands	dsettings

'POLARDIST 2000

Defines the snap increment when polar snap (*snaptype*) is enabled. When polar distance is set to 0, it inherits the value assigned to snap *X* spacing. Snap (*snapmode*) and polar tracking (*autosnap*) must be on for polar distance to take effect. This setting can be changed when you enter a value in the Polar Distance box from the *dsettings* Snap and Grid tab.

Initiate Command By
Command: **polardist**

Variable Settings

Initial default:	0.0000
Subsequent default:	Registry file
Value:	Real
Related Variables	autosnap, snapmode, snaptype
Associated Commands	dsettings

'POLARMODE 2000

Maintains the settings for polar and object snap tracking. This value is set by selecting the Additional Angles and Object Snap Tracking Settings radio buttons from the *dsettings* Polar Tracking tab and by selecting an Alignment Point Acquisition radio button from the *options* Drafting tab.

Initiate Command By
Command: **polarmode**

Options

Polarmode is bit-coded, and its value is the sum of the following:

Polar angle measurements

    0   Polar angles are measured based on the current UCS and are absolute.

    1   Polar angles are measured relative to last segment.

Object snap tracking

    0   Track orthogonally only.

    2   Track using all polar angle settings.

Use additional polar tracking angles

    0   *polaraddang* is inactive.

    4   *polaraddang* is active.

Acquire object snap tracking points

    0   Acquire points automatically.

    8   Acquire points by pressing the Shift key.

Variable Settings

Initial default:	1
Subsequent default:	Last value used in the drawing
Value:	Integer
Related Variables	trackpath
Associated Commands	dsettings, options, preferences

---

polyface   *see PFACE*

POLYGON   Draw toolbar

Creates 2D polygons. The number of sides ranges between 3 and 1,024. You can draw the polygon by inscribing or circumscribing about an imaginary circle. Since polygons are closed polylines, you can use the *pedit* command for editing. Polygons are drawn counterclockwise.

Initiate Command By
Command: **polygon**
Alias: **pol**
Draw → Polygon

Options

```
Enter number of sides <4>:
Specify center of polygon or [Edge]:
Enter an option [Inscribed in circle/Circumscribed about circle] <I>:
Specify radius of circle:
```

center of polygon

Specifies the center point about which the polygon will be drawn. All vertices are equidistant from the center point.

Edge

Specifies the size by picking the endpoints of one edge.

Inscribed in circle

The vertices touch the circumference of an imaginary circle. When you use the inscribed option and pick a point to show the radius, that point determines the location for the first vertex as well as the rotation angle.

Circumscribed about circle

The midpoint of each edge touches the circumference of an imaginary circle. When you use the circumscribed option and pick a point to show the radius, that point determines the location for the midpoint of the first edge as well as the rotation angle.

Tips & Warnings

Polygons are drawn with line width 0 regardless of the default polyline width and contain no tangent information. You can use *pedit* and assign widths and tangents once the polygon has been created.

Related Variables   polysides

Associated Commands   pedit, pline

Example

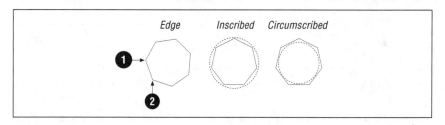

Edge   Inscribed   Circumscribed

---

polyline

see PLINE

'POLYSIDES

Maintains the default number of sides (3–1,024) for polygons. This value is set with *polygon*.

Initiate Command By
Command: **polysides**

Variable Settings

Initial default:	4
Subsequent default:	Initial default
Value:	Integer

Associated Commands   polygon

'POPUPS

Maintains the status of the display driver.

Initiate Command By
Command: **popups**

Options

0   Display driver does not support dialog boxes, toolbars, or pull-down and icon menus.

1   Display driver supports dialog boxes, toolbars, or pull-down and icon menus.

Variable Settings

Initial default:	1, read-only
Subsequent default:	Initial default
Value:	Integer

Associated Commands   options, preferences

PREFERENCES 2000mod   *see OPTIONS*

PREVIEW   Standard toolbar

Shows how the drawing will look when it is plotted. The plotting parameters are based on the current plot configuration. You can *zoom* and *pan* around the drawing using the shortcut menu. The *plot* command provides a Preview button so you can verify the plot setup without exiting the command.

Initiate Command By
Command: **preview**
Alias: **pre**
File → Plot Preview

Associated Commands   plot

'PROJECTNAME

Specifies the folders in which AutoCAD searches for external references. This variable is based on the Project Files Search Path settings located in the *options* Files tab. Each drawing can be assigned to only one project name.

Initiate Command By

Command: **projectname**

Variable Settings

Initial default:	" " (none)
Subsequent default:	Last value used in the drawing
Value:	String

Associated Commands   options, preferences, xattach, xref

'PROJMODE

Maintains the current projection mode for *bextend, btrim, extend,* and *trim.* This value is set using *trim* and *extend.*

Initiate Command By

Command: **projmode**

Options

0   No projection, true 3D mode.

1   Project to the *XY* plane of the current UCS.

2   Project to the current view plane.

Variable Settings

Initial default:	1
Subsequent default:	Registry file
Value:	Integer

Related Variables   extmode

Associated Commands   bextend, btrim, extend, trim

PROPERTIES 2000   Standard toolbar

Activates the Properties dialog box, which lists many of the drawing's default settings. These settings can be changed from this dialog box, or you can go to the individual commands to make changes. When selecting one or more objects, the fields displayed in the dialog box change to show the common properties of those objects. It provides a quick and easy way to view an object's settings and make any necessary changes. It combines many AutoCAD commands such as *change*, *chprop, color, ddedit, elevation, layer, lengthen, lweight,* and *linetype.* Some of the properties provide a down arrow or a pick point button. The down arrow lists available choices; the pick point button lets you select a point on the drawing. These symbols appear when an appropriate property is selected. For example, color, layer, and lineweight provide drop-down lists; *X, Y,* and *Z* provide a pick point button.

Initiate Command By

Command: **properties**
Alias: **mo, ch, ddmodify, props, ddchprop,** or Ctrl-1
Tools → Properties
Modify → Properties

Options

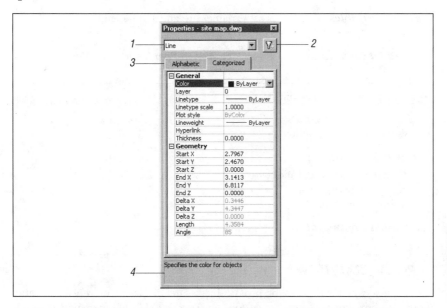

1. **Top drop-down list.** Lists the types of objects selected. If there is more than one object selected of the same type, it lists the type of object and in parentheses it provides the number of items. If more than one object type is selected, the word "All" is displayed along with the number of selected items. If you want to see objects of the same type, use the drop-down list and select an object type.

2. **Quick select.** Locates and selects objects based on their properties as opposed to you physically selecting the objects from the drawing with your pointing device. See the *qselect* command for more detailed information.

3. **Alphabetic/Categorized.** List the properties alphabetically or by category.

4. **Text box.** Lists descriptions of highlighted properties.

Tips & Warnings

- The Properties dialog box provides some of the same information as the *list* command. Use *list* if you want to save the information and copy it to a text editor or word processor. You also can save any information displayed at the command line to an ASCII log file by checking the "Maintain a log file" box in the *options* Open and Save tab.

- As an alternative, use *matchprop* if you want an object to inherit one or more properties from another object. *change* and *chprop* let you change properties assigned to objects, but they aren't as extensive as *properties*.

- The linetype scale sets the *celtscale* for individual objects not the global *ltscale*.

- See "Selection Sets" in Chapter 2, *Command Index and Global Topics*, for more information.

Related Variables   Most variables are affected depending on the selected objects.

Associated Commands   change, chprop, propertiesclose, qselect

---

PROPERTIESCLOSE 2000   Properties toolbar

Closes the Properties window.

Initiate Command By

Command: **propertiesclose**
Alias: **prclose**, Ctrl-1
Tools → Properties

Associated Commands   properties

'PROXYGRAPHICS

Determines whether images of proxy objects are displayed or replaced with a bounding box. Proxy objects are custom objects created from other software applications. This variable is set by checking the "Save proxy images of custom objects" box from the Options button on the Save and Saveas dialog box.

Initiate Command By

Command: **proxygraphics**

Options

0   Images are not saved with the drawing, and a bounding box is displayed.

1   Images are saved with the drawing.

Variable Settings

Initial default:	1
Subsequent default:	Last value used in the drawing
Value:	Integer
Related Variables	proxynotice, proxyshow
Associated Commands	save, saveas

'PROXYNOTICE

Displays a message when a proxy is created. Proxy objects are created when opening a drawing that had objects created from another application that is not present. A proxy is also created when unloading a custom object's parent application. This variable is set when checking the "Show Proxy Information dialog box" box from the *options* Open and Save tab.

Initiate Command By

Command: **proxynotice**

Options

0 No proxy messages are provided.

1 Proxy messages are provided.

Variable Settings

Initial default:	1
Subsequent default:	Registry file
Value:	Integer
Related Variables	proxygraphics, proxyshow
Associated Commands	options, preferences

'PROXYSHOW

Determines how custom objects or proxy images are displayed in drawings. This variable is set when selecting an option from the "Proxy images for custom objects" box from *options* Open and Save tab.

Initiate Command By

Command: **proxyshow**

Options

0 Proxy objects are not displayed.

1 Proxy objects (graphic images) are displayed for all proxy objects.

2 The bounding box is displayed for all proxy objects.

Variable Settings

Initial default:	1
Subsequent default:	Registry file
Value:	Integer
Related Variables	proxygraphics, proxynotice
Associated Commands	options, preferences

PSDRAG

Determines the display of PostScript images dragged into place with *psin.*

Initiate Command By
Command: **psdrag**

Options

0 The image's bounding box and filename are displayed as it is being dragged on the screen. It is much quicker to have only the bounding box displayed when using *psin.*

1 The rendered PostScript image is displayed as it is being dragged on the screen.

Tips & Warnings

If *psquality* is set to 0, *psdrag* has no effect.

Related Variables	psquality
Associated Commands	import, psin

-PSETUPIN
see PSETUPIN

PSETUPIN 2000

Copies page setups (*pagesetup*) defined in other drawing files and template files into the current drawing. Activate the command by selecting the Page Setup Name button from the *pagesetup* dialog box. The information retained with the *pagesetup* command includes parameters that define the plotter configuration, plot style table, what to plot, plot location (file or plotter), paper size and paper units, drawing orientation, plot area, plot scale, and plot offset. You can use -*psetupin* so all prompts and options appear at the command line.

Initiate Command By
Command: **psetupin**

Options

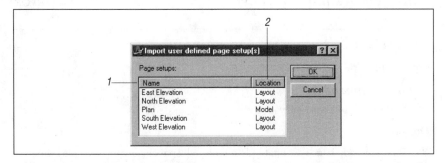

1. **Name.** Lists page setups already defined in an existing drawing.

2. **Location.** Indicates the space where the settings were defined.

Associated Commands   pagesetup, plot

PSFILL

Fills polyline outlines with PostScript patterns. The patterns are defined in the file named *acad.psf*. The patterns are not displayed on the screen; they show only after you print the file to PostScript (*psout*) and open that file with other computer programs or use *psin*.

Initiate Command By

Command: **psfill**

Options

```
Select polyline:
Enter PostScript fill pattern name (. = none) or [?] <.>:
```

.   Resets the default *psfill* to None.

?   Lists the PostScript fill patterns defined in the *acad.psf* file. This file is located in AutoCAD's support folder. The available patterns are Grayscale, RGBcolor, AIlogo, Lineargray, Radialgray, Square, Waffle, Zigzag, Stars, Brick, and Specks.

*   Placing an asterisk (*) before the pattern name omits the polyline outline when the PostScript pattern is plotted.

Related Variables   psquality

Associated Commands   export, import, psin, psout

PSIN—encapsulated PS (*.eps)   *see IMPORT*

'PSLTSCALE

Controls linetype scaling in layout space.

Initiate Command By

Command: **psltscale**

Options

0   When layout space is enabled, all model space viewports display linetype dash lengths based on their viewport zoom magnification.

1   When layout space is enabled, all model space viewports, regardless of their magnification, display linetype dash lengths identically. The scaling is based on paper space drawing units.

Variable Settings

Initial default:	1
Subsequent default:	Last value used in the drawing
Value:	Integer

Tips & Warnings

- When changing the *psltscale* value, you may need to regenerate (*regenall*) the viewports in order to see the changes.

- Use *ltscale* to set a global scale factor value. All objects are multiplied by the current *ltscale* setting. Use *celtscale* to control individual object linetype scaling.

Related Variables   celtscale, ltscale

Associated Commands   linetype, ltscale

Example

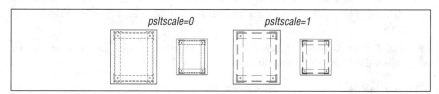

PSOUT—encapsulated eps (.eps)*   *see EXPORT*

PSPACE

Switches from drawing in model space to drawing in paper space. This command is available when layout space is active and at least one viewport is available. Viewports are created with *mview.* If the Model tab is active, *pspace* is not available. Model space is used to create and dimension your model. Paper space is used to annotate, compose, and plot 2D or 3D drawings. Model space and paper space each retain its own grid, snap, UCS icon, and views. You cannot edit objects created in paper space while in model space and vice versa. Plotting in model space plots only the current viewport; plotting in paper space plots all the active viewports.

If you are in model space and want to work in paper space, double-click outside the viewport border, type **pspace** at the command line, or click on the word "MODEL" located on the status bar. If you are in paper space and you want to activate a model space viewport, double-click inside the viewport border, type **mspace** at the command line, or click on the word "PAPER" located on the status bar.

You know you are working in paper space when the word "PAPER" appears on the status bar, the paper space UCS icon is displayed, and the drawing's crosshairs are displayed outside any defined viewports.

Initiate Command By

Command: **pspace**
Alias: **ps**
Status bar: PAPER

Tips & Warnings

- Dimensioning in model space gives you more flexibility. You can take advantage of associative dimensioning when editing your drawing.

- You cannot use most commands geared toward 3D when paper space is active. Some of those commands include *dview, plan, render, vpoint, 3darray, 3dclip, 3dcorbit, 3ddistance, 3dorbit, 3dpan, 3dswivel,* and *3dzoom.*

- Copy objects from model space to paper space by using *copybase* or *copyclip,* or by creating a block. Move objects using *cutclip.*

Related Variables	tilemode
Associated Commands	layout, mspace, mview, ucsicon

References O–P

Example

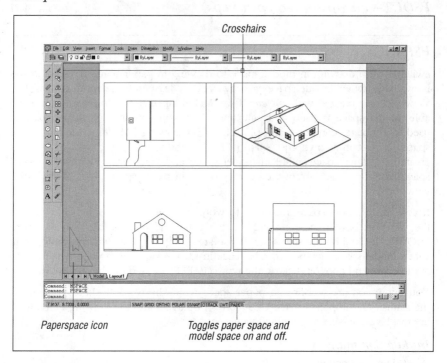

Crosshairs

Paperspace icon

Toggles paper space and
model space on and off.

'PSPROLOG

Assigns the name of a custom prologue section added in the *acad.psf* file. When
the *psout* command is issued, it will reference that customized section of the file.
This is ·used when customizing the appearance of PostScript output such as
assigning line widths for different colors or creating special linetypes.

Initiate Command By

Command: **psprolog**

Variable Settings

Initial default:	None
Subsequent default:	Registry file
Value:	String

Associated Commands   export, psout

'PSQUALITY

Controls the rendering quality of imported PostScript images.

Initiate Command By

Command: **psquality**

Options

0

Shows a PostScript image by its outline and filename.

greater than 0

Sets the number of pixels per AutoCAD drawing unit for the PostScript resolution. PostScript images are solid filled.

less than 0

Sets the number of pixels per AutoCAD drawing unit using the absolute value. PostScript image paths are shown as outlines.

Variable Settings

Initial default:	75
Subsequent default:	Registry file
Value:	Integer
Related Variables	psdrag
Associated Commands	import

'PSTYLEMODE 2000

Determines whether the current drawing is in a named plot style or color-dependent mode.

Initiate Command By

Command: **pstylemode**

Options

0 Named plot styles are used in the current drawing.

1 Color-dependent plot style tables are used in the current drawing.

Variable Settings

Initial default:	1, read-only
Subsequent default:	Registry file
Value:	Integer
Associated Commands	plot, plotstyle

'PSTYLEPOLICY 2000

Controls whether there is an association between an object's color property and its plot style setting.

Initiate Command By

Command: **pstylepolicy**

Options

0   An object's plot style is not associated to its color. The *defplstyle* determines the plot style for new objects; *defplstyle* determines the default plot style for new layers.

1   An object's plot style is associated with its color.

Variable Settings

Initial default:	1
Subsequent default:	Registry file
Value:	Integer
Related Variables	deflplstyle, defplstyle, visretain
Associated Commands	options, plotstyle, preferences

'PSVPSCALE 2000

Sets the scale factor for new viewports created in paper space. These viewports are created using *mview* and *vports*. When you use *vports*, *psvpscale* is used by the *Active Model Configuration* and Single options when Change View To is set to *Current*. When *psvpscale*'s value is set to 0, it means scaled to fit.

Initiate Command By

Command: **psvpscale**

Variable Settings

Initial default:	0
Subsequent default:	Last value used in the drawing
Value:	Real
Associated Commands	mview, viewports, vports, zoom

'PUCSBASE 2000

Stores the name of the UCS that defines the origin and orientation of orthographic UCS settings in paper space.

Initiate Command By

Command: **pucsbase**

Variable Settings

Initial default:	"" (none)
Subsequent default:	Last value used in the drawing
Value:	String
Related Variables	tilemode, ucsbase
Associated Commands	pspace, ucs

PURGE

Deletes unused blocks, dimension styles (dimstyle), layers, linetypes (ltypes), plot styles (plotstyle), shapes, text styles (styles), and multiline styles (mlstyles). You are prompted for a confirmation before each item is removed. If any of the named objects you want to purge is not listed, it is because that named object is being used or is referenced by something else in the drawing. For example, blocks can be nested and drawn on multiple layers, and you can purge only one reference level at a time. You should repeat the purge command until you receive the message "No unreferenced ..... found." Purging drawings reduces file size.

Initiate Command By

Command: **purge**
Alias: **pu**
File → Drawing Utilities → Purge

Options

```
Purge unused Blocks/Dimstyles/LAyers/LTypes/SHapes/STyles/
Mlinestyles/All:
```

All

Deletes all unused blocks, dimension styles, layers, linetypes, plot styles, shapes, text styles, and multiline styles. You are prompted individually for each item.

Tips & Warnings

- Use the *laydel* command if you want to delete layers and objects residing on those layers.

- You cannot purge layer 0, the Continuous linetype, the multiline style named Standard, or the text style named Standard. The dimension style Standard can be renamed and then purged, but you are always required to have at least one dimension style defined in a drawing.

- The following commands have their own methods of removing named items from the drawing: *group, layer, layout, light, lslib, matlib, pagesetup, scene, style, ucs, view,* and *vports.*

- Drawings still reference raster images and external references even when they are erased from a file. Use *image* detach and *xref* detach to actually remove any references to those files.

Associated Commands   laydel

QDIM ![2000]

Dimension toolbar

Quickly creates a series of baseline, continuous, staggered, ordinate, radius, or diameter dimensions. The dimensions take on the current dimension style (*dimstyle*) settings.

Initiate Command By

Command: **qdim**
Dimension → qdim

Options

```
Select geometry to dimension:
Specify dimension line position, or
[Continuous/Staggered/Baseline/Ordinate/Radius/Diameter/
datumPoint/Edit] <Continuous>:
```

Select geometry to dimension

Lets you select the objects to dimension. You may get unexpected results if an object was made longer by adding an additional piece rather than stretching, lengthening, extending, or gripping the endpoint of the original object.

dimension line position

Automatically defaults to the continuous option unless you select another option.

Continuous

Creates a series of horizontal or vertical continued dimensions. This is similar to *dimcontinue*.

Staggered

Creates a series of horizontal or vertical staggered dimensions. The dimension lines begin from the innermost location and work their way to the outermost dimension.

Baseline

Creates a series of horizontal or vertical baseline dimensions. This is similar to *dimbaseline*.

Ordinate

Creates a series of ordinate dimensions. This is similar to *dimordinate*.

Radius

Creates a series of radius dimensions. This is similar to *dimradius*.

Diameter

Creates a series of diameter dimensions. This is similar to *dimdiameter*.

datumPoint

Creates a series of ordinate dimensions, but it also lets you temporarily define the location for 0,0. This is similar to *dimordinate*.

Edit

Lets you add and remove existing points from existing dimensions. The Remove mode places an X at each point that can be edited; the Add mode lets you pick new places to add dimension lines.

Associated Commands   dimbaseline, dimcontinue, dimdiameter, dimlinear, dimordinate, dimradius, dimstyle

Example

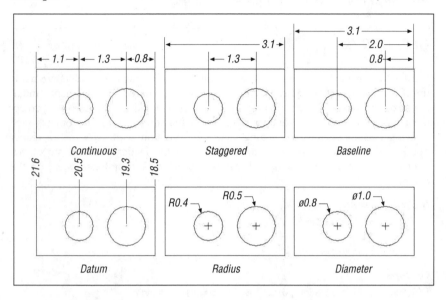

QLATTACH

Attaches a leader line created with *qleader* or *leader* to multiline text, tolerance dimensions, or a block.

Initiate Command By

Command: **qlattach**
Express → Dimension → Leader Tools → Attach Leader to Annotation

Tips & Warnings

- Detach leaders using *qldetachset*.
- You can add leaders to single-line text by converting single-line text to multiline text with *txt2mtxt* and creating a leader without annotation.

Associated Commands   expresstools, qldetachset, txt2mtxt

QLDETACHSET

Detaches leader lines created with *qleader* or *leader* from multiline text, tolerance dimensions, and blocks.

Initiate Command By

Command: **qldetachset**
Express → Dimension → Leader Tools → Detach Leaders from Annotation

Tips & Warnings

Attach leader lines with *qlattach*.

Associated Commands   expresstools, qlattach

QLEADER 2000

Dimension toolbar

Creates leader lines that are used to enter callouts on a drawing. Leaders are made up of the following: arrowheads, straight or splined (curved) line segments, multi-line text, and dimension information. All of the parts making up the leader (except the annotation) are associative or dynamic in that they act as one object. Each drawing remembers the last settings used for this command. *dim* has a leader option, but it is not as flexible and each part of the leader is a separate object. *leader* is almost the same as *qleader*, but all prompts and options appear on the command line.

Initiate Command By

Command: **qleader**
Alias: **le**
Dimension → Leader

Options

Specify first leader point, or [Settings]<Settings>:

The Annotation Tab

The Annotation tab defines the type of annotation to attach to the leader line.

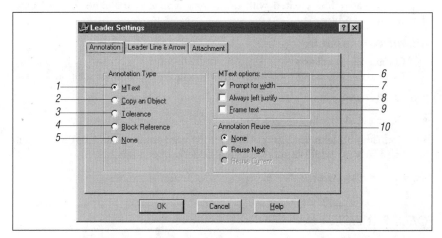

1. **Mtext.** Prompts you to place multiline text once the leader lines are drawn. Selecting this option activates both the MText Options section and the Attachment tab.

2. **Copy an Object.** Copies an existing single-line text, multiline text, block, or tolerance and places it as the annotation. It does not work for associative dimensions.

---

3. **Tolerance**. Activates the Geometric Tolerance dialog box. See *tolerance* for more detailed information.

4. **Block Reference**. Inserts a block as the annotation. You can activate a dialog box if you use a tilde (~) when prompted for the block name. See *-insert* for more detailed information.

5. **None**. Ends the leader command without placing anything at the end of the leader line.

6. **MText options**. This option is available only when the Annotation Type is set to MText and is not available for the *leader* command.

7. **Prompt for width**. Prompts for the width of the multiline text annotation.

8. **Always left justify**. Determines if multiline text is always left justified. When this box is checked, it automatically deactivates the Prompt for Width checkbox.

9. **Frame text**. Determines whether a box is placed around the multiline text.

10. **Annotation Reuse**. Determines whether you want to reuse the annotation last placed in the drawing for all subsequent leaders. This option is not available for the *leader* command.

The Leader & Line Arrow Tab

The Leader & Line Arrow tab defines how the leader lines and arrowhead will be displayed.

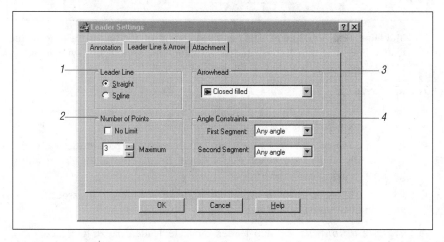

1. **Leader Line**. Determines whether the lines are straight or splined (curved line) segments. The *leader* command lets you change this setting up to the time you have completed drawing all of the leader lines.

2. **Number of Points**. Defines the maximum number of lines that can be created for each leader. Valid values range between 2 and 999. You also can set this with the No Limit checkbox. This setting is not available with the *leader* command.

3. **Arrowhead**. Lets you select the type of arrowhead for the leader line. The arrowhead size is based on the current dimension style settings. The *leader*

command offers only two choices, Arrow and None, but you can change this setting up to the time you have completed drawing all of the leader lines. The value is maintained by the *dimldrblk* system variable.

4. **Angle Constraints**. Lets you determine whether specific angles should be used for leader lines. The available angles are any angle, horizontal, 90°, 45°, 30°, and 15°. This setting is not available with the *leader* command.

The Attachment Tab

The Attachment tab determines how the leader line is attached to the annotation.

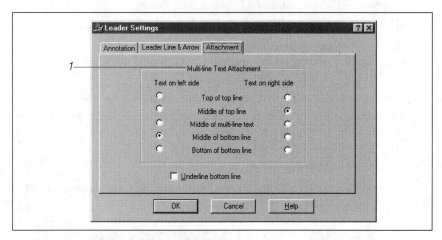

1. **Multi-line Text Attachment**. Defines the location of the text in relation to the leader line. This tab is available only when the Annotation Type is set to MText. You also can underline the last line of text.

Tips & Warnings

- Leaders use some of the default dimensioning style values since they default to the current dimension style setting (*dimstyle*).

- Canceling out of *qleader* before completion leaves that part of the leader that was already created. Canceling out of *leader* before completion erases all the geometry associated to the leader.

- Disassociate leaders and their annotation using *qldetachset*. Reassociate leaders to annotation using *qlattach*.

Associated Commands   dim–leader, dimstyle, leader, mtext, tolerance

Example

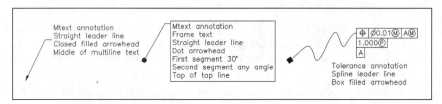

QSAVE

Saves your drawing file without requesting a filename. If it's the first time the drawing is saved, the Save Drawing As (*saveas*) dialog box is displayed. If the drawing is write-protected, you can create a new file by using *saveas*. Each time you use *qsave*, the previous saved drawing is renamed as the backup (*.bak*) drawing. This assumes that *isavebak* is set to 1. You should periodically save your drawing during each editing session.

You also can save files by using the automatic save feature (*savetime*), *save*, *saveas*, and *quit*. *save* and *saveas* activate the Save Drawing As dialog box; *quit* exits AutoCAD but gives you the opportunity to save your file if any commands were issued after the last *qsave*, *save*, or *saveas* command.

Initiate Command By

    Command: **qsave**, Ctrl-S
    File → Save

Tips & Warnings

* *undo* eventually will reset your drawing to the state it was in when you first opened it for editing, regardless of the amount of *qsaves* and *saves* you initiated. If you know that you do not want to *undo* past a certain point, you can always save, close, and re-open the file.

* If *filedia* is set to 1, a dialog box is activated; if *filedia* is set to 0, you are prompted on the command line. When *filedia* is set to 0, or off, entering a tilde (~) on the command line temporarily activates the dialog box.

Related Variables	filedia, isavebak, isavepercent, rasterpreview, savetime, tempprefix
Associated Commands	quit, save, saveas

QSELECT 2000mod

Creates selection sets based on object properties. Some of these properties include layer, color, lineweight, linetype, linetype scale, hyperlink, and plot style assignments. You can combine properties to make the selection set very complex. You use this in addition to or in place of the standard selection set options. Once you define and locate the objects, use "previous" as your response to the "Select object" prompt.

You also can select objects with *filter*, *getsel*, and *select*. *select* lets you select the objects based on any of the selection set options. It is straightforward and not very sophisticated. *filter* lets you select objects based on their object type, layer, color, linetype, linetype scale, location, and size. It does not include features such as lineweight, hyperlink, and plot style assignments. However, you can save your search criteria for future use. *getsel* lets you select objects based on their layer assignment and object type.

You can quickly activate this command with the shortcut menu when no other command is active.

Initiate Command By

Command: **qselect**
Tools → Quick Select

Options

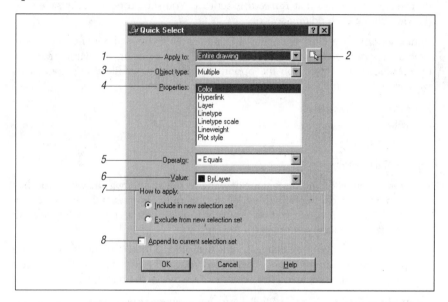

1. **Apply to.** Determines if the selection set is based on the entire drawing or to the current selection. The current selection is listed when a selection set was defined with *grips* before activating *qselect* or when you pick the Select Objects button located to the right.

2. **Select Objects.** Lets you select objects from the drawing to which to apply the filtering or properties criteria. This changes the Apply To option from "Entire drawing" to "Current selection." This is available only when the "Include in new selection set" radio button is selected and the "Append to current selection set" box is not checked.

3. **Object type.** Determines the object type to filter. Multiple is the default. If there is no selection set, all objects are listed in the drop-down list. If there is a selection set, only those object types contained in the selection set are listed.

4. **Properties.** Depends on the properties that are assigned to the object type. If Multiple is selected, the list is fairly generic. The list is ordered either alphabetically or by category and is based on the sort order of the Properties window.

5. **Operator.** Determines the range of the filter. The drop-down list varies and is based on the Properties selection. The options may include Equals (=), Not Equal (<>), Greater Than (>), Less Than (<), Wildcard Match (*).

6. **Value.** Defines the property value of the filter. The drop-down list varies and is based on the Properties selection. If the value is unknown, you must enter the value. For example, if you want to locate all lines whose length equals 5', set the following options: the Object type is Line, the Properties selection is Length, the Operator is Equals, and you enter 5' for the Value.

7. **How to apply.** Determines if you want the selection set to include or exclude the selected filtering parameters.

8. **Append to current selection set.** Determines if the selection set is added to an existing selection set or if it replaces the current selection set.

Tips & Warnings

See "Selection Sets" in Chapter 2, *Command Index & Global Topics* for more information.

Associated Commands   filter, properties, select

QTEXT

Determines whether text, multiline text, and attributes are displayed as text strings or as boxes representing the text. The box is the approximate height of the text string. The length is sometimes distorted and looks much longer then the actual text string. Turning *qtext* on can save you time whenever you redraw and regenerate the drawing. *qtext*'s value is maintained by the *qtextmode* variable. This command is set when selecting "Show text boundary frame only" from the *options* Display tab.

Initiate Command By

Command: **qtext**

Options

Enter mode [ON/OFF] <OFF>:

ON

Displays text strings as boxes.

OFF

Displays text strings normally.

Tips & Warnings

* When *qtext* is on and you use *change, ddedit,* or *properties* to edit the text or you use the *list* command for database information, the actual text is edited or listed.

* *qtext* affects all text strings regardless of their viewport, model space, or paper space location.

Related Variables   qtextmode

Associated Commands   options, preferences

Example

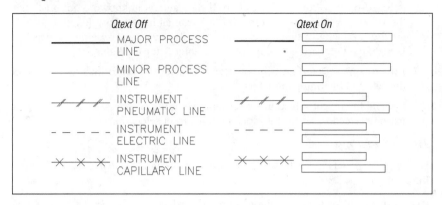

'QTEXTMODE

Determines whether text, multiline text, and attributes are displayed as text strings or as boxes representing the text. This value is set using *qtext* or by selecting "Show text boundary frame only" from the *options* Display tab.

Initiate Command By

Command: **qtextmode**

Options

0   Turns *qtextmode* off; characters are displayed.

1   Turns *qtextmode* on; characters are not displayed.

Variable Settings

Initial default:	0
Subsequent default:	Last value used in the drawing
Value:	Integer

Tips & Warnings

- When *qtext* is on and you use *change*, *ddedit*, or *properties* to edit the text or you use the *list* command for database information, the actual text is edited or listed.

- *qtext* affects all text strings regardless of their viewport, model space, or paper space location.

Associated Commands   options, preferences, qtext

Example   see QTEXT.

QUIT

Exits AutoCAD and returns you to Windows. If your drawing was modified since the last *qsave, save,* or *saveas,* you are given the opportunity to save your changes, quit without saving, or cancel from the *quit* command and return to the drawing screen. If you have multiple drawings open, you are prompted to save changes to each file if appropriate. *close* is similar, but it only closes the current drawing and doesn't exit you from the AutoCAD drawing session.

Initiate Command By

> Command: **quit**
> Alias: **exit**
> File → Exit

Tips & Warnings

If you made changes to a drawing that is write-protected and you want to save the changes, use the *save* or *saveas* command to create a new drawing with a different name.

Related Variables   isavebak, isavepercent, rasterpreview

Associated Commands   qsave, save, saveas

'RASTERPREVIEW

Determines whether a preview raster image of the current drawing display is saved as part of the drawing file. Preview drawing images are displayed in the Preview window when using the *insert, open, recover, saveas,* and *xref* commands. This variable is set when selecting "Save a thumbnail preview image" from the *options* Open and Save tab.

Initiate Command By

> Command: **rasterpreview**

Options

0   A preview image is not created. An advantage to this option is that it creates smaller file sizes.

1   A preview image is created.

Variable Settings

Initial default:	1
Subsequent default:	Registry file
Value:	Integer

Tips & Warnings

Drawings saved prior to Release 13 could not create a preview drawing image so the Preview window is empty. The browse and search feature of the *insert, open, recover, saveas,* and *xref* commands shows those files as a rectangle with diagonal lines crossing to the endpoints.

Associated Commands   end, options, preferences, qsave, save, saveas

---

RAY

Draw toolbar

Creates semi-infinite lines. Once you create a ray, the command repeats by asking for another through-point location. You can change a ray's properties (layer, location, coordinates, color, linetype, lineweight, linetype scale) using *change, chprop,* and *properties.* Rays convert to lines when edited with commands such as *trim, break,* and *fillet.*

Initiate Command By

    Command: **ray**
    Draw → Ray

Options

    Specify start point:
    Specify through point:

Specify through point:
    Select a second point, determining direction and angle for the ray. This second point extends to infinity.

Tips & Warnings

zoom–all and *zoom–extents* do not take rays into account. If the drawing contains only rays, then *zoom–all* and *zoom–extents* are based on the *limits.* Use *zoom–vmax* if you want to display rays outside the drawing limits.

Associated Commands   xline

RECOVER

Attempts to restore damaged drawings. If AutoCAD detects a damaged drawing during the *open* command, it automatically tries to repair it. An ASCII report file describing any problems and actions taken can be generated by turning on the *auditctl* variable. This report is created in the same folder as the current drawing. Its name is the same as the drawing file, with the extension *.adt.* Every time an audit report is created, it writes on top of any existing audit reports for that same drawing file. You can delete audit files without doing any harm to the associated drawing file.

Initiate Command By

    Command: **recover**
    File → Drawing Utilities → Recover

Tips & Warnings

- Files damaged with versions of AutoCAD earlier than Release 11 cannot be restored with *recover*.

- If *filedia* is set to 1, a dialog box is activated; if *filedia* is set to 0, you are prompted on the command line. When *filedia* is set 0, or off, entering a tilde (~) on the command line temporarily activates the dialog box.

Related Variables   auditctl, filedia

Associated Commands   audit, open

RECTANGLE

Draw toolbar

Creates a closed rectangular polyline. You define two diagonal points that determine length and width. You also can opt to have the corners chamfered or filleted and assign an elevation, thickness, and line width. If you don't use any of those options during the command, you can always edit the rectangle later using *chamfer, elevation, fillet, pedit,* and *thickness.*

Use *ai_box* to create 3D wireframe boxes and *box* to create 3D solid boxes. Extruding a rectangle creates a solid box with the option to include a taper.

Initiate Command By

Command: **rectangle** or **rectang**
Alias: **rec**
Draw → Rectangular

Options

```
Specify first corner point or [Chamfer/Elevation/Fillet/
Thickness/Width]:
Specify other corner point:
```

Tips & Warnings

Any chamfer, fillet, elevation, thickness, or width settings assigned to a rectangle remain the default for any other rectangles created during that drawing session. Even the *undo* command does not affect those settings.

Associated Commands   chamfer, elevation, fillet, pedit, pline, thickness

Example

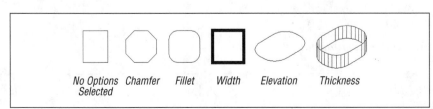

No Options Selected — Chamfer — Fillet — Width — Elevation — Thickness

REDEFINE

see UNDEFINE

REDIR 2000

Finds and replaces hardcoded directory paths for the current drawing's references to styles, shapes, external references, images, and remote text.

Initiate Command By

> Command: **redir**
> Express → Tools → Path Substitution

Options

```
Current REDIRMODE: Styles,Xrefs,Images,Rtext
Find and replace directory names
Enter old directory (use '*' for all), or ? <options>:
```

Current REDIRMODE:

> Lists the type of references that will be redirected. The settings are based on the last time this command was used.

old directory (use '' for all)*

> Specifies the directory to replace. The asterisk (*) wildcard character globally updates all the directories that match the Redirmode setting. You also are asked for the replacement directory. Pressing Enter without a response causes AutoCAD to look for the files in the directories specified in the support file search path located in the *options* File tab.

options

> Activates the Redirmode dialog box. This sets the status for which file types are redirected.

Associated Commands   expresstools

REDO

Standard toolbar

Reverses the effects of the last *undo* or *u* command. You can redo only the last *undo* or *u* command, and it must be the first command after the *undo* or *u*.

Initiate Command By

> Command: **redo**
> Edit → Redo
> Alias: Ctrl-Y

Associated Commands   u, undo

'REDRAW

see REDRAWALL

'REDRAWALL/REDRAW

Standard toolbar

redraw cleans up the current viewport. *redrawall* cleans up all the viewports. If *blipmode* is active, blips are removed. Any objects or parts of objects that disappeared or seemed erased due to editing are redrawn. Grid dots are redrawn if grid is on. Some commands, like turning grid on or off or turning layers on, automatically execute a redraw. Objects are redrawn on layers that are turned off even though they are not seen; objects on frozen layers are not redrawn.

Initiate Command By

Command: **redrawall**, **redraw**
Alias: **ra** or **r**
View → Redraw

Tips & Warnings

- If curved objects, such as circles, arcs, and ellipses, appear as if they are made up of straight line segments, use the *regen* command to smooth their appearance.

- *redraw* affects only the current space (model or paper).

Related Variables   sortents

Associated Commands   regen, regenall

REFCLOSE 2000

Refedit toolbar

A subset of the *refedit* command. *refclose* lets you save or discard changes made to external reference files or blocks. The only modifications that can be accomplished are the adding and removing of objects.

Initiate Command By

Command: **refclose**
Modify → In-place Xref and Block Edit → Save Reference Edits
Modify → In-place Xref and Block Edit → Discard Reference Edits

Options

Enter option [Save/Discard reference changes] <Save>:

Save
Permanently saves any changes made to the block definition in the current drawing or to the external reference source drawing. Objects removed from the external reference source drawing become part of the current drawing.

Discard reference changes
Discards any changes made to blocks and external reference files.

References Q-R

Tips & Warnings

Once the external reference drawing is modified, the drawing preview image for that file is no longer available until the next time that drawing is opened and saved.

Related Variables	refeditname, xedit, xfadectl
Associated Commands	refedit, refset, xref .

-REFEDIT 2000

see REFEDIT

REFEDIT 2000

Refedit toolbar

Lets you select a block or external reference file for editing. The only modifications that can be accomplished are the adding and removing of objects. Once the block or external reference is selected, use *refset* to add and remove objects and *refclose* to save or discard changes. You can achieve the same results using *-refedit* so all prompts and options appear on the command line.

Initiate Command By

Command: **refedit**
Modify → In-place Xref and Block Edit → Edit Reference

Options

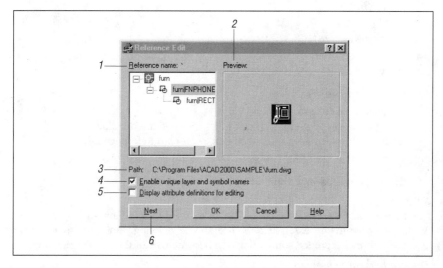

1. **Reference name.** Lists the reference selected for editing and any references nested within the selected reference. You can edit only one reference or block at a time. If you need to edit more than one reference or block, you

must complete the command and restart it for the next modification. Objects placed in a drawing due to *minsert* and OLE objects can never be edited.

2. **Preview.** Displays a preview image of the currently selected block or external reference.

3. **Path.** Displays the location of the selected external reference file. Paths are not displayed if the selected item is a block.

4. **Enable unique layer and symbol names.** Determines whether symbol and layer names, extracted from reference files, retain their original name or whether their name includes a unique identifier. The unique identifier includes the original filename followed by a dollar sign ($), a sequential number, and another dollar sign. The sequential number is incremented if an item by the same name already exists. This naming convention is the same used when binding external reference files.

5. **Display attribute definitions for editing.** Determines whether attribute definitions can be modified. Attributes tagged as constant can never be modified. Changes to attributes have no effect on attributes already existing in the drawing. This makes changes to only any new attributes inserted into the drawing. See *attredef* if you want to change existing attributes.

6. **Next.** Cycles through each nested level of the reference file.

Tips & Warnings

Once objects have been selected, the rest of the drawing becomes inactive. Depending on the *xfadectl* setting, the inactive portion of the drawing can be displayed faded.

Related Variables	refeditname, xedit, xfadectl
Associated Commands	refclose, refset, xref

'REFEDITNAME 2000

Stores the name of the reference file that is selected for editing with *refedit*.

Initiate Command By

Command: **refeditname**

Variable Settings

Initial default:	" ", read-only
Subsequent default:	Initial default
Value:	Integer
Related Variables	xedit, xfadectl
Associated Commands	refclose, refedit, refset

REFSET 2000

Refedit toolbar

A subset of *refedit. refset* lets you add and remove objects from external reference files and blocks.

Initiate Command By

Command: **refset**
Modify → In-place Xref and Block Edit → Add to Working set
Modify → In-place Xref and Block Edit → Remove from Working set

Options

```
Transfer objects between the Refedit working set and host drawing...
Enter an option [Add/Remove] <Add>:
```

Add

Adds objects to external references and blocks and removes them from the current drawing.

Remove

Removes objects from external references and blocks, and places them in the current drawing.

Tips & Warnings

Once the external reference drawing is modified, the drawing preview image for that file is no longer available until the next time you *open* and *save* that drawing.

Related Variables   refeditname, xedit, xfadectl

Associated Commands   refclose, refedit, xref

REGEN

see REGENALL

REGENALL/REGEN

regen cleans up the current viewport. *regenall* cleans up all the viewports. When a drawing is regenerated, all the data and geometry associated with each object are recalculated and reindexed. Changes made to some existing objects require a regeneration before they are made visible. You can stop a regeneration by pressing Escape. You can control automatic regenerations with the *regenauto* command. Objects on layers turned off are regenerated even though they are not seen; objects on frozen layers are not regenerated. *zoom–all* and *zoom–extents* always force a regen; *zoom–vmax* never requires a regen.

Initiate Command By

Command: **regenall** or **regen**
Alias: **rea** or **re**
View → Regenall
View → Regen

Tips & Warnings

- For best results, regenerate your drawing before it is printed.

- If curved objects, such as circles, arcs, and ellipses, appear as if they are made up of straight line segments, use the *regen* command to smooth their appearance.

- Regenerating a drawing that contains rendered objects causes those objects to default to the last *shademode* setting.

Related Variables   regenmode, sortents, vsmax, vsmin

Associated Commands   redraw, redrawall, regenauto, viewres

Example

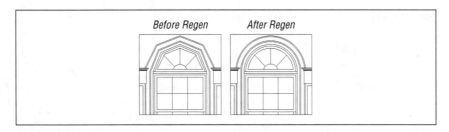

Before Regen   After Regen

'REGENAUTO

Suppresses some (not all) regenerations. When you want to regenerate the drawing, you can turn this value on or use *regen* or *regenall*. You also can use *zoom–all* or *zoom–extents* since they always force a regeneration. This value is maintained by the *regenmode* variable. Depending on the drawing complicity, completing a regeneration may take some time. Setting *regenauto* off lets you partially control the frequency of those regenerations, thus saving time.

Initiate Command By
    Command: **regenauto**

Options
    Enter mode [ON/OFF] <ON>:

ON
    Enables all drawing regenerations.

OFF
    Suppresses most drawing regenerations.

Tips & Warnings

regenauto off can suppress regenerations caused by changes to commands such as *layer*, *ltscale*, and *style*.

Related Variables   expert, regenmode

Associated Commands   regen, regenall, viewres

References
Q–R

'REGENMODE

Controls the automatic regeneration of a drawing. This value is set with *regenauto*.

Initiate Command By
Command: **regenmode**

Options

0   Turns drawing *regenauto* off.

1   Turns drawing *regenauto* on.

Variable Settings

Initial default:	1
Subsequent default:	Last value used in the drawing
Value:	Integer
Related Variables	expert
Associated Commands	regen, regenall, regenauto

REGION

Draw toolbar

Creates a solid from existing closed objects. These objects can be any combina-tion of arcs, circles, ellipses, elliptical arcs, lines, polylines, and splines. All the objects must form a closed shape or loop and cannot overlap or leave any gaps. Regions take on the current layer, linetype, color, and lineweight settings. You can create composite regions by using *intersect*, *subtract*, and *union*. Set *delobj* to 0 if you want to keep the original object(s). You can *explode* a region, turning some of the objects back to their original definitions. Polylines and any shapes made out of polylines such as ellipses (*pellipse* = 1) and polygons convert to lines and arcs.

Initiate Command By
Command: **region**
Alias: **reg**
Draw → Region

Related Variables	delobj
Associated Commands	boundary, explode, intersect, subtract, union

RE-INIT

Reinitializes the I/O (input/output) digitizer port, digitizer, and program parame-ters (*acad.pgp*) files. This variable is set with *reinit*.

Initiate Command By
Command: **re-init**

Options

re-init is bit coded and its value is the sum of the following:

1   Digitizer port reinitialization.

4   Digitizer reinitialization.

16 PGP file reinitialization.

Variable Settings

Initial default:	0
Subsequent default:	Initial default
Value:	Integer

Associated Commands   reinit

REINIT

Reinitializes the I/O (input/output) digitizer port, digitizer, and program parameters (*acad.pgp*) file. A reinitialization dialog box has you check which modes need to be reinitialized. The *re-init* variable controls the various choices for *reinit*.

Initiate Command By

    Command: **reinit**

Related Variables   re-init

-RENAME 2000

see RENAME

RENAME 2000mod

Lets you rename blocks, dimension styles, layers, linetypes, text styles, UCSs, views, and viewport configurations. You can achieve the same results using *-rename* (*-ren*) so all prompts and options appear on the command line.

If you have to rename the same items for more than one drawing, create a script file to automate the process. Named items are not case sensitive. You cannot rename layer 0, external reference layers, and the linetypes named Continuous, ByLayer, and ByBlock.

Initiate Command By

    Command: **rename**
    Alias: **ren**
    Format → Rename

References Q–R

Options

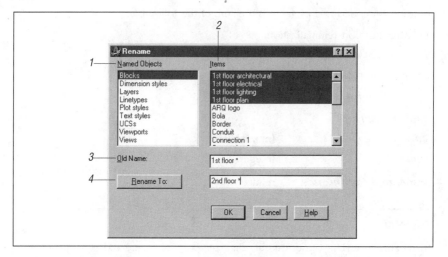

1. **Named Objects**. Lists the groups of items that can be renamed.

2. **Items**. Lists the individual items that can be renamed based on the Named Objects selection. You can rename more than one item at a time using wildcards, and you can select more than one item using the Shift and Ctrl keys.

3. **Old Name**. Lists the item selected from the Items list.

4. **Rename To**. Pressing "Rename To" after entering a valid name causes the Items list to update. Clicking on the OK button causes the item to be renamed and exits you from the dialog box.

Tips & Warnings

To rename a drawing file, use the *saveas* command or the Windows Explorer program. Rename layers and linetypes by selecting the Show Details button displayed in each of their dialog boxes and typing in a replacement in the Name box. *group*, *layout*, *lman*, and *mlstyle* each have their own rename option. You also can rename dimension styles (*dimstyle*) and UCSs (*dducs*) by right-clicking on top of the name you want changed.

RENDER

Render toolbar

Creates a realistic shaded image of objects. The drawing can be rendered based on predefined scenes, selected objects, or the current display. Light sources and different types of material can be assigned to the drawing or selected objects. All of the default values for the *render* command are based on the render preference (*rpref*) settings. Once you've set the preferences, you can always change the settings when rendering.

rmat attaches rendering material to objects, *saveimg* saves a rendered image to a file, *replay* displays rendered files, and *stats* provides rendering statistics. Anytime you change the display of rendered objects (such as *pan*, *regen*, and *zoom*), the objects lose their rendered status and default to the last *shademode* setting. Changing some of the settings in the *render* dialog box affects the *rpref* command and vice versa. See *rpref* for more detailed information.

Initiate Command By

Command: **render**
Alias: **rr**
View → Render

Tips & Warnings

- If you are using an older drawing that contains objects created with AME (Advanced Modeling Extension), use *ameconvert* to convert those objects to AutoCAD objects before using *render*.

- If the Render dialog box does not display, check the Rendering Procedure option of the Rendering Preferences (*rpref*) dialog box. When the Skip Render box is checked, it disables the Render dialog box.

Associated Commands   background, light, lsedit, lslib, lsnew, replay, rmat, rpref, saveimg, scene, stats

---

REPLAY

Displays *.bmp*, *.tga*, and *.tiff* images. Using *redraw*, or any command that causes a redraw, clears the image from the screen. If you want to make that image a permanent part of the drawing, use *image*.

Initiate Command By

Command: **replay**

Options

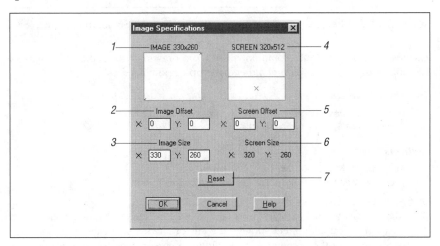

1. **Image**. Determines how much of the image is displayed on the screen (in pixels). The default displays the whole image. The values are reflected in the Image Offset and Image Size boxes. You can pick two points in the Image Tile, graphically showing which part of the image should be displayed, or enter values in the Image Offset boxes.

2. **Image Offset**. Determines the X,Y coordinate of the image's lower-left corner position. This value can also be set by selecting points in the Image Tile.

3. **Image Size**. Determines the size of the image area in pixels. This value also can be set by selecting points in the Image Tile.

4. **Screen**. Determines the location of the image (in pixels). The default displays the whole image starting from the lower-lefthand corner. You select a new location point by selecting the Screen Tile.

5. **Screen Offset**. Determines the X,Y coordinate of the image's lower left corner position in the display. This value also can be set by selecting a point in the Screen Tile.

6. **Screen Size**. Determines the maximum size, in pixels, of the image that can appear on the screen. This value also can be set by selecting a point in the Screen Tile.

7. **Reset**. Restores Image Offset, Image Size, and Screen Offset to their original values.

Tips & Warnings

saveimg and *render* create *.bmp*, *.tga*, and *.tiff* images. *export* creates *.bmp* files.

Associated Commands   render, rpref, saveimg

'RESUME   *see SCRIPT*

REVCLOUD 2000mod   Express Standard toolbar

Creates a revision cloud commonly used on drawings to depict a design or drafting change. The revision cloud is made up of polyline arcs.

Initiate Command By

Command: **revcloud**
Express → Draw → Revision Cloud

Options

```
Arc length = 0.5000, Arc style = Normal
Specify cloud starting point or [eXit/Options] <eXit>:
```

Specify cloud starting point
Allows you to pick a start point and move the cursor counterclockwise to create the cloudlike effect. Moving the cursor clockwise creates a cloud inside out. Complete the command by moving the cursor back to the starting point or by pressing Escape or Enter.

Options

Lets you change the cloud's appearance and the size of the arcs. Any changes made to the *revcloud* settings are retained the next time you begin a new AutoCAD design session.

The Revcloud Options Dialog Box

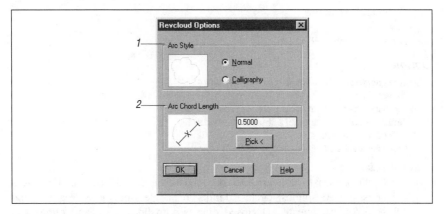

1. **Arc Style.** Normal clouds are created with the polyline width set to 0. Calligraphy clouds begin each polyline arc segment with a 0 width and end each segment with a width greater than zero.

2. **Arc Chord Length.** Determine the arc chord length for each polyline segment. You can enter a new number or use the Pick option. The Pick option lets you pick two points on the AutoCAD display screen, graphically defining the new arc chord length. This value is then multiplied by *dimscale*.

Related Variables	dimscale
Associated Commands	expresstools, pedit, pline

Example

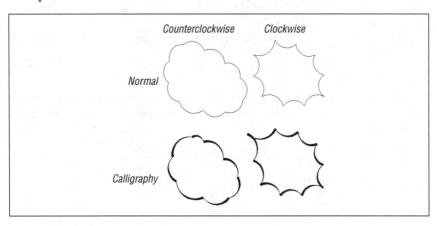

REVOLVE

Solids toolbar

Generates a 3D solid by revolving a 2D object about an axis.

Initiate Command By

Command: **revolve**
Alias: **rev**
Draw → Solids → Revolve

Options

```
Current wire frame density:  ISOLINES=4
Select objects:
Specify start point for axis of revolution or
define axis by [Object/X (axis)/Y (axis)]:
Select an object:
Specify angle of revolution <360>:
```

Select objects
Select 2D objects to convert into 3D solids. The 2D objects can be closed polylines, closed splines, circles, donuts, rectangles, polygons, regions, and ellipses. You can create 2D closed objects with lines, arcs, and plines and then convert them into a closed pline using *pedit–join, pljoin,* or *region.* You cannot *revolve* objects defined as blocks or polylines whose segments intersect.

Specify start point for axis of revolution or define axis by [Object/X (axis)/Y (axis)]
Define the first and second points of the axis of revolution.

Object
Select an existing line or polyline that defines the axis.

X
Uses the positive *X* axis of the current UCS.

Y
Uses the positive *Y* axis of the current UCS.

Specify angle of revolution <360>:
Specify an angle of revolution or press Return to revolve the object 360 degrees.

Tips & Warnings

Use *ddvpoint, dview, vpoint,* and *3dorbit* to view the revolved surface at different angles and elevations. Use *hide, render,* and *shademode* to enhance the revolved surface's display.

Related Variables

delobj, dispsilh, isolines

Example

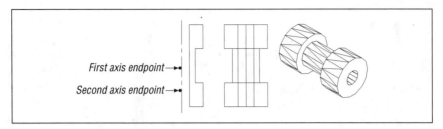

First axis endpoint →•

Second axis endpoint →•

REVSURF

Generates a 3D polygon mesh (surface) by revolving a selected profile or path curve around an axis. You can edit a revsurf object with *pedit*.

Initiate Command By

Command: **revsurf**

Draw → Surfaces → Revolved Surface

Options

```
Current wire frame density:  SURFTAB1=24  SURFTAB2=24
Select object to revolve:
Select object that defines the axis of revolution:
Specify start angle <0>:
Specify included angle (+=ccw, -=cw) <360>:
```

Select object to revolve:

Select an existing line, circle, arc, ellipse, elliptical arc, polyline, spline, closed polyline, polygons, closed spline or donut.

Select object that defines the axis of revolution:

The path curve defines the *N* direction of the surface polygon mesh. The profile or path curve can be made up of a single line, arc, circle, polyline, or 3D polyline. If you use a polyline, the revolution axis is considered a line from the first vertex to the last vertex, omitting any other vertices.

Specify start angle <0>:

Determine the start of the surface of revolution. It can be offset from the path curve.

Specify included angle (+=ccw, −=cw) <360>:

Determine the distance of revolution around the axis.

Tips & Warnings

Use *ddvpoint*, *dview*, *vpoint*, and *3dorbit* to view the revsurf at different angles and elevations. Use *hide*, *render*, and *shademode* to enhance the revsurf's display.

Related Variables   surftab1, surftab2

Associated Commands   3D, 3dmesh

Example

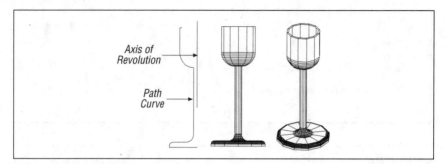

Axis of
Revolution

Path
Curve

RMAT

Render toolbar

Lets you create, modify, preview, import, export, and delete finishing materials. It
also lets you assign these finishes to individual objects and to layers. Use *showmat*
to find out the material type and attachment method assigned to selected objects.

Initiate Command By

Command: **rmat**
View → Render → Materials

Options

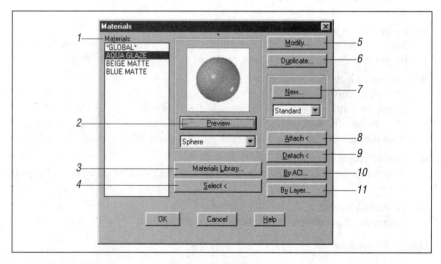

1. **Materials**. Lists the materials currently loaded in the drawing. *GLOBAL* is the
   default for objects with no attached material.

2. **Preview**. Shows how materials will be displayed on objects. Only one material can be previewed at a time. Select the material from the Materials list. You

---

can preview the material and see how it would display on a sphere or cube by selecting either option from the drop-down list located under the Preview button.

3. **Materials Library.** Displays a list of materials defined in the Materials Library. See *matlib* for more detailed information.

4. **Select <.** Displays the drawing and lets you select objects to determine how the material is to be attached. The information is displayed at the bottom of the dialog box.

5. **Modify.** Modifies a material selected from the Materials list. See the Modify Standard Material dialog box.

6. **Duplicate.** Creates a new material based on the values of an existing material. See the Modify Standard Material dialog box.

7. **New.** Creates a new material. See the Modify Standard Material dialog box.

8. **Attach <.** Displays the drawing and lets you assign the current material to the selected objects.

9. **Detach <.** Displays the drawing and lets you unassign or detach material assigned to objects.

10. **By ACI.** Lets you attach materials to objects based on the object's color assignment.

11. **By Layer.** Lets you attach materials to objects based on the object's layer assignment.

The Modify Standard Material Dialog Box

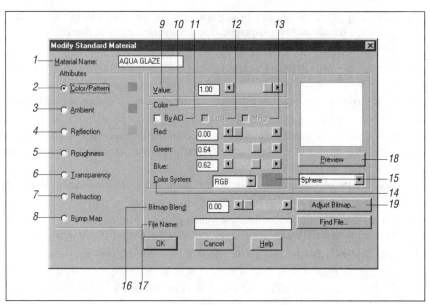

1. **Material Name.** Shows the name of the material being modified in the text box. If you type over the existing name, it will rename the material. If you are creating a duplicate or new material, you must enter the new material name.

2. **Color/Pattern.** Sets the main or diffuse color of the material. You set this using the Value and Color controls.

3. **Ambient.** Sets the material's ambient or shadow color. The ambient settings also determine the color reflected from ambient light. Setting this value too high makes the rendering looked washed out. You set this using the Value and Color controls.

4. **Reflection.** Sets the material's reflective or specular color. You set this using the Value and Color controls.

5. **Roughness.** Sets the roughness or shininess of the material. This determines the size of the reflected highlight. You set this using the Value control. Setting this to a lower number gives the rendering a smoother and less rough surface. In order for this value to have an effect, you must enter a value for Refraction.

6. **Transparency.** Sets the transparency of the object. You set this using the Value control. This value can be from 0 to 1.0. The higher the number, the longer it takes to render. You can use an opacity map with the material by entering a file name and setting the Bitmap Blend value. Bitmap Blend allows you to blend a pattern and color.

7. **Refraction.** Sets a refraction index for transparent materials. Refraction values have no effect unless you enter a nonzero value for transparency. This applies to photo raytrace rendering. Set the Value control to adjust how refractive the material is.

8. **Bump Map.** Determines the brightness of a bump map object. Bump Map values are translated into apparent changes in the height of the surface of an object.

9. **Value.** Adjusts the selected attribute (color/pattern, ambient, reflection, roughness, transparency, or refraction) value.

10. **Color.** Adjusts the selected attribute (color/pattern, ambient, or reflection) value.

11. **By ACI.** Lets you attach materials to objects based on the object's color assignment. This option is available only for color/pattern, ambient, and reflection attributes.

12. **Lock.** Locks the attribute's color to the main color. This option is available only for ambient and reflection attributes.

13. **Mirror.** Creates mirrored reflections when using the photo real or the photo raytrace renderer. This option is available only for the reflection attribute.

14. **Color System.** Contains the choice of the RGB or the HLS color system.

    Red, Green, Blue
    > Sets the color's RGB values. You can enter the values or use the scrollbars.

Hue, Lightness, Saturation
> Sets the color's HLS values. You can enter the values or use the scroll-bars. The hue changes the color's shade; the lightness changes the color's brightness; and the saturation increases the color's purity.

15. **Color Swatch.** Activates the Color window, which provides an alternative means of setting the RGB or the HLS color system.

16. **Bitmap Blend.** Determines how much of an impact a bitmap has in rendering. A material can have a bitmap specified for color/pattern, reflection, transparency, and bump map. The blend is based on the file chosen in the File Name text box.

17. **File Name.** Assigns a bitmap file name to color/pattern, reflection, transparency, and bump map. Each attribute can have its own bitmap file association. The Bitmap Blend controls how much of an impact the bitmap has in rendering.

18. **Preview.** Shows how materials will be displayed on objects. You can preview the material and see how it would display on a sphere or cube by selecting either option from the drop-down list located under the Preview button.

19. **Adjust Bitmap.** Displays the "Adjust material bitmap placement" dialog box where you can define how the bitmap is placed on the objects.

Associated Commands   lsedit, lslib, lsnew, matlib, render, showmat

---

ROTATE

Modify toolbar

Moves objects around a pivot or base point. If you *move* or *copy* objects and then want to rotate the same objects, you can quickly select the objects using the previous selection set option. *grips* has its own rotate routine that lets you create multiple copies at the same time. *mocoro* lets you move, copy, rotate, and scale objects. Use *align* instead of *rotate* if you plan to rotate and move the same set of objects. *images, insert, minsert*, and *xref* all have their own rotate option.

Rotating a viewport in paper space causes the viewport center point to rotate about the base point while keeping the viewport border parallel to the edges of the graphics display area. In essence, it basically does nothing but moves the viewport.

Initiate Command By
> Command: **rotate**
> Alias: **ro**
> Modify → Rotate

Options
```
Current positive angle in UCS:
ANGDIR=counterclockwise  ANGBASE=0
Select objects:
Specify base point:
Specify rotation angle or [Reference]:
```

base point
> Defines a reference point about which the objects are rotated.

rotation angle
> Determines the angle objects are rotated from their current orientation. A positive number creates a counterclockwise rotation; a negative number creates a clockwise rotation.

Reference
> Prompts for a reference angle and a new rotation angle relative to the reference angle.

Tips & Warnings

- Use the rotate option of *solidedit* if you want to rotate 3D solid planar faces.

- When rotating associative dimension objects, the dimension text retains its original orientation. You can rotate associative dimension text using *dimtrotate*, *dimtedit*, or *dimedit*.

- If you want to rotate your drawing's cross hairs and work at a different rotation angle, use the rotate option of *snap* or define a UCS.

Related Variables angbase, angdir

Associated Commands align, grips, insert, minsert, mocoro, rotate3d

Example

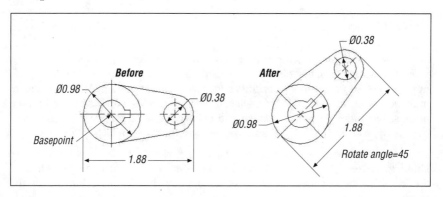

ROTATE3D

Rotates objects about an arbitrary 3D axis.

Initiate Command By

> Command: **rotate3d**

Options

```
Current positive angle:  ANGDIR=counterclockwise  ANGBASE=0
Select objects:
Specify first point on axis or define axis by
[Object/Last/View/Xaxis/Yaxis/Zaxis/2points]:
Specify second point on axis:
Specify rotation angle or [Reference]:
```

Object

Aligns the axis of rotation with an existing line, circle, arc, or polyline.

Last

Uses the last axis of rotation.

View

Aligns the axis of rotation with the viewing direction that passes through the selected point.

Xaxis, Yaxis, Zaxis

Aligns the axis of rotation with one of the standard axes that pass through the selected point.

2points

Allows you to enter two points defining the axis of rotation.

rotation angle

Rotates the object about the selected axis.

Reference

Specifies the reference angle and a new angle.

Related Variables   angbase, angdir

Associated Commands   align, rotate

RPREF   Render toolbar

Sets rendering preferences and uses the same dialog boxes as *render*. Changing any of the parameters while using the *render* command automatically changes the *rpref* settings and vice versa.

Initiate Command By

Command: **rpref**
Alias: **rpr**
View → Render → Preferences

Options

The Rendering Preferences dialog sets the default options for the rendering command.

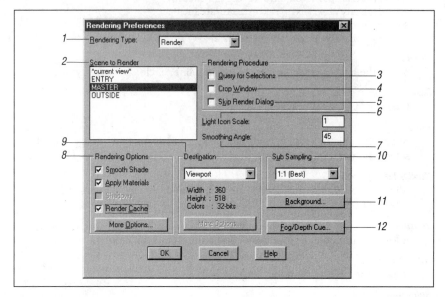

1. **Rendering Type.** There are three levels of rendering: render, photo real, and photo raytrace. Although it is easy enough to use any one of the options, your choice may be determined by whether you need a quick and fast render or a more precise but time-consuming method.

   Render
   The most basic and fastest of the rendering types. This is similar to the hidden line removal performed by *hide* but with color added in to help distinguish surface orientation.

   Photo Real
   Shades faces in a model so they appear smooth with a highlight. Displays bitmapped and transparent materials and generates volumetric and mapped shadows.

   Photo Raytrace
   The most realistic and accurate rendering method. It provides shadows, reflections, and refraction. It is also the slowest method and is often performed as the final rendering.

2. **Scene to Render.** Lists the scenes defined in the drawing. The default, "current view," uses the current screen display and all the lights defined in the drawing. If no lights are defined, it uses an "over-the-shoulder" distant light source with an intensity of 1 and an ambient light intensity of 0.

   Once light sources are defined with *light,* you can combine one or more light sources to a *view* and create a *scene.* Drawings usually have more than one scene. For example, you may have one scene defining a kitchen in a house but a different scene when viewing the house's exterior.

3. **Query for Selections.** Select the objects to render. Objects not selected are invisible once the rendering is complete.

4. **Crop Window.** Creates a rectangle around the area to render. Objects outside of the rectangle are invisible once the rendering is complete.

5. **Skip Render Dialog.** Determines whether the Render dialog box is displayed before the drawing is rendered.

6. **Light Icon Scale.** Determines the size of the blocks assigned to lights. The three types of lights are point, distant, and spotlight. The overhead block is assigned to pointed light; the direct block is assigned to distant light; and sh_ spot is assigned to spotlight.

7. **Smoothing Angle.** Determines the angle for defining edges. The default is 45 degrees. Angles less than 45 degrees are smoothed; angles 45 degrees and greater are defined as edges.

8. **Rendering Options.** Determines the rendering display. The options change depending on the current rendering type (render, photo real, and photo raytrace).

Smooth Shade
Smooths the edges of multifaceted surfaces by blending colors between adjacent faces.

Apply Materials
Determines whether the rendering applies the materials assigned to objects or to the ACI (AutoCAD Color Index) in the drawing. When this is not selected, all the objects assume the color, ambient diffuse, reflection, roughness, transparency, refraction, and bump map attribute values defined for the *Global* material. Materials are assigned with the *rmat* command.

Shadows
Generates shadows when photo real or photo raytrace is active.

Render Cache
Sends rendering information to a cache file for subsequent renders. This cache file us reused as long as the drawing geometry or view is unchanged. It saves time since AutoCAD doesn't have to retessellate when rendering solids.

More Options
The available options change depending on the active rendering type: render, photo real, or photo raytrace. See the following sections for more detailed information.

9. **Destination.** Determines the location of the rendering output.

Viewport
Renders the image in the current viewport.

Render window
> Renders the image to the Render window. From this window you can save the file as a *.bmp*, *.dib*, or *.rle*. You also can change the pixel display and color depth and have the image automatically change its size to preserve the aspects ratio of the image when the size of the Render window changes.

File
> Renders the image directly to a file.

More options
> Activates the File Output Configuration dialog box. It is available only when the destination is set to File. See the following section, "The File Output Configuration Dialog Box."

10. **Sub Sampling**. Renders a fraction of all pixels, reducing rendering time and image quality. A ratio of 1:1 is the best quality and 8:1 is the fastest.

11. **Background**. See *background* for more detailed information.

12. **Fog/Depth Cue**. See *fog* for more detailed information.

The Render Options Dialog Box

The Render Options dialog defines the rendering display.

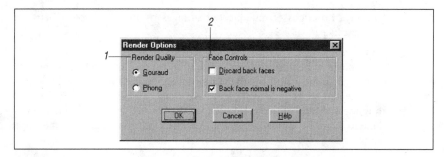

1. **Render Quality**. Controls the type of shading—Gouraud or Phong—when smooth shading is enabled. Gouraud determines light intensity at each vertex and interpolates intermediate intensities. This shading is faster than Phong. Phong is more sophisticated than Gouraud. It generates shading with more realistic highlights. Phong shading calculates light intensity at each pixel and therefore is slower than Gouraud.

2. **Face Controls**. Controls the faces of 3D solids. Discard Back Faces controls the calculation of back faces for 3D solid objects. Turning this option on speeds up the rendering process since it ignores the back faces. The "Back face normal is negative" checkbox controls which faces are considered back faces of objects. This is based on how the objects were created.

The Photo Real Render Options Dialog Box

The Photo Real Render Options dialog controls the photo raytrace rendering options.

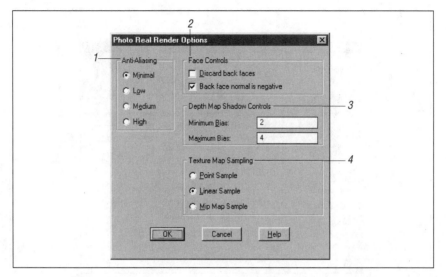

1. **Anti-Aliasing**. Determines how straight and curved edges are calculated and displayed. When anti-aliasing is set to Minimal, the edges appear jagged, and when set to High, the edges appear smooth and straight. When anti-aliasing is set to High, it takes longer to render and lines end up thicker than when it is set to minimal.

2. **Face Controls**. Controls the faces of 3D solids. Discard Back Faces controls the calculation of back faces for 3D solid objects. Turning this option on speeds up the rendering process since it ignores the back faces. The "Back face normal is negative" checkbox controls which faces are considered back faces of objects. This is based on how the objects were created.

3. **Depth Map Shadow Controls**. Controls the shadow relative to the shadow-casting object. Minimum Bias sets the lowest value in the range. The range is usually set to a value between 2.0 and 20.0. Maximum Bias sets the highest value in the Range. Maximum Bias should be no more that 10.0 greater than the Minimum Bias value.

4. **Texture Map Sampling**. Determines how to display a texture map when it's projected onto an object smaller than itself.

The Photo Raytrace Render Options Dialog Box

The Photo Raytrace Render Options dialog controls the photo raytrace rendering options.

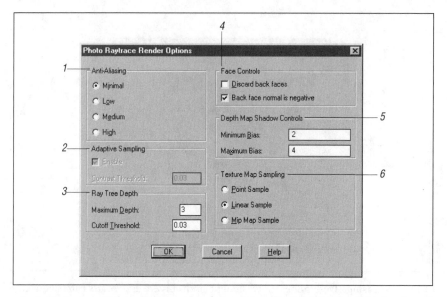

1. **Anti-Aliasing.** Determines how straight and curved edges are calculated and displayed. When anti-aliasing is set to Minimal, the edges appear jagged, and when set to High, the edges appear smooth and straight. When anti-aliasing is set to High, it takes longer to render and lines end up thicker than when it is set to Minimal.

2. **Adaptive Sampling.** This further refines the anti-aliasing process when anti-aliasing is set to Low, Medium, or High. When adaptive sampling is enabled the contrast threshold can set between 0.0 and 1.0. The higher the setting, the faster the rendering speed.

3. **Ray Tree Depth.** Controls the ray tree depth that tracks reflected and refracted rays. The greater the value, the more accurate the render, but also the slower the rendering speed. You may not want to set the maximum depth greater than 10.

4. **Face Controls.** Controls the faces of 3D solids. The "Discard back faces" checkbox controls the calculation of back faces for 3D solid objects. Turning this option on speeds up the rendering process since it ignores the back faces. The "Back face normal is negative" checkbox controls which faces are considered back faces of objects. This is based on how the objects were created.

5. **Depth Map Shadow Controls.** Controls the shadow relative to the shadow-casting object. Minimum Bias sets the lowest value in the range. The range is usually set to a value between 2.0 and 20.0. Maximum Bias sets the highest value in the range. Maximum Bias should be no more that 10.0 greater than the Minimum Bias value.

6. **Texture Map Sampling**. Determines how to display a texture map when it's projected onto an object smaller than itself.

The File Output Configuration Dialog Box

The File Output Configuration dialog defines the file type and screen resolution output.

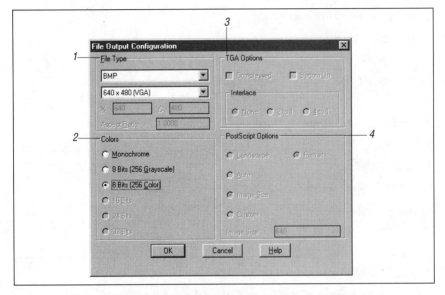

1. **File Type**. Lets you save your rendered image to .*bmp*, .*pcx*, .*ps*, .*tga*, and .*tif* files. You also can define the resolution of those files. The higher the number, the greater the resolution and file size. Selecting User Defined lets you manually enter the *X*-to-*Y* ratio as well as the aspect ratio of width to height.

2. **Colors**. Sets the colors in the output file. The available options are determined by the type of file that is being created.

3. **TGA Options**. Sets the file compression, scan line direction, and interlacing for .*tif* and .*tga* files.

4. **PostScript Options**. Sets the orientation, image size, and image scaling for PostScript files.

Associated Commands   background, fog, light, render, scene

RSCRIPT

see SCRIPT

'RTDISPLAY

Determines how raster images are displayed when using the real-time pan and zoom features.

Initiate Command By
Command: **rtdisplay**

Options

0   Displays the raster image. This setting increases the amount of time it takes to complete a real-time pan or zoom.

1   Displays the raster image outline.

Variable Settings

Initial default:	1
Subsequent default:	Registry file
Value:	Integer
Associated Commands	image, pan, zoom

RTEDIT 2000

Edits remote text objects. See *rtext* for more detailed information.

Initiate Command By
Command: **rtedit**

RTEXT 2000

References the content of ASCII text files or the value of Diesel expressions. It is similar to the concept of external references in that remote text objects are loaded into the drawing file each time you open the file for editing. This is especially useful when many people need to reference the same files and they want to make sure they are looking at the most up-to-date information. Edit remote text (rtext) objects with *rtedit*; convert rtext to multiline text (mtext) with *explode*.

If the rtext file is moved from its reference location, the message "RTEXT: file open error" is displayed instead of the rtext. To correct this, you can move the text file back to its referenced location using Windows Explorer or reassign the path to the rtext's location. You can reassign the path to the rtext's location through *rtedit*, *redir*, or *properties*.

Initiate Command By
Command: **rtext**
Express → Text → Remote Text

Options

```
Current settings: Style=Standard  Height=0.2000  Rotation=0
Enter an option [Style/Height/Rotation/File/Diesel] <File>:
Enter an option [Style/Height/Rotation/Edit]:
```

Style

Changes the current style default. See *style* for more detailed information.

Height

Assigns a text height.

Rotation

Specifies the text angle.

File

Specifies the name of an ASCII text file.

Diesel

Displays the results of Diesel code, or allows you to enter text strings. An example of Diesel code is the following:

```
$(getvar, "dwgprefix")$(getvar, "dwgname").
```

Entering this code in the Diesel dialog box produces the directory path and file name upon completion of the *rtext* command.

Edit

Lets you edit the ASCII file or Diesel expression.

Tips & Warnings

- If *filedia* is set to 1, a dialog box is activated; if *filedia* is set to 0, you are prompted on the command line. When *filedia* is set to 0, or off, entering a tilde (~) on the command line temporarily activates the dialog box.

- Use *list* or *properties* to find out the file name and location.

- If you plan to move a drawing file containing rtext files to another computer or to a diskette, you need to include any rtext files. Use *pack* to help you accomplish this.

Related Variables   filedia, textfill, textqlty, textstyle

Associated Commands   arctext, dtext, expresstools, mtext, pack, rtedit

---

RTPAN

see PAN

RTZOOM

see ZOOM

RULESURF

Surfaces toolbar

Generates a 3D polygon mesh (surface) depicting the ruled surface between two curves. You can edit a rulesurf object with *pedit*.

Initiate Command By

Command: **rulesurf**
Draw → Surfaces → Ruled Surface

Options

```
Current wire frame density:   SURFTAB1=12
Select first defining curve:
Select second defining curve:
```

Select first defining curve/Select second defining curve

The defining curves can be a point, line, arc, circle, spline, ellipse, 2D polyline, or 3D polyline. If one defining curve is a circle, ellipse, closed polyline, or closed spline, then the other boundary must also be closed. The ruled surface for a circle starts at the 0-degree quadrant. The ruled surface for a closed polygon starts at the last vertex and is constructed backward.

When constructing ruled surfaces for open curves, the endpoints nearest the selection pick points determine the start of the ruled surface. You cannot use a point to define both boundaries. However, a point can be used with any open or closed boundary.

Tips & Warnings

Use *ddvpoint, dview, vpoint,* and *3dorbit* to view the rulesurf at different angles and elevations. Use *hide, render,* and *shademode* to enhance the rulesurf's display.

Related Variables   snapang, surftab1

Associated Commands   3d, 3dmesh

Example

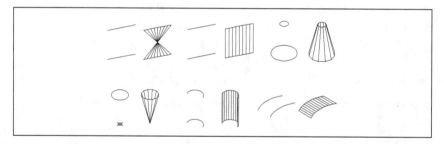

SAVE

Updates your drawing file by activating the Save Drawing As dialog box. The current drawing filename is the default name. If you specify another folder and/or filename, a copy is created, but your active drawing remains current. This is similar to *saveas* except that *saveas* saves the drawing to a different name, and that becomes the current drawing. See *saveas* for more detailed information.

You do not have to include the drawing extension *.dwg*; it is assumed. Each time you save, the previous saved drawing is renamed as the backup (*.bak*) drawing, assuming that *isavebak* is set to 1. You can control file size with *isavebak, isavepercent,* and *rasterpreview.* If you made changes to a drawing that is write-protected and you want to save the changes, use the *save* or *saveas* command and create a new drawing with a different name.

Initiate Command By

Command: **save**

Tips & Warnings

- You also can save files by using the automatic save feature, *qsave*, *saveas*, *close*, and *quit*. *qsave* saves the drawing without prompts and dialog boxes; *saveas* activates the Save Drawing As dialog box; *close* ends the current file; and *quit* exits the AutoCAD program. *close* and *quit* give you the opportunity to save your file if any commands were issued after the last *qsave*, *save*, or *saveas* command.

- If *filedia* is set to 1, a dialog box is activated; if *filedia* is set to 0, you are prompted on the command line. When *filedia* is set to 0, or off, entering a tilde (~) on the command line temporarily activates the dialog box.

- If you want to copy the file and all its dependencies to a user-specified location, use *pack*. File dependencies include images, external references, fonts, shapes, plot styles, plotter configuration files, remote text, and fontmap.

Related Variables	dwgname, dwgprefix, dwgtitled, filedia, indexctl, isavebak, isavepercent, proxygraphics, rasterpreview, savename, savetime, tempprefix
Associated Commands	close, options, pack, preferences, qsave, quit, saveas

---

SAVEAS

Lets you update your drawing file by activating the Save Drawing As dialog box. The current drawing file is the default name. If you specify another folder and/or filename, a copy is created and becomes your current drawing.

You do not have to include the drawing extension *.dwg*; it is assumed. If you enter a new name and/or drive or folder, the original file is not updated. It remains as it was when you first began the drawing session or when you last saved that file. If you made changes to a drawing that is write-protected and you want to save the changes, use *save* or *saveas* and create a new drawing with a different name.

Initiate Command By

Command: **saveas**
File → Save As

Options

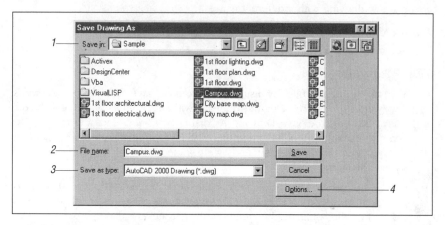

1. **Save in**. Lets you determine the folder in which to save your file. This value is maintained by the *dwgprefix* system variable.

2. **File name**. Lets you determine the filename. This value is maintained by the *dwgname* system variable.

3. **Save as type**. You can save the file as a template file (*.dwt*), drawing interchange file (*.dxf*), AutoCAD LT file (*.dwg*), or to a previous version of AutoCAD. The *.dxf* files are compatible with AutoCAD Release 12, 13, 14, and 15, and AutoCAD LT 2, 95, 97, and 98. The *.dwg* files are compatible with AutoCAD Release 13, 14, and 15 and AutoCAD LT 95, 97, and 98.

4. **Options**. Controls various DWG and DXF settings. See the following dialog boxes for more detailed information.

The DWG Options Tab

The DWG Options tab controls the drawing index and proxy images and determines the default file type.

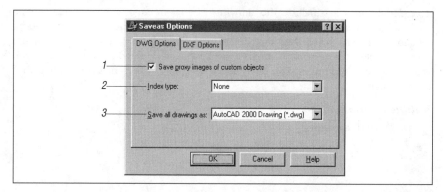

1. **Save proxy images of custom objects**. Determines if proxy images are displayed as images or as bounding boxes. Proxy images are custom objects created by developers of third-party software. This value is maintained by the *proxygraphics* variable.

2. **Index type**. Determines whether layer and spatial indexes are created and saved in drawing files. These indexes are used to improve performance during demand loading (*partiaload, partialopen*). A spatial index organizes objects based on their location in 3D space; a layer index is a list tracking which objects are on which layer. This value is maintained by the *indexctl* variable.

3. **Save all drawings as**. Sets the default for the file type saved whenever the *save, saveas*, and *qsave* commands are issued. This can also be set with the Save As option from the *options* Open and Save tab.

The DXF Options Tab

The DXF Options tab determines the default parameters when saving to a drawing interchange file (*.dxf*).

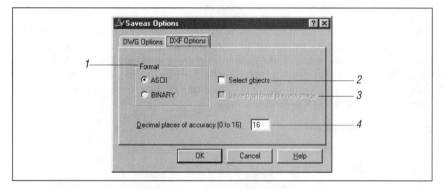

1. **Format**. Drawing interchange files can be created in ASCII or binary format. ASCII formats are much larger files, but they can be read with an ASCII text editor and are more widely used by other software programs. Binary files contain the same information and are saved in a more compact form. Your decision will be based on the software requirements of the program receiving this file.

2. **Select objects**. Determines whether the whole drawing is saved in the *.dxf* format or if you can select the objects through any of the standard object-selection methods.

3. **Save thumbnail preview image**. Determines whether an image is saved with the drawing file. This image is displayed in the Preview window of the Select File dialog box. The *insert* and *open* commands use this dialog box. This value is maintained by the *rasterpreview* variable.

4. **Decimal places of accuracy (0 to 16)**. Determines how many places past the decimal point is saved when creating a drawing interchange file. This value may be determined by the software requirements of the program receiving this file.

Tips & Warnings

- If *filedia* is set to 1, a dialog box is activated; if *filedia* is set to 0, you are prompted on the command line. When *filedia* is set to 0, or off, entering a tilde (~) on the command line temporarily activates the dialog box.

- *qsave* and *save* act like the *saveas* command when a file is saved for the first time.

- You can control file size with *isavebak, isavepercent,* and *rasterpreview.*

Related Variables	dwgname, dwgprefix, dwgtitled, filedia, indexctl, proxygraphics, rasterpreview, savename, savetime, tempprefix
Associated Commands	options, preferences, qsave, quit, save

SAVEASR12 (obsolete) *see SAVEAS*

'SAVEFILE 2000mod

Stores the filename of the file created when the automatic save feature is enabled. If you want to retrieve and use the drawing file created with this feature, you must rename the drawing file and assign it a *.dwg* file extension. The *savefile*'s extension is always *.sv$*. The *savefilepath* variable determines the location of these files. You can turn off the automatic save feature by checking the Automatic Save box located on the *options* Open and Save tab.

Initiate Command By
Command: **savefile**

Variable Settings

Initial default:	Varies, read-only
Subsequent default:	Registry file
Value:	String
Related Variables	savefilepath, savetime
Associated Commands	options, preferences

'SAVEFILEPATH 2000

Stores the location of the file created when the automatic save feature is enabled. You can turn off the automatic save feature by checking the Automatic Save box located on the *options* Open and Save tab. You set the file's path location with the "Temporary drawing file location" option located on the *options* Files tab.

Initiate Command By
Command: **savefilepath**

Variable Settings

Initial default:	C:\Windows\Temp\
Subsequent default:	Registry file
Value:	String

Related Variables	savefile, savetime
Associated Commands	options, preferences

SAVEIMG

Saves the drawing in *.bmp*, *.tga*, and *.tif* formats. This is especially useful for rendered drawings. The *render* command can also save *.bmp*, *.tga*,and *.tif* files. Use *replay* to display the images.

Initiate Command By

Command: **saveimg**
Tools → Display Image → Save

Options

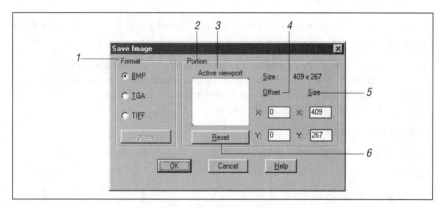

1. **Format.** Determines if the file is saved as a *.bmp*, *.tga*, or *.tif* image. *.tga* files can be compressed into run-length-encoded images; *.tif* files can be compressed using Macintosh packbits run-length-encoded image. To set the file compression, select the Options button.

2. **Portion.** Determines the portion of the drawing to save as an image file. The default (in pixels) is to save the whole image. The values are reflected in the Offset and Size text boxes. You can pick two points in the Active Viewport window, graphically showing which part of the image should be saved, or enter values in the Offset and Size text boxes.

3. **Active viewport.** Saves the active viewport. Picking two diagonal points inside the window defines a portion of the active viewport to save to an image file.

4. **Offset.** Determines the lower-left *X,Y* position of the image selection area.

5. **Size.** Determines the upper-right *X,Y* position of the image selection area.

6. **Reset.** Resets the Active Viewport window and the Offset and Size boxes to their default settings.

Associated Commands   render, replay, rpref

'SAVENAME

Stores the folder location and name of the current drawing once it's been saved.

Initiate Command By
Command: **savename**

Variable Settings

Initial default:	" ", read-only
Subsequent default:	Initial default
Value:	String

Related Variables tempprefix

Associated Commands qsave, save, saveas

'SAVETIME

Determines the frequency of automatic saves. *savetime* is activated as soon as you make any changes to the drawing. It is reset every time you issue a *qsave, save,* or *saveas* command. This variable is set when selecting the Minutes Between Saves option from the *options* Open and Save tab.

Initiate Command By
Command: **savetime**

Options

0   Disables *savetime.*

1–600
Sets the frequency of automatic saves in minutes.

Variable Settings

Initial default:	120
Subsequent default:	Registry file
Value:	Integer

Tips & Warnings

Once the *savetime* interval is reached, the next command reactivates the *savetime* feature. *savetime* works only if you are actively using the computer. If the time has expired and you are not actually using the computer, no *save* is issued.

Related Variables savefile, savefilepath

Associated Commands options, preferences, qsave, save, saveas, time

SCALE

Modify toolbar

Changes the size of objects. You cannot scale *X*, *Y*, or *Z* values independently. If you need to have different *X*, *Y*, and *Z* values, you can create a *block* and then use *insert* to assign different values to *X*, *Y*, and *Z*.

You can change the size or scale of most objects using *grips, lengthen, properties,* and *stretch. properties* and *lengthen* let you change only one object at a time. *grips* has its own scale routine that lets you create multiple copies simultaneously. *mocoro* lets you move, copy, rotate, and scale objects.

Initiate Command By

Command: **scale**
Alias: **sc**
Modify → Scale

Options

```
Select objects:
Specify base point:
Specify scale factor or [Reference]:
```

base point
Defines a reference point about which the objects are scaled.

scale factor
Provides a value to multiply the *X*, *Y*, and *Z* dimensions. A value greater than 1 enlarges the objects; a value between 0 and 1 reduces the size of the objects.

Reference
Prompts you to specify a reference length and the new length you want the reference length to become.

Tips & Warnings

Since drawings normally are drawn full size, use the *plot* options to scale your output to the plotter.

Associated Commands

align, grips, insert, minsert, mocoro

Example

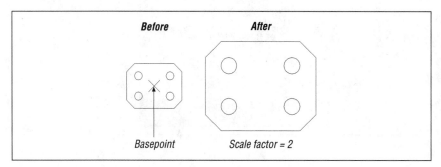

SCENE

Render toolbar

Provides a method of creating, modifying, and deleting scenes. Scenes are created by combining a named view with one or more light sources. Once one or more scenes have been defined, they are used to enhance the rendering of drawings.

Initiate Command By

Command: **scene**

View → Render → Scene

Options

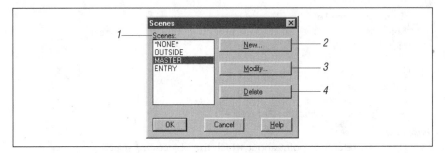

1. **Scenes**. Lists the names of scenes already created. This list also is displayed when using the *render* command. The default, *NONE* uses the display from the active viewport and all the lights defined in the drawing. If no lights are defined, it uses an "over-the-shoulder" distant light source with an intensity of 1 and an ambient light intensity of 0.

2. **New**. Activates the New Scene dialog box and lets you create new scenes.

3. **Modify**. Makes changes to existing scenes. This activates the Modify Scene dialog box, which has the same options as the New Scene dialog box.

4. **Delete**. Removes the scene selected from the Scenes list.

The New Scene Dialog Box

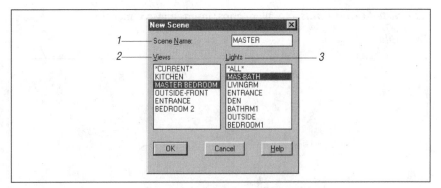

1. **Scene Name.** Assigns an 8-character name to a scene.

2. **Views.** Lists the views created with the *view* command. Only the views created in model space are displayed. Selecting a view assigns it to the scene. You can assign only one view to a scene.

3. **Lights.** Lists the lights created with the *light* command. Select one or more lights to add to the scene. Selecting a highlighted light removes the light from the scene. Selecting *ALL* uses all the lights in the drawing.

Associated Commands   light, render, view

'SCREENBOXES

Stores the maximum number of lines that can be displayed on the Screen menu. This number varies based on your video configuration. The Screen menu is turned on when checking the Display Screen Menu box located on the *options* Display tab.

Initiate Command By
Command: **screenboxes**

Variable Settings

Initial default:	0, read-only
Subsequent default:	Registry file
Value:	Integer

Associated Commands   options, preferences

'SCREENMODE

Keeps track of the current graphics/text state of your AutoCAD display.

Initiate Command By
Command: **screenmode**

Options

screenmode is bit-coded, and its value is the sum of the following:

0   Text screen is displayed.

1   Graphics screen is displayed.

2   Dual screen is displayed.

Variable Settings

Initial default:	Varies, read-only
Subsequent default:	Initial default
Value:	Integer

'SCREENSIZE

Maintains the size of the current viewport (*X, Y*) in pixels.

Initiate Command By

Command: **screensize**

Variable Settings

Initial default:	Varies, read-only
Subsequent default:	Initial default
Value:	2D point

SCRIPT/DELAY/RESUME/RSCRIPT

Script files automate routine tasks. A script file is an ASCII text file created with a text editor containing commands and responses in the exact order of execution. The file has the extension .*scr.* A script file is activated with *script* to perform the series of commands. The default script name is the current drawing filename. *delay, resume,* and *rscript* control the running of scripts.

Scripts often are used to display slide shows, plot drawings, and reset system variables. If you change drawing standards and need to update existing drawings, use script files to do the work.

Initiate Command By

Command: **script**
Alias: **scr**
Tools → Run Script

Options

Delay

Creates a pause, in milliseconds, between commands. The maximum delay is 32,767, or just under 33 seconds. The actual number of seconds may vary depending on the computer's hardware.

Resume

Reactivates a script that was interrupted. If the script stopped in the middle of a command, you may need to type **resume** with a leading apostrophe ('**resume**). You can stop a script by pressing the Backspace key or Escape.

Rscript

Repeats the script file. This command is placed as the last entry of a script file. You stop the script by pressing the Backspace key or Escape.

Tips & Warnings

- When using the *rscript* option, you may want to turn off the *undo–control– none* and log file features since the files will continuously increase in size and take up disk space.

- If *filedia* is set to 1, a dialog box is activated; if *filedia* is set to 0, you are prompted on the command line. When *filedia* is set to 0, or off, entering a tilde (~) on the command line temporarily activates the dialog box.

- The *undo* command considers a script sequence as one group. Therefore, you can reverse the effects of a script with a single *u* command.

- Suppress the display of nonfatal error messages and plot dialog boxes during script routines by setting *plquiet* to 1.

Related Variables	filedia, plquiet
Associated Commands	vslide

'SDI 2000

Single Document Interface controls the ability to have one or more files open during an AutoCAD drawing session. This variable is set when selecting the "Single-drawing compatibility mode" option of the *options* System tab.

Initiate Command By
Command: **sdi**

Options

0   Multiple-drawing interface is enabled.

1   Multiple-drawing interface is disabled.

2   Multiple-drawing interface is disabled when using a third-party application that does not support this feature.

3   Multiple-drawing interface is disabled by the end user and by a third-party application that does not support this feature.

Variable Settings

Initial default:	0
Subsequent default:	Registry file
Value:	Integer
Associated Commands	lispinit
Associated Commands	new, open, options, preferences

SECTION

Solids toolbar

Creates a region from the cross section of a 3D solid at a designated plane.

Initiate Command By
Command: **section**
Alias: **sec**
Draw → Solids → Section

Options

```
Select objects:
Specify first point on Section plane by
[Object/Zaxis/View/XY/YZ/ZX/3points] <3points>:
```

Object

Aligns the sectioning plane with an arc, elliptical arc, circle, ellipse, polyline, or spline.

Zaxis

Determines the sectioning plane by an origin point on the *Z* axis of the plane.

View

Aligns the sectioning plane with the current viewport's viewing plane.

XY

Aligns the sectioning plane with the *X, Y* plane of the current UCS.

YZ

Aligns the sectioning plane with the *Y,Z* plane of the current UCS.

ZX

Aligns the sectioning plane with the *Z,X* plane of the current UCS.

3points

Identifies three points on a sectioning plane. See the following example.

Associated Commands   region, slice

Example

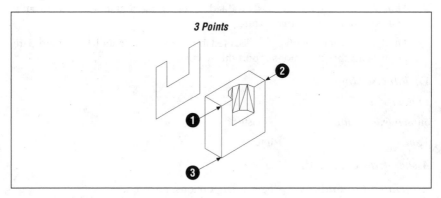

3 Points

SELECT

Lets you pick objects that are retained and can be recalled when using the previous (P) selection set option. Select often is used in macros and AutoLISP and other programming routines. See "Selection Sets" in Chapter 2, *Command Index and Global Topics*, for more detailed information.

You also can select objects with *filter*, *getsel*, and *qselect*. *filter* and *qselect* let you select objects based on the object type, layer, color, lineweight, linetype, linetype scale, hyperlink, and plot style assignments. *getsel* lets you select objects based on their layer assignment and object type.

Initiate Command By
Command: **select**

Tips & Warnings

You cannot select model space objects when working in paper space and vice versa.

Related Variables	highlight, pickadd, pickauto, pickbox, pickdrag, pickfirst
Associated Commands	filter, grips, pickbox, qselect

SELECTURL (obsolete)　　　　　　　*see HYPERLINKOPTIONS*

'SETVAR

Sets system variables. These are variables or data that are saved as integers, reals, points, or text strings. Some of the variables are saved in the drawing file and others in the Windows registry. Some are retained only for the current editing session, and others are read-only. Scripts and macros as well as AutoLISP and other programming routines frequently access system variables. The current units settings determine how values are displayed for real numbers.

Most variables can be accessed at the command prompt without using *setvar*. A few commands and variables (*aperture, area, blipmode, dragmode, ltscale,* and *ucsicon*) share the same name. The only way to access those variables is by first entering *setvar* at the command prompt and then entering the variable name. Most variables are automatically modified through AutoCAD commands. See the individual variables for more detailed information. See "Transparent Commands and Variables" in Chapter 2, *Command Index and Global Topics*, for a complete listing of all the transparent commands and variables.

Initiate Command By
Command: **setvar**
Alias: **set**
Tools → Inquiry → Set Variable

Options
Enter variable name or [?]:

Enter variable name
Enter the name of a variable to change.

? Activates the wildcard options for reviewing variable settings. The default, an asterisk, displays a sorted listing of all variables. You can use any of the wildcard options to create a more specific list.

You can access the variables with *setvar* or by typing the variable name directly on the command line. Since a few of the variables share the same names with commands, you can access only those variables by first issuing the *setvar* command. The following variables can only be accessed by first issuing *setvar*.

APERTURE

Controls the size of the target box located at the intersection of the crosshairs during object snap selection. The size of the aperture box may be changed by specifying its height in pixels (1–50). A pixel is the smallest visible dot that appears on the screen. Set the default to four or six pixels for the best visibility. This value is set when selecting the Aperture Size option from the *options* Drafting tab.

Variable Settings

Initial default:	10
Subsequent default:	Registry file
Value:	Integer
Related Variables	osmode
Associated Commands	aperture, osnap

AREA

Maintains the latest value of the *area* command.

Variable Settings

Initial default:	0.0000, read-only
Subsequent default:	Initial default
Value:	Real
Related Variables	perimeter
Associated Commands	area, dblist, list, massprop, properties

BLIPMODE

Controls the display of the small temporary blips or cross marks that appear when entering points or selecting objects.

0 (off)
    Suppresses blips.

1 (on)
    Generates blips.

2 (auto)
    Automatically enables drag for any command that supports dragging.

Variable Settings

Initial default:	1
Subsequent default:	Last value used in the drawing
Value:	Integer
Associated Commands	blipmode

DRAGMODE

Controls the way objects are displayed as they are dragged about the drawing.

0 (off)
> Ignores all dragging requests.

1 (on)
> Enables dragging when requested.

2 (auto)
> Automatically enables drag for any command that supports dragging.

Variable Settings

Initial default:	2
Subsequent default:	Last value used in drawing
Value:	Integer
Related Variables	dragp1, dragp2
Associated Commands	dragmode

LTSCALE

Assigns a global scale multiplier for all linetypes.

Variable Settings

Initial default:	1.0000
Subsequent default:	Last value used in the drawing
Value:	Real
Related Variables	celtscale, psltscale
Associated Commands	layer, linetype, ltscale

UCSICON

Determines the visibility and location of the ucsicon in the current viewport. The *ucsicon* is bit-coded and its value is the sum of the following:

0 The UCS icon is invisible.

1 The UCS icon is visible.

2 The UCS icon at the origin of the current UCS (0,0,0). If the origin is off the screen viewing area, the icon is shown in the lower-left corner.

Variable Settings

Initial default:	3
Subsequent default:	Last value used in the drawing
Value:	Integer
Related Variables	ucsfollow, ucsname, ucsorg, ucsxdir, ucsydir, worlducs
Associated Commands	dview, mspace, pspace, ucs, ucsicon, ucsman

---

SHADE 2000mod   *see SHADEMODE*

'SHADEDGE

Specifies how faces and edges are displayed when shaded. *shadedge* affects all viewports.

Initiate Command By
    Command: **shadedge**

Options

0   Faces are shaded, and the edges are not highlighted.

1   Faces are shaded, and the edges are drawn in the background color.

2   Faces are not filled, and the edges are in the object's color.

3   Faces are in the object's color, and edges are in the background color.

Variable Settings

Initial default:	3
Subsequent default:	Last value used in the drawing
Value:	Integer

Related Variables	shadedif
Associated Commands	shademode

'SHADEDIF

Specifies how the geometry is illuminated. It is the ratio of diffuse reflective light to ambient light. The value can be set anywhere from 0 to 100. A higher setting increases diffuse lighting and adds more reflectivity and contrast to the image. *shadedif* affects all viewports. This variable is active when *shadedge* is set to 0 or 1.

Initiate Command By
    Command: **shadedif**

Variable Settings

Initial default:	70
Subsequent default:	Last value used in the drawing
Value:	Integer

Related Variables	shadedge
Associated Commands	shademode

SHADEMODE 2000

Produces a shaded rendering of the objects in the current viewport. Once the objects are shaded, they can be edited. Only one light source is used, and there is a fixed amount of ambient light. The light source is located behind and over the left shoulder of the viewer. *shademode* combines the *shade* command and *shadedge* variable. The Shade toolbar (shown above) can be activated by right-clicking on an existing toolbar and selecting Shade.

Initiate Command By

    Command: **shademode**
    View → Shade

Options

    Current mode: 2D wireframe
    Enter option [2D wireframe/3D
    wireframe/Hidden/Flat/Gouraud/fLat+edges/gOuraud+edges] <2D wireframe>:

2D wireframe
    Produces an image showing only lines and curves. Raster images, linetypes, lineweights, and objects that should be hidden are displayed. Even if the compass is on, it is not displayed.

3D wireframe
    Produces an image showing only lines and curves. Raster images, linetypes, and lineweights are not displayed. Objects that should be hidden are displayed. The compass is displayed when on.

Hidden
    Produces an image showing only lines and curves. Raster images, linetypes, lineweights, and objects that should be hidden are not displayed. The compass is displayed when on.

Flat
    Shades objects between the polygon faces based on their color assignment. Raster images, linetypes, lineweights, and objects that should be hidden are not displayed. The compass is displayed when on. The shaded image is flatter and less smooth than the Gouraud-shaded objects.

Gouraud
    Shades and smooths objects between the polygon faces based on their color assignment. Raster images, linetypes, lineweights, and objects that should be hidden are not displayed. The compass is displayed when on.

fLat+edges
    Combines the 3D wireframe and flat options.

gOuraud+edges
    Combines the 3D wireframe and Gouraud options.

Tips & Warnings

- *zoom* previous takes you back to the last shademode you created as well as the last zoom.

- You can access the *shademode* command while 3D orbit is active by using the shortcut menu.

- Objects remain shaded even when the drawing is closed and reopened for editing. A regeneration has no effect on the shaded objects. Use the 2D or 3D wireframe options if you want to see the object's outline.

- For a more realistic view of your drawing, use *render*. Materials that have been assigned to objects with *rmat* are not displayed unless you use *render*.

- Anytime you change the display of rendered objects (such as *zoom, pan, regen*) the objects lose their rendered status and default to the last *shademode* setting.

Associated Commands   render

SHAPE

Inserts shapes into the drawing. Shapes are an alternative to blocks, and their definitions are stored in shape files. Each shape file can contain numerous symbol definitions. Shape files also are used to produce special text fonts and symbols. The shape file must be compiled with *compile*. The extension for a compiled shape file is *.shx*. Once the shape file is compiled, it must be loaded with *load* before it can be used. Shapes also can be used to create complex linetypes when using *mkltype*.

Shapes regenerate much faster than the same symbols stored as blocks and take up less memory. Even though shape definitions require less memory, they are not as desirable as block definitions. They cannot be exploded or scaled differently in *X* and *Y* directions. Complex shape definitions are tedious and time-consuming to create manually; use *mkshape* to quickly create shapes. Shapes are external to the drawing file and must always accompany the drawing. Shapes cannot include attribute definitions, but blocks may contain both shapes and attributes.

Initiate Command By

Command: **shape**

Options

? Activates wildcard options for reviewing the names of shapes defined in the drawing. The default, an asterisk, displays a listing of all loaded shapes. You can use any of the wildcard options to create a more specific list.

Tips & Warnings

If you plan to move a drawing file containing shapes to another computer or to a diskette, you need to include any referenced shape files. Use *pack* to help you accomplish this.

Related Variables	shpname
Associated Commands	block, compile, load, mkltype, pack

'SHORTCUTMENU 2000

Defines the right mouse button assignment. The shortcut menu can be set to Default, Edit, and Command modes. These modes are available when right clicking in the drawing area. Shortcut menus are defined by the current menu. This variable is set when selecting an option from the Windows Standard Behavior section located in the *options* User Preferences tab.

Initiate Command By

Command: **shortcutmenu**

Options

shortcutmenu is bit-coded, and its value is the sum of the following:

0   Causes clicking on the right mouse button to act as an Enter key. The Default, Edit, and Command modes are inactive.

1   Activates Default mode shortcut menus

2   Activates Edit mode shortcut menus.

4   Activates the Command mode shortcut menus whenever a command is active.

8   Activates the Command mode shortcut menus only when command options are available from the command line.

Variable Settings

Initial default:	11
Subsequent default:	Registry file
Value:	Integer
Related Variables	menuname
Associated Commands	menu, menuload, menuunload, options, preferences

SHOWMAT

Lists the material and the attachment method assigned to selected objects.

Initiate Command By

Command: **showmat**

Associated Commands   rmat

SHOWURLS 2000

Lists and locates the drawing's Internet address (Uniform Resource Locator, or URL). You also can edit the URL name with *showurls*. URLs are created with the *hyperlink* command. See *expresstools* if the Express pull down menu and toolbars aren't available.

Initiate Command By

Command: **showurls**
Express → Tools → Show URLs

Options

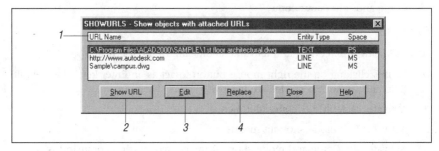

1. **URL Name, Entity Type, Space.** Lists the hyperlinks defined in the drawing, the type of object it is attached to, and the space (paper or model) where it resides. Double-clicking on a URL name causes the URL location to be displayed on the screen for a few seconds. You must be in model space to view model space locations and paper space to view paper space locations.

2. **Show URL.** Displays, for a few seconds, the URL location for the URL that is highlighted in the Show URLs window. You must be in model space to view model space locations and paper space to view paper space locations.

3. **Edit.** Allows you to edit the URL name.

4. **Replace.** Performs a case-sensitive search and replace on the URL name.

Associated Commands   expresstools, hyperlink

'SHPNAME

Sets and maintains the default shape name. This value is set with the *shape* command.

Initiate Command By

Command: **shpname**

Options   Resets the value to no default

Variable Settings

Initial default:	" " (none)
Subsequent default:	Initial default
Value:	String

Associated Commands   shape

SKETCH

Lets you draw freehand, creating contiguous short line segments, with an imaginary pen. You first specify line segment length, then sketch temporary line segments. A record option stores the line segments when you are finished. You have the option of setting *skpoly* to sketch either lines or polylines. You must use a pointing device such as a mouse or digitizer.

You can toggle *snap*, *grid*, and *ortho* on and off while sketching. To get smoother sketch lines, keep *snap* off. If an extrusion value (*thickness*) is set, line segments are extruded once the record option is selected. You also can extrude sketch lines by using *change*, *chprop*, or *properties*. You cannot turn Tablet mode on and off while sketching.

Initiate Command By

Command: **sketch**

Options

```
Record increment <0.1000>:
Sketch.  Pen eXit Quit Record Erase Connect.
```

Record increment <0.1000>

Determines the length of the sketch lines. When *snap* is on the segment lengths are based on the snap value. This value is maintained by the *sketchinc* variable.

Pen

Acts as a toggle switch for the up or down pen position. Sketching proceeds while the pen is down until you press P on the keyboard or release the pick button on your pointing device.

eXit

Records temporary line segments and exits the *sketch* command.

Quit

Discards temporary line segments and exits the *sketch* command.

Record

Records temporary line segments and remains in the *sketch* command.

Erase

Erases temporary line segments in the opposite order from which they were entered as you move your pointing device back over the line segments.

Connect

　Connects to an existing sketch object.

. (period)

　Draws a single line segment from the last point to the current pointing device location.

The buttons on a pointing device are redefined during the Sketch mode to the settings shown in the following table.

Puck	Keyboard	Function
0	P	pen up/down
1	.	single line
2	R	record lines
3	X	exit
4	Q	quit
5	E	erase
6	C	connect

Tips & Warnings

Since *sketch* requires a lot of disk space, try using *line*, *pline*, or *spline* as alternatives.

Related Variables　　　　sketchinc, skpoly

Associated Commands　　line, pline

Example

```
Command: sketch
Record increment <0.100000>: Press Enter
Sketch.  Pen eXit Quit Record Erase Connect. Pick point 1
<Pen down> P
<Pen up> Pick point 2
<Pen down> Press Enter
58 lines recorded
```

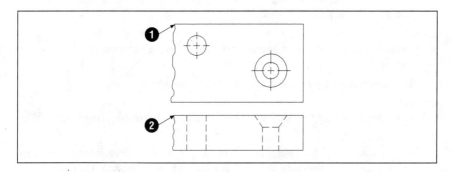

'SKETCHINC

Retains the record increment for *sketch*. When *snap* is on, it overrides the *sketchinc* setting. If the increment accuracy is important, set the value with a negative number. This number is considered positive, but the negative sign activates a special error-checking mode. This value is set when using the record increment option of the *sketch* command.

Initiate Command By

Command: **sketchinc**

Variable Settings

Initial default:	0.1000
Subsequent default:	Last value used in the drawing
Value:	Real

Related Variables	skpoly
Associated Commands	sketch

'SKPOLY

Determines the type of lines generated by the *sketch* command.

Initiate Command By

Command: **skpoly**

Options

0   Sketch with lines.

1   Sketch with polylines.

Variable Settings

Initial default:	0
Subsequent default:	Registry
Value:	Integer

Related Variables	sketchinc
Associated Commands	line, pline, sketch

SLICE

Solids toolbar

Cuts a 3D solid with a cutting plane. You determine whether to retain both sides of the solid or which side to keep.

Initiate Command By

Command: **slice**
Alias: **sl**
Draw → Solids → Slice

Options

```
Specify first point on slicing plane by
[Object/Zaxis/View/XY/YZ/ZX/3points] <3points>:
Specify a point on desired side of the plane or [keep Both sides]:
```

Object

Aligns the cutting plane with an arc, circle, ellipse, elliptical arc, polyline, or spline.

Zaxis

Determines the cutting plane by an origin point on the Z axis of the plane.

View

Aligns the cutting plane with the current viewport's viewing plane.

XY

Aligns the cutting plane with the X,Y plane of the current UCS.

YZ

Aligns the cutting plane with the Y,Z plane of the current UCS.

ZX

Aligns the cutting plane with the Z,X plane of the current UCS.

3points

Identifies three points on the cutting plane. See the following example.

Specify a point on desired side of the plane or [keep Both sides]:

Let you save both sides of the solid or select the side that remains in the drawing.

Associated Commands   section

Example

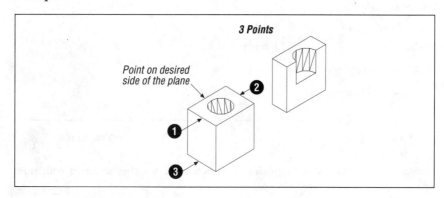

SNAP 2000mod

Restricts your crosshairs' movement to a specified increment. You can modify the increment value and turn the setting on or off. Snap also lets you work in Isometric mode. Each model space viewport and layout space tab contains their own snap settings. Snap is inactive during perspective views. You can change your snap settings from the Snap and Grid tab of the *dsettings* dialog box. You can create a rotated rectangular array by setting the snap rotation angle.

Typed coordinates, typed distances, and object snaps override *snap*. You will not snap to a grid point unless *snap* is on and is set to an even multiple of the grid increment.

Initiate Command By

Command: **snap**, Ctrl-B, or F9
Alias: **sn**
Tools → Drafting Settings → Snap and Grid
Status Bar: SNAP (left-clicking toggles snap on and off; right-clicking activates the *dsettings* Snap and Grid tab)

Options

Specify snap spacing or [ON/OFF/Aspect/Rotate/Style/Type] <0.5000>:

snap spacing
Sets the *X* and *Y* snap increment. Changing the snap spacing automatically turns *snap* on. This value is maintained by the *snapunit* variable.

ON
This value is maintained by the *snapmode* variable.

OFF
This value is maintained by the *snapmode* variable.

Aspect
Sets individual horizontal (*X*) and vertical (*Y*) snap increments. This option is not available if you are in Isometric mode. This value is maintained by the *snapunit* variable.

Rotate
Rotates the snap (and grid) by any specified angle about a base point. When working in Isometric mode, you should use the style option. Setting rotate is not as flexible, and the style option has greater functionality. This setting is maintained by the *snapbase* and *snapang* variables.

Style
Allows selection of the standard or isometric styles. Isometric sets the isometric snap and grid style on. Standard sets the normal drawing mode on. See *isoplane* for more detailed information. This value is maintained by the *snapstyl* variable.

Type
Sets the snap type to polar snap or grid snap. When polar snap is active, the crosshairs snap along polar angle increments; when grid snap is active, the

crosshairs snap along the grid. This value is maintained by the *snaptype* system variable.

Tips & Warnings

- To use the aspect option while in the *dsettings* dialog box, you must first set the *X* spacing, then the *Y* spacing.

- Screen crosshairs are oriented to the current snap rotation angle. *ortho* forces lines to be drawn orthogonally in relation to the crosshair orientation.

- You can control hatch pattern placement by setting the snap base point (use the rotate option) or the variable *snapbase* to a point at which you want the hatch pattern to originate.

Related Variables	snapang, snapbase, snapisopair, snapmode, snapstyl, snaptype, snapunit
Associated Commands	dsettings, grid, isoplane

'SNAPANG

Sets the snap/grid rotation angle for the current viewport. Keeping *ortho* on forces the crosshairs to maintain the *snapang* setting unless you use object snap over-rides or manually enter numeric values from the keyboard or from your pointing device. This value is set with the rotate option of the *snap* command or by selecting the Angle option from the *dsettings* Snap and Grid tab.

Initiate Command By

Command: **snapang**

Variable Settings

Initial default:	0
Subsequent default:	Last value used in the drawing
Value:	Real

Tips & Warnings

- You can create a rotated rectangular array by setting the snap rotation angle before using the *array* command.

- Use the snap's Isometric Snap option when working in the Isometric mode. Setting *snapang* is not as flexible.

Related Variables	snapbase, snapisopair, snapmode, snapstyl, snaptype, snapunit
Associated Commands	dsettings, grid, snap

Example

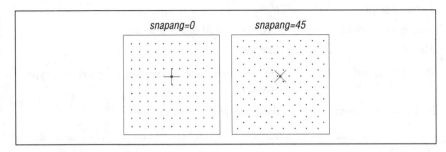

snapang=0   snapang=45

'SNAPBASE

Sets the snap/grid origin point for the current viewport. Grid locations are based on the *snapbase* value. This value is set with the rotate option of the *snap* command or by selecting the *X* Base and *Y* Base options from the *dsettings* Snap and Grid tab.

Initiate Command By

Command: **snapbase**

Variable Settings

Initial default:	0.0000,0.0000
Subsequent default:	Last value used in the drawing
Value:	2D point

Tips & Warnings

You can control hatch pattern placement by setting *snapbase* to a point at which you want the hatch pattern to originate.

Related Variables	snapang, snapisopair, snapmode, snapstyl, snaptype, snapunit
Associated Commands	dsettings, grid, snap

'SNAPISOPAIR

Determines the isometric plane for the current viewport. Isometric mode must be enabled (*snapstyl* set to 1) in order for *snapisopair* to function.

Initiate Command By

Command: **snapisopair**, F5, or Ctrl-E

Options

0   Left plane

1   Top plane

2   Right plane

References
S–T

Variable Settings

Initial default:	0
Subsequent default:	Last value used in the drawing
Value:	Integer

Related Variables   snapang, snapbase, snapmode, snapstyl, snaptype, snapunit

Associated Commands   dsettings, grid, isoplane, snap

'SNAPMODE

Sets snap on and off in the current viewport. This value can be set with the on or off option of the *snap* command, by selecting the Snap On option from the *dsettings* Snap and Grid tab, or by clicking on the SNAP button on the status bar.

Initiate Command By

Command: **snapmode**, F9, or Ctrl-B

Options

0   Snap off.

1   Snap on.

Variable Settings

Initial default:	0
Subsequent default:	Last value used in the drawing
Value:	Integer

Related Variables   snapang, snapbase, snapisopair, snapstyl, snaptype, snapunit

Associated Commands   dsettings, grid, snap

'SNAPSTYL

Determines whether the Standard or Isometric mode is active in the current viewport. This value is set with the style option of the *snap* command or by selecting the Isometric Snap option from *dsettings* Snap and Grid tab.

Initiate Command By

Command: **snapstyl**

Options

0   Standard mode is active.

1   Isometric mode is active.

Variable Settings

Initial default:	0
Subsequent default:	Last value used in the drawing
Value:	Integer
Related Variables	snapang, snapbase, snapisopair, snapmode, snaptype, snapunit
Associated Commands	dsettings, grid, isoplane, snap

'SNAPTYPE [2000]

Sets the snap type to polar snap or grid snap. This value is set with the type option of the *snap* command or by selecting the Snap Type & Style option from the *dsettings* Snap and Grid tab.

Initiate Command By

Command: **snaptype**

Options

0 Grid or standard snap is enabled. The crosshairs snap along the grid.

1 Polar snap is enabled. The crosshairs snap along polar angle increments.

Variable Settings

Initial default:	0
Subsequent default:	Registry file
Value:	Integer
Related Variables	snapang, snapbase, snapisopair, snapmode, snapstyl, snapunit
Associated Commands	dsettings, snap

'SNAPUNIT

Sets the snap spacing for the current viewport. This can also be set with the aspect option of the *snap* command or by selecting the Snap X Spacing and Snap Y Spacing options from the *dsettings* Snap and Grid tab.

Initiate Command By

Command: **snapunit**

Variable Settings

Initial default:	0.5000,0.5000
Subsequent default:	Last value used in the drawing
Value:	2D point

Related Variables	snapang, snapbase, snapisopair, snapmode, snapstyl
Associated Commands	dsettings, grid, snap

SOLDRAW

Solids toolbar

Hatches section views and places the hatches on layers created with *solview*. The section views are converted to 2D objects. The hatch pattern (*hpname*), angle (*hpang*), and scale (*hpscale*) are based on the current settings. Do not place any information on the layers created with *solview* since *soldraw* deletes and adds objects to those layers. Use the back option of the *undo* command if you want to reverse the effects of the *soldraw* command.

Initiate Command By

Command: **soldraw**
Draw → Solids → Setup → Drawing

Related Variables	hpang, hpname, hpscale, tilemode
Associated Commands	bhatch, slice, solprof, solview

Example

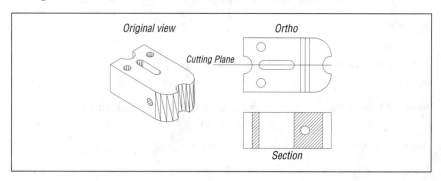

SOLID

Surfaces toolbar

Draws solid filled polygons. These areas can be triangular or quadrilateral. If *fill* or the system variable *fillmode* is on, the areas are filled. You can save time during regenerations and redraws by turning *fill* off. To see the results of turning *fill* on or off requires a drawing regeneration. If *grips* are enabled, the solid's grip definition points are the vertices. Picking any of the grip points of the solid lets you change the size and location. You must be in plan view to see the solid filled in.

Initiate Command By

Command: **solid**
Alias: **so**
Draw → Surfaces → 2D Solid

Related Variables   fillmode

Associated Commands   fill, grips

Example

'SOLIDCHECK

Turns solid validation on or off for the current AutoCAD session.

Initiate Command By

Command: **solidcheck**

Options

0   Turns solid validation off.

1   Turns solid validation on.

Variable Settings

Initial default: 1

Subsequent default: Initial default

Value: Integer

Associated Commands   solidedit

SOLIDEDIT `2000`   Solids Editing toolbar

Lets you edit faces, edges, and bodies of 3D solids. The edit options vary depending on which part of the solid you pick to edit. The Solids Editing toolbar (shown above) can be activated by right-clicking on an existing toolbar and selecting Solids Editing.

Initiate Command By

Command: **solidedit**
Modify → Solids Editing

Options

```
Solids editing automatic checking:  SOLIDCHECK=1
Enter a solids editing option [Face/Edge/Body/Undo/eXit] <eXit>:
```

Face

Lets you extrude, move, rotate, offset, taper, delete, copy, or change the color of 3D faces. Most of these options let you add and remove faces from the selection set. You also can cancel the selected faces you added most recently with the undo option.

Extrude

Extrudes one or more planar faces of a 3D solid object to a specified height or along a path. You can extrude the face longer or shorter by entering a positive or negative value. You also can taper the extruded portion by changing the angle to a value other than 0. Setting the angle to a positive value causes the face to taper in; a negative value causes the face to taper out. The path can be a line, circle, arc, ellipse, elliptical arc, polyline, or spline. The path should lie in a different plane from the face, and it should not contain a high curvature area. See the following example showing 3D solid faces extruded.

Move

Stretches one or more planar faces of a 3D solid object longer or shorter. Choosing the all option is the same as using the *move* command. Use this when different 3D solids are fused together with commands such as *union* and *subtract* and you want to move one or more of the fused objects.

Rotate

Rotates one or more faces on a solid about a specified axis. The axis of rotation can be defined in a number of ways: with two points, an existing object, or the viewing direction of the current viewport that passes through the selected point, or by aligning the axis of rotation with the axis that passes through the selected point.

Offset

Lets you offset planar faces parallel to itself by specifying a distance or a point through which the object will pass. A positive value increases the size; a negative value decreases the size.

Taper

Tapers faces with an angle. A positive angle tapers the face in; a negative angle tapers the face out. Valid angles are between –90 and 90 degrees.

Delete

Removes faces, chamfers, and fillets.

Copy

Copies faces as a region or a body.

coLor

Changes the color of faces.

Edge
> Lets you copy and change the color of edges.

Body
> Lets you imprint, separate, shell, clean, and check 3D solid objects.

> *Imprints*
> > Fuses an object (arc, circle, line, polyline, ellipse, spline, region, 3D solid) to a 3D solid. The object must intersect one or more faces of the 3D solid. Delete imprints with the clean option.

> *Shell*
> > Creates parallel lines for one or more faces. See the following example showing this option performed on a 3D rectangle. A positive value places the shell to the inside perimeter of the solid; a negative value places the shell to the outside perimeter.

> *cLean*
> > Deletes overlapping edges and vertices including imprinted and unused geometry. Once you select the 3D solid to clean, it automatically removes overlapping edges and vertices and imprinted and unused geometry.

> *Check*
> > Confirms the 3D solid object is an ACIS solid.

Undo
> Undoes the last edit.

eXit
> Exits the command.

Associated Commands   chamfer, fillet, section, slice

Related Variables   solidcheck

Example
```
Command: Solidedit
Solids editing automatic checking:  SOLIDCHECK=1
Enter a solids editing option [Face/Edge/Body/Undo/eXit] <eXit>: F
Enter a face editing option
[Extrude/Move/Rotate/Offset/Taper/Delete/Copy/coLor/Undo/eXit] <eXit>: E
Select faces or [Undo/Remove]: Pick point 1
2 faces found.
Select faces or [Undo/Remove/ALL]: Press Enter
Specify height of extrusion or [Path]: .5
Specify angle of taper for extrusion <0>: 0
Solid validation started.
Solid validation completed.
Enter a face editing option
[Extrude/Move/Rotate/Offset/Taper/Delete/Copy/coLor/Undo/eXit] <eXit>: X
```

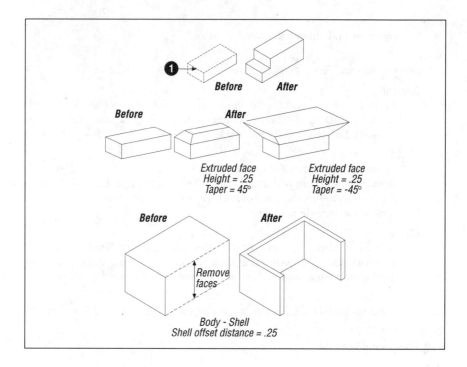

SOLPROF

Solids toolbar

Creates profile images of 3D solids. These images display the edges and silhouettes of curved surfaces for the current view. The profiles are stored as blocks and can be exploded. You can have the object lines reside on one layer and the hidden lines on another. Layer names are generated automatically by AutoCAD. They are all assigned names that are based on their viewport border's handle. This handle is prefaced by PV- (paper space visible) for object lines and PH- (paper space hidden lines) for hidden lines. This command can be used only when a layout tab (*tilemode* = 0) is active, and there is at least one viewport. Once a profile is created, it is not linked to the original solid. You can *explode* profiles and move them to other layers.

Initiate Command By

Command: **solprof**
Draw → Solids → Setup → Profile

Options

```
Select objects:
Display hidden profile lines on separate layer? [Yes/No] <Y>:
Project profile lines onto a plane? [Yes/No] <Y>:
Delete tangential edges? [Yes/No] <Y>:
One solid selected.
```

Display hidden profile lines on separate layer? [Yes/No] <Y>:
> Determines if you want hidden lines to reside on their own layer or be placed on the same layer as the object lines. The linetype for object lines is ByLayer. If the Hidden linetype is loaded the hidden lines are assigned to that linetype.

Project profile lines onto a plane? [Yes/No] <Y>:
> Determines whether the profile is created with 2D or 3D objects.

Delete tangential edges? [Yes/No] <Y>:
> Determines whether tangential edges are created. A tangential edge is where lines are drawn between two tangent faces. See the following example.

Related Variables   tilemode

Associated Commands   layout, mview, soldraw, solview, viewports, vports

Example

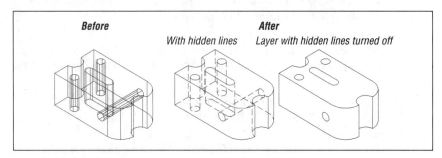

Before
With hidden lines

After
Layer with hidden lines turned off

SOLVIEW   Solids toolbar

Creates orthographic, sectional, and auxiliary views of 3D solids. It combines various commands to create the views including *layer, layout, mview,* and *view*. Layer names are generated automatically by AutoCAD. These layers are created so that visible lines, hidden lines, dimensions, and viewport borders are placed on their own layers. The layer names are prefaced by the view name with a hyphen followed by the type of object associated to that view: VIS (visible lines), HID (hidden lines), HAT (hatch lines), and DIM (dimensions). The viewport borders are placed on a layer named VPORTS. Do not place any other information on the VIS, HAT, and HID layers since *soldraw* deletes and updates objects on those layers. Dimensions are not created automatically, but you can use the DIM layer to create dimensions.

Since *solview* uses layout tabs, it will create one if necessary. If a layout tab already exists, it uses the last one that was active. It's best if you create a layout tab and make that current before issuing the *solview* command.

Initiate Command By
> Command: **solview**
> Draw → Solids → Setup → View

Options

        `Enter an option [Ucs/Ortho/Auxiliary/Section]:`

Ucs

Creates a profile view relative to a User Coordinate System (UCS). Once the command is complete, the UCS is saved with the view (*ucsview* is set to 1).

[Named/World/?/Current] <Current>:

Specify whether the User Coordinate System is be a saved UCS, the current UCS, or the WCS (World Coordinate System). The viewport projection is created parallel to the X, Y plane of the UCS with the axis facing right and the Y axis upward. If you don't remember the name of a saved UCS, you can enter a question mark (?) and receive a listing of saved UCSs.

Enter view scale <1.0000>:

The view scale is the *zoom–xp* scale factor. It scales the magnification of a model space view relative to paper space.

Specify view center <specify viewport>:

Determine the center location of the profile view. You can change the location as often as you like. Press Enter once you have determined the location.

Specify first corner of viewport, Specify opposite corner of viewport

Create the viewport for the profile view.

Enter view name:

Create a view name for the profile view. This name must be unique.

Ortho

Creates an orthographic view from an existing view. Once the command is complete, the UCS is saved with the view (*ucsview* is set to 1).

Specify side of viewport to project:

Pick the top, bottom, left or right edge of the viewport. When you select the side of the viewport, it automatically lines up the orthographic view since object snap is set to midpoint.

Specify view center <specify viewport>:

Determine how far away the orthographic view is from the existing view. You can change the location as often as you like. Press Enter once you have determined the location.

Specify first corner of viewport, Specify opposite corner of viewport

Create the viewport for the orthographic view.

Enter view name:

Create a view name for the orthographic view. This name must be unique.

Auxiliary

Creates an auxiliary view from an existing view. Auxiliary views are views obtained by projection on any plane other than the horizontal, frontal, and profile projection planes. Once the command is complete, the UCS is saved with the view (*ucsview* is set to 1).

Specify first point of inclined plane, Specify second point of inclined plane

Define the inclined plane. Both points must be located in the same viewport.

Specify side to view from:

Determine the side from which to create the auxiliary view.

Specify view center <specify viewport>:

Determine how far away the auxiliary view is from the existing view. You can change the location as often as you like. Press Enter once you have determined the location.

Specify first corner of viewport, Specify opposite corner of viewport

Create the viewport for the auxiliary view.

Enter view name

Create a view name for the auxiliary view. This name must be unique.

Section

Creates a sectional view from an existing view. Typical of section views, hidden lines are not displayed. *soldraw* adds hatch lines to the section. Using *soldraw* on a section converts that 3D solid object into 2D objects. See *soldraw* for an example of a hatched section view.

Specify first point of cutting plane, Specify second point of cutting plane

Define the cutting plane.

Specify side to view from:

Determine the side from which to create the section view.

Specify view center <specify viewport>:

Determine how far away the section view is from the existing view. You can change the location as often as you like. Press Enter once you have determined the location.

Specify first corner of viewport, Specify opposite corner of viewport

Create the viewport for the section view.

Enter view name:

Create a view name for the section view. This name must be unique.

Related Variables   tilemode, ucsview

Associated Commands   layer, layout, mview, soldraw, solprof, view

Example

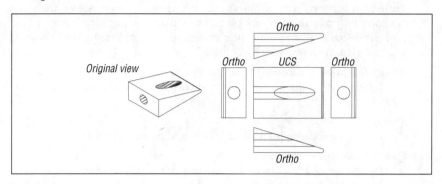

'SORTENTS

Controls the display of object sort order operations. The *draworder* command turns on all the values. Sorting can slow down certain operations depending on how many objects are being sorted. This variable is set when selecting the Object Sorting Methods option from the *options* User Preferences tab.

Initiate Command By

Command: **sortents**

Options

sortents is bit-coded and its value is the sum of the following:

0   Disables sortents.

1   Sorts for object selection.

2   Sorts for object snap (osnap).

4   Sorts for redraws.

8   Sorts for mslide creation.

16 Sorts for regenerations.

32 Sorts for plotting.

64 Sorts for PostScript output.

Variable Settings

Initial default:	96 (plotting and PostScript)
Subsequent default:	Last value used in the drawing
Value:	Integer
Related Variables	treedepth
Associated Commands	draworder, options, preferences

'SPELL

Checks the spelling of multiline and single-line text in a drawing. You can check the spelling of objects located in model space and paper space by using the selection set All. Spell does not check text that is part of a block, attribute, or external reference. It also ignores text on locked and frozen layers.

Initiate Command By

Command: **spell**
Alias: **sp**
Tools → Spelling

Options

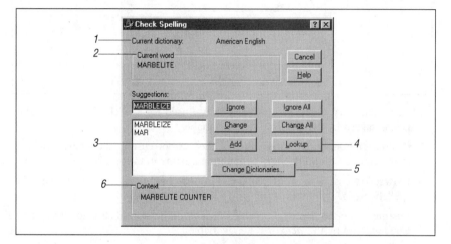

1. **Current dictionary**. Lists the default dictionary. This value is maintained by *dctmain*.

2. **Current word**. Lists the words, one by one, that are not listed in the dictionary.

3. **Add**. Adds the current word to the custom dictionary. The maximum length is 63 characters.

4. **Lookup**. Checks the spelling of the word in the Suggestions box.

5. **Change Dictionaries**. Displays the Change Dictionaries dialog box. See "The Change Dictionaries Dialog Box" later in this command description for more information.

6. **Context**. Displays the phrase in which the current word was located.

The Change Dictionaries Dialog Box

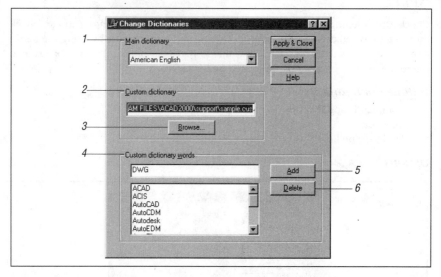

1. **Main dictionary.** Selects a dictionary to use used for spellchecking. This value is maintained by the *dctmain* system variable.

2. **Custom dictionary.** Lists the name of the current custom dictionary You can start a new custom dictionary by entering a name in the text box.

3. **Browse.** Selects a custom dictionary to use with the main dictionary for spellchecking.

4. **Custom dictionary words.** Lists the words in the custom dictionary. This value is maintained by the *dctcust* system variable.

5. **Add.** Adds the word listed in the Custom Dictionary Words text box to the custom dictionary.

6. **Delete.** Removes the word listed in the Custom Dictionary Words text box from the custom dictionary.

Tips & Warnings

- If all the words are spelled correctly, the Check Spelling dialog box does not appear.

- If you want to change the main dictionary default or the custom dictionary default, you can change the individual variables *dctmain* and *dctcust* or you can enter text that is not a word in order to activate the Check Spelling dialog box.

- *properties* and *ddedit* let you change the spelling of single-line and multiline text, dimensions, and attribute definitions. *change* lets you edit single-line text; *mtprop* lets you edit multiline text. Attributes can be edited with *attedit*.

Related Variables   dctmain, dctcust

SPHERE

Solids toolbar

Creates a 3D solid sphere. Use *ai_sphere* to create 3D wireframe spheres.

Initiate Command By   Command: **sphere**
Draw → Solids → Sphere

Options

```
Current wire frame density: ISOLINES=4
Specify center of sphere <0,0,0>:
Specify radius of sphere or [Diameter]:
```

center of sphere
Defines the sphere's center.

radius of sphere
Defines the sphere's radius.

Diameter
Defines the sphere's diameter.

Tips & Warnings

Use *ddvpoint*, *dview*, *vpoint*, and *3dorbit* to view the sphere at different angles and elevations. Use *hide*, *render*, and *shademode* to enhance the sphere's display.

Related Variables   dispsilh, isolines

Associated Commands   ai_sphere

Example

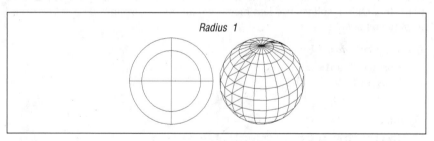

Radius 1

'SPLFRAME

Determines the display of splines, spline-fit polyline frames, and edges of 3D faces. You can change the visibility of 3D faces with the *properties* dialog box.

Initiate Command By

Command: **splframe**

Options

0   Hides spline frames and invisible edges of 3D faces.

1   Displays spline frames and invisible edges of 3D faces.

Variable Settings

Initial default:	0
Subsequent default:	Last value used in the drawing
Value:	Integer

Associated Commands edge, mpedit, pedit, pface, pline, spline, 3dface

Example

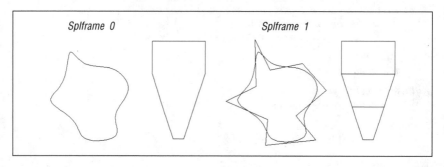

Splframe 0   Splframe 1

SPLINE

Draw toolbar

Creates a smooth curved object. This spline type is known as a nonuniform rational B-spline (NURBS) curve. Entering *u* (*undo*) at the "Specify next point" prompt undoes the last spline segment and returns you to the previous point. You can edit polylines (*pedit*) to create splines, but these are linear spline approximations. In addition, splines use less memory than polyline splines. Use *splinedit* and *grips* to edit splines.

Initiate Command By

> Command: **spline**
> Alias: **spl**
> Draw → Spline

Options

```
Specify first point or [Object]:
Specify next point:
Specify next point or [Close/Fit tolerance] <start tangent>:
Specify start tangent:
Specify end tangent:
```

Object
> Converts spline-fitted polylines (including 3D polylines) to spline objects.

Close
> Indicates that the starting and ending points are coincident and tangent.

Fit tolerance
> Determines how close the spline fits to the control points you specified. The lower the tolerance, the closer the spline is drawn to the control points. Zero tolerance places the spline through your control points.

Associated Commands   pedit, splinedit, 3dpoly

Example

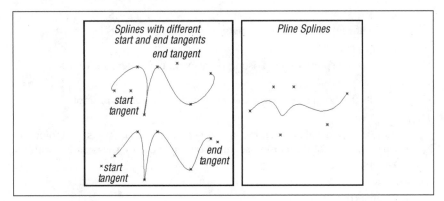

Splines with different start and end tangents — end tangent — start tangent — end tangent — start tangent

Pline Splines

SPLINEDIT   Modify II toolbar

Edits spline objects by modifying the control and fit data points. Splines created from polylines (*pedit–spline*) have control points; splines created from the *spline* command have fit data points. Selecting splines to edit causes the control or fit points to display in the current grip color setting.

Initiate Command By

Command: **splinedit**
Alias: **spe**
Modify → Spline

Options

Enter an option [Fit data/Close/Move vertex/Refine/rEverse/Undo]:

Fit data

Lets you edit fit data points using any of the following options:

Add

Creates new fit data points.

Close/Open

Closes an open spline, making its tangent continuous at its endpoints, or opens a portion of the closing segment of a spline if one was added with the close option.

Delete

Removes fit data points and adjusts the spline through the remaining points.

Move

Moves fit data points to a new location.

Purge

Removes a spline's fit data from the drawing's database. This also exits you from the fit data submenu and returns you to the *splinedit* prompt.

Tangents

Modifies the first and last tangents of a spline.

Tolerance

Refits the spline to the existing points with new tolerance values.

Exit

Exits the fit data submenu and returns to the *splinedit* prompt.

Close/Open

Closes an open spline, making its tangent continuous at its endpoints, or opens a portion of the closing segment of a spline if one was added with the close option.

Move vertex

Relocates control points.

Next

Moves to the next control point.

Previous

Moves back to the previous control point.

point

Lets you select a control point.

Exit

Exits the move vertex submenu and returns to the *splinedit* prompt.

Refine

Increases the spline's precision.

Add control point

Adds control points to the spline.

Elevate Order

Increases the number of control points for the whole spline. This number must be greater than or equal to the current setting. Using the same value has no effect on the spline. Using a greater value increases the number of control points. The maximum value is 26. Once a spline is "elevated," it cannot be reduced.

Weight

Changes the weight at various control points. Weight is the distance between the spline and a given control point.

Exit

Exits the refine submenu and returns to the *splinedit* prompt.

rEverse

Reverses the spline's direction.

Undo

Undoes, in reverse order, each change you made while in the command. This is different from the *undo* command, which reverses the changes made for each command.

Tips & Warnings

As soon as you select a splined polyline to edit, it is automatically converted into a spline. This occurs even if you cancel and don't complete the command. Use *undo* if you need to keep it as a polyline object.

Related Variables	splframe
Associated Commands	spline

'SPLINESEGS

Defines the number of line segments generated for each polyline spline segment. The greater the number, the smoother the curve, but it can also slow down the time it takes for drawing redraws and regenerations. You can have anywhere from –32,768 to 32,767 spline segments. Negative numbers are converted to their absolute value, and a fit curve made up of arcs is assigned to those segments.

Initiate Command By

Command: **splinesegs**

Variable Settings

Initial default:	8
Subsequent default:	Last value used in the drawing
Value:	Integer
Related Variables	splinetype
Associated Commands	mpedit, pedit, pline

'SPLINETYPE

Defines the type of spline curve generated with the spline option of *pedit*.

Initiate Command By

Command: **splinetype**

Options

5   Quadratic B-spline

6   Cubic B-spline

Variable Settings

Initial default:	6
Subsequent default:	Last value used in the drawing
Value:	Integer
Related Variables	splinesegs
Associated Commands	mpedit, pedit, pline

Example

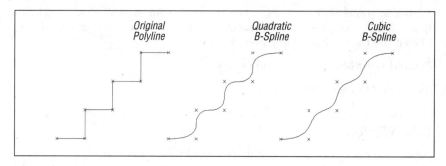

| Original Polyline | Quadratic B-Spline | Cubic B-Spline |

STATS

Render toolbar

Displays a dialog box containing information about your last rendering for that drawing. You can save the information, in ASCII format, by writing it to a file. Once the file is created, you can continue appending more rendering statistics to that file.

Initiate Command By

Command: **stats**
View → Render → Statistics

Options

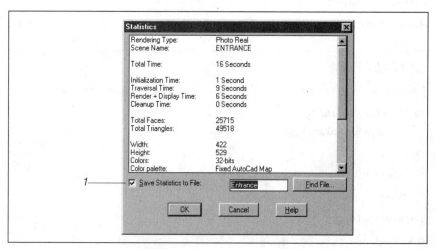

1. **Save Statistics to File**. Saves the dialog box information to an ASCII file when the checkbox is selected and a filename is entered in the text box. If the file exists, the information is appended to that file.

Associated Commands   render

'STATUS

Displays a text screen of information on the current drawing's limits, extents, display, drawing aid settings (*dsettings*), and some system information. The status' numeric display format is based on the current units system. The information is based on the current space—model space or layout space. Drawing extents specify the actual size of the drawing regardless of the limits setting.

Initiate Command By

Command: **status**
Tools → Inquiry → Status

Tips & Warnings

Use *status* at the "Dim:" prompt to get a listing of the current dimension variable settings; use *stats* to gather information about the last rendering that was issued during the current drawing session.

Related Variables	cecolor, celtype, celweight, clayer, cplotstyle, elevation, extmax, extmin, fillmode, gridmode, gridunit, insbase, limcheck, limmax, limmin, orthomode, osmode, qtextmode, snapmode, snapunit, tabmode, thickness
Associated Commands	base, color, dsettings, elev, fill, grid, layer, limits, linetype, mspace, ortho, osnap, pspace, qtext, snap, tablet, units

STLOUT

Saves a single solid to a file (.*stl*) in the Stereo-Lithography Apparatus format. This file can be saved in an ASCII or binary format. The *facetres* variable determines how the solid is triangulated. A higher value creates a finer mesh and a more accurate representation of the solid. However, it also creates a larger file.

Initiate Command By

Command: **stlout**

Tips & Warnings

If *filedia* is set to 1, a dialog box is activated; if *filedia* is set to 0, you are prompted on the command line. When *filedia* is set to 0, or off, entering a tilde (~) on the command line temporarily activates the dialog box.

Related Variables	facetres, filedia

STRETCH

Modify toolbar

Dynamically lengthens or shortens objects by placing a crossing window or crossing polygon around the endpoints of the objects to be stretched and specifying a displacement by keyboard entry or dragging. If you want to stretch more than one crossing window or crossing polygon, use *mstretch*.

You can stretch 3D faces, 3D meshes, arcs, lines, leaders, multilines, polylines, rays, solids, and traces. Object endpoints that lie outside the crossing window or crossing polygon remain fixed. Endpoints inside the crossing window or crossing polygon change. Text, dimension text, blocks, circles, and ellipses move if their definition points are within the crossing window or crossing polygon. The definition point for blocks, shapes, and text is the insertion point; for dimension text, the node or definition point at the end of the extension lines; for circles, the center point.

Stretching dimension text may leave the text offset from the dimension line. If the dimension line no longer has a reason to be split, the line closes up and becomes one object. You can restore the dimension text to the center of the dimension line with the hometext or tedit option of the *dim* command or with *dimedit* or *dimtedit*.

Stretching a viewport border in paper space increases or decreases the area of model space that is visible in the viewport. Placing the crossing window or crossing polygon at a corner stretches the viewport both horizontally and vertically. You cannot *stretch* circles, ellipses (*pellipse* set to 0), regions, or 3D solids. If you use the *mledit* cut options on a multiline, the *stretch* command does not work on the ends that were edited.

Initiate Command By

Command: **stretch**
Alias: **s**
Modify → Stretch

Options

```
Select objects to stretch by crossing-window or crossing-polygon...
Specify base point or displacement:
Specify second point of displacement:
```

Select objects to stretch by crossing-window or crossing-polygon
Unlike most commands that prompt with "Select objects," *stretch* requires a crossing window or crossing polygon. If you enter the *stretch* command from the keyboard, or repeat the command by pressing Enter, you must type a C (crossing window) or CP (crossing polygon) to select objects. If you pick more than one crossing window or crossing polygon, *stretch* uses only the last crossing selection.

base point
Determine a point of reference. Think in terms of "from where." After locating your reference point, you can drag your object(s) to the new location at the "second point" prompt, or you can enter the direct distance or absolute or relative coordinates. Use object snaps on intersections, center points, or other logical locations to set the base point.

displacement
Enter the distance for X, Y, Z and press Enter at the "Specify second point of displacement" prompt.

Tips & Warnings

- If dimension text was created with associative dimensioning enabled (*dimaso*), then *stretch* updates the dimension text. A definition point (defpoint) must be within the crossing at the time of the stretch.

- *extend, lengthen,* and *trim* are similar to *stretch. grips* has its own stretch routine that even lets you create multiple copies at the same time.

- Using the point option of *change* is similar to using *stretch*. However, if you change to a point with *ortho* off, all the selected lines converge at that point.

- You can stretch 3D solid planar faces using the move and offset options of *solidedit.*

Related Variables	grips
Associated Commands	change, extend, lengthen, mstretch, trim

Example

```
Command: Stretch
Select objects to stretch by crossing-window or crossing-polygon...
Select objects: c
Specify first corner: Pick point 1
Specify opposite corner: Pick point 2
8 found
Select objects: Press Enter
Specify base point or displacement: Pick any point
Specify second point of displacement: @1'<180
```

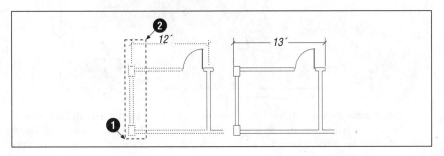

-'STYLE

see STYLE

'STYLE

Defines text formats. It determines the font, height, width, angle, and a few other properties that define the way text is displayed on the drawing. "Text" refers to any annotation such as single-line text (*text* and *dtext*), multiline text (*mtext*), attributes (*attdef*), remote text (*rtext*), arc text (*arctext*), and dimensions. You can achieve the same results using *-style* so all prompts and options appear on the command line.

You may want to create typical styles in your drawing template file to save time and maintain drawing standards. You also can insert styles from one drawing to another using the AutoCAD DesignCenter. The last style referenced during the *style, properties,* or text (*dtext, text*) command is the default for text.

If you plan to move a drawing file containing styles to another computer or to a diskette, you may need to include custom-designed styles. Use *pack* to help you accomplish this.

Initiate Command By

Command: **style**
Alias: **st**
Format → Text Style

Options

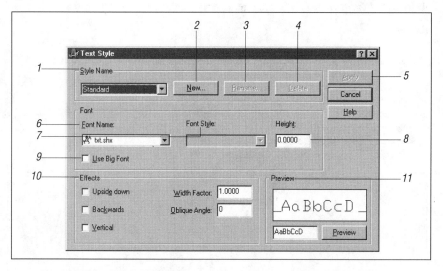

1. **Style Name**. Lists the styles already defined in the drawing. The default style is the one listed when the dialog box is first opened. If you select a different style for the default, the Cancel button changes to Close and you can save your settings. If you don't change any of that style's properties but just use the default, pressing Escape also makes that style current. This value is maintained by the *textstyle* variable.

2. **New**. Defaults to the word style followed by an incremental number (i.e., style1, style2, etc.). You can accept that name or enter another name. Depending on *extnames,* style names can contain up to 255 characters.

3. **Rename**. Lets you rename the style listed in the Style Name text box. You cannot rename Standard unless you use the *rename* command.

4. **Delete**. Removes the style listed in the Style Name text box. Any styles being referenced cannot be deleted. You cannot delete the style named Standard although you can rename it with the *rename* command. *purge* also removes any unused styles.

5. **Apply**. Applies any changes made to a style to the text or annotation referencing that style.

6. **Font Name**. Includes all registered TrueType fonts and all AutoCAD compiled shape (*.shx*) fonts in a drop-down list. You can have multiple styles assigned to the same font name.

7. **Font Style**. Lists special formatting that you can assign to many of the fonts. Most of the TrueType fonts offer the options of Bold, Bold Italic, Italic, and Regular. Depending on the font, the choices may vary. The AutoCAD fonts do not take advantage of this feature.

8. **Height**. Sets a fixed text height for single-line and dimension text. If you want to be prompted for text height, set it to 0.

9. **Use Big Font**. Handles Asian languages that use text fonts with thousands of non-ASCII characters. Only the AutoCAD font files take advantage of this feature.

10. **Effects**. Allows you to display the text upside down, backward, or vertically. You also can set an obliquing angle and change the width. Vertical orientation is available for some of the AutoCAD font files, and the width expands or compresses text. Setting the obliquing angle with a positive number slants the text toward the right; a negative number slants the text toward the left. Values can be between –85 and 84.9 degrees.

   If you redefine a style's font and/or its horizontal or vertical orientation, all text strings created with that style will update globally. If you change the other settings, they affect only new text. If you use *change* or *properties* and re-enter the style name, the text takes on all the latest settings of that style.

11. **Preview**. Displays a sampling of how the text will appear on the drawing. You can enter characters in the smaller text box and click on Preview to see specific characters. You do not get a true representation of text height until you enter it in the drawing.

Tips & Warnings

- You can reassign a new style to existing text with *arctext, change, dimstyle, matchprop, mtprop, properties*, and *rtedit*. *mtprop* changes multiline text; *dimstyle* changes associative dimensions; *rtedit* changes remote text; and *arctext* changes arc text.

- Unlike blocks, font file definitions (*.shx, .pfb, .pfa, .ttf*) are stored external to the drawing file and must accompany the drawing file. This includes drawings converted to *.dxf* format.

- You can assign a text style to a dimension style by selecting "Text style" from the *dimstyle* Text tab.

Related Variables	dimtxt, extnames, fontalt, fontmap, textsize, textstyle
Associated Commands	adcenter, arctext, attdef, dtext, mtext, pack, rtext, text

STYLESMANAGER 2000

Provides access to the Add-A-Plot Style Table wizard and the Plot Style Table Editor. Double-click on the Add-A-Plot Style Table wizard to add a new plot style, and double-click on the other icons to modify existing plot styles. Plot style filenames ending in *.ctb* are color dependent, and those ending in *.stb* are named plot styles. Use the *plottermanager* command to add a new plotting device. See *plotstyle* for more detailed information.

Initiate Command By

Command: **stylesmanager**
File → Plot Style Manager

Options

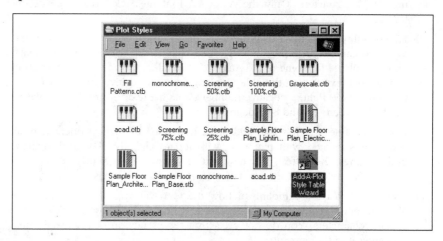

Associated Commands   plot, plotsytle

SUBTRACT   Solids Editing toolbar

Creates a composite solid or region by subtracting one set of solids from another set of solids or one set of regions from another set of regions. Exploding subtracted objects has various results depending on the original object and whether part of the object was deleted due to the subtract process. You can obtain detailed information concerning the subtract result with *massprop*. Edit 3D solids using *solidedit*.

Initiate Command By

Command: **subtract**
Alias: **su**
Modify → Solids Editing → Subtract

Associated Commands   interfere, intersect, union

Example

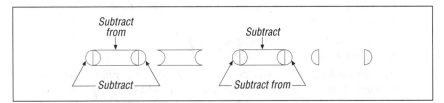

SUPERHATCH 2000

Express Standard toolbar

Uses raster images, blocks, external reference files, and wipeout objects as hatch patterns. You cannot use *superhatch* on splines, circles in nonuniformly scaled block inserts or ellipses, single-line text and multiline text within block inserts.

Superhatch objects are bound together and are considered groups. The group name is automatically assigned and is considered "unnamed." You can find out the name with *list* or by checking the Include Unnamed box located on the *group* dialog box. You also can temporarily ungroup the hatch with the selectable option of the *group* command or by pressing Ctrl-A.

Initiate Command By

Command: **superhatch**
Express → Draw → Super Hatch

Options

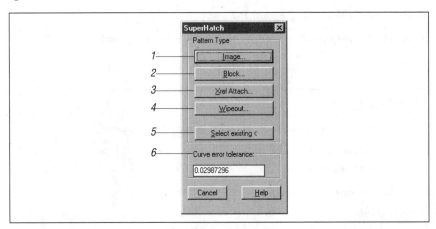

1. **Image.** Activates *imageattach*. Once the image is inserted into the drawing, you have the option to move the image to its starting point (inside the hatch boundary area). If parts of the image are clipped due to the size and shape of the border, you can turn the rest of the image on using *imageclip*.

2. **Block.** Activates *insert*.

3. **Xref Attach**. Activates the external reference (*xref*).

4. **Wipeout**. Selects a wipeout object as a hatch pattern. See *wipeout* for more detailed information.

5. **Select existing**. Selects an existing image, block, external reference or wipeout object as the hatch pattern.

6. **Curve error tolerance**. Defines the error tolerance for curved boundaries, and determines how to convert arc segments to straight line segments. The error distance defines the maximum distance from the midpoint of an arc to the midpoint of the straight line segment. If the number is too small, it will decrease drawing and plotting performance.

Associated Commands	bhatch, expresstools, group, hatch

'SURFTAB1

Sets the number of tabulations generated for *rulesurf* and *tabsurf* and the mesh density in the *M* direction for *revsurf* and *edgesurf*.

Initiate Command By
Command: **surftab1**

Variable Settings

Initial default:	6
Subsequent default:	Last value used in the drawing
Value:	Integer
Related Variables	surftab2
Associated Commands	edgesurf, revsurf, rulesurf, tabsurf
Example	See SURFTAB2.

'SURFTAB2

Sets the mesh density in the *N* direction for *edgesurf* and *revsurf*.

Initiate Command By
Command: **surftab2**

Variable Settings

Initial default:	6
Subsequent default:	Last value used in the drawing
Value:	Integer
Related Variables	surftab1
Associated Commands	edgesurf, revsurf

Example

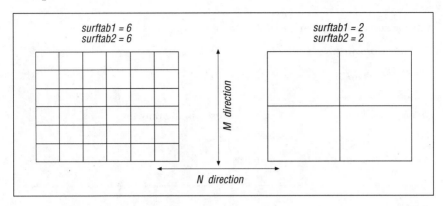

surftab1 = 6
surftab2 = 6

surftab1 = 2
surftab2 = 2

M direction

N direction

'SURFTYPE

Determines the type of surface fitting when using the smooth option of the *pedit* command.

Initiate Command By

Command: **surftype**

Options

5   Quadratic B-Spline surface

6   Cubic B-Spline surface

8   Bezier surface

Variable Settings

Initial default:	6
Subsequent default:	Last value used in the drawing
Value:	Integer

Related Variables   surfu, surfv

Associated Commands   mpedit, pedit, pline

Example

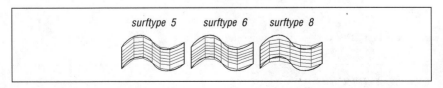

surftype 5   surftype 6   surftype 8

References
S-T

'SURFU

Sets the surface density in the *M* direction for 3D meshes.

Initiate Command By   Command: **surfu**

Variable Settings

Initial default: 6

Subsequent default: Last value used in the drawing

Value: Integer

Associated Commands   3dmesh

'SURFV

Sets the surface density in the *N* direction for 3D meshes.

Initiate Command By
    Command: **surfv**

Variable Settings

Initial default: 6

Subsequent default: Last value used in the drawing

Value: Integer

Associated Commands   3dmesh

'SYSCODEPAGE

Indicates which language is used by your version of AutoCAD. See AutoCAD's *Command Reference* located in the Help section for more detailed information.

Initiate Command By
    Command: **syscodepage**

Variable Settings

Initial default: Varies, read-only

Subsequent default: Initial default

Value: String

Related Variables   dwgcodepage

---

system variables   *see SETVAR*

SYSWINDOWS

Lets you quickly organize how drawings are displayed on your screen when you have more than one open at a time. This is similar to other programs also using the Windows operating system. You can have the windows cascade, tile horizontally, or tile vertically, or you can have all the files that are minimized line up at the bottom of the AutoCAD display.

Initiate Command By

Command: **syswindows**
Window → Cascade or Tile Horizontally or Tile Vertically or Arrange Icons

TABLET

Configures and calibrates a digitizing tablet. Configuring with the *tablet* command defines tablet areas for tablet menus and the screen pointing area. Calibrating aligns the tablet to a paper drawing for digitizing or tracing. The tablet and screen menus are interactive; you can pick commands off the tablet that activate screen menus. When digitizing, use Ctrl-T or F4 to toggle the Tablet mode on and off. Your pointing device must be a digitizer to access this command.

Initiate Command By

Command: **tablet**, F4, or Ctrl-T
Alias: **ta**
Tools → Tablet

Options

Enter an option [ON/OFF/CAL/CFG]:

ON

Enables the Tablet (digitizing) mode. This value is maintained by the *tabmode* variable. When *tablet* is on, you cannot change viewports or select commands from the screen.

OFF

Disables the Tablet (digitizing) mode. This value is maintained by the *tabmode* variable.

CAL

Calibrates the tablet with the coordinates of a paper drawing or photograph. Calibration is effective only in the space in which the calibration took place. Before calibrating, configure for 0 tablet menu areas and enlarge the screen pointing area. This gives you more digitizing space for your paper drawing.

CFG

Reserves portions of the tablet for menus and the screen pointing area. You can have a maximum of four tablet menu areas.

Tips & Warnings

- The current UCS is the digitizing plane when calibrating a tablet. You will need to recalibrate the tablet if you change the UCS; otherwise, digitized points will be projected onto the UCS.

- When using the tablet as a digitizer, you lose the coordinate settings once you end the drawing session.

Related Variables	tabmode

'TABMODE

Turns the tablet on and off. This value is set using the on/off option of the *tablet* command. Your pointing device must be a digitizer to access this command.

Initiate Command By

Command: **tabmode**

Options

0	Disables Tablet mode.
1	Enables Tablet mode.

Variable Settings

Initial default:	0
Subsequent default:	Initial default
Value:	Integer

Associated Commands	tablet

TABSURF

Surfaces toolbar

Generates a 3D polygon mesh (surface) by extruding an object (path curve) through space along a direction vector.

Initiate Command By

Command: **tabsurf**

Options

```
Select object for path curve:
Select object for direction vector:
```

object for path curve

The path curve can be a line, arc, ellipse, circle, polyline, or 3D polyline. The surface starts at the endpoint nearest your pick point on the path curve. If you use a polyline for the direction vector, only the first and last vertices are recognized.

object for direction vector

The direction vector can be a line, an open polyline, or 3D polyline.

Tips & Warnings

Use *ddvpoint, dview, vpoint,* and *3dorbit* to view the tabsurf at different angles and elevations. Use *hide, render,* and *shademode* to enhance the tabsurf's display.

Related Variables   surftab1

Associated Commands   3d, 3dmesh

Example

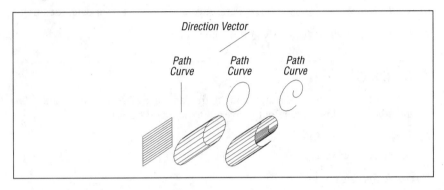

Direction Vector

Path Curve   Path Curve   Path Curve

'TARGET

Defines the camera target's location for the current viewport.

Initiate Command By
Command: **target**

Variable Settings

Initial default: 0.000,0.000,0.000, read-only

Subsequent default: Last value used in the drawing

Value: 3D point

Related Variables   viewdir, worldview

Associated Commands   camera, dview, UCS, ucsman, view, 3dorbit, 3dswivel

---

TBCONFIG   *see TOOLBAR*

'TDCREATE

Maintains, in Julian format, the local time and date the drawing was created. The *dwgprops* and *time* commands report this variable but convert it to standard format.

Initiate Command By
Command: **tdcreate**

Variable Settings

Initial default:	Varies, read-only
Subsequent default:	Last value used in the drawing
Value:	Real

Related Variables	cdate, date, savetime, tdindwg, tdupdate, tdusrtimer
Associated Commands	dwgprops, new, time

'TDINDWG

Lists the total amount of editing time in the drawing. The *dwgprops* and *time* commands report this variable but convert it to standard format.

Initiate Command By
Command: **tdindwg**

Variable Settings

Initial default:	Varies, read-only
Subsequent default:	Last value used in the drawing
Value:	Real

Related Variables	cdate, date, tdcreate, tdupdate, tdusrtimer
Associated Commands	dwgprops, time

'TDUCREATE 2000

Stores the universal time and date the drawing was created.

Initiate Command By
Command: **tducreate**

Variable Settings

Initial default:	Varies, read-only
Subsequent default:	Last value used in the drawing
Value:	Real

Related Variables	cdate, date, tdcreate, tdindwg, tdupdate, tdusrtimer
Associated Commands	new

'TDUPDATE

Maintains the local time and date the drawing was last saved. The *dwgprops* and *time* commands report this variable but convert it to standard format.

Initiate Command By
Command: **tdupdate**

Variable Settings

Initial default:	Varies, read-only
Subsequent default:	Last value used in the drawing
Value:	Real
Related Variables	cdate, date, tdcreate, tdindwg, tdusrtimer
Associated Commands	dwgprops, qsave, save, saveas, time

'TDUSRTIMER

Maintains the time spent during the current drawing session. This can be reset and turned on and off with the *time* command.

Initiate Command By
Command: **tdusrtimer**

Variable Settings

Initial default:	Varies, read-only
Subsequent default:	Last value used in the drawing
Value:	Real
Related Variables	cdate, date, tdcreate, tdindwg, tdupdate, tduupdate
Associated Commands	dwgprops, qsave, save, saveas, time

'TDUUPDATE 2000

Maintains the universal time and date of the last save.

Initiate Command By
Command: **tduupdate**

Variable Settings

Initial default:	Varies, read-only
Subsequent default:	Last value used in the drawing
Value:	Real
Related Variables	cdate, date, tdcreate, tdindwg, tdupdate
Associated Commands	qsave, save, saveas

'TEMPPREFIX

Maintains the folder location where temporary files are stored. This value is set with the "Temporary drawing file location" option from the *options* Files tab.

Initiate Command By
Command: **tempprefix**

Variable Settings

Initial default:	Varies, read-only
Subsequent default:	Initial default
Value:	String
Associated Commands	options, preferences

TEXT
see DTEXT

'TEXTEVAL

Determines how text strings are evaluated during AutoLISP routines. *dtext, mtext,* and *text* always read the leading parenthesis (() and exclamation point (!) as text strings regardless of the *texteval* setting.

Initiate Command By
Command: **texteval**

Options

0   Responses to prompts for text strings and attribute values are taken literally.

1   Any text string starting with a left parenthesis or exclamation point is evaluated as an AutoLISP expression. This works only for *-mtext.*

Variable Settings

Initial default:	0
Subsequent default:	Initial default
Value:	Integer
Associated Commands	dtext, -mtext, text

'TEXTFILL

Controls the filling of TrueType fonts when you use the *plot* and *psout* commands.

Initiate Command By
Command: **textfill**

Options

0   Displays the outline of text.

1   Displays text filled in.

Variable Settings

Initial default:	1
Subsequent default:	Registry file
Value:	Integer

Related Variables	textqlty
Associated Commands	attdef, dtext, mtext, text

TEXTFIT

Express Text toolbar

Expands or contracts single-line text to fit between two points.

Initiate Command By

Command: **textfit**
Express → Text → Text Fit

TEXTMASK 2000mod

Express Text toolbar

Lets you assign a border around text. The border can be a wipeout, 3D face, or solid. This border helps text stand out when text is place on top of other objects. Remove text masks with *textunmask.* Any changes made to the *textmask* settings are retained the next time you begin a new AutoCAD design session.

Initiate Command By

Command: **textmask**
Express → Text → Text Mask

Options

```
Current settings: Offset factor = 0.350000, Mask type = Wipeout
Select text objects to mask or [Masktype/Offset]:
```

text objects to mask
Lets you select single-line or multiline text.

Masktype
Lets you define the border as a wipeout, 3D face, or solid object. If you want to toggle the wipeout or 3D face masks on and off, use *tframes.*

Offset
Lets you enter an offset factor relative to text height.

*References
S–T*

Tips & Warnings

- Textmask objects are associated to text through the *group* command. When you move the text, the textmask object also moves. When the selectable option for *group* is off, the mask remains in its original location. Remove the mask with *wipeout* or *tframes* and remask the text in its new location. You could turn the wipeout border on and move both the text and mask at the same time.

- Update the textmask around modified text by remasking the text.

- Wipeout objects are raster images (except for their boundaries). If you have problems plotting, make sure your output device can support raster image plotting. If you use a wipeout in paper space to hide model space objects, make sure the "Plot paperspace last" option in the *plot* Plot Settings tab is not checked.

Associated Commands   group, textunmask

Example

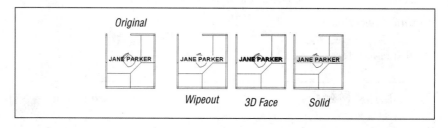

Original

Wipeout   3D Face   Solid

'TEXTQLTY

Controls the resolution of TrueType fonts when you use *plot* and *psout*. Resolution values are between 0 and 100. The higher the setting, the finer the resolution, but the longer it takes to plot. The lower the setting, the coarser the resolution, but the less time it takes to plot.

Initiate Command By

Command: **textqlty**

Variable Settings

Initial default:	50
Subsequent default:	Initial default
Value:	Integer
Related Variables	textfill
Associated Commands	attdef, dtext, mtext, text

'TEXTSCR

see GRAPHSCR

'TEXTSIZE

Sets the default text height for attributes, single-line text, and multiline text. This value is set using *attdef, dtext, mtext,* and *text.* Styles containing a preset text height override the *textsize* setting.

Initiate Command By
Command: **textsize**

Variable Settings

Initial default:	0.2000
Subsequent default:	Last value used in the drawing
Value:	Real
Related Variables	textstyle
Associated Commands	attdef, dtext, mtext, text

'TEXTSTYLE

Maintains the default text style for attributes, single-line and multiline text. This value is set using *attdef, dtext, mtext, style,* and *text.* The various textstyle options are created with the *style* command.

Initiate Command By
Command: **textstyle**

Variable Settings

Initial default:	Standard
Subsequent default:	Last value used in the drawing
Value:	String
Related Variables	textsize
Associated Commands	arctext, attdef, dtext, mtext, rtext, style, text

TEXTUNMASK 2000

Remove text borders or masks created with *textmask.*

Initiate Command By
Command: **textunmask**
Express → Text → Unmask Text

Associated Commands	textmask

'THICKNESS

Maintains the current 3D thickness (height) for the following objects:

arc	ellipse (*pellipse* = 1)	rectangle
attribute definition	line	shape
circle	point	solid
dimension text	polyline	text
donut	polygon	trace

This value is set with the *elev* and *properties* commands. You can reassign an object's thickness with *change*, *chprop*, *matchprop*, or *properties*. You can assign a thickness to single-line text, multiline text, and attributes once the text is placed on the drawing by using *change*, *chprop*, or *properties*. *sketch* does not show a thickness until the lines are recorded. *rectangle* lets you define a thickness during its construction.

Initiate Command By

Command: **thickness**
Alias: **th**
Format → Thickness

Variable Settings

Initial default:	0.0000
Subsequent default:	Last value used in the drawing
Value:	Real

Associated Commands   elev

Example

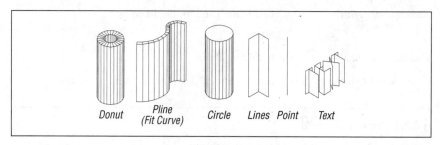

Donut   Pline (Fit Curve)   Circle   Lines   Point   Text

TIFFIN (obsolete)   *see IMAGE*

'TILEMODE `2000mod`

Determines whether tiled model space or layout space (floating model space and paper space) is enabled. The fastest way to change the *tilemode* setting is to click on the Model and Layout tabs.

Initiate Command By

Command: **tilemode**
Alias: **tm** or **ti**

Options

0   Tiled model space is enabled. Since you cannot see or access layout space objects, you can save time during regenerations and redraws.

1   Layout space (floating model space and paper space) is enabled. You can control layer visibility per viewport (*vplayer*) and overlap and plot multiple viewports.

Variable Settings

Initial default:	1
Subsequent default:	Last value used in the drawing
Value:	Integer
Associated Commands	model, mspace, pspace

'TIME

Displays the current date and time, the date and time the drawing was created, the date and time the drawing was last updated, the amount of time spent in the current editing session, and the amount of time left before the next automatic save. In addition, you can set an elapsed timer. Time is displayed to the nearest millisecond using military format. The Statistics tab in the *dwgprops* command contains the same information except that it does not have an elapsed timer, and it does not list how long it will be till the next automatic save.

Initiate Command By

Command: **time**
Tools → Inquiry → Time

Options

Enter option [Display/ON/OFF/Reset]:

Display
Shows the status of the time command.

ON
Activates the elapsed timer.

OFF
Stops the elapsed timer.

Reset
> Resets the elapsed timer to zero.

Tips & Warnings

- The time spent inserting a drawing or block and plotting the drawing does not add to the existing time.

- The time you work on a drawing will not be saved if you use the *quit* command.

Related Variables   cdate, date, savetime, tdcreate, tdindwg, tducreate, tdupdate, tdusrtimer

Associated Commands   qsave, save, saveas

TOLERANCE

Dimension toolbar

Creates geometric dimensioning and tolerance (GD&T) annotations. You can activate this feature when using *qleader* or the annotation option of *leader*. You can modify tolerance objects with the text override option of the *properties* command and with *ddedit*. You cannot *explode* tolerance objects.

Initiate Command By

> Command: **tolerance**
> Alias: **tol**
> Dimension → Tolerance

Options

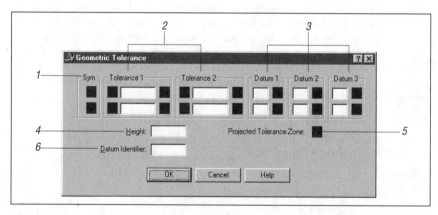

1. **Sym.** Selects a symbol representing the various geometric constraints. The symbols are shown in the figure that follows.

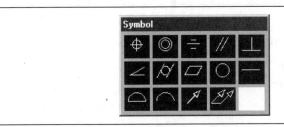

2. **Tolerance 1, Tolerance 2.** Creates the first and second (if applicable) tolerance value, in the feature control frame. Selecting the black box to the left inserts the diameter symbol; selecting the black box to the right inserts a material condition symbol, shown in the following figure.

3. **Datum 1, Datum 2, Datum 3.** Creates the datum references in the feature control frame. Selecting the black box to the right inserts a material condition symbol, shown in the previous figure.

4. **Height.** Creates a projected tolerance zone value in the feature control frame.

5. **Projected Tolerance Zone.** Inserts a projected tolerance zone symbol.

6. **Datum Identifier.** Creates a datum-identifying symbol.

Related Variables   dimclre, dimclrt, dimgap, dimtxsty, dimtxt

Associated Commands   dimstyle, leader, qleader

Example

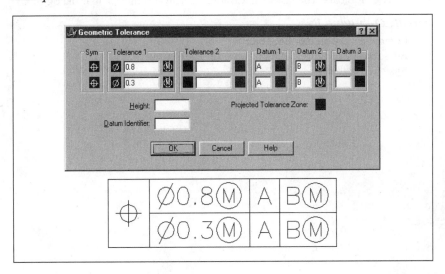

-TOOLBAR

Displays, hides, and positions toolbars from the command line.

Initiate Command By

Command: -**toolbar**

Options

```
Enter toolbar name or [ALL]:
Enter an option [Show/Hide/Left/Right/Top/Bottom/Float] <Show>:
```

Enter toolbar name or [ALL]:

Lets you enter the name of a toolbar to display or hide. The all option selects all the toolbars. *toolbar* or *tbconfig* provides a listing of the toolbar names.

Show

Displays the toolbar(s).

Hide

Closes the toolbar(s).

Left, Right, Top, Bottom

Docks the toolbar to the left, right, top, or bottom of the display.

Float

Switches the toolbar from docked to floating.

Related Variables   tooltips

Associated Commands   toolbar

TOOLBAR

Displays, hides, and creates toolbars. Right-clicking on any toolbar button lists all the available toolbars. The last item, Customize, activates the Toolbar dialog box.

Initiate Command By

Command: **tbconfig**, **toolbar**
Alias: **to**
View → Toolbars

Options

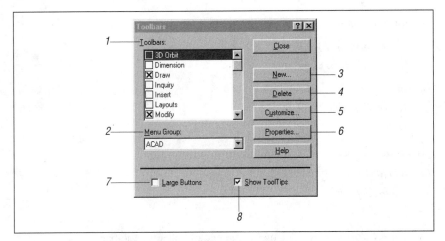

1. **Toolbars.** Lists all of the available toolbars. Clicking in the checkbox toggles the toolbar display on and off.

2. **Menu Group.** Lists the menu groups assigned to menus loaded with *menuload*. Each menu group may contain additional toolbars. Select the Express menu group to load the Express routines. If the Express menu group is unavailable, type **expresstools** or **expressmenu** at the command line. You may have to install that portion of the software if it wasn't initially loaded.

3. **New.** Lets you create your own toolbar. Once you create the toolbar, you can add toolbar buttons by selecting the Customize button.

4. **Delete.** Deletes the highlighted toolbar. If you accidentally delete a toolbar that comes with the AutoCAD software, you can reload the *acad.mnu* file to retrieve the original toolbars. During this process any customized toolbars will be lost. See the online help's *Customization Guide* to learn how to save your customized toolbars.

5. **Customize.** Lets you pick and drag toolbar buttons to any toolbar on the display screen. You also can move toolbar buttons by dragging a button from one toolbar to another. If you want to copy a toolbar button, hold the Ctrl key while dragging the button. Delete buttons by dragging them onto your display screen. You also can customize the code assigned to each button.

6. **Properties.** Displays the name of the toolbar that is used by AutoCAD for tracking purposes.

7. **Large Buttons.** Changes the size of the toolbar buttons.

8. **Show ToolTips.** Toggles tooltips on and off.

Related Variables	tooltips
Associated Commands	expressmenu, expresstools, menu, menuload, -toolbar

'TOOLTIPS

Controls the visibility of tooltips.

Initiate Command By
Command: **tooltips**

Options

0 Tooltips are not displayed.

1 Tooltips are displayed.

Variable Settings

Initial default:	1
Subsequent default:	Registry file
Value:	Integer

Associated Commands menu, menuload, tbconfig, toolbar

TORUS   Solids toolbar

Creates a 3D solid torus. Use the *ai_torus* command to create a 3D wireframe torus.

Initiate Command By
Command: **torus**
Alias: **tor**
Draw → Solids → Torus

Options

```
Current wire frame density:  ISOLINES=4
Specify center of torus <0,0,0>:
Specify radius of torus or [Diameter]:
Specify radius of tube or [Diameter]:
```

Current wire frame density: ISOLINES=4
Specifies the number of lines that will be displayed. It is for visualization only and does not affect the actual objects.

center of torus
Defines the torus's center.

radius of torus or [Diameter]
Defines the torus's radius or diameter. Create a torus without the center hole by specifying the tube's diameter greater than the torus's diameter.

radius of tube or [Diameter]
Defines the tube's radius or diameter.

Tips & Warnings

Use *ddvpoint, dview, vpoint,* and *3dorbit* to view the torus at different angles and elevations. Use *hide, render,* and *shademode* to enhance the torus's display.

Related Variables   dispsilh

Associated Commands   ai_torus

Example

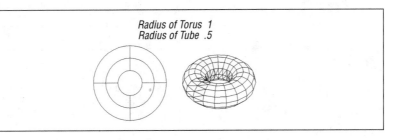

Radius of Torus 1
Radius of Tube .5

TRACE

Creates line segments that can be assigned a width. *trace* also automatically calculates the miter for adjacent segments, but only after the endpoint of the next segment is entered. Traces assigned a width other than 0 ignore the *lineweight* setting. If *fill* is on, all traces are displayed as solid filled. Traces cannot be *exploded.* Object snap modes treat traces the same as solid fills. You can object-snap to the four vertices and midpoint of a trace. While drawing a trace, you do not have undo and close options like those in the *line, mline, polyline,* and *spline* commands.

Initiate Command By

Command: **trace**

Prompts

```
Specify trace width <0.0500>:
Specify start point:
Specify next point:
```

Tips & Warnings

- Polylines also create line segments that can be assigned a width, but they are much more flexible and versatile than traces.

- You cannot use the following editing commands on a trace: *change–point, extend, offset,* and *trim.* However, you can use *grips* and achieve most of the functionality of those commands.

- Use the *digitizer* command if you want to trace over a drawing on paper.

Related Variables   fillmode, tracewid

Associated Commands   mline, pline

Example

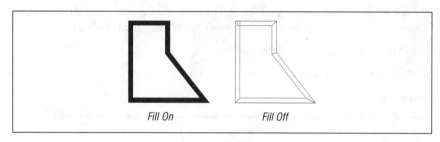

Fill On   *Fill Off*

'TRACEWID

Sets the default width of traces. This value is set using *trace*.

Initiate Command By

Command: **tracewid**

Variable Settings

Initial default:	0.0500
Subsequent default:	Last value used in the drawing
Value:	Real

Associated Commands   trace

'TRACKPATH 2000

Controls the display of object snap and polar tracking alignment paths. This value is set when checking the AutoTrack Settings checkboxes located in the *options* Drafting tab.

Initiate Command By

Command: **trackpath**

Options

0   The full screen object snap tracking path is displayed.

1   The object snap tracking path is displayed between the alignment point and From point to cursor location.

2   Polar tracking path is not displayed

3   Polar or object snap tracking paths are not displayed.

Variable Settings

Initial default:	0
Subsequent default:	Registry file
Value:	Integer

Related Variables   polarmode

Associated Commands   options, preferences

TRANSPARENCY

Reference toolbar

Controls the display of images sharing the same space. This works only for images that are bitonal and nonbitonal. Images are automatically attached with transparency set off.

Initiate Command By

Command: **transparency**

Modify → Object → Image → Transparency

Options

On

Turns transparency on. Objects under the image are visible.

Off

Turns transparency off. Objects under the image are not visible.

Tips & Warnings

Change the display order of objects with *draworder.*

Related Variables   pickfirst

Associated Commands   draworder, image, imageadjust, imageattach, imageclip, imageframe, imagequality

---

TREEDEPTH

Determines the maximum number of times the tree-structured spatial index can divide into branches. *treemax* helps control *treedepth* by limiting the number of nodes in the spatial index. This is one of the few variables that cannot be used transparently.

Initiate Command By

Command: **treedepth**

Options

0

Suppresses the spatial index. Objects are always processed in database order. The *sortents* system variable is inactive.

greater than 0

Enables *treedepth.* The value can be an integer of up to four digits. The first two numbers refer to model space; the second two numbers refer to paper space.

less than 0
> Treats model space objects as two-dimensional. This is used for two-dimensional drawings and provides a more efficient use of memory without a loss in performance.

Variable Settings

Initial default:	3,020
Subsequent default:	Last value used in the drawing
Value:	Integer

Related Variables   sortents, treemax

Associated Commands   treestat

'TREEMAX

Limits memory usage during drawing regeneration by limiting the number of nodes in the spatial index. This setting is based on the amount of available RAM.

Initiate Command By
Command: **treemax**

Variable Settings

Initial default:	10,000,000
Subsequent default:	Registry file
Value:	Integer

Related Variables   treedepth

Associated Commands   treestat

'TREESTAT

Displays information concerning the drawing's current spatial index. The spatial index tracks an object's location in space. This index is tree structured, and its two major branches are paper space (quadtree) and model space (oct-tree). *treestat* tracks the number of nodes, number of objects, maximum depth of the branch, and average number of objects per node.

Initiate Command By
Command: **treestat**

Related Variables   treedepth, treemax

TRIM

Clips portions of objects to the cutting edge or implied cutting edge of objects. You can have more than one cutting edge, and an object can be both a cutting edge and an object to trim. You can trim objects and define cutting edges only for the space (model or layout) in which they objects were created. Use *btrim* if you want objects defined in blocks as boundaries.

The following table shows the trim results of various object types.

Object	Object to trim	Cutting Edge	Object	Object to trim	Cutting Edge
arc	Yes	Yes	ray	Yes	Yes
associative dimensions	Yes	No	region	No	Yes
block	No	No	shape	No	No
circle	Yes	Yes	solid	No	No
ellipse (polyline)	Yes	Yes	spline	Yes	Yes
ellipse (true)	Yes	Yes	text	No	Yes
leader	No	Yes	trace	No	No
line	Yes	Yes	viewport[a]	No	Yes
multiline	No	Yes	xline	Yes	Yes
multiline text	No	Yes	3D face	No	No
pface	No	No	3D mesh	No	No
point	No	No	3D poly	Yes	Yes
polylines	Yes	Yes	3D solids	No	No

[a] Only when paper space is active.

Initiate Command By

> Command: **trim**
> Alias: **tr**
> Modify → Trim

Options

> Current settings: Projection=UCS Edge=None
> Select cutting edges ...
> Select objects:
> Select object to trim or [Project/Edge/Undo]:

cutting edges
> Lets you determine the cutting edge(s) for the objects you want to trim. Pressing Enter without selecting objects automatically selects all the objects assigned to layers that are on and thawed. It is possible to select more than one cutting edge per object. The object will trim to the first edge and stop.

Pick the object again, and it will trim to the next cutting edge. Trimming circles requires two intersections with a cutting edge.

object to trim

Lets you select the part of the object to delete. You can select multiple objects by using the fence selection set method. Objects trim to the center of wide polyline cutting edges and to each line of a multiline object. Ends of wide polylines are always square. Trimming a wide polyline at an angle results in a portion of the polyline width extending past the cutting edge. You cannot decurve a splined polyline that has been trimmed. The polyline becomes permanently curved polyline segments. When trimming an associative linear dimension, the entire dimension updates.

Project

Determines the projection mode used for finding cutting edges. This value is maintained by the *projmode* variable.

None

Specifies no projection. Only objects that intersect with the cutting edge in 3D space are trimmed.

UCS

Specifies projection onto the *XY* plane of the current UCS. Objects that do not intersect with the boundary edges in 3D space are trimmed.

View

Specifies projection along the current view direction. All objects that intersect with the cutting edge in the current view are trimmed.

Edge

Determines whether the object trims to the implied intersection or whether it must actually intersect the boundary edge. This value is maintained by the *edgemode* variable.

Extend

Trims to the cutting edge or to the implied cutting edge.

No extend

Trims only if it actually intersects the cutting edge.

Undo

Restores the last object trimmed.

Tips & Warnings

At times, you can use *break, chamfer, change–point, fillet, grip* editing, *properties*, and *lengthen* to trim most objects. None of these commands requires a boundary edge.

Related Variables   edgemode, projmode

Associated Commands   btrim, change, extend, extrim, lengthen, stretch

Example

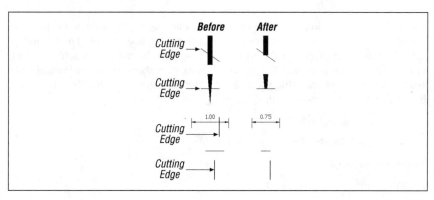

'TRIMMODE

Determines whether the original objects being filleted and chamfered are modified. This value is set using the trim/no trim option of *chamfer* or *fillet*.

Initiate Command By

Command: **trimmode**

Options

0   Does not modify selected edges.

1   Trims selected edges to the endpoints of chamfer lines and fillet arcs.

Variable Settings

Initial default:	1
Subsequent default:	Registry file
Value:	Integer

Associated Commands   chamfer, fillet

Example

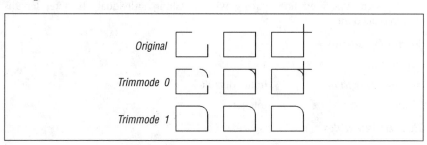

'TSPACEFAC ▢2000▢

Determines the spacing between lines of multiline text. The values are between .25 and 4.0. The distance is measured as a factor of text height. The *tspacetype* variable determines whether the spacing is based on the tallest character (at least) or is based on the specified line spacing (exactly) without taking individual character sizes into account. This value is set when selecting the Line Spacing option from the *mtext* Line Spacing tab.

Initiate Command By

Command: **tspacefac**

Variable Settings

Initial default:	1
Subsequent default:	Initial default
Value:	Real
Related Variables	tspacetype
Associated Commands	mtext

'TSPACETYPE ▢2000▢

Determines if the line spacing between lines of multiline text is based on an exact number or on the tallest character in the text string. The *tspacefac* variable determines the spacing. This value is set when selecting the Line Spacing option from the *mtext* Line Spacing tab.

Initiate Command By

Command: **tspacetype**

Options

1 (At least)
    Uses the tallest character.

2 (Exactly)
    Uses the specified line spacing without taking individual character lengths into account.

Variable Settings

Initial default:	1
Subsequent default:	Initial default
Value:	Integer
Related Variables	tspacefac
Associated Commands	mtext

'TSTACKALIGN 2000

Sets the vertical alignment of multiline stacked text. You can set this value using the *mtext* shortcut menu. Once the characters have been stacked, use the shortcut menu and select properties to change this setting.

Initiate Command By   Command: **tstackalign**

Options

0   Stacked text is bottom-aligned. It aligns the bottom of the fraction with the text baseline.

1   Stacked text is center-aligned. It centers the fraction vertically to the center of the text line.

2   Stacked text is top-aligned. It aligns the top of the fraction with the top of the text line.

Variable Settings

Initial default:	1
Subsequent default:	Last value used in the drawing
Value:	Integer
Related Variables	tstacksize
Associated Commands	mtext

Example

$$20'-0\tfrac{13}{16}''\qquad 20'-0\tfrac{13}{16}''\qquad 20'-0\tfrac{13}{16}''$$

   Top   *Center*   *Bottom*

'TSTACKSIZE 2000

Determines the height of multiline stacked text. The height is based on a percentage of the text size. The values range from 1 to 127. Once the characters have been stacked, use the shortcut menu and select properties to change this setting.

Initiate Command By

Command: **tstacksize**

Variable Settings

Initial default:	70
Subsequent default:	Last value used in the drawing
Value:	Integer

References S–T

Related Variables   tstackalign

Associated Commands   mtext

TXT2MTXT

Converts single-line text (*dtext*, *text*) to multiline text (*mtext*).

Initiate Command By   Command: **txt2mtxt**
                          Express → Text → Convert Text To Mtext

Options

    Select text objects, or [Options]<Options>:

text objects
  Lets you select the single-line text for conversion.

Options
  Activates the Text to MText Options dialog box. This dialog box lets you
  determine how text is ordered. Text ordering can be based on the order in
  which text is selected or the order of the descending *Y* value. You also determine if word wrap is enabled or if each string of text begins a new multiline
  text (*mtext*) line.

Associated Commands   dtext, mtext, text

TXTEXP   Express Text toolbar

Explodes single-line (*text*, *dtext*) and multiline (*mtext*) text into polylines and
polyline arcs. Exploding the polylines and polyline arcs converts them into lines
and arcs. Text that is solid filled loses that property.

Initiate Command By

  Command: **txtexp**
  Express → Text → Explode Text

Associated Commands   dtext, mtext, text

Example

Before — **Exploded text**   After — Exploded text

U   Standard toolbar

Reverses the effects of the last command. You can undo back to the beginning of
the drawing session. *undo* is similar, but it has additional features. *redo* reverses
the effects of the *u* command. You can *redo* only once, and it must be the first

---

command after *u*. *undo* views a script command sequence as a group. Therefore, you can reverse the whole script with one *undo* command. Some commands such as *appload, attext, dxfout, mslide, plot, syswindows*, and *wblock*, and the loading and unloading of rendering software cannot be undone.

ddedit, dim, dview, extend, grips, leader, lengthen, line, mledit, mline, mvsetup, pedit, pline, splinedit, and *trim* have an undo option built into their commands. If you use *u* without exiting the command, the last change or action is undone. If you exit the command and issue a *u*, whatever was done during that command sequence is undone.

Initiate Command By

    Command: **u**
    Alias: Ctrl-Z
    Edit → Undo

Tips & Warnings

Even though you may use the *qsave* and *save* commands, you can still undo past those commands until you return to the beginning of the drawing session. If you want to make sure you do not undo past a certain point, use the *save* and *close* commands and then *open* the drawing for editing.

Associated Commands   redo, undo

UCS ▐2000mod▐   Standard toolbar

Redefines the location of 0,0 and the direction of the *X*, *Y*, and *Z* axes. The original location, the WCS (World Coordinate System), can never be altered. The UCS icon (*ucsicon*) graphically displays the origin and viewing plane of the current UCS. The *view* command lets you assign a named UCS to a view.

Initiate Command By

    Command: **ucs**
    Alias: **dducs**
    Tools → Move UCS
    Tools → New UCS

Options

    Enter an option [New/Move/orthoGraphic/Prev/Restore/Save/Del/Apply/?/
    World] <World>:

New

    Creates a new UCS.

    Specify origin of new UCS

        Lets you specify a new origin point while retaining the direction of the *X*, *Y*, and *Z* axes. If a *Z* coordinate is not given, it uses the current elevation value.

    ZAxis

        Lets you specify a new origin point and a positive *Z* axis.

3point

Lets you specify a new UCS origin and the direction of its positive X and Y axes.

OBject

Defines a new UCS with the same orientation as a selected object. The origin is determined by the object type. This option does not work for 3D polylines, ellipses, leaders, meshes, multilines, multiline text, rays, regions, 3D solids, splines, viewport borders, and xlines.

Face

Lets you select the face of a 3D solid object and aligns the UCS to that face. Once the face is chosen, you can flip the UCS about the X and Y axes by 180 degrees. You also can change the face to either the adjacent face or the back face of the selected edge. AutoCAD chooses the face.

View

Defines a new UCS parallel to the screen. The origin point does not change. This gives you the ability to create annotation right side up regardless of the UCS's location.

X

Rotates the current UCS around the X axis. This value is maintained by the *ucsaxisang* variable.

Y

Rotates the current UCS around the Y axis. This value is maintained by the *ucsaxisang* variable.

Z

Rotates the current X and Y axes about the Z axis. This value is maintained by the *ucsaxisang* variable.

Move

Lets you change the Z depth of the current UCS. The XY plane does not change.

orthoGraphic

Lets you set the UCS to one of the preset standard orthographic views: top, bottom, front, back, left, or right.

Prev

Restores the previous UCS. You can backtrack up to 10 previous coordinate systems for paper space and 10 previous coordinate systems for model space. This is the same as selecting *PREVIOUS* and Current from the UCS Names list of the *ucsman* dialog box.

Restore

Lets you retrieve a previously saved UCS. Responding with a question mark (?) activates the wildcard options for reviewing the names of UCSs defined in the current drawing. The default, an asterisk, gives a sorted listing of the named UCSs. You can use any of the wildcard options to create a more specific list. If the current UCS is unnamed, it is listed as *WORLD* or *NO NAME*, depending on its orientation. This is the same as looking at the UCS Names list of the *ucsman* Named UCSs tab. The *ucsname* variable retains the name of the last UCS saved or restored.

Save

Stores the current UCS with a name you specify, up to 31 characters long. Responding with a question mark (?) is the same as using the ? option. Depending on the *extnames* setting, UCS names can contain up to 255 characters. The *ucsname* variable retains the name of the last UCS saved or restored.

Del

Deletes a saved UCS. You cannot delete World, Previous, and Unnamed.

Apply

Applies the current UCS to a specified viewport or to all viewports.

?

Activates the wildcard options for reviewing the names of UCSs defined in the current drawing. The default, an asterisk, gives a sorted listing of the named UCSs. You can use any of the wildcard options to create a more specific list. If the current UCS is unnamed, it is listed as World or Unnamed. This is the same as the UCS Names list of the *ucsman* dialog box.

World

Restores the World Coordinate System (WCS). This is the same as selecting World from the *ucsman* Named UCSs tab.

Tips & Warnings

- Only one UCS can be current.

- If you get lost locating a UCS, return to the WCS and start over. The location of the WCS can never be altered.

- Each viewport retains its own UCS setting.

Related Variables   extnames, ucsaxisang, ucsbase, ucsfollow, ucsicon, ucsname, ucsorg, ucsview, ucsxdir, ucsydir, viewctr, viewdir, viewmode

Associated Commands   plan, ucsicon, ucsman, view

Example:

```
Command: Ucs
Current ucs name: *WORLD*
Enter an option [New/Move/orthoGraphic/Prev/Restore/Save/Del/Apply/?/
World] <World>: N
Specify origin of new UCS or [ZAxis/3point/OBject/Face/View/X/Y/Z]
<0,0,0>: 3
Specify new origin point <0,0,0>: Pick point 1
Specify point on positive portion of X-axis <2.0000,1.0000,0.0000>: Pick
point 2
Specify point on positive-Y portion of the UCS XY plane
<1.0000,2.0000,0.0000>: Pick point 3
Command: Ucs
Current ucs name: *NO NAME*
Enter an option [New/Move/orthoGraphic/Prev/Restore/Save/Del/Apply/?/
World] <World>: S
Enter name to save current UCS or [?]: RIGHT
```

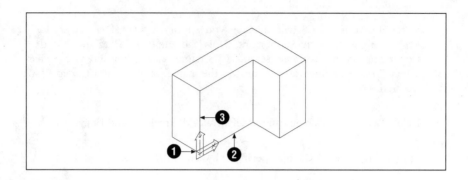

'UCSAXISANG 2000

Stores the default angle when creating a new UCS by rotating the UCS around the X, Y, or Z axis. Valid default values are 5, 10, 15, 18, 22.5, 30, 45, 90, and 180.

Initiate Command By
Command: **ucsaxisang**

Variable Settings
Initial default:	90
Subsequent default:	Registry file
Value:	Integer

Associated Commands   ucs

'UCSBASE 2000

Maintains the name of the UCS that defines the origin and orientation of orthographic UCS settings. The UCS names are created with the save option of the *ucs* command. To reset the *ucsbase* to *World* enter a period (.).

Initiate Command By
Command: **ucsbase**

Variable Settings
Initial default:	*World*
Subsequent default:	Last value used in the drawing
Value:	String

Related Variables   pucsbase

Associated Commands   ucs, view

'UCSFOLLOW

Determines whether a change in the current viewport's UCS causes the drawing to display in plan view relative to the new UCS. Once the drawing is in plan view, you can always use *dview, plan, view, vpoint,* or *3dorbit* to change the drawing's viewing direction. Paper space treats this variable as though it were always set to 0. This value is set when checking the "Update view to plan when UCS is changed" box from the *ucsman* Settings tab.

Initiate Command By

Command: **ucsfollow**

Options

0   A change in the UCS does not affect the view.

1   A change in the UCS causes an automatic change to the plan view of the new UCS.

Variable Settings

Initial default:	0
Subsequent default:	Last value used in the drawing
Value:	Integer
Related Variables	viewmode
Associated Commands	plan, ucs, ucsman

'UCSICON 2000mod

Determines the visibility and location of the User Coordinate System (UCS) icon. It is used as a marker to graphically display the origin and viewing plane of the current UCS. You can control the display during *3dorbit* by using the shortcut menu. The system variable (*setvar*) that maintains this setting is also named *ucsicon.*

Initiate Command By

Command: **ucsicon**
View → Display → UCS Icon

Options

Enter an option [ON/OFF/All/Noorigin/ORigin] <ON>:

ON
Displays the UCS icon in the current viewport.

OFF
Turns the UCS icon display off in the current viewport.

All
Displays changes to the UCS icon in all active viewports.

Noorigin

Displays the UCS icon at the lower-left side of the viewport regardless of the current UCS definition.

ORigin

Displays the UCS icon at the origin of the current UCS (0,0,0). If the origin is off the screen's viewing area, the icon is shown in the lower-left corner.

The following figure illustrates the different icon features.

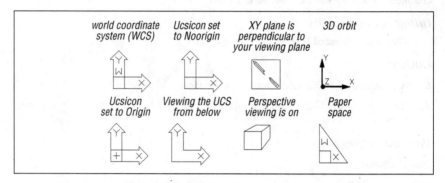

W

The UCS is the same as the WCS.

+

The icon is located at the origin point of the UCS.

Box

The UCS is viewed from a positive *Z* direction.

Box with a broken pencil

The *XY* plane of the UCS is perpendicular to your viewing plane.

Cube in perspective

Perspective viewing is on. This is a result of the Distance option of the *dview* command.

Related Variables   ucsicon, worlducs

Associated Commands   dview, mspace, pspace, setvar, ucs, ucsman, 3dorbit

---

UCSMAN [2000]   UCS toolbar

Manages the User Coordinate System (UCS). The UCS allows you to redefine the location of 0,0 and your viewing direction. You can assign a name to each UCS for future retrieval. *ucsman* lets you restore saved UCSs and orthographic UCSs. It also lets you access *ucsicon* settings and settings for viewports. The UCS toolbar (shown above) can be activated by right-clicking on an existing toolbar and selecting UCS.

Initiate Command By

Command: **ucsman**
Tools → Named UCS

Options

The UCS dialog has three tabs that are covered in detail in this section.

The Named UCSs Tab

The Named UCSs tab lists User Coordinate Systems and changes the current UCS. The *dducs* command also activates this dialog box.

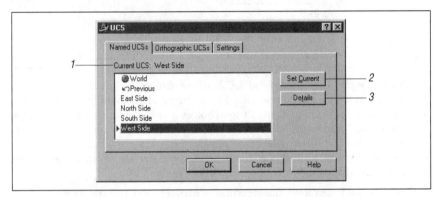

1. **Current UCS**. Lists the UCSs that have been saved with the *ucs* command. World is always listed and will return you to the World Coordinate System (WCS). This cannot be renamed or deleted. When Previous is listed it lets you return to the previous UCS setting. Unnamed appears when the current UCS has not been assigned a name. Use the save option of the *ucs* command to save a UCS. You can identify the current UCS by the arrow highlighting the name of the UCS. Double-clicking on any of the choices sets it current when you exit the command. This value is maintained by the *ucsname* system variable.

2. **Set Current**. Sets the highlighted UCS current. You also can double-click on the UCS name and pick OK.

3. **Details**. Lists the origin and the *X*, *Y*, and *Z* axes of the current UCS. You can display this information relative to another UCS.

The Orthographic UCSs Tab

The Orthographic UCSs tab lists predefined orthographic User Coordinate Systems and lets you set the current viewport to any of those settings. The *dducsp* command also activates this dialog box.

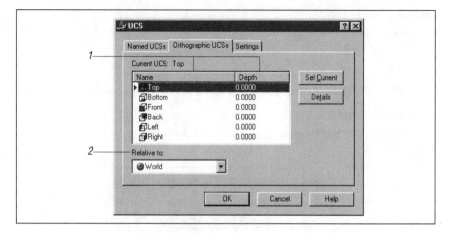

1. **Name, Depth**. Lists predefined UCSs. These cannot be renamed or deleted. You can identify the current UCS by the arrow highlighting the name of the UCS. Double-clicking on any of the choices sets it current when you exit the command. The Depth field lists the distance between the orthographic coordinate system and the parallel plane passing through the origin of the UCS base setting. You can change the depth setting by using the shortcut menu. This value is maintained by the *ucsbase* system variable.

2. **Relative to**. Determines the direction of the selected UCS relative to a base coordinate system.

The Settings Tab

The Settings tab controls the visibility and location of the UCS icon and the behavior of the UCS settings in viewports.

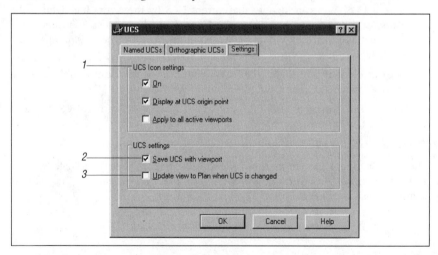

1. **UCS Icon settings**. Determines the visibility and location of the UCS icon. This value is maintained by the *ucsicon* system variable. See *ucsicon* for more detailed information.

2. **Save UCS with viewport**. Determines if the UCS in each viewport changes to match the current UCS or if each viewport retains its own UCS setting. This value is maintained by the *ucsvp* system variable.

3. **Update view to Plan when UCS is changed**. Determines whether a change in the current viewport's UCS causes the drawing to display in plan view relative to the new UCS. This value is maintained by the *ucsfollow* system variable.

Related Variables   ucsbase, ucsfollow, ucsorg

Associated Commands   ucs, ucsicon

'UCSNAME 2000mod

Maintains the name of the current UCS. This value gets reset whenever the latest save or restore options of the *ucs* and *ucsman* commands are used. This value is blank when the current UCS is unnamed.

Initiate Command By
    Command: **ucsname**

Variable Settings

Initial default:	None, read-only
Subsequent default:	Last value used in the drawing
Value:	Text string

Associated Commands   ucs, ucsman

'UCSORG 2000mod

Maintains the origin point of the current UCS. The value is stored as a world coordinate. This value is set with the *ucsman* and *ucs* commands.

Initiate Command By
    Command: **ucsorg**

Variable Settings

Initial default:	0.0000,0.0000,0.0000, read-only
Subsequent default:	Last value used in the drawing
Value:	3D point

Associated Commands   ucs, ucsman

'UCSORTHO 2000

Determines if the UCS setting changes to match restored orthographic views. These views and UCS settings are set by checking the "Restore orthographic UCS with view" box located on the *view* command's Orthographic & Isometric Views tab.

Initiate Command By
Command: **ucsortho**

Options

0   The UCS setting remains unchanged when an orthographic view is restored.

1   The UCS setting changes to match restored orthographic views.

Variable Settings

Initial default:	1
Subsequent default:	Registry file
Value:	Integer

Associated Commands   ucs, ucsman, view

'UCSVIEW [2000]

Determines whether the current UCS is saved by the *view* command. This value is set when creating a *view* and checking the "Save UCS with view" box located in the New View dialog box.

Initiate Command By   Command: **ucsview**

Options

0   The current UCS is not saved when creating new views.

1   The current UCS is saved when creating new views.

Variable Settings

Initial default:	1
Subsequent default:	Registry file
Value:	Integer

Associated Commands   ucs, view

'UCSVP [2000]

Determines if the UCS in each viewport changes to match the current UCS or if each viewport retains its own UCS setting. This value is set when checking the "Save UCS with viewport" box on the *ucsman* Settings tab.

Initiate Command By
Command: **ucsvp**

Options

0   The UCS changes to match the UCS of the current viewport.

1   Each viewport retains its own UCS setting.

Variable Settings

Initial default:	1
Subsequent default:	Last value used in the drawing
Value:	Integer
Associated Commands	ucs, ucsman

'UCSXDIR `2000mod`

Maintains the *X* direction of the current UCS. This value is set with the *ucsman* and *ucs* command.

Initiate Command By
Command: **ucsxdir**

Variable Settings

Initial default:	1.0000,0.0000,0.0000, read-only
Subsequent default:	Last value used in the drawing
Value:	3D point
Associated Commands	ucs, ucsman

'UCSYDIR `2000mod`

Maintains the *Y* direction of the current UCS. This value is set with the *ucsman* and *ucs* command.

Initiate Command By
Command: **ucsydir**

Variable Settings

Initial default:	0.0000,1.0000,0.0000, read-only
Subsequent default:	Last value used in the drawing
Value:	3D point
Associated Commands	ucs, ucsman

UNDEFINE/REDEFINE

undefine disables built-in AutoCAD commands so they can be replaced with other commands of the same name and is usually used in conjunction with AutoLISP, ADS, or ARX programs. *redefine* restores the original AutoCAD command. Attempting to execute an undefined command causes an "Unknown command" error message. You can use *redefine* and *undefine* only for commands, not for command options. For example, you can undefine the complete *layer* command, but not the specific layer options.

Initiate Command By

Command: **undefine** or **redefine**

Options

Command name:

Tips & Warnings

• *redefine* and *undefine* are valid only for the current editing session.

• Preceding an undefined command name with a period (.) recalls the original AutoCAD command for that single condition.

UNDO

Lets you sequentially reverse previous commands individually, in groups, or to the beginning of the current drawing session. *redo* reverses the effects of the *undo* command. You can *redo* only once, and it must be the first command after *undo*. *undo* views a script command sequence as a group. Some commands such as *appload, attext, dxfout, mslide, plot, syswindows,* and *wblock* and the loading and unloading of rendering software cannot be undone.

ddedit, dim, dview, extend, grips, leader, lengthen, line, mledit, mline, mvsetup, pedit, pline, splinedit, and *trim* have an undo option built into their commands. If you use *u* without exiting the command, the last change or action is undone. If you exit the command and enter undo 1, whatever was done during that command sequence is undone.

Initiate Command By   Command: **undo**

Options

Enter the number of operations to undo or
[Auto/Control/BEgin/End/Mark/Back] <1>:

the number of operations to undo or <1>

Specifies the number of commands to undo. The default, 1, is the same as using the *u* command.

Auto

Marks a menu macro as one command when on. Auto off treats each command in a menu macro as an individual command.

Control

Limits or disables the *undo* command. This value is maintained by the *undoctl* variable.

All

Enables all the *undo* prompts and options.

None

Disables the *undo* and *u* commands. The auto, begin, and mark options are not available when none is active.

One

> Allows only the last command to be undone. The auto, begin, and mark options are not available when this option is active.

BEgin/End

> Begin treats a sequence of commands as one. End terminates this process. This is similar to the way auto behaves with menu macros. This value is maintained by the *undoctl* variable.

Mark/Back

> Mark sets a marker before issuing a series of commands. You can have as many markers as you want. The back option undoes commands up to the last marker. Once you reach the first marker, you will receive the message "This will undo everything. OK? <Y>." This value is maintained by the *undomarks* variable.

Tips & Warnings

Even though you may use the *qsave* and *save* commands, you can still undo past those commands until you return to the beginning of the drawing session. If you want to make sure you do not undo past a certain point, use the *save* and *close* commands, and then *open* the drawing for editing.

Related Variables	undoctl, undomarks
Associated Commands	redo, u

'UNDOCTL

Maintains the settings for the auto and control options of the *undo* command.

Initiate Command By

Command: **undoctl**

Options

undoctl is bit-coded, and its value is the sum of the following:

0	Undo is disabled.
1	Undo is enabled.
2	Only one command can be undone.
4	Auto group mode is enabled.
8	A group is currently active.

Variable Settings

Initial default:	13, read-only
Subsequent default:	Initial default
Value:	Integer
Associated Commands	undo

'UNDOMARKS

Tracks the number of marks that have been placed with the *undo* command.

Initiate Command By
Command: **undomarks**

Variable Settings

Initial default:	0, read-only
Subsequent default:	Initial default
Value:	Integer

Associated Commands   undo

UNION

Solids Editing toolbar

Creates a composite solid or region from two or more solids or regions by combining one set of solids with another set of solids or one set of regions with another set of regions. The objects do not have to share the same coordinates. Exploding unions has various results depending on the original objects and whether parts of the object were deleted due to the union process. You can obtain detailed information concerning the union's result with *massprop*. Edit 3D solids using *solidedit*.

Initiate Command By
Command: **union**
Alias: **uni**
Modify → Solids Editing → Union

Associated Commands   interfere, intersect, subtract

Example

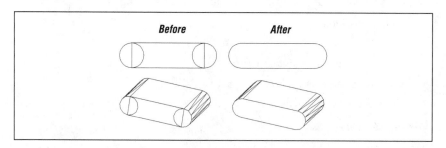

Before   After

'UNITMODE

Controls the displays of fractions, feet and inches, and surveyor's angles. You can have the units displayed with a hyphen separating the feet and inches (standard format) or without the hyphen (user input format). You can have angular units displayed with spaces between values (standard format) or without spaces (user input format). *unitmode* affects commands such as *list* and *area* and the status bar coordinates. However, dimensioning always shows the standard format as the default.

Initiate Command By

Command: **unitmode**

Options

0   Displays units in standard format.

1   Displays units in user input mode.

Variable Settings

Initial default:	0
Subsequent default:	Last value used in the drawing
Value:	Integer
Associated Commands	units

'-UNITS 2000

see UNITS

'UNITS 2000mod

Controls the input and display formats of coordinates, distances, and angles. You specify the system of units, the precision, the system of angle measure, the precision of angle display, and the direction of angles. You can achieve the same results using *-units (-un)* so all prompts and options appear at the command line.

The Advanced Setup and Quick Setup wizards of the *new* command request the units settings. The Quick Setup requests only the units of measure; the Advanced Setup requests the units of measure and the precision, the angle of measure, and the precision and the angle direction.

Initiate Command By

Command: **units**
Alias: **un**
Format → Units

Options

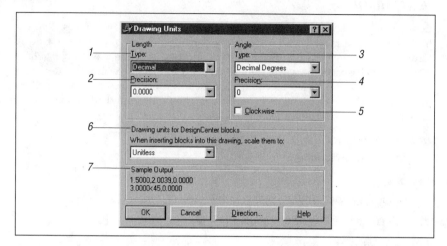

1. **Type.** Specifies the units of measure: scientific, decimal, engineering, architectural, or fractional. This value is maintained by the *lunits* system variable.

2. **Precision.** Specifies the number of digits past the decimal place or the smallest fraction of an inch to display. This value is maintained by the *luprec* system variable.

3. **Type.** Specifies the format for angle measurements: decimal degrees; degrees, minutes, and seconds; grads; radians; or surveyor's units. This value is maintained by the *aunits* system variable.

4. **Precision.** Select the precision with which angles are displayed. This value is maintained by the *auprec* system variable.

5. **Clockwise.** Determines whether positive angles are calculated in a clockwise direction. This value is maintained by the *angdir* system variable.

6. **Drawing units for DesignCenter blocks.** Determines the unit of measure used for blocks inserted through the AutoCAD DesignCenter. Blocks created with a different set of units are scaled and inserted in the specified units. If you want blocks inserted as they were created and not scaled to match the specified units, set the value to Unitless. This value is maintained by the *insunits* system variable.

7. **Sample Output.** Displays an example of the selected length and angle settings.

The Direction Control Dialog Box

The Direction Control dialog determines the 0 degree location when AutoCAD calculates angles.

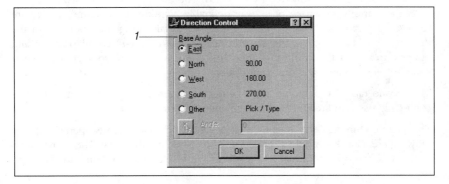

1. **Base Angle**. Determines the direction of the base angle. The default direction for the 0 angle is East. You can select an angle on the screen and type the angle in the text box when Other is selected. The base angle is relative to the User Coordinate System (UCS) setting. This value is maintained by the *angbase* system variable.

Tips & Warnings

- The format for entering 3'-5½" is 3'5-1/2 or 3'5-1.5. The inch character (") is optional.

- You can override the current angle format and enter angles in decimal degrees relative to AutoCAD's default orientation (0 degrees equals 3 o'clock) and direction (counterclockwise) by preceding the angle with two angle brackets (<<). Preceding the angle with three angle brackets (<<<) overrides only the orientation and direction and allows the angle to be specified in the current angle units format.

- Civil engineering drawings are usually created in decimal units, with the convention that 1.0 equals 1'-0". If you change the *units* to architectural, 1.0 becomes 1". If necessary, you can *scale* the drawing 12 times to have 1.0 equal to 1'-0".

Related Variables   angbase, angdir, aunits, auprec, insunits, lunits, luprec, unitmode

---

'-VIEW ⬛2000⬛   *see VIEW*

'VIEW 2000mod

View toolbar

The View dialog box is divided by two tabs. The first tab, Named Views, lets you save the current viewport or a user-definable window to a name, for future retrieval. It provides a way to return quickly to certain designated portions of the drawing. You can achieve the same results using -*view* (-*v*) so all prompts and options appear at the command line. You can use the *view* command transparently but only when using the -*view* option.

The second tab, Orthographic & Isometric Views, provides preset standard views commonly used on architectural and engineering drawings.

The *open* command lets you preselect a view to display before opening up the drawing file. Check the Select Initial View box to define the view. The partial open option lets you open a drawing to a specific view and lets you define the layers to load.

The *plot* command gives you the option of plotting a view. The advantage is that it will plot only those objects or parts of objects contained within the view. You can assign a *hyperlink* to a view.

Initiate Command By

Command: **view**
Alias: **v**
View → Named Views

Options

The View dialog contains two tabs, which are covered in detail in this section.

The Named Views Tab

The Named View tab creates, sets, and deletes named views.

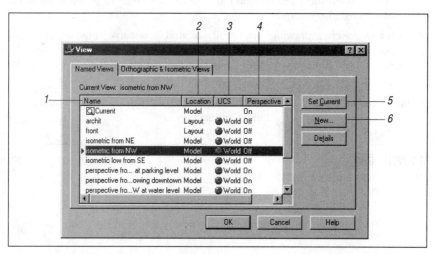

1. **Name**. Lists the names of views defined in the drawing. The Current view is always present and is based on your current viewport. Clicking on Name in the status bar does not sort the views by ascending or descending order, as is common for most Windows programs. If the view names contain three dots (...), it is because the name is truncated. Stretching the Name bar causes the complete name to display. Rename views by right-clicking on the view name or by using the *rename* command. Press the Delete key to remove the view name highlighted by the arrow.

2. **Location**. Tells you whether the view was created in model space or layout space.

3. **UCS**. Lists the UCS assigned to the view. If no UCS is defined but the "Save UCS with view" box in the New View dialog is checked, it defaults to World. When that box is unchecked, the UCS entry is empty.

4. **Perspective**. Lets you know if the view was created with perspective viewing enabled. Perspective viewing is set with *3dorbit* or *dview–distance*.

5. **Set Current**. Restores the named view, selected from the view list, as the current view when exiting the dialog box. Double-clicking on a view name is the same as selecting this button. If you restore a model space view while working in layout space, you are asked to select a viewport. The viewport must be on and active. You then are switched to model space. You can restore a layout space view while working in model space if *tilemode* is off (0). View will not let you restore any layout space views if model space is active and *tilemode* is on (1).

6. **New**. Activates the New View dialog box. This dialog box lets you define a new view by creating a name and location and assigning an optional UCS.

The New View Dialog Box

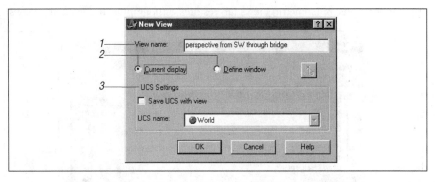

1. **View name**. Enter a view name. Depending on the *extnames* setting, view names can contain up to 255 characters.

2. **Current display, Define window**. A view is created by either saving your current display or by creating a window around an area defining the view.

3. **UCS Settings**. You can save the view with a predefined UCS. Checking the "Save UCS with view" box turns on the *ucsview* variable and lets you select a UCS from the UCS name drop-down list.

The View Details Dialog Box

The View Details dialog box lists various settings that were active when the view was created. This is especially helpful when creating new views with similar settings. The "Relative to" drop-down list sets the orientation of the selected view relative to the WCS or UCS' saved in the current drawing.

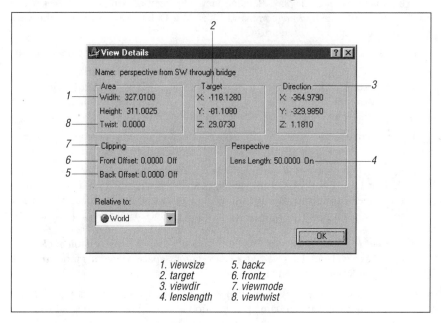

1. viewsize
2. target
3. viewdir
4. lenslength
5. backz
6. frontz
7. viewmode
8. viewtwist

The Orthographic & Isometric Views Tab

The Orthographic & Isometric Views tab restores orthographic and isometric views.

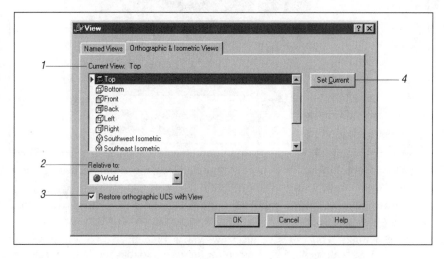

1. **Current View**. Lets you select a view from a list of predefined orthographic and isometric views. The views are relative to the UCS listed in the Relative To drop-down list.

2. **Relative to**. Sets the orientation of the selected view relative to the WCS or to a UCS saved in the current drawing via a drop-down list. This value is maintained by the *ucsbase* system variable.

3. **Restore orthographic UCS with View**. Restores the associated UCS when making an orthographic view current. This value is maintained by the *ucsortho* system variable.

4. **Set Current**. Sets the named view, selected from the view list, as the current view when exiting the dialog box. Double-clicking on a view name is the same as selecting this button.

Tips & Warnings

- *zoom–previous* includes restored views.

- Gain more control when rendering a drawing by creating views and light sources, then use the *scene* command to link the various lights to different views.

Related Variables	backz, extnames, frontz, lenslength, target, ucsbase, ucsortho, ucsview, viewdir, viewmode, viewsize, viewtwist
Associated Commands	light, open, rename, render, scene, 3dorbit

'VIEWCTR

Maintains the current viewport's center point.

Initiate Command By
Command: **viewctr**

Variable Settings

Initial default:	Varies, read-only
Subsequent default:	Last value used in the drawing
Value:	3D point
Related Variables	target, viewdir, viewtwist
Associated Commands	ddvpoint, dview, pan, ucs, ucsman, vpoint, vports, zoom, 3dorbit, 3dswivel

'VIEWDIR

Maintains the current viewport's viewing direction in UCS coordinates.

Initiate Command By
Command: **viewdir**

Variable Settings

Initial default:	0.0000,0.0000,1.0000, read-only
Subsequent default:	Last value used in the drawing
Value:	3D Vector
Related Variables	target, viewdir, viewtwist
Associated Commands	3dorbit, ddvpoint, dview, ucs, ucsman, view, vpoint, vports

'VIEWMODE

Maintains the current viewport's viewing mode. This value is set with *3dclip* or *dview*.

Initiate Command By
Command: **viewmode**

Options

viewmode is bit-coded, and its value is the sum of the following:

0   Viewmode is disabled.

1   Perspective view is active.

2   Front clipping is on.

4   Back clipping is on.

8   Ucsfollow mode is on.

16   Front clipping is not at eye level.

Variable Settings

Initial default:	0, read-only
Subsequent default:	Last value used in the drawing
Value:	Integer
Related Variables	backz, frontz, ucsfollow
Associated Commands	dview, view, vports, 3dorbit, 3dswivel

VIEWPORTS   *see VPORTS*

VIEWRES

Controls the display resolution of arcs, circles, splines, spheres, and tori in the current viewport.

Initiate Command By

Command: **viewres**

Options

```
Do you want fast zooms? [Yes/No] <Y>:
Enter circle zoom percent (1-20000) <100>:
```

Do you want fast zooms? [Yes/No] <Y>:

The fast zoom feature no longer has any effect. It was left in the system for compatibility with custom scripts and macro routines from previous versions.

Enter circle zoom percent (1–20000) <100>:

Entering a value greater than 100 provides a smoother resolution display but increases regeneration times. Lower values decrease the resolution display (objects are drawn with short line segments) but also decreases regeneration time.

Tips & Warnings

- The *viewres* setting has no effects on objects when *whiparc* is set to display arcs and circles as smooth.

- Regardless of the *viewres* setting, the objects are always printed at the plotter's resolution.

- To produce the best rendering quality, set *viewres* to a higher number.

- Broken linetypes can appear as continuous lines due to *viewres* and the current zoom level. Forcing a regeneration or zooming in closer may display the linetype correctly.

Related Variables	facetres, whiparc
Associated Commands	pan, render, view, zoom

Example

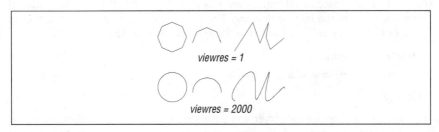

viewres = 1

viewres = 2000

'VIEWSIZE

Maintains the height of the current viewport.

Initiate Command By

Command: **viewsize**

Variable Settings

Initial default:	9.0000, read-only
Subsequent default:	Last value used in the drawing
Value:	Real
Associated Commands	ddvpoint, dview, view, vpoint, vports, zoom, 3dswivel

---

'VIEWTWIST

Maintains the view twist angle for the current viewport. This value is set with the *dview* and *3dorbit* commands. The *properties* window displays this value as Roll Angle.

Initiate Command By

Command: **viewtwist**

Variable Settings

Initial default:	0, read-only
Subsequent default:	Last value used in the drawing
Value:	Real
Related Variables	viewctr, 3ddistance, 3dzoom
Associated Commands	dview, view, vports, 3dorbit, 3dswivel

'VISRETAIN

Determines whether an external reference's layer settings and changes made to the paths of nested external references are based on the external reference's original values or those of the current drawing. The value is set when checking the "Retain changes to Xref layers" box located in the *options* Open and Save tab.

Initiate Command By

Command: **visretain**

Options

0   The external reference's layer and path settings are defined and displayed by the external reference file settings. You can temporarily change the external reference's linetype, color, lineweight, plotstyle (if *pstylepolicy* is set to 0), and layer visibility, as well as paths of nested external references. However, this is only temporary. Once you reload, attach, or end the session, that information is forgotten.

1   The external reference's layer settings and paths of nested external references are defined and displayed by the current drawing.

Variable Settings

Initial default:	1
Subsequent default:	Last value used in the drawing
Value:	Integer
Related Variables	pstylepolicy
Associated Commands	layer, options, preferences, xref

VPCLIP 2000   Viewports toolbar

Changes the shape of layout space viewports. Viewports are created with *mview*, *viewports*, and *vports*.

Initiate Command By

Command: **vpclip**
Modify → Clip → Viewport

Options

Select clipping object or [Polygonal/Delete] <Polygonal>:

Select clipping object
Lets you assign a circle, closed spline, closed polyline, ellipse, or region to replace an existing viewport. The object must reside in paper space.

Polygonal
Creates a new boundary from an existing viewport. This boundary, made up of polylines, can be irregular shaped.

Delete
Removes the polygonal object and replaces it with the viewport object.

Tips & Warnings

Create clipping boundaries for raster images with *imageclip*, for external references and blocks with *xclip* or *clipit*, and for all objects with *wipeout*.

Associated Commands   mview, viewports, vports

Example

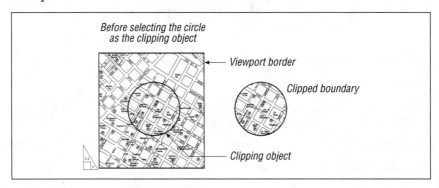

Before selecting the circle
as the clipping object

Viewport border

Clipped boundary

Clipping object

VPLAYER

Controls layer visibility per viewport when layout space is active. Viewports are created with *mview, viewports, -vports,* and *vports.* The *layer* command contains the *vplayer* options as part of its dialog box options.

Initiate Command By

Command: **vplayer**

Options

```
Enter an option [?/Freeze/Thaw/Reset/Newfrz/Vpvisdflt]:
Enter an option [All/Select/Current] <Current>:
```

?

Displays a listing of the frozen layers for the current viewport. If you are in model space, you are temporarily switched to paper space for viewport selection.

Freeze

Lets you specify layers to freeze. You can list layer names separated by commas or use wildcard characters. Once you name the layers, you select the viewport(s).

Thaw

Lets you select layers to thaw. You can list layer names separated by commas or use wildcard characters.

Reset

Restores the default visibility setting for layers based on the *vpvisdflt* setting.

Newfrz

Lets you create new layers that are frozen in all viewports. Create more than one layer at a time, separating layer names with commas.

Vpvisdflt

Viewport visibility default determines layer visibility defaults before creating viewports. You can set more than one layer by using wildcard characters.

All

Lets you select all paper space viewports including those that are not visible.

Select

Lets you select paper space viewports using standard object selection methods. If you are in model space, you are temporarily switched to paper space for viewport selection.

Current

Selects the current viewport.

Tips & Warnings

vplayer cannot override layer command settings. Layers must be thawed and on in order to be affected by the *vplayer* command.

Related Variables	tilemode
Associated Commands	layer, mview, viewports, -vports, vports

VPOINT

Specifies the direction and angle for viewing a drawing by selecting a 3D view-point. Issuing the command regenerates the drawing in parallel projection from the 3D point that you specify. You have three ways to define a viewpoint: enter *X,Y,Z* values; supply an angle in the *XY* plane from the *XY* plane; or pick a point on the compass icon. You also can view objects in 3D with *ddvpoint, 3dorbit,* and *view. vpoint* can only display parallel projection. To generate perspectives, use *dview* or *3dorbit.* You cannot control the distance at which you are viewing an object, only the orientation. To control the distance, use *3dorbit* or *dview.* Specify a viewpoint of 0,0,1 to return to plan view, or use the *plan* command.

Initiate Command By

Command: **vpoint**
Alias: **-vp**

Options

    Current view direction: VIEWDIR=0.0000,0.0000,1.0000
    Specify a view point or [Rotate] <display compass and tripod>:

view point
Specify a viewing direction by entering *X,Y,Z* coordinates relative to 0,0,0.

Rotate
Specify the viewpoint by entering two angles: the angle in the *XY* plane from the *X* axis and the *Z* angle from the *XY* plane.

display compass and tripod
A compass and axis tripod is displayed to assist in selecting a viewpoint. The compass represents a 2D globe. The center point is the north pole, the inner ring is the equator, and the outer ring is the south pole.

Tips & Warnings

* The viewpoint is always viewed through 0,0,0 of the WCS or UCS depending on the setting of the *worldview* variable. If you want to view your drawing through a different point, use *dview* or *3dorbit.*

* Issuing *vpoint* in a drawing containing rendered objects causes those objects to default to the latest *shademode* setting.

Related Variables	target, viewctr, viewdir, viewsize, vsmax, vsmin, worldview
Associated Commands	camera, ddvpoint, dview, plan, 3dorbit

Example

The following options can be located from the View → 3D Views pull-down menu.

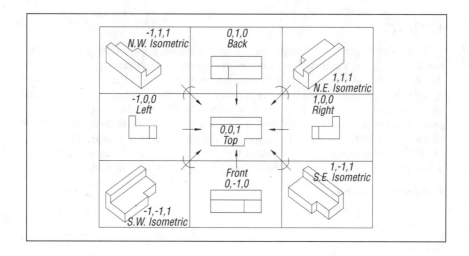

-VPORTS `2000`

see VPORTS

VPORTS/VIEWPORTS `2000mod`

Viewports toolbar

Creates, restores, and deletes viewports. Viewports let you divide your screen into several viewing areas. Each viewport can display a different view of your drawing and has independent settings for commands such as *dview, 3dorbit, grid, snap, ucsicon, viewres, vpoint,* and *isometric* settings. You can independently *pan, redraw, regen,* and *zoom* in each viewport. You can achieve the same results using the *-vports* command so all prompts and options appear on the command line.

Viewports are interactive. You can begin most drawing and editing commands in one viewport and click into another viewport to complete the drawing or editing command. Only one viewport can be current at a time. The current viewport is surrounded by a wider border, and the crosshairs are present only within that viewport.

Viewports are called "tiled" when model space (*tilemode* = 1) is active. Tiled viewports cannot overlap, and you cannot dynamically move, copy, or change their size. You can plot only the current viewport. Viewports are called "floating" when paper space (*tilemode* = 0) is active. Floating viewports can overlap, and you can dynamically move, copy, or change their size. You can control layer visibility per viewport and plot multiple viewports at multiple scales. You cannot see the viewports created in model space in layout space and vice versa. You cannot create named viewport configurations in paper space.

You also can create viewports in layout space using the *mview* command. *mview* creates and restores named viewports, controls viewport visibility, and performs hidden line removal during paper space plots. Creating a new layout with the *layout* command can automatically create a new viewport. This is accomplished

---

when the "Create viewport in new layouts" box, located in the Display tab of the *options* command, is checked.

Initiate Command By

Command: **vports** or **viewports**
View → Viewports

Options

The Viewports dialog contains two tabs, which are covered in detail in this section.

The New Viewports Tab

The New Viewports tab creates new viewport configurations. When model space is active, the viewports are tiled or fixed; when layout space is active, the viewports are floating.

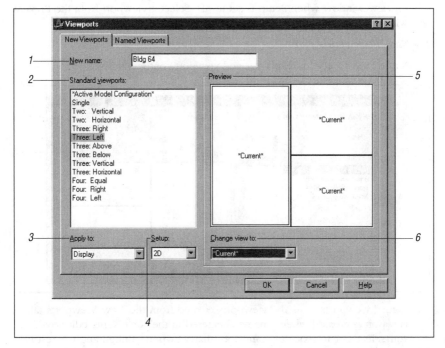

1. **New name.** Saves the current viewport configuration with a name. It also remembers how the objects are displayed in each viewport. Depending on the *extnames* setting, viewport names can contain up to 255 characters. This option is not available when paper space is active.

2. **Standard viewports.** Lists predefined viewport configurations. *Active Model Configuration* refers to the viewport configuration currently displayed on the screen. All drawings have at least one viewport, and it is considered Single. When paper space is active you can retrieve the viewports, but you must select two diagonal points to define the size of the viewport configuration. This is similar to *mview*.

3. **Apply to.** Defines the area where the viewport creation takes place. You can have your whole screen change to match the Standard viewports selection, or you can change the current viewport to match the Standard viewports selection.

4. **Setup.** Determines the viewport's viewing direction. When Setup is set to 2D, the viewing direction is based on the current viewport. If the drawing is already displayed in a 3D mode, it retains that setting. When Setup is set to 3D, it automatically changes the viewing direction of most of the viewports. The Preview window lists the viewing direction for each viewport. You can change the viewing direction by selecting another option from the Change View To drop-down list.

5. **Preview.** Graphically displays how your screen will look based on the selection in the Standard Viewports window.

6. **Change view to.** Changes the viewing direction assigned to a viewport in the Preview window when Setup is set to 3D. Select a viewport from the Preview window and choose the viewing direction from the drop-down list.

The Named Viewports Tab

The Named Viewports tab displays saved viewport configurations.

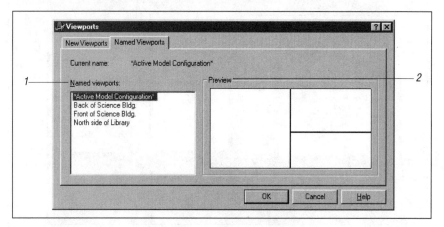

1. **Named viewports.** Lists the viewports created from the New Viewports tab. A viewport is created when a name is entered in the New Name edit box. Once you select OK to exit the command, that viewport configuration is restored. You can delete and rename the viewports with the shortcut menu.

2. **Preview.** Displays the viewport configuration for the named viewport currently selected in the Named Viewports window.

Tips & Warnings

- *redraw* and *regen* affect only the current viewport. You can redraw and regenerate all the displayed viewports with *redrawall* and *regenall*.

- Use Ctrl-R to toggle between different viewports.

- You can preset the scale factor of viewports with the *psvpscale* variable.

- Use the *mview* or *-vports* command if you want to create circular and irregular-shaped viewports in paper space.

Related Variables	cvport, extnames, maxactvp, psvpscale, tilemode, viewctr, viewdir, viewsize, vsmax, vsmin
Associated Commands	layoutwizard, mview, redrawall, regenall, -vport

---

VSLIDE

Displays a slide file in the current viewport. Slides often are used for slide show presentations and as references. A slide file has the extension *.sld*. You create slides with the *mslide* command. Using *redraw* or any command that causes a redraw usually clears the slide. If that doesn't work, use the *zoom* or *pan* command. Since slide files do not retain any of the data associated with objects, recalling slides is accomplished at redraw speed. Slides cannot be edited or plotted. This value is maintained by the *insbase* system variable.

Initiate Command By

Command: **vslide**

Tips & Warnings

If *filedia* is set to 1, a dialog box is activated; if *filedia* is set to 0, you are prompted on the command line. When *filedia* is set to 0, or off, entering a tilde (~) on the command line temporarily activates the dialog box.

Related Variables	filedia
Associated Commands	delay, mslide, script

'VSMAX

Maintains the upper-right corner of the current viewport's virtual screen.

Initiate Command By

Command: **vsmax**

Variable Settings

Initial default:	Varies, read-only
Subsequent default:	Last value used in the drawing
Value:	3D point
Related Variables	vsmin
Associated Commands	ddvpoint, dview, limits, regen, vpoint, vports, zoom, 3dorbit, 3dswivel

'VSMIN

Maintains the lower-left corner of the current viewport's virtual screen.

Initiate Command By
Command: **vsmin**

Variable Settings

Initial default:	Varies, read-only
Subsequent default:	Last value used in the drawing
Value:	3D point
Related Variables	vsmax
Associated Commands	ddvpoint, dview, limits, regen, vpoint, vports, zoom, 3dorbit, 3dswivel

-WBLOCK 2000

see WBLOCK

WBLOCK 2000mod

Writes a drawing, part of a drawing, or a block to a file as a new drawing. This file can be inserted into other drawings using *insert*, *xref*, or the AutoCAD Design-Center feature. Use the AutoCAD DesignCenter or the *open* command to edit this file directly. You can achieve the same results using *-wblock* where all prompts and options appear on the command line.

Initiate Command By
Command: **wblock**
Alias: **w**

Options

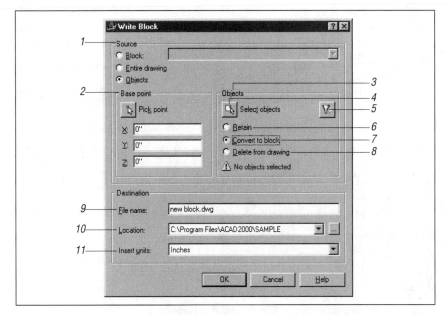

1. **Source.** Lets you determine what defines the geometry making up the block by choosing Block, Entire Drawing, or Objects. Depending on your response, different options are available within the rest of the dialog box. Block is accessible only when you have blocks already defined in the current drawing. When using this option, you must select the block name from the drop-down list. Entire Drawing is the same as using *saveas*. Objects lets you select specific geometry, which can include blocks. The Base Point and Objects portions of the dialog box are activated when you select the Objects option.

2. **Base point.** Determines the insertion base point of the new file. This section is available when Objects has been chosen as the Source. This base point is used when inserting or externally referencing the file into another drawing. The *base* command can always be used to reset the base point. You can set the base point using the Pick Point button or entering the *X*, *Y*, and *Z* coordinates.

3. **Objects.** Defines the objects making up the write block and the action taken once these objects are selected. This section is available when Objects has been chosen as the Source.

4. **Select objects.** Selects the objects or geometry making up the write block through any of the standard selection sets. If you select external references, they become external references in the new file. Objects residing in paper space convert to model space if you open the file after it has been created. If you insert the file, you can have the objects reside in paper space if paper space is active. Viewports that are *wblocked* and *inserted* into paper space in another drawing are inactive or off. Use the on option of the *mview* command to make them active.

5. **Quick select icon.** Activates the *qselect* dialog box.

6. **Retain.** Keeps the selected objects in the drawing after you exit the command.

7. **Convert to block.** Converts the selected objects into a block and keeps them in the drawing after you exit the command.

8. **Delete from drawing.** Removes the selected objects from the drawing when you exit the command.

9. **File name.** Defaults to *new block.dwg*. This is always the default name. The name can contain up to 255 characters. The file extension *.dwg* is applied automatically. This value is maintained by the *dwgname* system variable.

10. **Location.** Specifies a path or folder location for the new file. The button to the right activates a dialog box that lets you select the path. This value is maintained by the *dwgprefix* system variable.

11. **Insert units.** Specifies the units used when the new file is *inserted* into another drawing as a block. This value is maintained by the *insunits* system variable.

Tips & Warnings

Make sure the desired UCS or WCS setting is current before wblocking objects. If you don't have it set properly, you may have unexpected results when inserting the file or using it as an external reference.

Related Variables	filedia, insbase, insunits
Associated Commands	base, block, export, insert

WEDGE

Solids toolbar

Creates a 3D solid wedge. Use negative values when referencing the negative direction of the current UCS *X*, *Y*, and *Z* axes. Use the *ai_wedge* command to create a 3D surface mesh wedge.

Initiate Command By

    Command: **wedge**
    Alias: **we**
    Draw → Solids → Wedge

Options

    Specify first corner of wedge or [CEnter] <0,0,0>:
    Specify corner or [Cube/Length]:
    Specify height:

Tips & Warnings

Use *ddvpoint*, *dview*, *vpoint*, and *3dorbit* to view the wedge at different angles and elevations. Use *hide*, *render*, and *shademode* to enhance the wedge's display.

Associated Commands	ai_wedge

Example

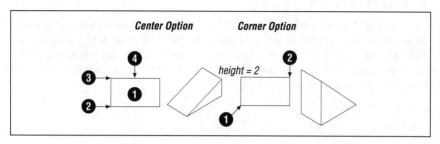

Center Option   Corner Option

height = 2

'WHIPARC 2000

Controls the display of circles and arcs as smooth or as a series of vectors.

Initiate Command By

Command: **whiparc**

Options

0   Circles and arcs are displayed as a series of vectors.

1   Circles and arcs are displayed as smooth.

Variable Settings

Initial default:	0
Subsequent default:	Registry file
Value:	Integer

Tips & Warnings

When changing the value from 0 to 1, you will need to use *regen* to see the results.

Associated Commands   viewres

Example

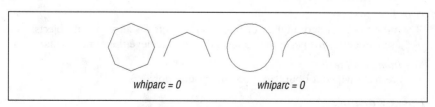

whiparc = 0   whiparc = 0

WHOHAS [2000]

Lets you find out who has drawings open. Once you select a filename from the "Select file to query" dialog box, you are given the date, time, and owner's name. The name is based on the current owner's computer name, the owner's login ID, and the owner's full name. This command works only if you and the other user have the *whohas.arx* program loaded.

Initiate Command By

Command: **whohas**

WIPEOUT [2000mod]

Express Text toolbar

Creates a closed polyline boundary that can hide objects occupying the same space. The interior of the wipeout image looks empty because it takes on the color of the AutoCAD display window. Wipeout objects can be edited the same as other polyline objects.

Wipeout objects are raster images (except for their boundaries). If you have problems plotting, make sure your output device can support raster image plotting. If you use a wipeout in paper space to hide model space objects, make sure the option "Plot paper space last" is not checked in the *plot* command Plot Settings tab.

Initiate Command By

Command: **wipeout**
Express → Draw → Wipeout

Options

```
Select first point or [Frame/New from Polyline] <New>:
Specify next point:
Specify next point or [Undo]:
Specify next point or [Close/Undo]:
Wipeout created.
```

first point

Creates a polygon boundary.

Frame

Turns the boundary outline or frame on and off for all wipeout objects. You also can enter *tframes* at the command line to achieve the same results.

New from Polyline

Creates a wipeout boundary from an existing polyline.

Tips & Warnings

• The *drawoder* command can change the order of objects causing selected objects to appear in front of the wipeout.

• Create clipping boundaries for raster images with *imageclip* and *clipit*, for viewports with *vpclip*, and for external references and blocks with *xclip*.

- If you create wipeout objects and they disappear on the screen, type **tframes** to toggle them back on.

Associated Commands   draworder, masktext

'WMFBKGND 2000

Determines the background color of files created with *wmfout*. Once these files are created, they usually are copied to the clipboard and pasted as a Windows metafile into AutoCAD or other programs supporting Windows applications.

Initiate Command By
Command: **wmfbkgnd**

Options

OFF (0)
The background is transparent.

ON (1)
The background color is the same as AutoCAD's background color.

Variable Settings

Initial default:	1
Subsequent default:	Initial default
Value:	Integer

Associated Commands   wmfin, wmfopts, wmfout

WMFIN

see IMPORT

WMFOPTS

Controls the way objects are defined when importing *.wmf* files.

Initiate Command By
Command: **wmfopts**

Options

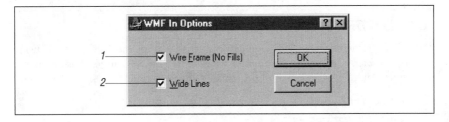

1. **Wire Frame (No Fills).** When the box is checked, objects are imported as wire-frames. When the box is empty, objects are imported as filled.

2. **Wide Lines.** When the box is checked, objects are imported maintaining their relative line widths. When the box is empty, objects' line widths are set to 0.

Tips & Warnings

Importing files as wireframe and with 0 line width helps speed up display commands (i.e., *regen, zoom*) and editing commands.

Related Variables	fillmode, wmfbkgnd
Associated Commands	import, wmfin

WMFOUT   *see EXPORT*

'WORLDUCS

Maintains the relationship between the UCS and WCS.

Initiate Command By

Command: **worlducs**

Options

0   UCS does not equal the WCS.

1   UCS equals the WCS.

Tips & Warnings

When the UCS equals the WCS, the letter W is displayed inside the UCS icon.

Variable Settings

Initial default:	1, read-only
Subsequent default:	Last value used in the drawing
Value:	Integer
Related Variables	ucsicon
Associated Commands	ucs, ucsicon, ucsman

'WORLDVIEW 2000mod

Determines whether the UCS temporarily changes to the WCS when using *ddvpoint, dview, vpoint,* and *3dorbit,* whether the UCS changes based on the *ucsbase* variable, or whether the UCS remains unchanged.

Initiate Command By

Command: **worldview**

Options

0 UCS doesn't change.

1 UCS changes to the WCS when using the *ddvpoint, dview, vpoint,* or *3dorbit* commands.

2 UCS changes relative to the UCS defined by the *ucsbase* variable.

Variable Settings

Initial default:	1
Subsequent default:	Last value used in the drawing
Value:	Integer
Associated Commands	ddvpoint, dview, vpoint, 3dorbit

'WRITESTAT 2000

Tracks the read/write status of AutoCAD files. This variable is set when opening up a drawing file for editing.

Initiate Command By

Command: **writestat**

Options

0 Drawings can't be modified.

1 Drawings can be modified.

Variable Settings

Initial default:	1, read-only
Subsequent default:	Initial default
Value:	Integer
Associated Commands	open

XATTACH

Reference toolbar

Lets you reference and view a drawing file within the current drawing. You can attach more than one file, but you must restart the command each time you want to attach another file. *xattach* is similar to *insert*, but the files are not permanently merged together. You also can access this command using the Xref Manager dialog box (*xref*) and the AutoCAD DesignCenter (*adcenter*) features.

Initiate Command By

Command: **xattach**
Alias: **xa**
Insert → External Reference

Options

The Select Reference File dialog box activates the standard file selection dialog box

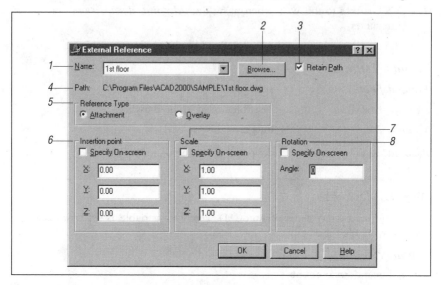

1. **Name.** Lists the drawing file selected from the Select Reference File dialog box. You also can access any existing external reference files from the drop-down list.

2. **Browse.** Replace the drawing file selected from the Select Reference File dialog box by reopening the Select Reference File dialog box.

3. **Retain Path.** Determines whether the drawing retains the path and folder location associated to the external reference. If the path isn't saved, AutoCAD uses the "Support file search path" and the "Project files search path" settings defined in the *options* Files tab.

4. **Path.** Lists the name and location of the file selected for attachment.

5. **Reference Type.** Determines the method of attachment: attached or overlaid. Overlaid references are similar to attached references. When referencing a file containing overlaid references, the overlaid references are not displayed in the current drawing, whereas attached references are always displayed.

6. **Insertion point.** When the Specify On-screen box is checked, you drag the external reference file around the screen until you pick an insertion point. When this box isn't checked, you preset the *X, Y,* and *Z* coordinates for the insertion point.

7. **Scale.** When the Specify On-screen box is checked, you use your pointing device to determine the *X, Y,* and *Z* scale factors. When this box isn't checked, you preset the *X, Y,* and *Z* scale factors.

8. **Rotation.** When the Specify On-screen box is checked, you use your pointing device to determine the rotation angle. When this box isn't checked, you preset rotation angle in the Angle box.

Tips & Warnings

Named items (layers, blocks, dimension styles, layouts, linetypes, text styles, and external references) in attached reference files remain separated from named items in other referenced files and from the base or master drawing. All attached reference-file named items are prefaced with their filename followed by the pipe symbol (|). The only exception is layer 0.

Related Variables   projectname

Associated Commands   adcenter, xref

XBIND

Reference toolbar

Makes selected external reference (*xref*) file information a permanent part of the current drawing. You can achieve the same results using *-xbind* (*-xb*) so all prompts and options appear on the command line. When specifying the referenced items at the command line, you can type in the named item, list multiple names separated with commas, or use wildcard characters. A similar command, *xref–bind*, adds the entire external reference file to your drawing.

Initiate Command By

Command: **xbind**
Alias: **xb**
Modify → Object → External Reference → Bind

Options

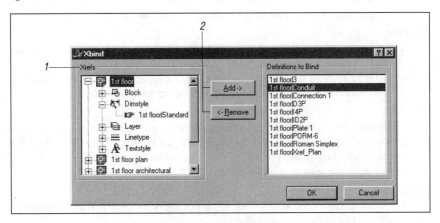

1. **Xrefs**. Lists xref files and named items associated to the files that are available for binding. Double-clicking on each filename lets you see a listing of the available categories; double-clicking on each category opens up a list of named items for binding. These named items include blocks, dimension styles, layers, linetypes, and text styles.

2. **Add, Remove**. Select named items from the Xrefs text box you want bound and choose the Add button. Select named items from the Definitions to Bind text box you don't want bound and choose the Remove button.

Tips & Warnings

Bound items are given names comprised of the external reference filename followed by a dollar sign ($), a sequential number, and another dollar sign. The number is incremented if an item by the same name already exists.

Associated Commands   xref

***

XCLIP

Reference toolbar

Lets you control how much of an external reference file or block you want displayed. You do this by creating a boundary around the area of the external reference or block you want shown.

Initiate Command By

Command: **xclip**
Alias: **xc**
Modify → Clip → Xref

Options

```
Select objects:
Enter clipping option
[ON/OFF/Clipdepth/Delete/generate Polyline/New boundary] <New>:
Specify clipping boundary:
[Select polyline/Polygonal/Rectangular] <Rectangular>:
```

Select objects

Lets you select one external reference or block if you are going to assign it a boundary. Select one or more if you are going to use any of the other options.

ON/OFF

Turns on or off the geometry located outside the boundary feature for the selected external references and blocks. When the boundary is on the external references and blocks are displayed clipped; when the boundary is off, the external references and blocks are shown in their entirety.

Clipdepth

Lets you define a front and back clipping plane passing through and perpendicular to the clipping boundary. You also can use the distance option that creates a clipping plane parallel to the clipping boundary. Delete the clipping planes with the remove option.

Delete

Removes the association of the clipping boundary to the external reference or block but doesn't delete the boundary.

generate Polyline

Creates a polyline from an existing boundary. This polyline can be edited and redefined as a boundary.

New

Creates a new boundary from an existing polyline or creates a polygonal or rectangular shape. If the polyline is opened, it is automatically closed from the start point to the endpoint. A polygonal shape can be an irregular-shaped polygon, but it cannot intersect itself. Once you have completed the boundary with the polygonal or rectangular shape, it automatically is hidden. The *xclipframe* variable maintains the visibility of the boundary.

Tips & Warnings

Create clipping boundaries for raster images with *imageclip* and *clipit*, for viewports with *vpclip*, and for all objects with *wipeout*.

Related Variables	xclipframe
Associated Commands	block, xref

'XCLIPFRAME

Reference toolbar

Controls the display of the clipping frame for external references and blocks. The clipping frames this affects are those created with the new (polygonal or rectangular) option of *xclip* and *clipit*.

Initiate Command By

Command: **xclipframe**
Modify → Object → External Reference → Frame

Options

0   Clipping boundary is not displayed.

1   Clipping boundary is displayed.

Variable Settings

Initial default:	0
Subsequent default:	Last value used in the drawing
Value:	Integer
Associated Commands	clipit, xclip

'XEDIT 2000

Determines whether a drawing that is externally referenced by another drawing can be edited. This value is set when checking the "Allow other users to refedit current drawing" from the *options* Open and Save tab.

Initiate Command By

Command: **xedit**

Options

0   A drawing that is externally referenced by another drawing can be edited.

1   A drawing that is externally referenced by another drawing cannot be edited.

Variable Settings

Initial default:	1
Subsequent default:	Last value used in the drawing
Value:	Integer
Related Variables	xfadectl
Associated Commands	options, preferences. refedit, xref

'XFADECTL 2000

Determines how objects are displayed when editing a reference file with *refedit*. The reference objects are displayed normally while the rest of the drawing objects fade into the background. Valid values can range from 0 percent fading (minimum value) to 90 percent fading (maximum value).

Initiate Command By

Command: **xfadectl**

Variable Settings

Initial default:	50
Subsequent default:	Registry file
Value:	Integer

Tips & Warnings

Using *shademode* with any option other than 2D wireframe causes the objects to remain the same and not fade.

Related Variables	xedit
Associated Commands	xref

Example

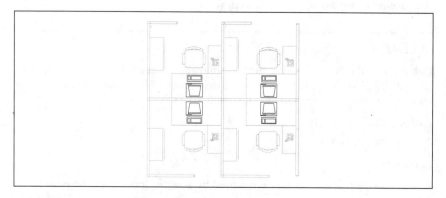

XLINE

Draw toolbar

Creates a line whose endpoints extend into infinity. The command repeats itself, asking for a new through point and using the same angle. *zoom–all* and *zoom–extents* do not take into account xlines. If the drawing contains only xlines, then *zoom–all* and *zoom–extents* are based on the *limits*. Use *zoom–vmax* if you want to display any xlines outside the limits.

Initiate Command By

> Command: **xline**
> Alias: **xl**
> Draw → Construction Line

Options

> Specify a point or [Hor/Ver/Ang/Bisect/Offset]:
> Specify through point:

point
> Lets you select a fixed starting point.

Hor
> Creates a horizontal xline passing through a selected point.

Ver
> Creates a vertical xline passing through a selected point.

Ang
> Creates an xline at a specified angle.

Bisect
> Creates an xline that bisects an angle.

Offset
> Creates an xline parallel to another object. You determine the offset distance.

through point
> Lets you select a second point determining direction and angle for the xline.

Tips & Warnings

- You can change a xline's properties (layer, location, color, linetype, linetype scale) using *change*, *chprop*, and *properties*.

- When edited with commands such as *trim*, *break*, and *fillet*, xlines convert to rays or lines.

Associated Commands   ray

XLIST

Express Block toolbar

Lists the object type, block name, layer name, color, and linetype of nested objects in blocks and external references.

Initiate Command By

Command: **xlist**

Express → Blocks → List Xref/Block Entities

Associated Commands   block, list, xref

'XLOADCTL

Determines the demand loading of external reference files. This value is set with the Demand Load Xrefs option from the *options* Open and Save tab.

Initiate Command By

Command: **xloadctl**

Options

0   The entire drawing is loaded, and demand loading is off.

1   The reference file is kept open, and demand loading is on.

2   A copy of the reference file is opened, and demand loading is on. The reference copy is stored in the temporary files folder. You can define this temporary folder in the "Temporary external reference file location" option of the *options* Files tab, or you can set the *xloadpath* variable.

Variable Settings

Initial default:	1
Subsequent default:	Registry file
Value:	Integer

Related Variables   indexctl, xloadpath

Associated Commands   open, save

'XLOADPATH

Maintains the folder location for temporary external reference files. This value is set with the "Temporary external reference file location" option from the *options* Files tab. If a folder location isn't provided, the temporary external reference files default to the temporary drawing location (*tempprefix*).

Initiate Command By

Command: **xloadpath**

Variable Settings

Initial default:	c:\windows\temp\
Subsequent default:	Registry file
Value:	String

Related Variables   tempprefix, xloadctl

Associated Commands   options, preferences

XPLODE `2000mod`

Converts complex objects (blocks, 3D solids, surfaces, dimensions, regions, polylines, and multilines) into their individual components. *xploding* some objects may result in a change in their color and linetype as they return to their original layer, color, and linetype definitions. Unlike *explode*, *xplode* allows you to control the color, layer, linetype, and lineweight of the exploded objects. For more details concerning xploded objects and what they revert to, see *explode*.

Initiate Command By

Command: **xplode**

Options

```
Enter an option [Individually/Globally] <Globally>:
Enter an option [All/Color/LAyer/LType/Inherit from parent block/Explode]
<Explode>:
```

Enter an option [Individually/Globally] <Globally>:
This prompt appears when more than one object is selected. You can globally or individually change the selected objects.

All
Provides the opportunity to change the color, layer, linetype, and lineweight for the xploded objects. If All is not selected, once you change the color, layer, or linetype, the command automatically ends.

Color
Determines the color of the xploded object(s). See *color* for more detailed information.

LAyer
Determines the layer of the xploded object(s). See *layer* for more detailed information.

LType
Determines the linetype of the xploded object(s). See *lineytpe* for more detailed information.

Inherit from parent block
Sets the color, layer, linetype, and lineweight of the xploded object(s) to the current color, layer, linetype, and lineweight settings if the object's original layer assignment was 0 and its color, linetype, and lineweight settings were set to ByBlock.

Explode
Converts the objects to their individual components, the same as in *explode*.

Tips & Warnings

- You may have to *xplode* a block more than once to break it down into its original components. This is referred to as nested levels of information. For example, blocks A, B, and C may make up a fourth block named D. *xploding* D leaves you with the original blocks A, B, and C.

- If you cancel *xplode* after making some changes, you will still need to undo whatever was performed from the time you began the command to the time you canceled the command.

Related Variables	explmode
Associated Commands	burst, explode

-XREF

see XREF

XREF

Reference toolbar

Attaches and manages external drawing files to your current drawing. These references are loaded into your drawing file each time you open the file for editing or initiate a plot. You can achieve the same results using *-xref* (*-xr*) so all prompts and options appear on the command line.

You can easily locate referenced items because they retain their filename followed by a vertical bar symbol (|) and then the item name. This keeps any blocks, dimension styles, layers, linetypes, and text styles containing the same names in both files from conflicting. Layer 0 does not get renamed when referenced by another drawing. External reference files help keep individual file sizes to a minimum.

If the layer named Defpoints exists in the external reference file but the current drawing does not, that layer name is created in the current drawing even if you detach the external reference.

You can maintain a log file each time you use the *xref* command. The file (in ASCII format) has the same name as the current drawing, but with the file extension *.xlg*. You may want to print and/or erase these files periodically. You activate the log file by setting *xrefctl* to 1. Only model space objects are referenced; paper space objects are ignored.

You can attach a drawing as an external reference with the AutoCAD Design-Center feature. To do this, you select the file and then activate the shortcut menu by right-clicking. You can create a boundary around an external reference defining how much of the external reference you want displayed using *xclip* and *clipit*. If you plan to move a drawing file containing external references to another computer or to a diskette, you need to include those external reference files. Use *pack* to help you accomplish this.

Initiate Command By

Command: **xref**
Alias: **xr**
Insert → External Reference

Options

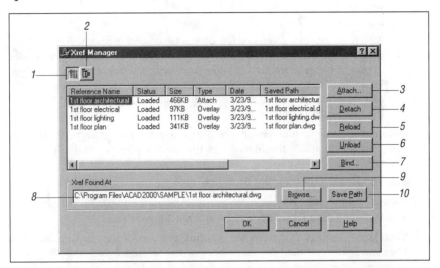

1. **List View (F3).** Shows the external references attached to the drawing. You can sort the list by selecting any of the columns except Status. Each time you press the column heading, you can change the listing from ascending to descending order.

   The Status column can have any of the following notations: Loaded, Unloaded, Reload, Not Found, Unreferenced, Unresolved, or Orphaned. Loaded, Unloaded, and Reload are directly related to the Reload and Unload buttons on the right. Not Found indicates that the external reference file cannot be located in the search path. Unreferenced indicates that the external reference is deleted from the drawing but is still attached. Unresolved means that a file cannot be read by AutoCAD. Orphaned means that the external reference is attached to another external reference that is unreferenced, unresolved, or not found. The Size and Date are left empty when the external reference is unloaded, not found, or unresolved. The Type column toggles between the attach and overlay attachment methods. You can change the size of each column by moving the cursor over the vertical bar and dragging the bar to the left (smaller) or to the right (larger). If you are in the Tree view and want to return to List view, you can press F3.

2. **Tree View (F4).** Shows the external references attached to the drawing. It provides the filenames and their assigned folders. If you are in the List view and want to return to Tree view, you can press F4.

3. **Attach.** Attaches a reference drawing to your current drawing. This is the same as using *xattach*. Attaching is similar to inserting, but the files are not permanently merged together.

   Retain Path

   Determines whether the external reference file's path is saved with the filename or if the file is saved without a path. If the path isn't saved, AutoCAD searches for the external reference file in the support file search path and the paths associated with the current project name defined in the Files tab of the *options* dialog box.

Reference Type

Attach an external reference file using one of two methods. Attaching an external reference lets you view any nested external reference files. The overlay option does not include any nested external reference files. Regardless of the method chosen, you can easily change it from within the Xref Manager dialog box by double-clicking on the Type setting of the externally referenced file.

4. **Detach.** Permanently removes attached external references from your drawing. You also can highlight the filename in the reference name list and press the Delete key.

5. **Reload.** Reloads reference files without exiting the drawing editor.

6. **Unload.** Temporarily removes the external reference file from the drawing. This is one method for saving redraw and regeneration time.

7. **Bind.** Makes the external reference a permanent part of the drawing file. You have the option to bind or insert the external reference file. The difference between these two methods is that named items (blocks, dimension styles, layers, linetypes, and text styles) merge when inserting but remain separate when binding. Binding a reference file causes the names of referenced items to change. The referenced item names are prefaced with the name of the external reference file followed by a dollar sign ($), a sequential number, and another dollar sign. The sequential number is incremented if an item by the same name already exists. If you want to bind items selectively, not the entire reference file, use *xbind*. Once a file is bound, it is converted into a block.

8. **Xref Found At.** Displays the location of the selected reference file.

9. **Browse.** Displays the Select New Path dialog box. You can select a different path or filename.

10. **Save Path.** Saves the path of the Xref Found At to the currently selected external reference.

Tips & Warnings

• The *layer* command lets you view all external-reference-dependent layers with the Named layer filters list. You also can use the invert filter to view those files that are not external-reference-dependent layers.

• Setting *visretain* to 1 retains any changes you make to the color, linetype, lineweight, plot styles, or layer visibility of referenced items. However, this is used only when you reference drawings and does not change the original drawing settings.

• You cannot *insert* or *explode* reference files. You can merge the external reference file using the *bind* option.

• *xlist* provides information about nested objects in a block or xref.

Related Variables   visretain, xrefctl

Associated Commands   clipit, pack, refedit, xattach, xbind, xclip, xedit

'XREFCTL

Determines whether an ASCII file is created when using external references. This file is a log of actions and is created in the same folder as the current drawing. Its name is the same as the drawing file, with the extension *.xlg*. You can delete reference (*.xlg*) files without affecting the associated drawing file.

Initiate Command By

    Command: **xrefctl**

Options

0   Does not create a *.xlg* file.

1   Creates a *.xlg* file.

Variable Settings

Initial default:	0
Subsequent default:	Registry file
Value:	Integer

Associated Commands   xref

'ZOOM

Standard toolbar

Zoom toolbar

Magnifies (zooms in) or shrinks (zooms out) the display in the current viewport. It does not physically change the size of the drawing; rather, it lets you view a small part of the drawing in detail or look at a greater part with less detail. Three zoom options are available as buttons on the Standard toolbar and on the Zoom toolbar, as shown above.

Initiate Command By

    Command: **zoom**
    Alias: **z**
    View → Zoom

Options

    Specify corner of window, enter a scale factor (nX or nXP), or
    [All/Center/Dynamic/Extents/Previous/Scale/Window] <real time>:
    Press Escape or Enter to exit, or right-click to display shortcut menu.

scale factor
    Allows you to enter a magnification number, which is relative to the *limits* setting. A scale factor of 1 displays the drawing limits, 2 displays the drawing twice as big, and .5 displays the drawing half its size.

nX

Zooms relative to the current viewport display. Enter the value followed by an *X* (times). The display center remains fixed.

nXP

Scales the magnification of a model space view relative to paper space. Layout mode and model space must be active. You can preset the sale factor of viewports with *psvpscale*.

All

When in plan view, it displays the drawing to the limits or to the drawing extents, whichever is greater. When in 3D view, it displays the drawing to the extents.

Center

Allows you to specify a center point and a new display height or magnification in drawing units. If you pick a new center and press Enter, the new point becomes the center of the screen without changing the zoom magnification. If you enter a magnification value, it is considered an absolute zoom. Entering a magnification value followed by an *X* zooms relative to the current factor. Entering a magnification value followed by an *XP* scales the magnification of the model space view relative to paper space.

Dynamic

Displays the entire generated portion of your drawing with a box representing the last zoom magnification. Dynamic is a graphical combination of *zoom–all*, *zoom–extents*, and *pan*. This box can be moved around the screen to simultaneously pan to another drawing area. You can change the size of the box by pressing the Pick button and moving the pointing device to resize the zoom box. Clicking the Pick button toggles you from relocating to resizing the box. Once the box size and location are satisfactory, press Enter.

Extents

Displays drawing objects as large as possible. Objects on layers that are turned off are also taken into account.

Previous

Restores a previous *dview, pan, view, zoom,* or *3dorbit* display. The *zoom* command retains the last 10 views for each viewport.

Window

Specifies a window area for the new display. You define a window by selecting two diagonal points. Often you will see more than the window area because the display area is extended to fill the graphics screen.

real time

Displays a magnifying glass letting you interactively zoom in and out by moving your pointing device up and down. Moving your pointing device up zooms in so you can see greater detail. Moving your pointing device down zooms out so you see less detail but more of the drawing. Press Escape or Enter to end the command.

Vmax

Zooms to the limits of the virtual screen's display space. This displays the maximum drawing area possible without causing a regeneration.

Tips & Warnings

- Plot multiple scaled views of the same drawing in one drawing by setting up viewports in layout space and using the *nXP* option.

- When perspective viewing is enabled, you must use the zoom option of *dview* or *3dorbit* to change the viewing magnification.

- *zooming* in a drawing containing rendered objects causes those objects to default to the last *shademode* setting.

Related Variables   extmax, extmin, viewctr, viewsize, vsmax, vsmin, zoomfactor

Associated Commands   ddview, dview, limits, pan, view, 3dzoom

Example

```
Command: zoom
Specify corner of window, enter a scale factor (nX or nXP), or
[All/Center/Dynamic/Extents/Previous/Scale/Window] <real time>: C
Specify center point: Pick point 1
Enter magnification or height <15.3114>: 2x
```

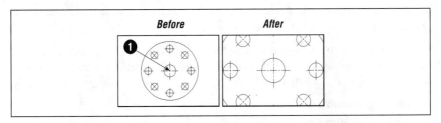

'ZOOMFACTOR 2000

Determines the zoom factor applied when turning the wheel on an IntelliMouse mouse. Valid values are integers between 3 and 100. The higher the number, the smaller the change. Rotating the wheel forward zooms in, backward zooms out.

Initiate Command By

    Command: **zoomfactor**

Variable Settings

Initial default:	10
Subsequent default:	Registry file
Value:	Integer

Associated Commands   zoom

3D

Activates nine 3D polygon mesh routines that create the following objects: box, cone, dish, dome, mesh, pyramid, sphere, torus, and wedge. Each of these objects has the appearance of being solid but is actually made up of meshes or surfaces. You can bring up the individual routines at the command line by adding the prefix *ai_* (artificial intelligence). For more information on these routines, see *ai_box*, *ai_cone*, *ai_dish*, *ai_dome*, *ai_mesh*, *ai_pyramid*, *ai_sphere*, *ai_torus*, and *ai_wedge*.

Initiate Command By

> Command: **3D**
> Draw → Surfaces → 3D Surfaces

Tips & Warnings

- Use *3dorbit*, *ddvpoint*, *vpoint*, and *dview* to look at these objects at different angles and elevations. Use *hide*, *render*, and *shademode* on these objects to make them appear solid.

- *exploding* any of the shapes converts the meshes into 3dfaces.

3DARRAY

Copies objects in 3D rectangular or polar (circular) patterns. Use this command when you to need to copy objects that are equidistant apart. You can copy objects in the *X*, *Y*, and/or *Z* directions.

Initiate Command By

> Command: **3darray**
> Alias: **3a**
> Modify → 3D Operation → 3D Array

Options

> Select objects:
> Enter the type of array [Rectangular/Polar] <R>:

Rectangular

> Copies objects in rows (*X* axis), columns (*Y* axis), and levels (*Z* axis). Designate the number of rows, columns, and levels and the distance between rows, columns, and levels. There always must be at least two rows, two columns, or two levels. Entering a negative distance causes the array to be located along the negative *X*, *Y*, and *Z* axes.

Polar

> Copies objects about an axis of rotation. You must specify the number of items, angle to fill, center point, and axis of rotation. The objects in the array may be optionally rotated.

Associated Commands   array, copy

Example

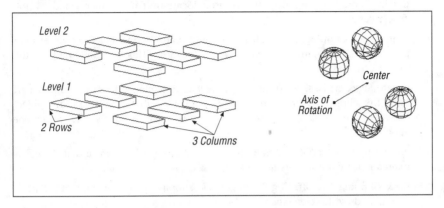

Level 2

Level 1

2 Rows

3 Columns

Center

Axis of Rotation

3DCLIP 2000 3D Orbit toolbar

Defines a front and back clipping plane for viewing 3D objects. *3dclip* activates the 3D orbit feature and opens the Adjust Clipping Plane window for defining the clipping planes. The Adjust Clipping Plane window displays objects rotated at a 90-degree angle from the current 3D orbit view. Once a clipping plane is defined it can be turned on or off. If you define a front and back clipping plane, you can slice the object and view only that portion residing between the two planes.You also can use *dview* to define the front and back clipping planes. However, *3dclip* is easier to use since it provides the Adjust Clipping Planes window and there are fewer steps required to set up the planes. *dview* would be the preferred choice if you know the exact coordinate locations of the clipping planes.

Initiate Command By
Command: **3dclip**

Options

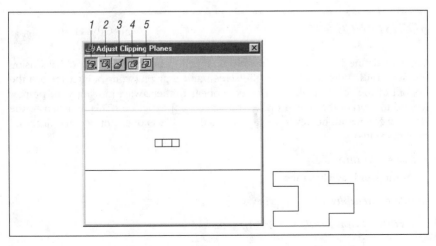

1. **Adjust Front Clipping**. Set the front clipping plane by moving the pointer over the line and dragging it to the desired location. This is maintained by the *frontz* variable.

2. **Adjust Back Clipping**. Set the front clipping plane by moving the pointer over the line and dragging it to the desired location. This is maintained by the *backz* variable.

3. **Create Slice**. Causes the front and back clipping planes to move together. If both the clipping planes are on, you only see that portion of the object between the two clipping planes. This is maintained by the *viewmode* variable.

4. **Front Clipping On/Off**. Toggles the front clipping plane on and off. This is maintained by the *viewmode* variable.

5. **Back Clipping On/Off**. Toggles the back clipping plane on and off. This is maintained by the *viewmode* variable.

Related Variables	backz, frontz, viewmode
Associated Commands	dview, 3dorbit

3DCORBIT 2000

3D Orbit toolbar

A variation of the *3dorbit* command that enables you to interactively view a drawing in 3D. You set the objects in continuous motion by clicking in the drawing area and dragging your pointing device in the direction of the rotation. The speed of the object's rotation is based on the speed of your pointing device movement when defining the rotation. While the drawing is rotating, you can activate the shortcut menu and change the projection, shading modes, visual aids, and preset views. See the *3dorbit* command concerning those options.

Initiate Command By	Command: **3dcorbit**
Associated Commands	3dorbit

3DDISTANCE 2000

3D Orbit toolbar

Lets you define how close or far objects appear when viewing 3D objects using the 3D orbit feature. Clicking on the screen and dragging your pointer toward the bottom of the screen makes the object appear further away; moving your pointer toward the top of the screen makes the objects appear closer. This is similar to the *3dzoom* command; however, the appearance of objects does not become distorted or exaggerated.

Initiate Command By
    Command: **3ddistance**

Related Variables	viewsize
Associated Commands	3dorbit, 3dzoom

3DFACE

Surfaces toolbar

Creates surfaces or opaque objects defined by either three or four corner points. If you specify varying *Z* coordinates for the corner points, you end up with nonplanar faces. Locating all the points in the same plane is equivalent to creating a region object. You can specify the visibility of each edge during the 3D face construction or use *edge* or *properties* and change the visibility of edges later. You can view all edges by setting the *splframe* variable to 1. This command is not used by itself so much as it is used by other AutoCAD routines to create surfaces.

Initiate Command By

Command: **3dface**
Alias: **3f**
Draw → Surfaces → 3D Face

Options

```
Specify first point or [Invisible]:
Specify second point or [Invisible]:
Specify third point or [Invisible] <exit>:
Specify third point or [Invisible] <exit>:
Specify fourth point or [Invisible] <create three-sided face>:
```

I (invisible)

Define the edge as invisible by entering an I before specifying the first point of the edge and before any coordinate input, filters, or object snaps.

Tips & Warnings

* The *hide* command displays 3d faces as opaque.

* All meshes are made up of one or more 3D faces.

* When extruding 3D faces, the invisible edges are modified and become visible.

Related Variables

splframe

Associated Commands

edge, grips, properties, 3dmesh

Example

```
Command: 3dface
Specify first point or [Invisible]: Pick point 1
Specify second point or [Invisible]: Pick point 2
Specify third point or [Invisible] <exit>: I
Specify third point or [Invisible] <exit>: Pick point 3
Specify fourth point or [Invisible] <create three-sided face>: Pick point 4
Specify third point or [Invisible] <exit>: Pick point 5
Specify fourth point or [Invisible] <create three-sided face>: Pick point 6
Specify third point or [Invisible] <exit>: Press Enter
```

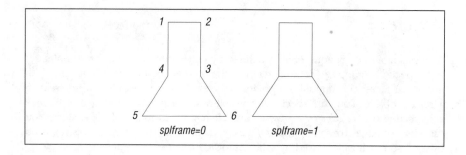

splframe=0   splframe=1

3DMESH

Creates 3D polygon meshes. These meshes are actually 3D faces fused together to act as one object. You specify the mesh size and location (X,Y,Z) in terms of the number of vertices in two directions, M and N.

Since the 3D mesh command is tedious, requiring you to input individual vertex points, it is recommended that you use the automated mesh commands: *edgesurf, revsurf, rulesurf,* and *tabsurf,* and *3d.*

Initiate Command By

    Command: **3dmesh**
    Draw → Surfaces → 3D Mesh

Options

    Mesh M size:
    Mesh N size:
    Vertex (0, 0):

Mesh M size

> Allows you to specify the number of vertices (2–256) in the M direction.

Mesh N size

> Allows you to specify the number of vertices (2–256) in the N direction. The N direction is considered the direction in which you begin to define the mesh.

Vertex (#, #)

> Prompts you to enter each M,N vertex.

Tips & Warnings

You can edit 3D meshes using *grips, pedit,* and *properties.*

Related Variables   surftype

Associated Commands   ai_mesh, 3dface

Example

    Command: **3dmesh**
    Enter size of mesh in M direction: **3**
    Enter size of mesh in N direction: **3**

```
Specify location for vertex (0, 0): 0,0,0
Specify location for vertex (0, 1): 0,1,.5
Specify location for vertex (0, 2): 0,2,0
Specify location for vertex (1, 0): 1,0,.5
Specify location for vertex (1, 1): 1,1,1
Specify location for vertex (1, 2): 1,2,.5
Specify location for vertex (2, 0): 2,0,0
Specify location for vertex (2, 1): 2,1,.5
Specify location for vertex (2, 2): 2,2,0
```

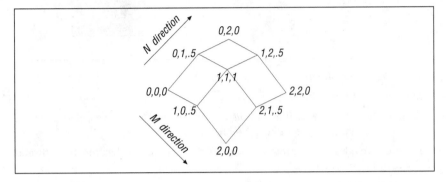

3DORBIT 2000   Standard toolbar/3D Orbit toolbar

An interactive tool for viewing 3D models. It is similar to *ddvpoint*, *dview*, and *vpoint*, but it is much more visual, faster, and easier to use. An arcball, a circle with four smaller circles at each quadrant, appears as soon as *3dorbit* is active. The center of the arcball, the target point, stays stationary. The camera location, or point of view, moves around the target. Picking and dragging your pointing device changes the viewing direction. Selecting one of the smaller circles on the top or bottom rotates the view around the horizontal or *X* axis; selecting one of the smaller circles on the left or right rotates the view around the vertical or *Y* axis. The available options are obtained by using the shortcut menu. Return to plan view using *plan*.

Initiate Command By

Command: **3dorbit**
Alias: **3do**, **orbit**
View → 3D Orbit

Options

Press the Escape or Enter key to exit, or right-click to display the shortcut menu.

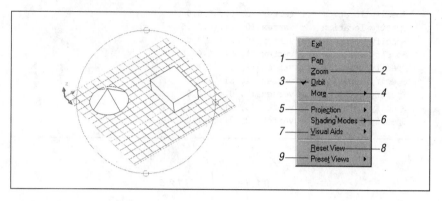

1. **Pan.** Activates *3dpan*.

2. **Zoom.** Activates *3dzoom*.

3. **Orbit.** Returns you to the *3dorbit* command after you have selected More, Pan, or Zoom from the shortcut menu.

4. **More.** Provides easy access to some of the commands that can be activated while *3dorbit* is enabled.

    Adjust distance
    Activates *3ddistance*.

    Swivel camera
    Activates *3dswivel*.

    Continuous orbit
    Activates *3dcorbit*.

    Zoom window
    Activates *zoom–window*.

    Zoom extents
    Activates *zoom–extents*.

    Adjust clipping planes
    Activates *3dclip*.

    Front clipping on
    Activates the front clipping plane option of *3dclip*.

    Back clipping on
    Activates the back clipping plane option of *3dclip*.

5. **Projection.** Provides the option to enable parallel or perspective viewing mode.

    Parallel
    Displays parallel lines as never converging at a single point regardless of how far away the objects appear.

    Perspective
    Displays parallel lines as converging at a single point the further they are from the viewing direction.

6. **Shading Modes.** Activates *shademode*.

7. **Visual Aids**. Provides aids to help determine the appropriate viewing direction.

Compass

Toggles the 3D sphere on and off. The sphere encircles the arcball showing the *X*, *Y*, and *Z* axes.

Grid

Toggles *grid* on and off. Ten horizontal and ten vertical lines are placed between major grid lines. The major grid lines are based on the *gridunit* setting.

UCSicon

Toggles the shaded UCS icon on and off using the *ucsicon* command. See *ucsicon* for more detailed information.

8. **Reset View**. Sets the viewing direction to its original location. This is the view prior to activating *3dorbit*.

9. **Preset Views**. Provides a selection of standard 3D views including top, bottom, front, back left, and right.

Tips & Warnings

You can opt to have only one object displayed on the screen while in the *3dorbit* command. This will save time and may work better with your video display. Once you exit *3dorbit*, the rest of the objects will display appropriately. You do this by selecting your objects before issuing the command. *pickfirst* must be set to 1 in order to preselect objects.

Related Variables	backz, compass, frontz, gridunit, lenslength, shadedge, target, viewctr, viewtwist, vsmax, vsmin
Associated Commands	camera, ddvpoint, dview, grid, shademode, ucsicon, vpoint, zoom, 3dclip, 3dcorbit, 3ddistance, 3dpan, 3dswivel, 3dzoom

---

3DPAN `2000`   3D Orbit toolbar

Lets you horizontally, vertically, and diagonally scroll around the drawing similarly to the *pan* command. When perspective viewing is enabled, you can use *3dpan*, but the scrollbars and *pan* are disabled. Perspective viewing is enabled using *3dorbit* or *dview.* You can opt to have at least one object displayed on the screen while using *3dpan*. This will save time and may work better with your video display. Once you exit *3dpan*, the rest of the objects display appropriately. You do this by selecting your objects before issuing the command. *pickfirst* must be set to 1 in order to preselect objects.

Initiate Command By

Command: **3dpan**

Related Variables	pickfirst
Associated Commands	dview, 3dorbit

3DPOLY

Creates a 3D polyline in which each vertex can be located anywhere in 3D space. 3D polylines cannot have arc segments, width, or tapers, and they support only continuous linetypes. The polyline edit (*pedit*) options available for 3D polylines are close, edit vertex, spline curve, decurve, and undo. End the command by pressing the Escape or Enter key.

Initiate Command By

> Command: **3dpoly**
> Alias: **3p**
> Draw → 3D Polyline

Options

```
Specify start point of polyline:
Specify endpoint of line or [Undo]:
Specify endpoint of line or [Close/Undo]:
```

Close

> Entering C (close) at the "Specify endpoint of line" prompt closes the polyline segments created during the command by connecting the start point to the endpoint. This option is available when at least two lines are created.

Undo

> Entering U (undo) at the "Specify endpoint of line" prompt undoes the last polyline segment and returns you to the previous point.

Tips & Warnings

You can convert 3D polylines into lines with *explode*. In order to convert a 3D polyline into a spline, you must first convert it into a polyline spline using *pedit*. Once you convert a 3D polyline into a spline, you cannot convert it back into a 3D polyline.

Associated Commands   pedit, spline

3DSIN

see IMPORT

3DSOUT

see EXPORT

3DSWIVEL 2000

3D Orbit toolbar

Lets you interactively define a target point when viewing 3D objects. This is similar to the concept of looking through a camera and turning to look at other objects through the camera lens. You can achieve the same results using the target option of the *dview* command. If you activate the shortcut menu, you can change the projection, shading modes, visual aids, and preset views, and access the *3dorbit* command. See *3dorbit* for more detailed information.

Command: **3dswivel**

Related Variables   target, viewctr, viewsize, viewtwist, vsmax, vsmin

Associated Commands   dview, 3dorbit

3DZOOM `2000`

3D Orbit toolbar

Magnifies (zooms in) or shrinks (zooms out) the display in the current viewport. It does not physically change the size of the drawing; rather, it lets you view a small part of the drawing in detail or look at a greater part with less detail. Picking and dragging your pointing device toward the top of the drawing makes the objects appear larger; dragging your pointing device toward the bottom of the drawing makes the objects appear smaller. It is similar to the real time option of the *zoom* command.

When perspective viewing is enabled, you can use *3dzoom,* but the scrollbars and the *pan* command are disabled. Perspective viewing is enabled using the *3dorbit* or *dview* command.

You can opt to have at least one object displayed on the screen while using *3dzoom.* This saves time and may work better with your video display. Once you exit *3dzoom,* the rest of the objects display appropriately. You do this by selecting your objects before issuing the command. *pickfirst* must be set to 1 in order to preselect objects.

Initiate Command By

Command: **3dzoom**

Related Variables   viewsize

Associated Commands   zoom, 3dorbit

PART III

Appendixes

APPENDIX A

Command Shortcuts

There are various ways to access commands. With your pointing device you can activate commands from the pull-down, toolbar, and status line menus. If your pointing device is a digitizer and puck you can select commands from the tablet or from the puck buttons. If you are using a mouse you have the right-click or shortcut menu, and by combining the Shift key with the right-click button you have even more options.

Command	Function Keys	Control Keys	Alias (ACAD.PGP)	Status Bar	Shift + 2nd Mouse Button
adcclose		Ctrl-2			
adcenter		Ctrl-2	adc		
align			al		
appload			ap		
arc			a		
area			aa		
array			ar		
-attdef			-att		
attdef			att, ddattdef		
-attedit			-ate, atte		
attedit			ate		
attext			ddattext		
autosnap (object snap tracking)	F11			✓	
autosnap (polar)	F10			✓	

Command	Function Keys	Control Keys	Alias (ACAD.PGP)	Status Bar	Shift + 2nd Mouse Button
bhatch			bh, h		
-block			-b		
block			b		
bmake			b		
-boundary			-bo		
boundary			bo		
break			br		
chamfer			cha		
change			-ch		
circle			c		
color			col, colour, ddcolor		
coords	F6	Ctrl-D			
copy			co, cp		
copyclip		Ctrl-C			
cutclip		Ctrl-X			
dbconnect		Ctrl-6	dbc		
ddatte			ate		
ddedit			ed		
ddvpoint			vp		
dimaligned			dal, dimali		
dimangular			dan, dimang		
dimbaseline			dba, dimbase		
dimcenter			dce		
dimcontinue			dco, dimcont		
dimdiameter			ddi, dimdia		
dimedit			ded, dimed		
dimlinear			dli, dimlin		
dimordinate			dor, dimord		
dimoverride			dov, dimover		
dimradius			dra, dimrad		
dimstyle			d, dst, dimsty		
dimtedit			dimted		
dist			di		
divide			div		
donut			do		

Command	Function Keys	Control Keys	Alias (ACAD.PGP)	Status Bar	Shift + 2nd Mouse Button
draworder			dr		
dsettings			ds, se		
dsviewer			av		
dtext			dt		
dview			dv		
ellipse			el		
erase			e		
explode			x		
export			exp		
extend			ex		
extrude			ext		
fillet			f		
filter			fi		
graphscr/textscr	F2				
grid	F7	Ctrl-G		✓	
-group			-g		
group			g		
hatch			-h		
hatchedit			he		
help, ?	F1				
hide			hi		
hyperlink		Ctrl-K			
-image			-im		
image			im		
imageadjust			iad		
imageattach			iat		
imageclip			icl		
import			imp		
-insert			-i		
insert			i, inserturl		
insertobj			io		
interfere			inf		
intersect			in		
isoplane	F5	Ctrl-E			
-layer			-la		
layer			la, ddlmodes		
-layout			lo		
leader			lead		

Command	Function Keys	Control Keys	Alias (ACAD.PGP)	Status Bar	Shift + 2nd Mouse Button
lengthen			len		
line			l		
-linetype			-lt,-ltype		
linetype			lt, ltype, ddltype		
list			li, ls		
ltscale			lts		
lweight			lineweight, lw	✓	
matchprop			ma		
measure			me		
mirror			mi		
mline			ml		
move			m		
mspace			ms		
mtext			mt, t		
-mtext			-t		
mview			mv		
new		Ctrl-N			
offset			o		
open		Ctrl-O			
options			op, pr		
ortho	F8	Ctrl-L		✓	
-osnap			-os		
osnap	F3		os, ddosnap	✓	✓
-pan			-p		
pan			p		
-partialopen			partialopen		
pasteclip		Ctrl-V			
pastespec			pa		
pedit			pe		
pline			pl		
plot		Ctrl-P	print		
point			po		
polygon			pol		
preview			pre		

Command	Function Keys	Control Keys	Alias (ACAD.PGP)	Status Bar	Shift + 2nd Mouse Button
properties		Ctrl-1	ch, mo, props, ddchprop, ddmodify		
propertiesclose		Ctrl-1	prclose		
pspace			ps		
purge			pu		
qleader			le		
qsave		Ctrl-S			
quit			exit		
rectangle, rectang			rec		
redo		Ctrl-Y			
redraw			r		
redrawall			ra		
regen			re		
regenall			rea		
region			reg		
-rename			-ren		
rename			ren		
render			rr		
revolve			rev		
rotate			ro		
rpref			rpr		
scale			sc		
script			scr		
section			sec		
setvar			set		
shade			sha		
slice			sl		
snap	F9	Ctrl-B	sn	✓	
solid			so		
spell			sp		
spline			spl		
splinedit			spe		
stretch			s		
style			st		
subtract			su		
tablet	F4	Ctrl-T	ta		

Command	Function Keys	Control Keys	Alias (ACAD.PGP)	Status Bar	Shift + 2nd Mouse Button
thickness			th		
tilemode			ti tm	✓	
tolerance			tol		
toolbar			to		
torus			tor		
trim			tr		
u		Ctrl-Z			
ucs			dducs		
union			uni		
-units			-un		
units			un		
-view			-v		
view			v		
vpoint			-vp		
-wblock			-w		
wblock			w		
wedge			we		
xattach			xa		
-xbind			-xb		
xbind			xb		
xclip			xc		
xline			xl		
-xref			-xr		
xref			xr		
zoom			z		
3darray			3a		
3dface			3f		
3dorbit			3do, orbit		
3dpoly			3p		

Command Modifiers

Description	Keyboard Shortcut	Shift + 2nd Mouse Button
center	cen	✓
endpoint	end	✓
extension	ext	✓
from	fro	✓
insertion	ins	✓

Description	Keyboard Shortcut	Shift + 2nd Mouse Button
intersection	int	✓
midpoint	mid	✓
nearest	nea	✓
node	nod	✓
none	non	✓
parallel	par	✓
perpendicular	per	✓
quadrant	qua	✓
quick	qui	✓
tangent	tan	✓

Miscellaneous

Description	Keyboard	Control Keys	Shift + 2nd Mouse Button
cancel	Esc		
next viewport		Ctrl-R	
point filters			✓

APPENDIX B

Scale Factor Chart and Drawing Limits

The following scale factor chart is helpful for those who lay out their drawing and plot in model space as well as those who use the layout feature (paper space) to plot their drawing. When plotting in model space, the size of your titleblock and text is based on the drawing scale of your plotted output.

For example, if you plan to plot out a C size drawing so that 1/8" = 1'-0", you will need to increase the size of the titleblock and any text 96 times. This is because when you plot the drawing, it will be drawn 96 times smaller. In addition, you will also want to change the size of your dimensions (*dimscale* = 96) and linetypes (*ltscale* = 96). You may find that once you set the linetype scale, it may be too large or small, and then you can modify that number to fit your needs.

The scale factor chart also provides standard drafting sheet sizes and how much space each sheet represents based on the various drawing scales. An arbitrary 1-inch nonprintable border was assumed for each sheet size. In other words, a C size drawing at 1/8" = 1'-0" represents a space that is approximately 128'-0" × 168'-0".

If you require more space you will need to change your sheet size and/or change the drawing scale factor. The column labeled "1/8" Plotted Text Height" lists the values you need to set for your text height so that it will plot out 1/8" high. Plotted scale is the value you set for the plot scale located in the Plot Settings tab of the *plot* command. For this example, 1" = 96 drawing units.

If you're taking advantage of the layout feature (paper space), you will need to set the scale of the viewports using the nXP option of the *zoom* command. The last column of the chart lists those values. The plotted scale value located in the Plot Settings tab of the plot command is always 1:1 (1 = 1 drawing unit).

| | Scale | | Model Space | | | | | | Layout Space |
Drawing Scale	Scale Factor	A: 8.5×11 (7.5×10)	B: 11×17 (10×16)	C: 17×22 (16×21)	D: 22×34 (21×33)	E: 34×44 (33×43)	1/8" Plotted Text Height	Plotted Scale	Zoom XP
					Architectural				
1"=1'	1	7"×10"	10"×1'	1'×1'	1'×2'	2'×3'	.125	1=1	1xp
3"=1'	4	2'×3'	3'×5'	5'×7'	7'×11'	11'×14'	.5"	1=4	1/4xp or .25xp
1 1/2"=1'	8	5'×6'	6'×10'	10'×14'	14'×22'	22'×28'''	1"	1=8	1/8xp or .0125xp
1"=1'	12	7'×10'	10'×16'	16'×21'	21'×33'	33'×43'	1.5"	1=12	1/12xp or .08333xp
3/4"=1'	16	10'×13'	13'×21'	21'×28'	28'×44'	44'×57'''	2	1=16	1/16xp or .0625 xp
1/2"=1'	24	15'×20'	20'×32'	32'×42'	42'×66'	66'×86'	3"	1=24	1/24xp or .04166xp
3/8"=1'	32	20'×26'	26'×42'	42'×56'	56'×88'	88'×114''	4"	1=32	1/32xp or .03125xp
1/4"=1'	48	30'×40'	40'×64'	64'×84'	84'×132'	132'×172'	6"	1=48	1/48xp or .02083xp
3/16"=1'	64	40'×53'	53'×85'	85'×112'	112'×176'	176'×229''	8"	1=64	1/64xp or .01562xp
1/8"=1'	96	60'×80'	80'×128'	128'×168'	168'×264'	264'×344'	12"	1=96	1/96xp or .01041xp
3/32"=1'	128	80'×106'	106'×170'	170'×224'	224'×352'	352'×458'	16"	1=128	1/128xp or .00781xp
1/16"=1'	192	120'×160'	160'×256'	256'×336'	336'×528'	528'×688'	24"	1=192	1/192xp or .00520xp
1/32"=1'	384	240'×320'	320'×512'	512'×672'	672'×1056'	1056'×1376'	48"	1=384	1/384xp or .00260xp
					Mechanical				
2"=1"	.5	3"×5"	5"×8"	8"×10"	10"×16"	16"×21"	.0625	1=.5	2xp
3/4"=1"	1.33	9"×13"	13"×21"	21"×27"	27"×43"	43"×57"	.167	1=1.33	3/4xp or .75xp
1/2"=1"	2	15"×20"	20"×32"	32"×42"	42"×66"	66"×86"	.25	1=2	1/2xp or .5xp
3/8"=1"	2.67	22"×29"	29"×42"	42"×56"	56"×88"	88"×114"	.33	1=2.67	3/8xp or .375xp
1/4"=1"	4	30"×40"	40"×64"	64"×84"	84"×132"	132"×172"	.5	1=4	1/4xp or .25xp
3/16"=1"	5.33	39"×53"	53"×85"	85"×111"	111"×175"	175"×229"	.66	1=5.33	3/16xp or .1875xp

| Scale | | Model Space | | | | | 1/8" Plotted | Plotted | Layout Space |
Drawing Scale	Scale Factor	A: 8.5×11 (7.5×10)	B: 11×17 (10×16)	C: 17×22 (16×21)	D: 22×34 (21×33)	E: 34×44 (33×43)	Text Height	Scale	Zoom XP
				Civil					
1"=10'	120	75'×100'	100'×160'	160'×210'	210'×330'	330'×430'	15"	1=120	1/120xp or .00833xp
1"=20'	240	150'×200'	200'×320'	320'×420'	420'×660'	660'×860'	30"	1=240	1/240xp or .00416xp
1"=30'	360	225'×300'	300'×480'	480'×630'	630'×990'	990'×1290'	45"	1=360	1/360xp or .00277xp
1"=40'	480	300'×400'	400'×640'	640'×840'	840'×1320'	1320'×1720'	60"	1=480	1/480xp or .00208xp
1"=50'	600	375'×500'	500'×800'	800'×1050'	1050'×1650'	1650'×2150'	75"	1=600	1/600xp or .00166xp
1"=60'	720	450'×600'	600'×960'	960'×1260'	1260'×1980'	1980'×2580'	90"	1=720	1/720xp or .00138xp
1"=80'	960	600'×800'	800'×1280'	1280'×1680'	1680'×2640'	2640'×3440'	120"	1=960	1/960xp or .00104xp
1"=100'	1200	750'×1000'	1000'×1600'	1600'×2100'	2100'×3300'	3300'×4300'	150"	1=1200	1/1200xp or .00083xp

Index

A

acad.lsp file, 25
acad.pgp files, reinitializing, 432
acad.psf file, custom prologue section
    in, 410
active tab, storing name of, 100
Add-A-Plot Style Table wizard, 506
Add-A-Plotter wizard, 396
Adjust Clipping Plane window, 591
.adt files, 56
Aerial View window, 185
AME (Advanced Modeling Extension),
    conversions to AutoCAD, 39
angles
  0, direction for, 39
  direction of, 40
  display/input formats, 551–553
  displayed, precision of, 57
  measurement format, 57
annotation, commands for, 14
aperture box
  size of during object snap
    selection, 41
  vs. target box, 380
apostrophe ('), ix
applications, third-party, 110
arbitrary polyface meshes, creating, 376
arcs, 43
  diameter, 132
  displaying, 571
  joining into one polyline, 387
  last drawn, location of last angle, 261
  multiple parallel, 321
  radial dimensions for, 150
  text for, 44
area, 45
arrays, 47
arrowheads, 122–123
  color, 129
  displaying separate symbol for each
    dimension, 151
  visibility, 153
arrows, two (>>) with transparent
    commands, 21
asterisk (*) wildcard character, 22
at sign (@) wildcard character, 22
Attribute dialog box, 51

attributes
  data, extracting from drawings, 53
  definitions of
    in blocks, modifying, 55
    retaining settings for, 30
  displayed as text string/box, 421–422
  editing, 52, 223
  inserted, 51
    controlling display of, 54
  text, 49
  values, prompting for, 55
AutoCAD
  accurate drawings, creating, 16–21
  conversions from AME, 39
  display, 463
  file formats, importing into, 249
  files, tracking read/write status
    of, 575
  full-screen display, 223
  language used, 510
  platform used, 383
  quitting, 423
  Release 13, optimizing formats, 95
  release/version number,
    displaying, 26
  screen, 4–6
  solid validation, 485
  Startup wizard, 4
  startup, applications loaded
    during, 41
AutoCAD 2000
  commands
    modified in this release, 10
    new to this release, 9
    obsolete with this release, 11
  new features, 3–11
  variables
    modified in this release, 10
    new to this release, 9
    obsolete with this release, 11
AutoCAD DesignCenter, 7
  starting, 27–29
  window
    closing, 27
    on/off settings, 30
Autodesk web site, viii
AutoLISP functions/variables,
    retaining, 288

opening, 346–349
  multiple, 6
  one or more simultaneously, 465
  saved automatically (see automatic
    saves)
  searching for, 7, 347
fill, 213, 216
fillets, 214–216
Find Files feature, 7
finishes, 440–443
fog, 220
folders, browsing, 348
fonts, 221
fractions, type displayed, 138
freehand drawing, 475–477
full-size drawing, 3

G

gap between dimension line and
  text, 139
geometry, creating from existing
  objects, 7
global scale factor, 142
graphics mode, switching to text
  mode, 224
grid, 225–227
grips, 228–230
groups, treated as individual
  objects, 382

H

handles, 233
hardcoded directory paths, 426
hatches, 63, 233–236
  double lines, 239
  optimizing formats, 95
  patterns, 240, 507
    angle for, 238
    line spacing for, 240
  on section views, 484
hatching, commands for, 12
hyperlinks, 241–243
hyphen (-) wildcard character, 22

I

illumination, 470
image filenames, presetting, 30

image files, importing into
  drawings, 247
Image Manager dialog box, loading
  images into, 244–245
images
  adjusting, 246
  loading into Image Manager dialog
    box, 244–245
  raster (see raster images)
incremental solid lines, 259
International Standards Organization
  (ISO) code, maintaining, 291
Internet, last used location, 251
isometric planes, 260
items, selecting more than one in
  dialog boxes, 6

J

justification for new multilines, 90

L

landscaped objects
  adding to drawings, 296
  editing, 294
Layer Properties Manager dialog
  box, 263
layer visibility, 8
layers, 262–269
  assignment, changing, 268
  current, saving settings for, 289–291
  deleting, 262
  freezing on selected objects, 267
  lineweight, assigning to, 300
  locking, 268
  number of loaded and displayed,
    controlling, 367
  overlays, acting as, 263–267
  renaming, 433
  selected, moving objects on, 268
  thawing, 272
  turning on/off, 267–269
  unlocking for selected objects, 272
  unused, deleting, 413
layout space
  controlling linetype scaling in, 408
  enabling, 521
layout tabs, assigning page setups
  to, 364

reverse quote (`) wildcard character, 22
revision clouds, 436

S

.sat files, ACIS version, 27
scenes, 462
Screen menu, 310, 463
screen, snapshot of, 327
scripts, 464
sections, 465
Select Menu File dialog box, 309
selected objects
    freezing layers, 267
    information about, 289
    manipulating, 324
    material and attachment method
        assigned to, 473
selection sets, 18–21
    creating, 217–218
        based on object
            properties, 419–421
    tips for using, 20
shape files (.shp files), 94, 472
    compiling, 94
    loading, 291
shapes
    default name, 474
    definitions, 318
    inserting into drawings, 472
    unused, deleting, 413
shortcut menus
    assigning right mouse button to, 473
    modes of, 7
    on right mouse button, 6
silhouette curves, displaying, 175
sketching, 475–477
slides, 567
snap, 479–484
snap increments, 398
snap settings, 360
snapshot of screen display, 327
solid validation, 485
solids
    3D, generated from 2D objects, 438
    combining sets of, 550
    creating
        composite, 257–258, 506
        from existing closed objects, 432

rendered and shaded, smoothness
    of, 212
    saving in Stereo-Lithography
        Apparatus format, 501
sort order operations, controlling
    display of, 492
spatial index, 529–530
spellcheck, 104, 493
spheres, 3D polygon mesh (surface), 36
splines, 496–499
Startup wizard, 4
status bar, adding text to, 325
Stereo-Lithography Apparatus
    format, 501
support folder path, 26
surface fitting, 509
symbols at end of dimensions, 124
system variables, setting, 467–469

T

tabulations, 508
target box, size of, 379
template files (.dwt files),
    opening, 346–349
temporary files, folder stored in, 516
text
    border around, 517
    copying, 98
    default height, 519
    dimension (see dimension text)
    displayed as text string/box, 421–422
    dynamic, 187–190
    finding in drawings, 218–220
    mirroring, 315
    multiple lines of (see multiline text)
    single-line
        converting to multiline text, 536
        exploding into polylines/polyline
        arcs, 536
        fitting between two points, 517
    stacked, 535
    styles, 503–505
text editor, assignment to
    commands, 333
text mode, switching to graphics
    mode, 224
text strings, evaluating, 516

W

warning messages, controlling display of, 367
WCS (World Coordinate System), 537
  UCSs and, 574
web site, Autodesk, viii
wedges, 3D polygon mesh (surface), 37
wildcard characters, 21
Windows clipboard
  copying
    drawings to, 99
    objects to, 97
  pasting contents into current
    drawing, 370
  OLE objects, 369
  pasting objects from, 370
Windows close button, 27
Windows Explorer, 7
World Coordinate System (see WCS)

Z

zoom, 587–589

About the Author

Dorothy Kent is a published author and veteran AutoCAD end user and trainer. Since 1983, she has taught hundreds of industry professionals and their support staff how to be productive with AutoCAD. This includes creating customized training and implementation programs. Dorothy, a registered Autodesk author, has been a guest speaker at Autodesk University, is a member of the Editorial Advisory Board of *Cadalyst* magazine, and has worked with Autodesk's Customer Education and Training Department developing training materials for their Learning Resource Series publications. Dorothy previously published an AutoCAD book with Springer Verlag.

Dorothy has also published her best seller *AutoCAD Reference Guide* with New Riders Publishing and was a contributor to *Inside AutoCAD, Special Edition*. For information regarding customized AutoCAD training programs, you can contact Dorothy via the Internet at *Dorothy_Kent@yahoo.com*.

Colophon

Our look is the result of reader comments, our own experimentation, and feedback from distribution channels. Distinctive covers complement our distinctive approach to technical topics, breathing personality and life into potentially dry subjects.

The animal appearing on the cover of *AutoCAD 2000 in a Nutshell* is an elk (*Cervus elaphus*), or wapiti. Elk populations were once distributed throughout North America, but they are now found only in the western United States from Canada to New Mexico and in parts of Michigan.

The elk is one of the largest members of the deer family. Males can weigh as much as 450 kg and stand 1.5 meters tall. They have long heads and strong, symmetrical antlers that grow as wide as 1.5 meters from tip to tip. A full-grown male usually has 12 points per antler. A long, dark mane covers the neck and chest area.

Elk prefer semi-open woodlands to dense forests. In summertime, they move up into the mountains, where they feed on grasses and wildflowers. In the winter months, they descend to the valleys where they eat what grass and woody growths they can find. They browse for food in the morning and evening and are mostly inactive during the day. Elk are social animals, living in matriarchal herds of up to 400 animals. In mating season, bulls join the herd, and their loud mating bugle, compared by some to a yodel, can be heard echoing in the mountains. Elk are the noisiest of all deer, from the time they're born and issue their first bleat. Outside of mating season, bulls are gentle and nonaggressive to other elk.

As stated earlier, elk were once widely distributed throughout North America. Their population was greatly diminished by a combination of hunting and increased land cultivation, which disturbed their habitat. The eastern subspecies *Cervus elaphus canadensis* is now extinct. Elk have no special conservation status, but limits on hunting and the efforts of individuals and government agencies have led to increases in the elk population and they are not considered to be in danger.

Melanie Wang was the production editor and proofreader for *AutoCAD 2000 in a Nutshell*; Norma Emory was the copyeditor; and Madeleine Newell and Jeff Liggett provided quality control. Judy Hoer, Maeve O'Meara, Anna Snow, and Abigail Myers provided production support. Mike Sierra provided FrameMaker technical support. Brenda Miller wrote the index.

Hanna Dyer designed the cover of this book, based on a series design by Edie Freedman. The cover image is a 19th-century engraving. Kathleen Wilson produced the cover layout with QuarkXPress 3.32 using Adobe's ITC Garamond font.

Alicia Cech designed the interior layout based on a series design by Nancy Priest. Mike Sierra implemented the design in FrameMaker 5.5.6. The text and heading fonts are ITC Garamond Light and Garamond Book. The illustrations that appear in the book were produced by Robert Romano and Megan Morahan using Macromedia FreeHand 8 and Adobe Photoshop 5. This colophon was written by Clairemarie Fisher O'Leary.

Whenever possible, our books use RepKover™, a durable and flexible lay-flat binding. If the page count exceeds RepKover's limit, perfect binding is used.

O'REILLY™

O'Reilly & Associates, Inc.
101 Morris Street
Sebastopol, CA 95472-9902
1-800-998-9938

Visit us online at:
http://www.ora.com/
orders@ora.com

O'REILLY WOULD LIKE TO HEAR FROM YOU

Which book did this card come from?

_____

Where did you buy this book?
- ❏ Bookstore
- ❏ Direct from O'Reilly
- ❏ Bundled with hardware/software
- ❏ Other _____
- ❏ Computer Store
- ❏ Class/seminar

What operating system do you use?
- ❏ UNIX
- ❏ Windows NT
- ❏ Other _____
- ❏ Macintosh
- ❏ PC(Windows/DOS)

What is your job description?
- ❏ System Administrator
- ❏ Network Administrator
- ❏ Web Developer
- ❏ Other _____
- ❏ Programmer
- ❏ Educator/Teacher

❏ Please send me O'Reilly's catalog, containing a complete listing of O'Reilly books and software.

Name _____ Company/Organization _____

Address _____

City _____ State _____ Zip/Postal Code _____ Country _____

Telephone _____ Internet or other email address (specify network) _____

Nineteenth century wood engraving
of a bear from the O'Reilly &
Associates Nutshell Handbook®
Using & Managing UUCP.

PLACE
STAMP
HERE

NO POSTAGE
NECESSARY IF
MAILED IN THE
UNITED STATES

BUSINESS REPLY MAIL
FIRST CLASS MAIL   PERMIT NO. 80   SEBASTOPOL, CA

Postage will be paid by addressee

O'Reilly & Associates, Inc.
101 Morris Street
Sebastopol, CA 95472-9902